THE
BIRMINGHAM
AND
GLOUCESTER
RAILWAY

Captain C.R. Moorsom, Chairman of the B&G 1841–43 (W.V. Awdry)

THE
BIRMINGHAM
AND
GLOUCESTER
RAILWAY

P.J. Long
AND
The Reverend
W.V. Awdry

ALAN SUTTON
1987

Alan Sutton Publishing
Brunswick Road · Gloucester GL1 1JJ

First Published 1987

British Library Cataloguing in Publication Data

Long, Peter
  The Birmingham & Gloucester Railway.
  1. Birmingham & Gloucester Railway Company — History
  I. Title   II. Awdry, W.
  385'.09424   HE3020.B5

  ISBN 0–86299–329–6

Jacket illustration: The Lickey Incline, *showing the first Norris A extra* Philadelphia, *by E.T. Dolby, The Science Museum.*

Typesetting and origination by
Alan Sutton Publishing Limited
Printed in Great Britain

CONTENTS

GENERAL NOTES

ABBREVIATIONS

B&B	Bristol and Birmingham Railway
BC	Birmingham Committee of the B&G
B&G	Birmingham and Gloucester Railway
BDJc	Birmingham and Derby Junction Railway
BoT	Board of Trade
BrG	Bristol and Gloucester Railway
CGWU	Cheltenham and Great Western Union Railway
CofE	Committee of Enquiry
GC	Gloucester Committee of the B&G
GCR	Grand Connections Railway
GJR	Grand Junction Railway
GWR	Great Western Railway
L&B	London and Birmingham Railway
LNWR	London and North Western Railway
M&B	Manchester and Birmingham Railway
MR	Midland Railway
OWW	Oxford Worcester and Wolverhampton Railway

Distances	OLD	NEW
The old system is used	1 mile = 1760 yds,	= 1.6 km.
	1 yard = 3ft.	= 0.9 m.
	1 foot or 1ft.	= 30.5 cm.
	1 inch or 1in.	= 2.54 cm.

Weights	OLD	NEW
The old system is used	1 ton = 20 cwt.	= 1016 kg.
	1 hundredweight = 112 lbs	= 50.8 kg.
	1 pound or (lb.)	= 0.45 kg.

Money	OLD	NEW
The old system is used	£1 = 20s.	= £1 = 100p.
	1s. = 1 shilling = 12d	= 5p
	1d. = 1 penny	= 0.8p
	1.2d.	= 1p.
	1 guinea = 21s.	= £1.05

ACKNOWLEDGEMENTS

I should like to thank the staff at the Public Records Office, Kew; Gloucester Records Office and Gloucester Public Library for their assistance. Special thanks to the Rev. Awdry, whose knowledge, wisdom, kindness, enthusiasm and hospitality have made this book possible.

P.J. Long

FOREWORD

This is unquestionably Peter's book. I have for many years, as is well known, lectured on the B&G and J.E. McConnell their outstanding locomotive engineer. I was also contemplating writing its history some day when I had collected further material.

However it was Peter who got in first with that laborious task. He called me for consultation, and I was happy to make available to him all the information that I had. In return he kindly allowed me to contribute the chapters on Locomotives, the Lickey and the B&G's tangled affairs at Gloucester; all of which are subjects which I have long considered as my own.

For the rest this book is all Peter's. I am full of admiration for the depth of his research and his skill in drawing maps and plans with which to elucidate the text. He has written a book based firmly enough on original sources to be authoritative, but which is yet an eminently readable and interesting account of the somewhat stormy history of one of Britain's pioneer railways hitherto strangely neglected by historians. A railway whose survival was once very much in doubt, but which now, in its 150th year, carries heavy traffic as part of an important trunk route.

W. Awdry
Stroud 1986

CHAPTER ONE

INTRODUCTION

The Birmingham and Gloucester Railway (B&G) in its short but eventful life became especially notorious in railway annals for two things:– the Lickey Incline, and the break of gauge at Gloucester. The Lickey Incline – 2 miles at 1 in 37½, is the steepest main line gradient in the British Isles. Thrifty directors insisted on it. They thought it the shortest and therefore the cheapest route for their railway, but it proved to be the most expensive of all their many expensive economies. From the first its operation was fraught with danger, and it was so costly to work that it kept the company in debt throughout its independent existence.

Special locomotives were needed to work it, from the Norris 'A Extras' to McConnell's *Great Britain*, right through to Fowler's *Big Emma* (1919–56). When the special Banker was not available, two, sometimes three, tank engines had to buffer up behind. As a pyrotechnical display of locomotive sound and fury, their performance could never be bettered. Those of us who have seen and heard *Big Emma*, or a trio of Jinties in full cry, will never forget the experience; but that era is now past. Today, with high powered diesels, there is no need to stop at Bromsgrove for a banker and, except for a slight diminuation of speed near the summit, passengers scarcely notice that they are climbing a gradient at all.

There were many other places in the West Midlands where narrow gauge (4ft. 8½in.) met broad gauge (7ft. ¼in.), but it was the break of gauge at Gloucester where the transfer of passengers and goods from one to the other caused most inconvenience.

The 'narrow gauge' B&G and its partner, the somewhat jimcrack 'broad gauge' Bristol and Gloucester (BrG), were parts of an important rail route between the manufacturing town of Birmingham and Bristol, the most important port and entrepôt of the west. Traffic, particularly in freight, was heavy, but no through-running was possible because at Gloucester the two gauges met. Freight and passengers had to be transferred with great labour and expense. Delays, damage and losses mounted up. Passengers and traders seethed with fury and a Government appointed Commission of Enquiry was set up. It began work in August 1845, and recommended that narrow gauge should be laid within the broad gauge between Gloucester and Bristol, to allow through running, and further that in their view 4ft. 8½in. should in future be the British standard gauge. This was a set-back for the Great Western Railway (GWR), and the second they had had in the area in just under a year. Too comfortably sure of their commanding position at Gloucester, and that the B&G and the BrG were fruit ripe for picking whenever they chose, the GWR had discovered, to their chagrin, that in January 1845 both B&G and BrG had been gathered into the Midland Railway's standard gauge net!

Born in 1836, the B&G had an independent life of barely ten years; but its story is full of incident and well illustrates the trials and tribulations of early railway promoters who, starting out with high hopes and little experience, had perforce to learn the hard way.

THE BIRMINGHAM AND GLOUCESTER RAILWAY, 1840–46

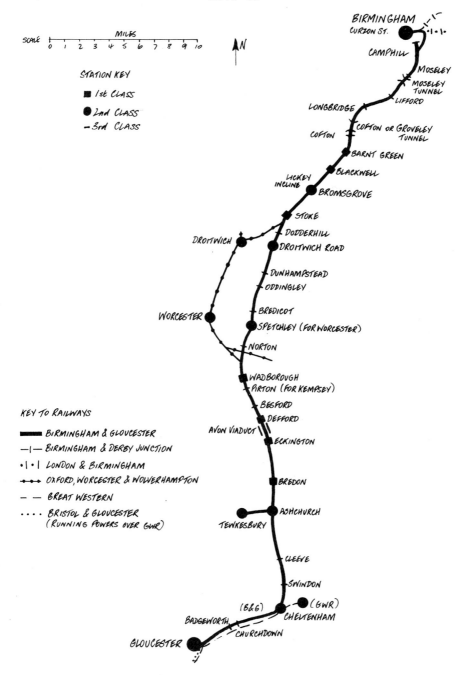

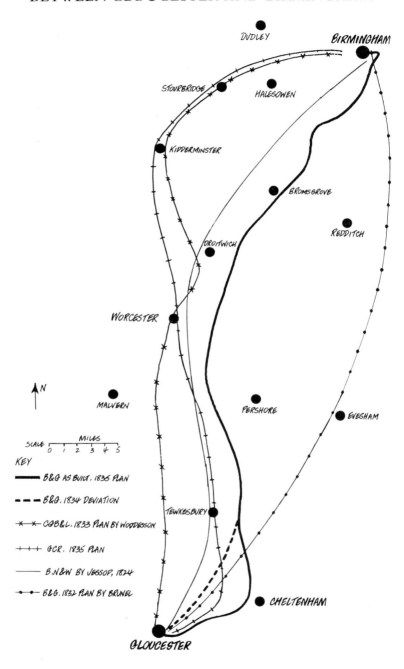

DUDLEY

BIRMINGHAM

STOURBRIDGE

HALESOWEN

KIDDERMINSTER

BROMSGROVE

REDDITCH

DROITWICH

WORCESTER

N

MALVERN

PERSHORE

EVESHAM

SCALE

MILES
0 1 2 3 4 5

KEY

━━━━ B&G AS BUILT, 1835 PLAN

━ ━ ━ B&G, 1834 DEVIATION

╳╳╳ C&B&L, 1833 PLAN BY WOODDESSON

+++ GCR, 1835 PLAN

───── B.N&W BY JESSOP, 1824

•─•─• B&G, 1832 PLAN BY BRUNEL

TEWKESBURY

CHELTENHAM

GLOUCESTER

CHAPTER TWO
DEVELOPMENT

The industrial growth of Birmingham had, in the eighteenth century, been phenomenal. This growth had earned for the town the sobriquet of 'Workshop of the World'. An impressive canal network linked the town with Liverpool, London and Worcester; via the river Severn, Bristol could be reached.

Bristol was a port of considerable antiquity, and by the eighteenth century it had become second only to London in size and prosperity. Its wealth was based largely on trade with the Americas and the West Indies. In this lay its attraction for Birmingham traders; but the passage for their wares down the Severn from Worcester was slow and chancy, vessels being at the mercy of wind and tide, to say nothing of constantly shifting sandbanks.

It was to bypass these hazards that the Gloucester & Sharpness Canal had been mooted. This canal, when opened in 1827 made Gloucester a much more desirable port than Worcester for Birmingham traders, for it was within 60 miles of their factory gates and could now offer easier access to Bristol than Worcester ever could.

Gloucester had, like Bristol, been a port from Roman times, and had been granted a charter by Queen Elizabeth I in 1580. Since then however, it had declined in importance; but the opening of the canal enabled ocean-going ships to reach the docks, and cargoes of merchandise began to flow in from the Americas, the West Indies, and Mediterranean ports. Timber also came in large quantities from the Baltic, but at first there was little for export in exchange except coal from the Forest of Dean and the Black Country, together with salt from Droitwich. It is not surprising therefore that Gloucester merchants began to look to Birmingham for export goods with which to balance their overseas trade; but it was the almost instant success of the Liverpool & Manchester Railway in 1830 which convinced traders in Gloucester and Birmingham that a railway could be the answer to their need. Bristolians too were thinking the same way, but as might be expected they were earlier in the field.

They had opened their floating harbour in 1809 and, needing abundant commerce to help recoup its cost, they began to think of railways as a supplement to existing waterways. From such thinking came two schemes launched in Bristol in 1824. These were the London and Bristol Railroad (later to develop into the Great Western Railway) and the Bristol, Northern & Western Railroad (BN&W). It is with the latter and its successors that we are mainly concerned.

On 13 December 1824 a meeting was held at the White Lion, Bristol, at which it was proposed to build a line of railway to Birmingham via Gloucester, Tewkesbury and Worcester. In addition to linking the above centres it would provide outlets for quarries and collieries in Coalpit Heath, the brick and clay traffic of Stourbridge, salt from Droitwich, and textiles from the valleys around Stroud. In spite of enthusiastic efforts, including a full survey by Josias Jessop, the concern was abandoned for financial and engineering reasons in 1826.

Nevertheless the BN&W idea was far from dead, but instead of being built by one concern, the Birmingham–Bristol line had to grow piecemeal. The first section was opened in 1834 from Cuckolds Pill to Coalpit Heath under the title of the Bristol and Gloucestershire Railway, and after a few years as a horse-hauled edge-rail railway it was expanded into the broad gauge steam worked Bristol and Gloucester Railway opened in 1844.

But to return to Gloucester and Birmingham. With the collapse of the BN&W, Birmingham's hopes had been temporarily dashed; but, as we have seen above, the opening throughout of the Gloucester and Sharpness Canal in 1827 made prospects brighter, for Gloucester was on the way to becoming a thriving port once more. It was situated more than half-way to Bristol, and the canal now greatly facilitated waterway access to that port.

The BN&W idea had a brief revival during 1829–30, but nothing practical was done until at last Birmingham traders, under the leadership of the Sturge Brothers (Joseph, Charles, and Edmund, corn merchants in Gloucester and Birmingham), engaged a young engineer, Isambard Kingdom Brunel to survey a route for a railway between Birmingham and Gloucester. The stipulation was that it should be a direct line avoiding centres of population *en route* with their inflated land values. From this it is clear that neither Birmingham nor Gloucester were in the least interested in intermediate traffic, but only in what the line could carry from town to port and vice versa. The exact route chosen by Brunel is not known, but it was to the east of the present line and skirted Evesham, Redditch and the Lickey Hills. It is said, and knowing the terrain it is a little hard to believe, that on Brunel's whole route there was to have been no gradient steeper than 1 in 300.

Brunel made his report, but the estimated cost of his line was considered too high. He was given £100 for his trouble, and the matter of the line was suspended. But the news about Brunel's survey soon became known, and complications set in. The BN&W proposals had raised the hopes of Tewkesbury, Worcester, Droitwich, Stourbridge, Kidderminster and Dudley. It was unthinkable to people in these places that a railway should be built which passed them by. They accordingly made their opposition felt. In November 1833 the Cambrian, Gloucester, Birmingham & London Railway (CGB&L) was promoted to run from Gloucester through Tewkesbury, Worcester, Kidderminster, Stourbridge and Dudley and thence to Birmingham. To counter this threat the Birmingham Committee in December of that year engaged Capt. W.S. Moorsom to survey a route for them.

He produced as nearly as possible a 'point to point' line which, on leaving Gloucester avoided Cheltenham, Tewkesbury, Worcester and Droitwich, strode straight up the Lickey, and joining the London & Birmingham (L&B) at Garrison Lane, proceeded to a joint L&B and B&G station at Curzon St. This survey was accepted and Capt. Moorsom was eventually paid £500 for his pains.

The fat was now well and truly in the fire! The Severn Valley rang with furious protests and the CGB&L railway proposals were now widely favoured, but its promoters must have been remarkably inept; for instead of cashing in on the situation they appear to have done little or nothing except talk. They also had the press on their side.

For instance in June 1835 the *Worcester Journal* noted that: '. . . It is currently reported that the Birmingham to Gloucester Railway project is about to be revived, and the proposed line will pass to the east of Worcester by a few miles. We allude to this report in the hope that our fellow citizens will take steps to prevent this course. The most desirable line not only for the city but for other places, is the one which shall pass through Kidderminster, Stourbridge and Dudley. Compared to this the line through the east of the country is barren of resources, not including any town of consequence between its two extremities.' This was certainly true. Capt. Moorsom's route was then, with one exception (the Cheltenham deviation), very much as it is today; but the overriding aim was to link Birmingham with Gloucester to provide exclusive transport for the 'Workshop of the World'. Nothing else seemed to matter to these short-sighted promoters, and it was the

Birmingham dog which wagged the Gloucester tail. This is shown in the first recorded entry in the Minute Books. It is dated September 19th 1835 and the Gloucester Committee (henceforth GC) resolved to meet the Birmingham Committee (henceforth BC) to '. . . arrange . . . the best mode of carrying the Undertaking into effect.'

A curious feature of the railway was that for some years it was managed by two committees of directors – the BC and the GC. They held a joint meeting at the Star Hotel, Worcester on 25 September 1835, approved Capt. Moorsom's plans, and agreed upon a prospectus. Thus was the B&G Railway conceived.

CHAPTER THREE

FROM PROSPECTUS
TO ACT OF
INCORPORATION

The prospectus issued in November 1835 was, as might be expected, couched in glowing terms: '. . . The Port of Gloucester exhibits a most rapid increase of traffic subsequent to the opening of the GB canal, from £14,717 in 1825 to £131,117 in 1834 . . . In 1828 imports . . . by canal were 111,787 Tons, in the present year . . . nearly 250,000 tons. The Severn Trade is estimated as being nearly half of that on the canal . . .'. Exports reached nearly 200,000 tons, and official evidence showed that 90 per cent of imports at Gloucester travelled northwards towards Birmingham and the number of road coaches between Gloucester, Cheltenham and Birmingham was nearly equal to those on the London to Birmingham road. Water transport was 60 miles by canal and river: '. . . the boats on which, independently of delay occasioned by frost flood and drought, consume several days in their passage. These facts seem to demand the establishment of a rapid communication between the two towns, commensurate with those established and in progress in other parts of the U.K. . . . the length of the line will be less than 50 miles passing through or near Cheltenham, Worcester, Tewkesbury, Pershore, Droitwich, Redditch and Broms-grove'. The capital required was estimated at £750,000, to be raised by the issue of shares of £100 each, which, it was calculated, would bring in a return to investors of 12 per cent. Passenger traffic which other railways had found to be just as profitable as goods – if not more so – was calculated to bring in £117,286 per annum, while the figure for merchandise (apart from heavy goods such as coal etc.), was put down as £70,371 per annum. Operating expenses were optimistically esti-mated at 50 per cent of revenue, thus giving a profit of some £91,529.

'. . . no subscriber will embark his capital in the undertaking without the fairest possible prospect of having made a profitable and advantageous investment.' They were certainly in for a shock.

Glowing and enthusiastic support came from newspapers both in Gloucester and Birmingham. They alleged that applications for shares came in at such a rate that the list could have been closed by mid October. However, as might be expected, these applications were few. Instead furious protests came from places by-passed by the proposed line which in reality was convenient only for Birmingham and Gloucester and avoided intermediate towns and cities by several miles. In addition the Cheltenham & Great Western Union Railway (CGWU), proposed to link with the GWR via Gloucester, Stroud and Swindon, now threatened the B&G's hoped for monopoly at Gloucester.

Cheltenham's development as a spa had been recent but rapid, and the people of Cheltenham had a high idea of their own importance. Since they had been by-passed by the B&G, they now wanted their own link with the outside world. The CGWU informed the B&G of their proposals and that they would be presenting their bill to Parliament during the Session of 1836. Since it was in this session that the B&G hoped to obtain their Act of Incorporation it was necessary for them to work fast to appease the aggrieved inhabitants of Worcester and Cheltenham. The B&G had to make expensive concessions in the form of a deviation or branch line to Worcester, and an uneasy relationship with the CGWU was developed as well. The CGWU planned to have a central terminus in Cheltenham, and I.K. Brunel, their engineer, proposed a junction with the B&G and a joint line thereafter to Gloucester before proceeding on their own up the Stroud valley.

At this stage, Capt. Moorsom's choice of line between Cheltenham and Gloucester was still unsettled. Gloucester, as the line's southern terminus, had to have a central passenger depôt and a goods depôt at the docks. Cheltenham however was more difficult. Although not a centre of commerce or industry, it had become a popular spa town, a favourite and fashionable place where high society visited and where majors and generals retired and expired. The affluence of Cheltenham's population made it a healthy consumer of coal and the gasworks was one of the country's earliest. Moorsom's 1834 plan had avoided Cheltenham by about 3 miles and naturally outraged its inhabitants. Feeling the rumbles of discontent, the GC in October 1835 told him to alter his line to '. . .approach Cheltenham as nearly as should be consistent with the interests' of the B&G and also to afford convenience for the CGWU line. He reported that he could approach to within one mile of the Plough Hotel, (bang in the centre of town), before engineering and land costs became astronomical. A depôt would be made on the road near Mauds Elm from whence the line veered away to Gloucester. Two alternative routes into Gloucester were planned. One terminated at the docks by the gaol but had a central passenger depôt at Southgate Street, while the other, necessary in case of high property costs and opposition, was to the south with a passenger depôt on the Bristol Road and a junction with the canal at High Orchard. Cheltenham people thought poorly of the depôt proposed for them at Mauds Elm. Pearson Thompson, a Cheltonian member of the GC submitted a proposition demanding that, since the depôt was: '. . . not in a situation calculated to accommodate the bulk of the population and width of Cheltenham,' and that since the mainline could not be deviated, a branch should be made to some '. . . central part of town'.

When this idea was rejected on the grounds of expense, Mr Pearson Thompson offered to build the branch at his own cost. This put a different complexion on things, and the GC in particular was much taken with the idea. When the two committees next met they heard the Gloucester division's engineer report that the branch would be more suitable than a depôt out at Mauds Elm, and so it was agreed. Two routes were chosen for submission to Parliament which terminated respectively at St George's Place, and Westall Green (see map). The former was close to the station site favoured by the CGWU, and on land owned by Pearson Thompson himself, who offered it to the B&G at £300 per acre. With Cheltenham partially pacified, the B&G now had to come to some sort of working arrangement with the CGWU.

The two railways had planned virtually identical sections of line between Cheltenham and Gloucester which were of paramount importance to each, the B&G wanting independence at Gloucester, and the CGWU at Cheltenham. Parliament would certainly not authorize both, and could possibly damage the interests of one or both railways at either end. It was necessary to present Parliament with a logical business-like agreement between both parties, and negotiations were begun in November towards achieving that end. Both companies threw out the others proposals for a 'joint' line. They both agreed that any arrangement must be on the basis of 'perfect reciprocity' and at least their disagreement on each others proposals was reciprocal! Both sides eventually agreed to the conditions which formed the basis of the relevant clauses in their subsequent Acts of Incorporation.

The B&G managed, whether by accident or design, to secure that their bill was heard in Parliament before that of the CGWU. The clauses relevant to the Cheltenham–Gloucester line may be summarised as follows:- their independent line to Gloucester and the branch to St Georges Place, Cheltenham was authorised, but should the CGWU'S bill be authorised then these powers would lapse (which they did), the

CGWU would build the line between Cheltenham and Gloucester, and the depôt of their choice for joint use. After completion, the B&G would pay a moiety of costs to the CGWU whereupon the CGWU would be the sole owners of the Cheltenham half of the line, but trustees only of the Gloucester half; the B&G occupying the Gloucester half as if it were their own. Each company was to have free access to each others depôts, receive the tolls over, and maintain their respective halves. As for the gauge, it was to be laid in the narrow gauge with the CGWU adding a third rail at their sole expense. Of paramount importance to the B&G was a clause requiring the CGWU to complete the line for the B&G's use: as soon as the Birmingham to Cheltenham section was complete. Last, but not least, the Gloucester and Cheltenham Tramway was to be purchased jointly by both companies at a cost of £35,000.

The tramway was an attractive proposition. It ran from near the gasworks at Cheltenham along the turnpike road to Gloucester then down to the dock basin. Neither company contemplated using the tramway's main line but both wanted to make use of the access it provided to Gloucester Docks (see Chapter 25).

You may wonder, quite rightly, what became of the B&G's extension down to the docks. It was authorised in the B&G's Act, but cancelled by the CGWU's some months later, leaving the B&G without a direct communication to the Docks. The only access which remained available to them was over the Tramroad. Transhipment was required here, which, though expensive and inconvenient, was nevertheless used until the Midland Railway (MR) completed the High Orchard branch (authorised in 1845) in 1848.

Turning now to Worcester. The city had for many years protested at being bypassed by the direct B&G line and these protests had gained momentum towards the end of 1835.

Public meetings were held, attended by B&G officials, to air the grievances of Worcester and seek a compromise with or alternative to the B&G. On 22 October 1835 at one such meeting, a large attendance heard a resolution requesting a branch line, but before further action could be taken, Mr Pierpoint (of whom much more later) interrupted and demanded a deviation of the main line to bring it closer to Worcester. He challenged Moorsom's statement that the topography prohibited such a deviation, he offered a practical example, and proposed such a line should be surveyed and if it proved practical, it was to be incorporated in the company's submission to Parliament.

Anxious to gain the city's support, the B&G acceded to these demands, and arranged a further meeting the following week. However, to satisfy both Worcester and Cheltenham's demands would be impossible without an increase in the £750,000 capital. A decision on the company's finances would be made on the same day as the proposed meeting, but time was running out for such late changes. Full plans had to be submitted to the Justice of the Peace for Worcestershire by 30 November 1835, to allow inclusion in the ensuing session of Parliament.

Prior to the next meeting the B&G deputation met their engineer and a Mr Varden who had surveyed Mr Pierpoint's proposed line. It was agreed that Moorsom's plan for a deviation from Oddingly to Abbotswood was superior as it approached to within 1 mile of the city centre. The cost for the 8¾ miles was a staggering £192,500, £120,500 more than the original 6 mile route between these places. In addition he presented plans of a 4 mile branch line into the city centre at Sansome Field costing £70,000. Armed with these, the deputation resolved to include deviation, branch and the original line in their application to Parliament. That way, surely, the Worcester people could not accuse them of neglecting the city, and Parliament would decide which line best served the interests of the public and the company alike.

These plans were however rejected outright by the public meeting to which they were presented later that day. The meeting resolved to '. . . sanction no railroad that does not bring the mainline close to or within one mile of the City of Worcester.'

Still smarting from their brusque reception, the B&G deputation resumed their labours that evening to decide upon the required increase in capital. They decided that two thousand extra shares should be issued and in order to impress upon the people of Worcester that their intentions were sincere, an advertisement was placed in the Worcester press stating that the extra shares were required in order to convince Parliament of the railway's ability to carry out its pledge to Worcester, and that prospective investors from the city would be given preference in buying the shares.

Meanwhile, rival schemes proliferated. A public meeting was held to 'consider a line of railway on the west side of the Severn between Birmingham and Gloucester passing close to the city of Worcester . . . with the view of immediately applying to Parliament'. Mr Pierpoint said an alternative line had been surveyed by a Mr Prosser (See Map 2.1) and had pronounced it superior to Moorsom's. A similar proposal, in which Mr Pierpoint played a prominent part, and which was later known as the Grand Connection Railway (GCR) promised a return of 17½ per cent. But it never became more than a set of proposals and a pawn in Worcester's fight to stop the B&G undermining the city's interests as a port.

Contemporary newspapers devoted much space to the railway fiasco at Worcester. The *Gloucester Journal*[1] could not understand how the B&G could be blamed for neglecting Worcester; first they moved

Brunel's line 3 miles closer, then they agreed to a branch, then a deviation, all at great additional expense. What more could they do? A correspondent claimed that the deviation would cost £50,000 more than the branch and would suffer every through passenger to travel and pay for an extra 3 miles just to approach to within 1 mile of Worcester. The branch however would penetrate the heart of the city and would have distinct trains running to Birmingham and to Gloucester without change of carriage. It was, he concluded, '. . . the better solution to the Company, the public and all.'

The chief obstacle in the way of obtaining either a branch or a deviation railway lay not in the obstinacy of Worcester or the B&G, but in that of the Rt. Hon. Robert Berkeley of Spetchley Park. Both would have to be built over his land, and in common with many landowners at that time, he was not favourable to railways and objected to the cutting up of his estate. Eventually sufficient alterations were made to the routes to meet his objections, and while preferring the proposals of the GCR, he gave grudging assent to the B&G's deviation and branch plans which were to be put before Parliament.

The bill was presented to Parliament in February 1836 and because of opposition from GCR supporters in Worcester both branch and deviation clauses were withdrawn in the committee stage. Meanwhile, much too late to be of any practical use, the GCR emerged from its shell, and thereby added greatly to the confusion. They asked for negotiations to prevent a collision of interests, but such was the protracted nature of these talks, that agreement when it came, was too late to save either the branch or the deviation in the current session of Parliament. So after all the effort of the past few months all Worcester had to show was an agreement between the B&G and the GCR which was to prove, as we shall see in the next chapter, very much to the B&G's detriment. We must now leave Worcester and follow up events on other parts of the line.

At the Birmingham end little opposition was met. The major problem was whether or not to incur the heavy expenditure involved in making a junction with the L&B (see Map 22.1). On balance, however, such was the importance of joining the L&B, GJR, and the proposed Birmingham and Derby Junction Railway (BDJc) that it was agreed to go ahead regardless of cost. In this connection the B&G achieved an important 'diplomatic coup' in that the L&B not only agreed to the junction between the two lines, but also that the B&G should, on payment of toll, use their Curzon Street station.

Preparations for putting the railway before Parliament in the 1836 session were well under way by November 1835. Compliance with 'Standing Orders' was an absolute necessity. This was a procedure which all private bills had to follow or risk being lost before being read before the House. For railways this involved, for instance: advertising in the local press the intention of applying for an Act; depositing accurate plans and books of reference of the property for which compulsory purchase was sought with the local Justice of the Peace; and also providing accurate traffic estimates and construction estimates to prove there would be a sufficient volume of traffic to justify the railway, a profit to be had for its proprietors, and that sufficient funds existed to complete its construction. All these were successfully completed on time by the B&G. Then counsel for the promotion of the bill in Parliament had to be engaged, support canvassed from local members of both Houses, and a canvass made likewise of all land-owners along the route.

Traffic estimates were obtained by visual observation on the high-ways and waterways, and from the account books of coach proprietors, carriers and canal companies. To ensure accuracy, observations were carried out over 28 days to iron out fluctuations. Passenger traffic estimates were at first doubled, later trebled, to allow for the marked increase in journeys which followed railway openings. All told the expected revenue would be £190,000, just over that stated in the prospectus (details in appendix). Capt. Moorsom supplied the engin-eering estimates (see appendix); a maximum of £920,000 was, he claimed, sufficient to complete the whole line, branches and all.

Early in February 1836, the bill was introduced into the House of Commons. Opposition was expected from certain parties in Wor-cester, discussed previously, but Tewkesbury fulfilled their threat to make a stand to protect its interests. Tewkesbury enjoyed not only great historical associations but a thriving coach establishment. Now, by leaving Tewkesbury off the main line of railway, the B&G proposed to sacrifice the town's position, trade, and the livelihood of its inhabitants for the benefit of Cheltenham and Gloucester.

The *Gloucester Journal* commented that the preamble of the bill mentioned the great advantage of the railway to the intermediate towns and districts.[2] 'It is curious but true that not a single intermediate town is touched upon . . . and the inhabitants of Tewkesbury quietly told to take their carts and wagons to join the train road at Ashchurch.' A petition was to be presented by the town to Parliament to register its disgust, but an amicable arrangement was made in the nick of time which promised a direct branch right into the centre of the town.

Unlike many Parliamentary battles between rival companies, the B&G's bill passed through peacefully, receiving the Royal Assent on 22 April 1836. The news was greeted in Worcester by shares falling from £10 to £7.10s.0d. premium!

The House of Commons committee report is interesting.[3] It proved an expected revenue of £156,000 yielding £100,000 profit per annum;

nearly 9,000 shares had been allotted, and the total cost of the construction etc. would be £940,000. Two inclined planes were to be traversed by passengers; the Lickey, split into two sections, 1½ miles at 1 in 54 worked by a 96 hp stationary engine, and 1¼ miles at 1 in 36 with a 121 hp engine; the other on the junction line with the L&B, 1 in 84 worked by 'an assistant locomotive engine'. At Gloucester the goods depôt at the canal (later nullified) was to be reached by an inclined plane at 1 in 30–48 and also worked by stationary power. On the main line, whose maximum gradient was 1 in 300, one tunnel at Grovely (Cofton) of 440 yards was required. (That at Moseley was later forced on the company by objectors.)

We have seen how the various clauses affected Gloucester, Cheltenham, Worcester and Birmingham; the remainder of the Act is quite lengthy and we quote here a few of the more important and interesting clauses. Engineering works were given 5 years for completion and interference with roads, rivers, canals, etc. forbidden; bridge dimensions are specified. Shareholders were to have two general meetings per year, at which 'lunatics and idiots' could only vote by committee.

Working of the line was outlined and appears to have been based upon the methods practised by canals, tramroads and turnpike roads. Rates and tolls (see appendix) were payable for all traffic transported, details of which were to be displayed at each depôt or toll station, where a toll collector would be stationed. Additional charges could be made by the company for use of depôts, maintenance, rolling stock and locomotive power (which had to consume its own smoke on penalty of £5 for each offence). Private wagons, carriages and locomotives could be used but only with the prior agreement of the company, who regulated the opening times, passage, timetable, speed and loading of all trains. The 'smoking of tobacco' was firmly prohibited. Customers of Travellers Fare will please note that: 'The said Company shall not erect or permit to be erected any Beer Shop, or Place for sale of Beer or Liquors on any part of the said line.' Parliament's concept of railway working was very primitive compared with that we are now used to but in practice the B&G operated on more familiar lines.

Constitution of the Board of Directors was a little complex. Eighteen members were allowed in two committees of nine (i.e. the BC and GC), each having power to make contracts and agreements independently of the other. Shareholders could replace or re-elect a certain number of directors on an annual basis. Finally, the company was allowed to borrow money up to one third of the authorised capital of £950,000.

CHAPTER FOUR
THE FIRST EIGHTEEN MONTHS:

AMENDMENT ACT AND VOTE OF CONFIDENCE

With the passing of their Act, both committees were eager to commence preparations for constructing the railway. As can be imagined, the preparatory work needed was immense; detailed surveys and plans of every bridge and all earthworks; property plans for land purchase; preparation of detailed contracts for executing the work; and so on. Capt. Moorsom's 'Division of Contracts', submitted to the Board in July 1836, split the entire line into 16 contracts of varying length and complexity; seven in the Gloucester division for which the GC had responsibility, and nine in the Birmingham division, the BC's responsibility. Starting with the heaviest earthworks in November 1836 he had hoped to complete the whole by December 1838. An optimistic prediction.

Moorsom's requirements for engineering staff were also brought before the directors. He, of course, was chief, at £1000 salary, with 4 assistants (2 per division at £500 salary each) to take charge of setting out the land and to attend to the construction in detail. Each had a sub-assistant (at £200) to survey, make working drawings and report on the progress of contracts. A surveyor, draughtsman and clerk completed the team. The engineer's contract forbade him to superintend more than one other railway: '. . . thus securing to the Company the time and talents of an engineer of great energy and zeal without the liability of having his attention too much diverted from this important service.'

Shareholders had the chance of hearing a progress report at their first general meeting in September 1836. The report, which was circulated to all proprietors before the meeting, told them that completion was expected in a much shorter time than any comparable railway yet constructed, and all its features were highly satisfactory. When asked why no visible start had been made, the directors replied that planning the work to perfection before entering into contracts was by far the safest plan, but this took time. Portions of the line had been staked out and a little purchased, but two months had been lost while waiting for the CGWU's Act in June which had prevented completion of the survey. The proprietors should be satisfied, concluded the report, that their line would be open two years after the letting of the first contract.

In October Moorsom told the BC that considerable progress had been made in staking out the line at the Birmingham end, and contracts were to be advertised in November. Unfortunately the purchase of the required land had not met with the same progress. Demands from landowners had been exhorbitant and negotiations had broken down. In cases of dispute on the price of compulsory purchase land, a jury could be convened by which both parties had to abide but this took time to arrange, and so the contracts were postponed indefinitely.

After Capt. Moorsom had presented his plans for laying down the permanent way (rails, sleepers, ballast; details in Way & Works, Chapter 15), a digression was provided by the GC. They had heard about improvements in locomotive engines consequent upon the use of a wider gauge which allowed bigger engines of higher power. This no doubt refers to Brunel's broad gauge engines, and it sparked the imagination of the GC; perhaps they thought such engines could flatten the Lickey Incline. Capt. Moorsom was asked to consult the leading locomotive builders, and Edward Bury of Liverpool thought that a gauge of 5ft. 6in. was an ideal compromise between power and the extra width of land required. Moorsom thought it injudicious to use a different gauge than that adopted by the connecting railways at Birmingham; luckily the BC also took this view. When both committees met to discuss this in December 1836, 4ft. 8½in. was decided upon despite pleas from the GC to adopt a wider gauge if the present locomotive experiments proved a success. The mind boggles at the thought of two gauge changes between Birmingham and Bristol!

Progress was slow. Frustrated proprietors, wondering why their shares, once at a premium, were now at discount, had little cheer at the February 1837 general meeting. They were thanked for the prompt payment of their first call, especially as, '. . . the general pressure upon the moneyed interest has affected . . . almost all classes of persons . . . the capital has been forthcoming with an alacrity which leaves no doubt of the whole being obtained at the various periods at which it may be required.' Some consolation was forthcoming; proprietors were glad to hear that the exorbitant demands for land were not met for the sake of a speedy start of construction. Several contracts would shortly be advertised.

In a report given to the Board, but not to the proprietors, Capt. Moorsom gave a fuller picture of affairs. He complained, not for the last time, about the lack of staff and facilities in his department. Assistant engineers' posts had only recently been filled, and the cheap, inexperienced draughtsmen employed delayed the proceedings instead of assisting. You will notice over the pages of this story how the use of cheap alternatives usually caused more expense in the long run. On the bright side: 38 miles were surveyed in the 'most perfect manner', 22 miles had property plans completed and 15 miles were staked out.

March of 1837 saw the first three contracts advertised, two of the BC's heaviest, between Camp Hill and Moseley, and the bridge over the river Avon at Eckington in the Gloucester division. Contracts for earthworks received several applications but all were considerably above the engineer's price. He had estimated £30,000 for the 1½ miles between Camp Hill and Moseley, but the lowest tender was £37,000! Similarly the other contract, 1½ miles between Moseley and Bredon's Cross was tendered for at £25,000 compared with the Engineer's estimate of £21,000. The B&G got cold feet! Gloucester directors looked at the existing funds of the company and estimated they could rapidly become exhausted if contracts were let. Britain was in the grip of a severe money shortage, and the GC calculated that a further call on the shareholders would soon be necessary and under present circumstances proprietors could not be expected to pay. The board resolved to suspend further consideration of contracts.

Staff in the engineering department were confined to preparing property plans, estimates and drawings for contracts endeavouring to reduce expenses as far as possible. A revised estimate for constructing the railway was made by Capt. Moorsom following new arrangements between Cheltenham and Gloucester. £877,000 would be needed, and with the allowance of 9 per cent contingency payment, it brought the total precariously close to the authorised capital of £950,000.

It will be remembered that the B&G lost both branch and deviation lines to Worcester in their 1836 bill while still negotiating with the GCR. Agreement was reached during March 1836, and the GCR issued a prospectus for a line from Worcester through the Black Country to Wolverhampton with a junction to the GJR. They were to drop their line to Gloucester and the B&G would construct, or co-operate with the GCR to construct, a branch to Worcester from Abbotswood. A bond carrying a penalty of £70,000 was entered into to ensure that the agreement was carried into effect.

Although their original intention was to make the branch from Bredicot to Sansome Fields, the Board honoured the bond and plans were submitted to Parliament for the 1837 session. So far, the directors had regarded the bond quite seriously. Then the GCR blew their cover. They had included the Abbotswood to Worcester section in their own bill. Mr Pierpoint, their chairman, defended this as a purely pre-cautionary object in case the B&G failed to apply, but the B&G decided they alone were going to build the branch, and opposed the GCR's application for a junction with their line at Abbotswood.

After a lengthy wait, in May 1837 the B&G received Parliament's authority to proceed with their branch to Worcester. However, should the GCR's bill be authorised, the B&G's powers would lapse. Later in the month Parliament threw out the entire GCR bill, which, according to the *Gloucester Journal* was: '. . . sufficient proof that the House is not disposed to countenance speculations of this description.'[1] So the B&G were left with powers to build a branch whose junction, route, and terminus they did not approve, all because of a bond with a company which did not legally exist!

At first, Tewkesbury was easier to please, although the end result for the town was a little 'Heath Robinson'. From its opposition to the Incorporating Act, Tewkesbury gained an agreement by which the B&G would build a branch line from their main line at Ashchurch, right through the centre of the town to a terminus near the quay on the river Avon (see Map 26.1). Proprietors were told at their September 1836 general meeting that the branch would: '. . . secure the transport of coals, goods and merchandise from Tewkesbury along the main line, which although not at first calculated in the present estimate of traffic, will add considerably to the revenue of the Company.' Parliament sanctioned the branch along with that to Worcester, in May 1837.

With the passing of the CGWU's bill in June 1836, powers for the B&G's Cheltenham to Gloucester line lapsed, and although the Act allowed a junction between the two companies, its location was, to the B&G, inconveniently situated for access to the town of Cheltenham. A deviation was therefore planned (see Map, 24.1) from Mauds Elm to join the CGWU near the new Gloucester turnpike road and authorised in the 1837 Amendment Act of the B&G.

The first general meeting of B&G, in September 1836, was an occasion for self congratulation and optimism for future prosperity: '. . . when it is considered that this line will connect the large and important manufacturing town of Birmingham with the rapidly incre-asing port of Gloucester; that it will obtain all the Northern traffic of Cheltenham with its large moving population: that it will open communications between the various towns and cities upon its immediate line; and above all will be throughout the whole extent the unrivalled medium of railway communication between Bristol and the whole West of England, Birmingham, Liverpool and the whole of the North; no one can doubt the superior claims of the B&G to the public confidence as a safe and profitable investment.' In addition, the directors personally felt very satisfied: '. . . in having been instrumental in promoting the commercial prosperity of their country by laying the foundation of a work which forms a portion of those great national undertakings which history will record as a lasting monument to the industry, enterprise and wealth of the age in which we live . . . the merchant of Gloucester can go to . . . [Birmingham] . . . to breakfast, spend the day in the transaction of his business and return again with the most perfect ease the same evening . . . and the manufacturer or merchant of Birmingham shall find the ships that are to convey his goods to the most distant lands brought within 2 hours ride of his own door: who can say to what an extent the commercial intercourse between these 2 places may be be carried out: who can tell to what pitch of importance one port and city may be raised by the completion of this great undertaking!' Until this meeting the term 'director' was, of course, a misnomer for 'Member of the Provisional Committee'. The first directors were elected at this general meeting, nine for the BC and nine for the GC, with £1000 between them for services to the company during the next 6 months. Having to hold a minimum of the shares, and often holding considerable numbers, the directors were, by nature of their position at the top, able to forsee and plan events which might lead to a rise or fall in the share prices. Certain proprietors were quick to notice this, and unsuccessfully demanded a prohibition on their trafficking in shares. There are always those who will blame the directors for anything and everything and no doubt this accusation was made by a proprietor anxious to nail the company's discounted shares on the director's abuse of their trust.

The constitution of the board was simplified during 1837. Both GC and BC were empowered by the Act of Incorporation to make important decisions without reference to the other and this led to confusion and a strained relationship. On the suggestion of the GC and with the proprietors' endorsement a new Board with 5 directors each from Birmingham and Gloucester and one each from Tewkesbury and Worcester was elected in August 1837. The two committees would continue; that at Gloucester meeting solely to attend to matters specific to the Gloucester division (Gloucester to Tibberton and the Tewkesbury and Worcester branches), leaving the BC to make the company's major policy decisions in addition to those specific to their own division (between Tibberton and Birmingham).

Capt. Moorsom's staff had been busy since contracts were halted in

April 1837. Progress was outlined to the proprietors at their August general meeting. The period of 'unexampled monetary difficulty' and the inability of proprietors to meet calls on their shares led to the postponement of contracts, but the company were now in a position to proceed immediately. The delay had proved advantageous. There had been reductions in cost and quantities of some materials; revision of plans and contracts had been made effecting savings in expenditure; and all the required land had been staked out. Property plans had progressed and several purchases had been made.

Certain proprietors were sceptical of Moorsom's capabilities, both as regards estimating the costs of construction and the suitability of his route in engineering and traffic terms. They succeeded in obtaining an adjournment of the meeting for six weeks to allow an independent report to be made on Moorsom's route by an 'eminent engineer'. Were it to prove unsuitable then it should be abandoned.

Joseph Locke, the engineer of the GJR accepted the task. It was to be confined to considering the suitability of the line for passengers, the fitness of the proposed engineering works and the estimates for their costs. Reporting back to the meeting in September, Mr Locke found: '. . . nothing to induce doubt or hesitation but the inclined plane. Gradients were such [Lickey excepted] that locomotive engines for conveying passengers may be properly applied.' It was a well selected line, other than the Lickey Incline, and Moorsom's estimations for the costs were endorsed, in fact Locke's only other criticism was in the lightness of the rails to be used.

Of the Lickey, Locke was concerned mainly about the safety of working it for the passenger trains. Samuel Baker, the B&G chairman stated how Parliament had examined the Lickey in detail and was well satisfied. Similar inclines on the Bolton and Leigh, and Canterbury Railways had carried 680,000 passengers over the past eight years without a single accident. Locke had to admit that he thought there was less risk to passengers on an inclined railway than on an inclined turnpike road.

Satisfied as regards engineering, the meeting then turned its attention to the traffic and (hopefully) the profit on offer. A bright prospect was reported: '. . . the present condition of your affairs is such as to insure the ultimate completion of the undertaking and the fulfilment of all the expections of advantage originally held out to the public . . .' Results of every railway yet opened had shown passenger revenue far higher than the most optimistic estimates, such were: '. . . the superior facilities of this mode of travelling . . . Add to this the connection at Birmingham with the GJR & L&B . . . The Directors believe that in proportion to the amount of capital expended, the traffic on this line will be little inferior to any railway in the Kingdom; it will be the connecting link between the whole of the West of England, South of Ireland, Liverpool and the great manufacturing districts of the North.' With such glowing prospects proclaimed who could ask for more? Well, two types of shareholders could. Those who genuinely doubted the viability of the concern, and those who were after the quickest and fattest returns.

Having heard Mr Locke's endorsement of the costs, the adjourned meeting debated the accuracy of the traffic estimates submitted to Parliament. Samuel Baker considered them an underestimate, but even if the line paid only 1 per cent it would be fair remuneration to those, who from other motives than gain, wished to see so great a national object carried into effect. Such motives, however, would not encourage shareholders to support the railway; he offered the following data.

The 39 coaches each way daily on the road between Gloucester, Cheltenham, Worcester and Birmingham, would produce, when doubled as was usual for railway estimates, £125,500 per annum. Merchandise, taking only a fraction of the present trade, gave £43,500. Working expenses, as recently calculated by Robert Stephenson, were on average £1000 per mile of railway per year, so for the B&G this was £55,000, giving a net income of £114,000, or 12 per cent on the capital. However, some railways had reported passenger loadings, four times that of the road traffic. He was delighted to witness a brighter prospect and had no doubt that works would be: '. . . vigorously prosecuted to a successsful issue.' Those shareholders who had called the adjournment had done their homework on the traffic and had surprised themselves. They calculated £171,000 income which gave 9 per cent return using the '50 per cent working expense' formula, or 12 per cent using the '£1000 per mile' one.

They could report the general propriety of the company and that an ample return was guaranteed. Perhaps the exercise was a genuine one, done for the benefits and assurance of the entire meeting. On the other hand, what better way could there be to stimulate and rekindle interest in the company and help push share prices upwards?

A further note of encouragement was struck in the *Gloucester Journal*.[2] A correspondent explained that the large discount on the B&G shares was due entirely to unsucc ssful speculation by shareholders who had taken on far too many shares. When they could not afford to pay the calls on them the market was saturated with unwanted shares which naturally caused their value to plummet. If only shares were held by bona fide local people, able to pay calls on time, he pleaded, then the works could quickly proceed and hasten a return on their investments. As for the prosperity of the B&G, explained the correspondent, look at the Liverpool & Manchester and GJR shares, they were worth double their original price and the number of passengers was over four times the previous coach traffic: 'Consider the railway as like a tree. Birmingham is the ground in which the tree stands; one great root strikes out for Liverpool, another to Manchester, sending their fibres off collecting sap from densely populated lines of the North which will flow into the trunk at Birmingham, extending to Stonehouse where one great stem diverges west to Bristol [i.e. the BrG] and the Bath extending its branches over the whole of the Southwest and another stem diverges towards London [CGWU] ramifying in all directions to the South.'

3:1 CHELTENHAM TO GLOUCESTER 1836

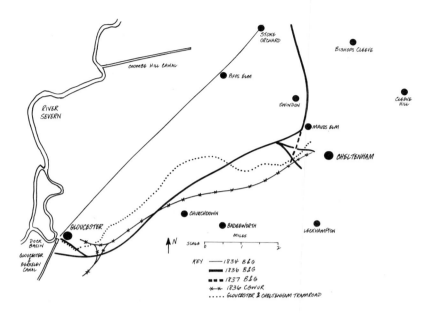

5:1 CHELTENHAM TO GLOUCESTER 1837–38

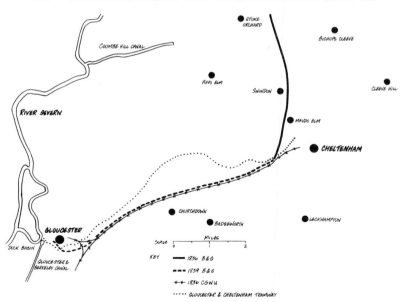

3:2 RAILWAYS TO WORCESTER, 1836

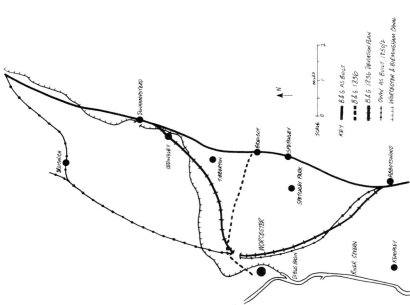

3:3 WORCESTER CITY CENTRE

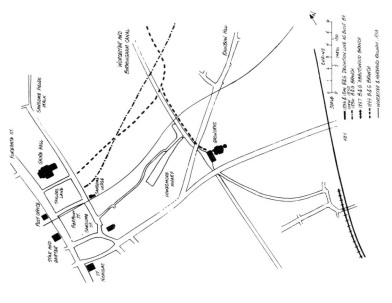

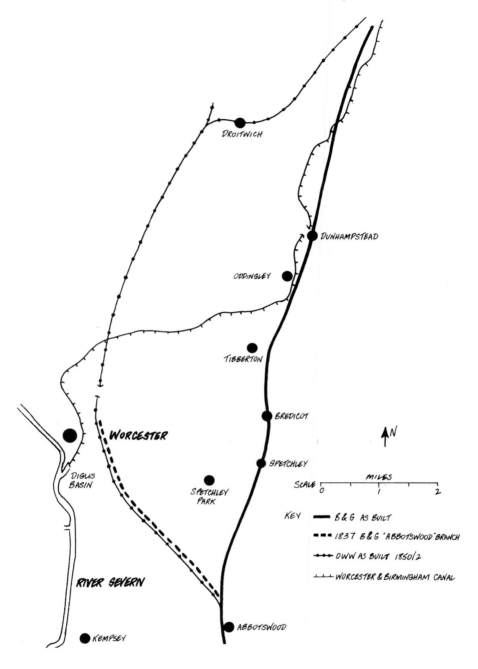

DROITWICH

DUNHAMPSTEAD

ODDINGLEY

TIBBERTON

BREDICOT

WORCESTER

SPETCHLEY

DIGLIS
BASIN

SPETCHLEY
PARK

↑ N

SCALE   MILES
         0   1   2

KEY   ━━━ B & G AS BUILT

       ▬ ▬ ▬ 1837 B & G "ABBOTSWOOD" BRANCH

       •—•—• OWW AS BUILT 1850/2

       ┴─┴─┴ WORCESTER & BIRMINGHAM CANAL

RIVER SEVERN

ABBOTSWOOD

KEMPSEY

5:2 RAILWAYS TO WORCESTER. THE ABBOTSWOOD AND BREDICOT BRANCHES COMPARED.

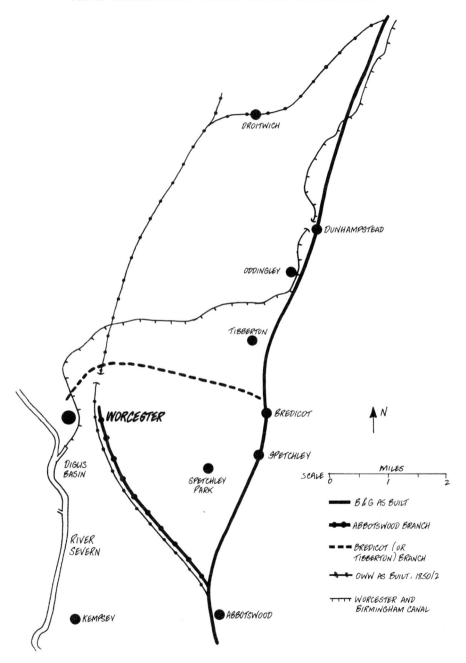

DROITWICH

DUNHAMPSTEAD

ODDINGLEY

TIBBERTON

WORCESTER

BREDICOT

DIGLIS BASIN

SPETCHLEY

SPETCHLEY PARK

RIVER SEVERN

KEMPSEY

ABBOTSWOOD

N

SCALE

MILES

0 — 1 — 2

━━━ B & G AS BUILT

●━●━● ABBOTSWOOD BRANCH

- - - BREDICOT (OR TIBBERTON) BRANCH

┤┤┤ OWW AS BUILT, 1850/2

┬┬┬ WORCESTER AND BIRMINGHAM CANAL

CHAPTER FIVE

THE CGWU AND WORCESTER REVISITED

With prospects of an early start of construction on the B&G, the same cannot be said for the CGWU on whom the B&G depended for access to Gloucester. In fact the CGWU were all but bankrupt after their lengthy opposition to the Cheltenham and Tring Railway. Their general meeting in November 1837 was informed that the Swindon to Kemble section would provide the quickest return and would therefore be constructed first. The Cheltenham to Gloucester line was thus deferred, but as powers for the compulsory purchase of land lapsed in June 1838, an application to Parliament for an extension of time would be necessary.

Naturally this decision outraged the B&G. They considered that the protecting clauses in their Act of Incorporation (Chapter 3) were inadequate: if the CGWU went bankrupt for instance, the B&G would be powerless to take over and complete the Cheltenham to Gloucester line. The Board instructed their solicitors to draw up clauses for insertion in the CGWU bill to compel them to complete the joint line by a certain date (to be decided). Penalty clauses would allow the B&G to buy out the CGWU's rights and build the line themselves.

The CGWU rejected these demands. Sufficient protection for the B&G already existed, they complained, and added that confrontation in Parliament would only further deplete both company's finances. The B&G however persisted with their opposition and even submitted plans for an independent line between Cheltenham and Gloucester (see Map 5.1). Fortunately for both sides a suggestion for binding arbitration was accepted instantly and the difficulties were settled by March 1838.

The bill with its protecting clauses became law on 11 June 1838. 'By these clauses', states the report to the August 1838 general meeting, 'a definite and short time is fixed by which the CGWU have to purchase the land [March 1839] and construct their line [June 1840] and should they fail to do either, this Company has the power to construct it for their own benefit . . .' Power was given to the CGWU to purchase a moiety of the Cheltenham to Gloucester line provided their line opened fully to Gloucester by June 1845, which purchase would revest the powers and provisions of the line with them. The provisions of the B&G Incorporating Act were now repealed and they were empowered to build their own depot at Gloucester. Rapid progress followed the passing of the Act. By November, the contracts were let, all land purchased, and works proceeded. The original agreement for joint depots at Cheltenham and Gloucester was terminated and separate stations adopted.

Work proceeded on the line and all was well between the two companies until November 1839. Then the bomb dropped. On the 21 November the B&G was informed that the Cheltenham to Gloucester line would not be completed by 21 June 1840 as stipulated in the Act. Although the trackbed was largely complete (except for the permanent way), all work ceased on it until June 1840 when the CGWU released it to the B&G who began a frenzied assault on its rapid completion.

Worcester had lost its chance of being on a main line between the GJR at Wolverhampton and the B&G at Abbotswood when the GCR Bill was thrown out by Parliament during May 1837. All it had was the promise of a branch line from Abbotswood, awarded to the B&G in the same session; one which the B&G did not approve but into which they had been trapped by their bond with the GCR. The GCR was a shabby affair. Conceived in 1835 to link Gloucester and Worcester with Birmingham and Wolverhampton, it had amputated its Gloucester and Birmingham section in the following year and failed miserably in Parliament. Resurrected again in 1837 as a local scheme between Stourbridge and Worcester, the promoters defended its contraction by describing their new proposal as 'in every way desirable'. However, the shareholders did not agree and called for the abandonment of the scheme and a rebate of whatever funds were left. Exit the GCR? No, not yet!

Such was the undesirability of Abbotswood branch to the B&G that they began to question the legality of the bond which held them bound to construct it. Although there is no record of its wording, it is certain that it was in the name of the GCR and since the GCR never became a corporate body how could the bond have legal validity? In December 1837 the B&G sought legal advice and decided upon the non-legality of the bond. They resolved that the '. . . branch from Abbotswood be not proceeded with but that the engineer be directed to report to a future meeting . . . the best branch for connecting the City of Worcester to the main line.'[1] Some have said that the B&G treated the city badly by avoiding it in the first place, while others take the opposite view, though perhaps it was more a case of 'six of one and half a dozen of the other'. Perhaps Worcester's chance of a connection with the main line was spoilt by having the town council (Worcester was a city yet all contemporary reports refer to a 'town council', 'town clerk', etc. – we have thus used this terminology throughout) Chamber of Commerce, and the GCR all claiming to represent the 'best interests' of the city. Had the B&G's original branch submission from Bredicot to Sansome Fields been authorised it would certainly have been built and served the centre of the City with equal favour to Birmingham and Gloucester. The Abbotswood line, however, terminated away from the centre and was a distinct disadvantage for those travelling to and from Birmingham; no wonder the B&G would not build it. The element in Worcester who did support it (i.e. the GCR party) obviously had eyes on its future extension through the Black Country to Wolverhampton – rather than on its position on the Birmingham to Gloucester route.

Towards the end of 1838 the B&G received a letter from Mr Pierpoint, the chairman of the GCR. He requested information on the progress of the Abbotswood branch, since that company was about to go to Parliament again for a shortened line between Worcester and Stourbridge. The *Gloucester Journal* warned: 'Another scheme is in agitation.' But agitate is all it did. Mr Pierpoint was bluntly told that the B&G 'did not recognise the existence of the GCR'. A deputation of the B&G attended a meeting of Worcester people and informed them of their intention to make a branch 'in a good situation'.

Worcester's response was delayed until the B&G sought powers in Parliament during the 1839 session to construct a branch to Gloucester Docks. Literally hours before the bill was 'committed' to the House (endorsed by the Parliamentary Committee), the town clerk of Worcester arrived to present a petition on behalf of the city's inhabitants to insert clauses in the bill compelling the B&G to make the Abbotswood branch – and none other – before their main line opened. In reply, the B&G repeated their resolve to abandon that line which had been pursued only because of the bond with the GCR and to make a branch with a central terminus. Furthermore they offered to leave the choice of junction to the Mayor and Mr Berkeley and would agree to the insertion of a penalty clause in the event of their failure to complete it by a date to be specified.

But no! Worcester insisted on Abbotswood or nothing and alas, the Parliamentary Committee agreed. For the B&G, it was a choice between the all important branch to Gloucester Docks, the unwanted one to Worcester or nothing. The board would not submit to Worcester and withdrew the bill! Of this the *Railway Times* commented:[2] '. . . in defeating the Bill they [Worcester] have released the Directors and the Company from the pledge which they had given and by which they considered themselves bound to construct the branch line . . .' Public opinion in Worcester towards the B&G was at a very low ebb. Worcester newspapers made a song and dance over their 'decided and important victory' but as the *Railway Times* remarked, by that 'victory' they had lost all chance of a railway in the forseeable future and must ultimately say: 'a few more such victories and we are undone'. Looking at it from the B&G's point of view, they had suffered an immense loss from the failure to get their branch to Gloucester Docks. After all, did not the B&G grow from the desire to link Birmingham with the docks at Gloucester? The loss of traffic in later years through not having this link had a profound effect on the B&G's fortunes.

Mr Pierpoint of the GCR rubbed salt into the wound. Through his solicitor, he had applied: '. . . for payment of £70,000 being the amount payable to him by the breach of the condition for a bond dated 14th October 1836 . . . by which the Company engaged to make a branch . . . to the City of Worcester.' What a nerve! Notice the phrase 'payable to him'! Needless to say the Board declined to pay, but did communicate to the Chamber of Commerce their willingness to make a suitable branch and supplied a report, compiled by Capt. Moorsom, of the B&G's policy.[3]

A branch, he thought, needed a central position for its terminus, a connection with the river Severn, a booking office for passengers in Sansome Fields (near Foregate St.) and had to be on the most direct and least expensive route. The Abbotswood line satisfied none of these requirements. It terminated 1 mile from the city centre, 30 miles from Birmingham and 20 from Gloucester. In contrast the 'Tibberton' [northerly] line was central, it would cost £10,000 to £15,000 less than the former, and by it Worcester would be only 25 miles from Birmingham, from and to which the principal traffic was expected. After due consideration, the Chamber of Commerce rejected the branch principle in favour of one that should be part of a main line from Worcester to the north. Back again to square one!

CHAPTER SIX

PROGRESS ON THE MAIN LINE

With the return to normality of the money supply, the long awaited commencement of construction was possible. Moorsom reported to the Board on 24 October 1837 the good news that work would start the following month which would allow the partial opening of the railway between Cheltenham and Tibberton, near Worcester, in June 1839 (i.e. the Gloucester division). The heavier earthworks in the Birmingham division would not however be completed until January 1841.

Contracts were advertised on 31 October 1837. Applications were to be approved by both committees and, according to Capt. Moorsom's principles, should be painstakingly compiled to avoid confusion, ambiguity and fraud. The efficient execution of the contracts would be ensured by the engineer's experience in the management and command of men as a result of his army experience. He said he would encourage the best possible work from all his subordinates, believing that this was best attained by encouraging their education and promotion. His efforts were often in vain. The BC thought they knew better than their engineer and sought economy rather than quality, often with the result that more was spent putting things right than ever was saved by their economies.

Visible progress on earthworks was reported by the engineer at the end of the year, but he was none too pleased with the Board's skinflint attitude towards the employment of staff. Not one draughtsman was employed in his office at Worcester, he complained, where working drawings for all the contracts were produced. His plea was answered during the ensuing months and the ranks of the engineering department were increased, and included a draughtsman named Herbert Spencer, who was later to provide an account of his experiences on the B&G in his autobiography.[1]

Of life in the offices at Worcester he recalled: 'The junior members of the B&G staff belonged largely to the ruling classes and had corresponding notions and habits. Our chief engineer, Capt. W.S. Moorsom having been a military man and having as his 2 resident engineers military men also, . . . showed his leanings or perhaps chiefly his friendships by gathering together as sub-engineers and draughtsmen, young fellows whose connections were in most cases military or naval. There were, however, some of other classes [Spencer was the son of a schoolmaster] . . . The superintendence was not rigid and the making of designs was interspersed . . . with stories not of an improving kind . . . with glances down on . . . passers by . . . females, and resulting remarks being a continuous accompaniment of whistling and singing . . . the code of morals . . . was not very high . . . However, sundry of them have turned out very respectable men . . .' Junior members had not unpleasant lives, their office hours being from 9 a.m. to 5 p.m. with Saturday afternoon off. 'In the office at Worcester there had been made not only drawings for engineering works but also those for buildings, stations, offices, engine houses, and so forth . . . we have a club consisting of all . . . the engineering department . . . we meet and dine together at Capt. Moorsom's every two months and in the evening subjects connected with the railway . . . are discussed, every individual being allowed to make observations. We have a club uniform which . . . I was forced to get rather against my will.' Good news awaited proprietors at the general meeting in February 1838. Work between Cheltenham and Droitwich was being accelerated to enable a partial opening by mid-1839 by which coach traffic could be transferred onto the line at Cheltenham to resume its journey to Birmingham at Droitwich. The remaining works at the Birmingham end were not being neglected but owing to the heavier earthworks would take until early 1841 to complete. Land purchase was nearly completed, and contracts let on advantageous terms to local people, thus avoiding bringing in a 'host of strangers' and 'those not of a desirable kind'. There was: 'no doubt whatever in the opinion of the Engineer that the subscribed capital of £950,000 will be fully sufficient to complete the undertaking'.

Shares (£12.10s.0d. paid up but selling at £5.10s.0d.) were reaching a wider market. The *Railway Times* remarked:[2] 'We confess . . . no little surprise . . . [at] . . . the quotation of shares in this undertaking . . . at the ruinous discount at which these have lately stood . . . the traffic on the line has been proved to be nearly equal to the GJR . . . .it is not always the best which are the most prosperous. . .'. From the *Cheltenham Looker-on*:[3] '. . . it poses . . . the singular feature of almost unprecedented cheapness of execution combined with . . . [potential] traffic of a large amount.'!

Six months later the proprietors heard that engineering progress was considerable; about half of the line with some of the heaviest earthworks was under construction and the projected opening was likely to be on schedule. Land juries had saved the Company thousands of pounds; one landowner claimed £12,000 for two pieces of land, but had been awarded only £1,600! Contracts were let within the engineer's estimate but in a different manner than on many other railways. They were divided into smaller portions than usual and let to contractors particularly conversant with each description of work which secured lower prices per mile than on other railways.

Financial matters began to improve. Shares (£20 paid up) were now only at 50 per cent discount on the market compared with 70 per cent at the last meeting. Samuel Baker thought this depreciation expressed a want of public confidence in the company. The directors would not, he said, worry about share prices or the fears and speculations of shareholders, they would act solely towards conducting the affairs of the company. But he would say that such were the prospects of the line that any shareholder who was alarmed for the future had only himself to blame. Traffic estimates were the usual 'carrot' or 'bribe' thrown at the shareholders, and plenty of them appeared in the report and the press.

Detailed analysis (see appendix) of the present coach traffic on the route would gross £104,000 for the railway and a further £26,000 would accrue from post and parcels. Conveyance of goods was discussed for the first time in detail, which seems a little odd considering that the original purpose of the railway was alleged to have been for goods traffic. Perhaps those concerned simply expected it to transfer from the canals and rivers to their line automatically. Charles Shaw, a merchant from Birmingham, alluded to the great advantage experienced by his colleagues in Birmingham from the quick transit of goods by the GJR, which despite taking them at low rates, realised at least 50 per cent profit. Bearing in mind the great traffic by canals to the western parts of England and also the serious interruptions to which that traffic was liable in the winter months he had, he said, no doubt that once the B&G was open it would at once be made use of as a cheap and speedy channel for merchandise.

Joseph Walker, the chairman, added that no other method of conveyance could compete with the railways in the carriage of goods; look at the GJR, he said, it had one of the finest lines of canal in the country along side it and had successfully made deep inroads into the canal traffic. What could go wrong?

Local newspapers often reported progress on the main line. In the latter part of 1838, the men employed between Camp Hill and Moseley[4] were, 'prosecuting their labours night and day as the weather permits.' Further south:[5] '. . . Workmen are engaged in laying the permanent way, which is constructed on a new and improved principle from which it is anticipated that the line will possess all the firmness and solidity as that of the GWR but free from its defects. Work at the Cheltenham and Tewkesbury depots has commenced . . . The Gloucester portion is rapidly reaching completion, earthworks are remarkably light, as is the masonry, of which the whole is being executed at prices hitherto unknown to railway proprietors. The engineer has solved the problem of lack of gravel by burning clay into a species of brick rubbish which appears to answer exceedingly well'.

The February 1839 general meeting promised to be a stormy one. In January, Burgess, the secretary, and Capt. Moorsom had investigated the financial affairs of the company and had had a shock. Parliamentary estimates for land had been £84,000 but the figure to date was £126,000, with that in the Birmingham division 100 per cent more than the estimate. Present expenditure and future liabilities totalled £1.1 millions, an excess of £160,000 (see appendix for details). Borrowing was the only solution and having successively promised that the existing capital would be quite sufficient, the present state of affairs was going to need some explaining at the general meeting. It would seem that the B&G had a good public relations man to write their reports as is apparent in the following precis.

Construction progress was good with one third of earthworks, brickwork and masonry complete; materials for the permanent way were in course of delivery and several sections laid. (That was the good news, now follows the bad!) To keep costs within targets, the business of the. company was conducted with a 'rigid regard for economy'; engineering costs were within the authorised capital but increases in the cost and amount of rolling stock required, the extension to Gloucester Docks, better station facilities and sundry other items of unforseen expenditure required an additional sum, the amount of which: '. . . cannot at present be exactly ascertained', but it should not exceed one half of the authorised borrowing powers of £316,000 (see appendix for full details). Proprietors should be satisfied, the report continued, to compare the B&G with other railways. The Liverpool and Manchester line overspent by 150 per cent, the GJR by 60 per cent, the L&B by 230 per cent, the Southampton Railway by 75 per cent.

An interesting footnote to the overspending on railways appeared in the *Railway Times*.[6] Capt. Moorsom wrote to defend 'the engineer', who, it would appear, always got the blame. By instancing the spending on the B&G which was under his control, he proved that the final total would be on or about the original estimate and the same was true on other railways at that time. The culprits were, he concluded, out-of-the-ordinary events such as weather but mostly the overall management of the companies by their directors. We shall return to this subject a little later!

Proprietors were then told that in November 1838 the Board had decided to postpone the opening between Cheltenham and Droitwich and to push on to Bromsgrove. Droitwich was a 'stage and a half' from Birmingham, had no coach establishment, and there was little hope of getting the Bristol to Birmingham coaches on the line for so short a distance. Now, were the line extended to Bromsgrove, an established coaching point 13 miles from Birmingham, then the coach traffic could be relied upon and it was confidently expected that this opening could be effected by December 1839.

The usual salvos of optimistic cliches were fired to appease the proprietors. Mr Tartt, an influential shareholder, (of whom more later) reassuringly said:[7] 'The B&G is an important line of communications between the North of England and the West and South. It passes through more places likely to contribute to its traffic than any other line of the same extent. [We wonder if he had studied a map] I believe it will create its own traffic.' Suitably calmed, the proprietors quietly went away without calling for heads to roll, and patiently waited the six months before the August general meeting would bring further news.

Capt. Moorsom reported that engineering work was proceeding steadily and without incident. Delay had been caused in several places by contractors, landowners and turnpike trustees, but the Cheltenham to Bromsgrove section would be ready early in 1840 (previous estimate December 1839) and the stations along this route were soon to be complete. Finally locomotives and rolling stock were in course of delivery (all details in relevant chapters).   To whet their appetites, the Board told the proprietors of the impetus given to travel by the opening of the L&B and GJR which had increased the traffic between Gloucester and Birmingham considerably (22 road coaches daily, double the previous number) while the completion of the BDJC and the passing of the BrG's Act would significantly add to that traffic. From Exeter to Newcastle railways were finished or being constructed making the B&G one of the main links in the chain of communication from north to south of the country which stretched for 350 miles.

With the partial opening to Bromsgrove in prospect for January 1840, the directors hoped a further section between Bromsgrove and Lifford could be opened by July of that year. Capt. Moorsom pointed out that this extension was nine miles in length and included the Lickey Incline, Grovely Lane Tunnel (Cofton in later years) and several large cuttings and embankments. Work on Grovely Tunnel had not yet begun but Capt. Moorsom considered that completion could be hastened if all attempt at approach cuttings were abandoned and the bore lengthened to 450 yards instead of the 150 he had planned for the sake of economy. But even by increasing the number of men employed, and offering incentive payments to the contractors he thought 11 months (i.e. November 1840) was the minimum time required to complete the whole section. Even that estimate of time was doubtful owing to the rain which had fallen continuously for the past few months and showed no sign of cessation. The additional expense of accelerating the works would be £10,000.

He added that progress on the Lifford to Camp Hill section was such that he could expect completion of the entire line by mid-January 1841. This would save the expense of a temporary station at Lifford if a further opening were delayed for six weeks. With further discussion, the board persuaded him to push for an opening to Lifford by the middle of September 1840 and he agreed, providing the weather was favourable.

Commenting on progress at Cheltenham, the *Cheltenham Looker-on* noted:[8] '. . . the extensive range of buildings near the offices and lodge are already erected and in a very forward state and unless retarded by the weather will be roofed over in a few days. A powerful locomotive is now constantly employed in removing ballast etc. along the line from Cheltenham to Tewkesbury and we believe it is the intention of the Directors to make their first experimental trip along it some day next week . . . The 32 miles cost will not exceed £1 million and traffic along the route has doubled since the GJR opened. The ultimate prospects of the Company are most promising.' During December 1839 and January 1840 the floodgates of publicity opened with local and national papers filled with glittering prospects for the B&G consequent on the shortly expected opening. A few are quoted. From the *Cheltenham Examiner*:[9] 'We have very little doubt that the B&G will turn out well. Everybody knows that the trade of Gloucester is vastly on the increase, her fine canal and capacious docks alike monuments of the enterprise of her citizens and the stupidity of certain Bristolians [!], crowded with vessels of every tonnage and from every country, afford clear indices of rapid commercial progress. The enormous increase of iron trade in the district of which Birmingham is the centre answers an increase of commerce there and hence will the B&G form the medium of carriage between two of the busiest spots in England and moreover into each end of which, whether from the North or West, other lines pour their contribution of traffic. We believe no line in England has been more economically or better constructed and we look forward to its success as all but certain.' One optimist writing in the *Railway Times*[10] thought the B&G's prospects were: '. . . as brilliant as . . . many at present in better odour with the public.' (Their shares were at a discount of 39 per cent!) Present coach traffic, he stated, consisted of 26 daily each way averaging 10 passengers per coach, which, when trebled, as was the usual way of estimating for railway traffic, would gross £240,000 per annum and assuming only a modest goods traffic of £250 weekly, gross overall takings would be £260,000. Deducting working expenses and interest charges left a net profit of £125,000 or: '. . . the rate of 14 per cent, nearly . . . can we look for a better investment? . . . parties investing absolutely secure to themselves a fortune . . . without the slighest risk.'!

At the general meeting of February 1840 we find: '. . . the subject of opening the line is that on which Proprietors must naturally have the greatest anxiety.' Quoting from the engineer's report: '. . . works on the entire line have been proceeding steadily towards completion although they have been most seriously retarded by a continued series of rain and tempest unexampled in the valley of the Severn for very many years . . . I have found it necessary to stop contractors in order to avoid absolute injury to the permanent works by a fruitless perseverance amongst mud and water . . . A few slips had occurred but of no consequence . . . Depôts and stations at Tewkesbury, Cheltenham, Spetchley, Droitwich, Bromsgrove, Ashchurch, Eckington, Defford and Bredon are either complete or in a forward state . . ..
The carrying department has 10 locomotives at work at various parts of the line helping with construction, more are on order and wagons and coaches are being delivered.' Capt. Moorsom thought it: '. . . imprudent to calculate upon opening the railway to Bromsgrove before the month of May . . . As regards the further opening . . . the railway may be opened to Lifford [9 miles from Bromsgrove] in October or November next, and to Camp Hill, Birmingham during the present year. The short Extension line to the L&B station . . . will occupy until the end of Spring 1841 . . .' Unfortunately the cost of the undertaking would probably exceed the authorised amount but this was wholly due to unforseen events, such as the increase in the cost and numbers required of locomotives and rolling stock, also of passenger accommodation at stations.

Further indecision over the opening occurred in April 1840. Having inspected the line between Bromsgrove and Barnt Green, including the Lickey, the directors thought: '. . . that with a trifling additional expense and only a little extra time the line could be opened to field No.24, Bromsgrove' which was near the road bridge at Barnt Green and 11 miles by road from Birmingham.[11]

Capt. Moorsom thought such an opening was possible by 1 July, and in a written reply to the Board he not only confirmed this, but made a bitter attack on the BC's lust for economy. First he complained of the lack of suitable locomotive power to work the Incline, having but one 'Heavy' engine (Norris A-extra) which was capable of working trains on it. Without extra power he could not manage to work trains on the Incline with any degree of reliability. There was no water supply at the proposed 'terminus' for the engines so a temporary supply would be required. Lastly, the additional expense of temporary buildings could not be easily estimated owing to: '. . . the way in which you act with me in respect of the Buildings and other erections at stations. You have hitherto refused to let me put up the erections at the proper time when I requested to have them and at present there is much hurry and effort making to get some of the buildings at other places partially erected in time.' We do believe that the engineer was looking forward to relinquishing his post! The directors nevertheless decided to pursue opening to Barnt Green.

Trial runs between Cheltenham and Eckington were reported in May by the *Cheltenham Examiner*.[12] '. . . several experimental trips have been made to this pleasant village about 13 miles from Cheltenham with a loaded train of 100 tons burden. The American engines, although small, appear to possess a concentration of power which rarely appertains to engines but of the largest size.' These trips were continued into June with Herbert Spencer[13] involved in experiments on the friction of locomotives: 'In the afternoon we happened to have . . . [by accident] . . . two engines going the same way on the two lines of rails and a race was the consequence; we went side by side at between 30–40 m.p.h. for a mile or so and shook hands from one train to another.'

A single line of railway was completed between Cheltenham and Bromsgrove on 30 May and private trains ran on the following two days. One trip was recorded by the *Gloucester Journal*:[14] '. . . a party of Directors assembled at Cheltenham with the view of proceeding along the line to Bromsgrove; two carriages, four wagons comprising the train . . . they proceeded to Bromsgrove . . .

At Bromsgrove they were met by an excellent band provided by one of the contractors, Mr Bayliss [he was actually the Resident engineer] who also furnished a number of flags, and as the party took the musicians, banners etc. with them on their return the train assumed a very gay appearance and led to the supposition that it was a public opening of the line, . . . further strengthened by the fact that five carriages also accompanied with music and banners joined the train at Ashchurch. The trip was highly satisfactory and not the slightest accident occured to mar the pleasance of the day.' Then the directors decided to alter the opening plans yet again. Lord Seymour's Railway bill, the first of the 'Regulation of the Railways Acts', was shortly to become law and contained a clause forcing all public railways to be inspected for safety and soundness by an officer of the Board of Trade (BoT) one month before opening. As this would interfere with the B&G's plans, they resolved not to proceed to Barnt Green, but to open the railway partially from Cheltenham to Bromsgrove by running 2 trains each way daily from 23 June for the conveyance of passengers, parcels, horses and carriages. The incomplete state of the line as a whole forced a postponement of goods traffic until early the following year.

Formal opening was delayed for a day, and took place on Wednesday 24 June 1840. There was no celebration, no speeches, no banquet or festivities; such were deemed an arrant waste of the company's precious funds by the Board, who preferred to squander capital in other parts of the undertaking!

From the local press[15] we discover that the inaugural train consisted of two 1st class and two 2nd class carriages hauled by the locomotive *W.S. Moorsom* [a rare complement to their engineer] and left Cheltenham at 9.10 a.m.: '. . . the signal for starting was given. A bugler played "God Save the Queen", the train . . . started off in gallant style quickly receding from the astonished gaze of the persons assembled . . . the pace was excellent, being at least 30 m.p.h.' At Eckington, reached at 9.45 a.m., they were met by '. . . passengers flocking to ride upon a train for the very first time in their lives, followed by a stop at Defford [which] crammed the carriages to capacity. When the train reached Spetchley road coaches were waiting to take up passengers for Worcester, this stop being used to enable the engine to take on water'. Arrival at Bromsgrove was at 10.50 a.m., and after a rapid turnround the train returned to Cheltenham arriving at 12.27 p.m. Share prices rose £13 to £75 (on £80 paid up), the best price for a long, long while.

Good news greeted the shareholders at their August meeting: '[Traffic] . . . has exceeded the most sanguine expected of the Directors . . . The cheering inference may be fairly drawn that when the whole line is in operation, the traffic will be increased to an amount far exceeding any calculations that have hitherto been made'.

A further opening to Cofton Farm, 8 miles from Birmingham was expected on or near 15 September. The Cheltenham and Gloucester section, dealt with in detail later, had been taken over by the B&G from the CGWU and was expected to be ready during November.

Finance was a subject for congratulation, said the directors, but we find it difficult to see why. All the authorised capital had been raised, mostly as a result of having to provide capital to take over the Cheltenham to Gloucester line from the CGWU, which meant nearly a third of a million pounds on loan at 4 or 5 per cent interest. This interest commitment hung like a lead collar around the directors' necks throughout the remainder of the railway's independent existence.

Re-calculation of the eventual outlay in June 1840 had foreseen a surplus of only £82,000 from the combined share and loan capital of £1,266,666 after allowing for the Worcester branch (when and if built) and only a moiety of the Cheltenham–Gloucester line. Now that the full cost of that section had to be borne, things were going to be tight. However, the directors were confident that they would be able to manage on existing funds.

Herbert Spencer throws a little light on how difficult the financial situation was.[16] 'Capt. Moorsom had no doubt made an underestimate of the cost of the line . . . but was creditably anxious to keep within the estimates, and hence was over-prone to to economy of construction. In some cases the effects were disastrous.' He refers, as an example, to the giving way of the wing walls of the Avon Bridge at Eckington, while we can think of the use of untreated timber in the permanent way which soon rotted as a further example.

However, we do think Spencer is a little unfair to Capt. Moorsom. The directors [especially the BC], whom he obeyed to the letter, had the major say in the materials and method of construction and the finger of blame should be pointed at their expensive 'economies'. It is easy, with hindsight, to condemn their stupidity; but in common with most of those who in the early days gaily promoted railways, they had no idea of the complexity of the problems in which they would become involved. The professionals whom they employed knew of course but even they had gained their knowledge the 'hard way'.

At first all had gone reasonably well, and the two committees were delighted to find that the first and easiest stretch of the line – that between Cheltenham and Bromsgrove – had been built comfortably within Capt. W.S. Moorsom's estimates. The stretch between Bromsgrove and Birmingham was however a very different matter. The Lickey Incline was in itself expensive, as also was Cofton Tunnel; while the country between Longbridge and Birmingham was by no means easy. It had been split up into short sections for contract purposes just as had been done with the lower stretch of the line. Capt. Moorsom, knowing the the nature of the ground and its geology, allowed for its difficulty in his estimates of what each section would cost. The BC, knowing nothing of geology, had only one criterion of cost, namely that of distance. If so many miles in Worcestershire had cost so much, they were quite unable to understand why a similar distance should cost so much more in Warwickshire. Accordingly they made the stupid blunder of thinking they knew better than their engineer, and accepted the lowest tenders rather than those nearest to his estimates. The results of this 'economy' was, as might have been expected, instead of saving money they squandered it. The 'cut-price contractors' either failed on site or skimped their work, and went bankrupt when made to do it properly. In either case, contracts had to be re-let to other contractors at higher and more realistic prices.

A further portion of the line was opened on 17 September to a temporary terminus at Cofton Farm, with 5 trains each way, Sundays excepted. Connecting road coaches at Cheltenham were arranged to take passengers to the west of England while connections with the L&B, GJR and BDJc were advertised. Goods traffic came in dribs and drabs, a wagonload here and there attached to the passenger trains prior to full arrangements which followed in March 1841.

How the railway worked its traffic is explained in later chapters, whilst the following pages describe the opening of the remainder of the B&G, and how its neighbour at Gloucester, the BrG, arrived.

CHAPTER SEVEN

FILLING IN THE GAPS

As we have seen above, the CGWU's decision in December 1839 not to honour their undertaking to build the Cheltenham–Gloucester line brought the penalty clauses into effect and by 24 June 1840 the B&G had taken the line over as the Act of 1838 entitled them to do.

Capt. Moorsom was in Liverpool at the time, and at that distance he could only give a provisional answer to the directors' questions concerning the completion of that section. He wrote saying that given the work already done on trackbed and structures, four and a half months would suffice for tracklaying, and that £5,000 per mile would cover the cost. Brunel and Moorsom met in July, and having agreed on the method of tracklaying for the two gauges, contracts for ballasting and tracklaying were immediately let. [Although the B&G would not lay the broad gauge rails, they would have to make allowances for clearances, etc.]

The B&G agreed to pay £20,000 monthly to the CGWU in respect of money expended by them in the construction of the joint line; a single payment of £17,500 also bought the CGWU's share in the Cheltenham and Gloucester Tramroad. The assessment of the precise amount of money owed by each company to the other through the joint line transaction remained in dispute for many years. Solicitors and accountants on both sides were kept busy well after 1843, when the GWR took over the CGWU. Indeed the dispute was not finally settled until after the MR had absorbed the B&G. The following brief summary shows how complicated the financial arrangements became.

All sums expended in construction prior to the B&G's takeover had to be repaid, with interest, and the CGWU presented a final account of

£118,000 for work done by them. Before paying the full amount however, the B&G decided to prepare a detailed estimate of how much the line would cost to build for the narrow gauge only. A comparison and a fair compromise could then be made, having in mind the Act's stipulations that work done solely for the broad gauge must be paid in full by the CGWU.

On checking the accounts, the secretary, Burgess, and solicitors found the contractor's accounts to be unsatisfactory; the amount of land and engineering works charged for was much greater than necessary. Legal and office costs had been charged for, yet they had no direct bearing on the construction of the line and should, they argued, be borne exclusively by the CGWU. Basically, the B&G disputed the accounts and resolved to make no further monthly payments until agreement had been reached. They had already paid £60,000 in addition to the tramroad moiety of £17,500. Solicitors acting for the CGWU called for immediate independent arbitration. This was agreed and the necessary steps taken, though nothing is minuted to record the outcome. Meanwhile, for reasons known only to themselves, the GC paid another £20,000 instalment, against the wishes of the Board, taking the amount paid to £80,000. There it remained right through to 1844 when the GWR, by then owners of the CGWU, repurchased their moiety. The whole financial position was eventually cleared up only after extensive investigation and the GWR had paid back £100,000 to redeem their rights in their half of the joint line. But we must return to 1840. Progress in track laying was slow owing to non-delivery of rails and Capt. Moorsom reckoned that opening could not be considered before October.

The *Gloucester Journal*,[1] reported a rumour that an engine was expected on the line and: '. . . great numbers of persons, anxious to gratify their curiosity, were attracted together to witness the arrival of the engine at Gloucester'. No engine appeared, much to their disappointment. However, a week or so later the *Gloucester Journal* announced that two experimental trips would be made over the Cheltenham to Gloucester line on 17 October and many hundreds arrived to witness this: '. . . novel sight . . . [and] . . . evidently much delighted with the prospects which the proceedings of the day afforded of the early application of this mode of travelling direct from this city to the North of England'.[2] A free ride was given from Gloucester to Cheltenham and back and was apparently remarkably pleasant; the carriages were described as 'handsome and commodious'. Opening was fixed for 2 November.

History was made on 21 October 1840 when Capt. Melhuish, R.E., performed the first BoT inspection of a new line of railway, between Cheltenham and Gloucester. He found the earthworks safe and sound.

The six months gap between cessation of work by the CGWU and the date of his inspection had allowed the works far greater time to settle than was usual. However, the permanent way, although 'laid down with great care', was incomplete. The Inspector was assured that two lines of rails would be laid before opening, which, together with repairing a defective bridge at Barnwood, delayed the opening until 4 November.

It was a cold, wet November morning which greeted the inaugural train. A correspondent to the *Railway Times* jubilantly reported:[3] '. . . we had the pleasure of travelling by railway to Gloucester, starting . . . at Lansdown at 9.00 we arrived in 16 minutes. There was a large concourse of people awaiting the arrival who appeared much gratified with the new system of travelling. The prospects on the journey are delightful, having in view the Leckhampton and Churchdown Hills nearly the whole of the distance.'

A service of four trains daily each way ran between Gloucester and Cofton, supplemented by four 'short trains' each way between Cheltenham and Gloucester. The public were pleased, but the shareholders were less so when they learned that the CGWU's defection and the B&G's acquisition of the line had forced expenses above their authorised capital by £60,000, pushing them still further into debt, and thus putting almost out of sight any prospect of a quick return on their investment.

We must return now to the Birmingham division. In November 1840, Capt. Moorsom announced that the completion of the railway between Camp Hill and Cofton could be expected on 15 December. The Board fixed the opening date at 15 December, and invited the BoT to inspect the line on the 12th, arrogantly ignoring the one month notice required by the BoT! Sir Frederick Smith of the BoT duly arrived to inspect the line and was not over-impressed. Heavy earthworks were required on that 8 mile section. Cuttings at Longbridge and Grovely were, he noted, unfinished and the slopes each side, especially at Grovely, were 'rugged and precipitous'. Embankments at Wychall, Northfield and the Rea Valley were lofty and did not appear to him to be sufficiently consolidated to ensure the public's safety.

Ballasting of the track was incomplete but Mr Hughes, the assistant engineer who accompanied Sir Frederick, said this would have to be a lengthy process which would continue over the next 12 months or so. The terminus at Camp Hill was in an imperfect state. It was only half-finished, with some rails not laid and no signals fitted.

Sir Frederick recommended that the opening be postponed, but if that was not possible, a 10 m.p.h. speed limit should be imposed on all trains until a further inspection in 12 months time. The Board, however, wished to open the line and knew they were not legally bound to adhere to the BoT's report. Through their secretary, Mr Burgess, they informed the BoT that since final arrangements for opening had already been made, they were unable to postpone it, but that immediate measures had been taken to ensure safety and they were satisfied that the railway was in: '. . . a fit and safe state to work at our normal velocity. . .'. Cuttings at Longbridge and Grovely were tidied up and a policeman stationed at the latter place in case of a slip. 'Embankments', Burgess continued, 'were firm and Camp Hill station had been put in a respectable condition including the red signal lamp'. Delayed by only a few days, that section was opened to the public on 17 December 1840, with the train service as before. Yet again, apart from the formal announcement there was no celebration, and the occasion was treated as just another ordinary working day in the life of the B&G.

To allay any doubts as to to the safety of the works on that portion, the Secretary joined the resident engineer, Mr Wetherall, and his assistant on a tour of inspection. 'As a whole ', he reported to the Board, 'the road may be said to be in excellent order, better than any portion of your railway has been . . . at the time of opening, in fact better than any railway that I have yet seen opened.' He had doubts about Grovely cutting, however, and said it did not look safe. He thought it might slip at any moment and suggested that land on either side be purchased in order to widen the cutting and thus decrease the slope, which they did.

With trains now running into Birmingham at Camp Hill, the chief urgency departed. The extension to the L&B station at Curzon St. was still under construction, and Capt. Moorsom hoped that this might be ready by June 1841 but in the end the usual crop of last minute difficulties delayed completion for another two months.

At Gloucester, despite their acquisition of the tramroad, the B&G still had no easy access to the docks from their 'temporary' depôt near the cattle market. They were therefore considering the building of a plateway spur from their goods shed to join the tramroad at the most convenient spot – 200 yards or so north of Barton crossroads. This would of course involve laborious transfer of goods to the tramroad wagons, but at least it was better than nothing.

Worcester meanwhile was still marooned 3 miles from the railway at Spetchley, and the B&G did their best to appease irate Worcester citizens by providing a free road coach service which met all trains. This arrangement, though well meant, was never satisfactory; for it added considerably to the B&G's working expenses while providing Worcester people with a continuous subject for complaint.

On the main line certain minor repairs to bridges and cuttings were necessary, but the engineering department staff were soon to be slashed. The engineer reported that a skeleton staff of 2 engineers and 3 or 4 clerks only could be kept after April 1841. Moorsom himself was anxious to leave. He had unsuccessfully applied for the post of engineering manager on the BrG in September 1840, and in February 1841 was asked to stay on as the B&G's consulting engineer only. Herbert Spencer recalled that,[4] '. . . the greater number of those who'd been employed . . . have gone; and now too I have received a notice that after April 25th my services will no longer be required . . . I was really quite pleased.'

Construction costs by then had passed the £1 million mark, yet various reports from the secretary in 1841 spoke of further liabilities of nearly £200,000; grand stations at Gloucester and at Lawley Street, Birmingham; improvements at the locomotive works at Bromsgrove and at various other stations. No mention was made of the docks branch or of a connection to Worcester!

On 14 August 1841, Sir Frederick Smith arrived to inspect the extension line to the L&B. This, he was told, would be used by all passenger trains running into the L&B Curzon St. station as well as by connecting freight traffic. Camp Hill would be used only for local goods, and a depôt for locomotives and rolling stock.

Sir Frederick made a very careful study of arrangements at the junction. As can be imagined (see Map, 16.1), the junction of two main lines offered considerable likelihood for accident. Certain precautions, such as the stopping of every train before it proceeded over or past the junction, were suggested and subsequently adopted (see Signalling, Chapter 16). Sir Frederick noted that engineering works on the line were in good order, and reported that the line was ready for opening subject to the adoption of special safety precautions at the junction.

With the opening of the line two days later, continuous railway communication were now possible between York, Hull, Leeds, Sheffield, Derby, Nottingham, Leicester, London, Liverpool, Birmingham, Cheltenham and Gloucester. This impressive chain of communication however still lacked one important link – that from Gloucester to Bristol – then under construction by the BrG.

From the first, as we shall see in a moment, both B&G and BrG had considered themselves as two parts of one whole. The BrG had in 1839, obtained their Act of Incorporation with B&G support on the understanding that the BrG's gauge was to be the same as the B&G's, and though subsequent plans for amalgamation had been temporarily dropped, there could be no doubt that, apart from some dissidents in Gloucester, most of those in the B&G camp felt that the fortunes of the BrG were closely bound up with their own.

As we have seen in Chapter 2, the Bristol Western & Northern Railway had had to be abandoned in 1826 as too large an enterprise for the time. But the idea was not dead and was revived from 1834 onwards by the advancement of more modest schemes of which the B&G was one. The BrG began more modestly still as a 9 mile horse tramway linking mines and quarries at Coalpit Heath with Bristol at Cuckolds Pill. It was incorporated as the Bristol & Gloucestershire Railway. That this enterprise was merely a step forward on the part of Bristol people to reach Birmingham, is shown by the fact that shortly after the opening in August 1835, a prospectus was issued for extending the line on to Gloucester to meet the then proposed B&G. It was to follow Jessop's route of 1824 and join the proposed CGWU at Stonehouse, over whose rails they would have running powers to Gloucester. This was the BrG. Gloucester was not impressed. All its efforts in attracting Birmingham's traffic via the B&G to their port would be wasted if a railway to Bristol by-passed it, so they set to work to destroy the extension plans.

A number of Gloucester merchants, many associated with the B&G, joined forces with more bona fide men from Bristol to promote the Gloucester and Bristol Railway (G&B) which offered all the advantages of the BrG but with a 'better line'. War was declared, insults exchanged, and inspite of the fact that the G&B had no intention of making a railway at all, they managed to succeed in delaying the BrG Act for some years. It received the Royal Assent however on 1 July 1839, having been warmly supported by the B&G. The B&G having failed as yet to gain direct access to Gloucester Docks, it is probable that they thought the best policy was to reach Bristol without delay.

The importance of the Bristol connection to the B&G was emphasised late in 1839 when they were in danger of losing it. Two vital sections of the Bristol to Birmingham route were owned by the CGWU: the Cheltenham–Gloucester on the B&G side and the Gloucester–Stonehouse section on the BrG. When the CGWU obtained authority to defer indefinitely the construction of those parts of their line, it left the Bristol & Birmingham companies facing each other over an unbridged gap. On 31 December 1839 the B&G Board resolved to negotiate with the CGWU and BrG with a view to amalgamation and completion of the route as one united company.

Working the B&G and BrG as one company was an obvious necessity but since each company depended upon unbuilt sections of the CGWU, it was equally important to bring them into the deal. Early in the New Year, the BrG, CGWU and B&G met to hear the latter's proposals. The CGWU had reservations, but both Gloucester companies agreed to unite and to purchase the CGWU and thus work the whole Birmingham to Bristol route as one united company.

Deputations of the B&G and BrG met in February 1840 and agreed to introduce a bill into Parliament to authorise their amalgamation and purchase of the CGWU. The CGWU was offered £750,000, but just in case they failed to agree, an alternative route between the B&G and BrG would be pursued.

At this point railway power politics upset their plans. The GWR had helped to fight off the L&B's challenge of a line to Cheltenham from Tring. In so doing they had through their puppet company (the CGWU) secured for themselves a commanding position in the Gloucester area. From that vantage point they intended to expand into south Wales, and possibly north and south as well. They therefore had no intention of allowing the CGWU to fritter that position away , and demanded to know what the CGWU was doing in conference with the B&G and BrG companies.

Their solicitor assured the GWR that they had no intentions of giving up their route. They desired the earliest possible completion and they did not wish to sell out at all, but, the 'embarassed state' of their finances, the weakness of a proportion of their proprietors and the 'anxiety of many to catch at any proposal offering an apparent advantage' had been the main cause of entertaining these negotiations. An immediate promise of financial help was forthcoming from the GWR to keep the CGWU intact and out of the hands of the narrow gauge faction, on condition of course that they broke off all negotiations for a sellout of the Standish Gloucester section, though possession by the B&G of the Cheltenham–Gloucester line could not now be prevented.

Meanwhile, the Bill for amalgamation had been considered by the Standing Orders committee and given a first reading in the House of Commons. Further progress of the Bill had to halt until the CGWU gave their assent, but when this was refused, for reasons given above, the B&G and BrG then tried an alternative approach. They proposed that they would amalgamate, and together, at cost price, buy out the CGWU's rights in the line between Cheltenham and Standish. To this the CGWU dared not agree. Since therefore the connecting line between their two systems was not available, both B&G and BrG felt that amalgamation would serve no useful purpose, and their bill was accordingly withdrawn. We suspect there was more to it than that. A memorial from Birmingham interests (directors and proprietors; some associated with the L&B) was read to the B&G board urging them against joining the BrG or CGWU since the implications 'were not fully understood'.

It is more likely that railway power politics played a part. The L&B element considered that the GWR's presence at Bristol and at Gloucester (via the CGWU) might prove overpowering to the limited Birmingham and Bristol Companies. They were appalled at the prospect of having the broad gauge forcing its way into Birmingham. Bristol shed no tears over the split. BrG proprietors congratulated their directors on the break off in negotiations at their general meeting in March 1840. They were convinced that their section would prove to be much more profitable and since the B&G had alienated Worcester, that city would implacably oppose each and every further application to Parliament they might require to make. (The town council had in fact resolved to oppose the amalgamation bill using their alleged bond as ammunition.)

No mention has yet been made of the gauge proposed by the BrG. Their Act specified only the alteration of that of the Bristol and Gloucestershire, which was 4ft. 8in., but the 4ft. 8½in. narrow gauge was implied in the preamble which notes the BrG's importance in the continuous chain of communication from the north to the west of England. This had been endorsed at the general meeting above referred to, it being '. . . essential to the interests of the undertaking that the line should be constructed of the same gauge as that of the railway from Gloucester to Birmingham.' Although they had dropped their plan for amalgamation, nonetheless both railways realised their interdependence for trade. The B&G directors told the proprietors in August 1840 that they were '. . . happy to learn that the BrG have commenced their works. This will be an important connecting line for the B&G, and in its success the B&G has a deep interest.' It would be almost four years before the BrG opened, during which time came frequent cries of despair from the B&G management. Without the BrG, they were '. . . a line only half opened . . . labouring under all the disadvantage incidental to a broken communication.'

CHAPTER EIGHT

WORKING THE
RAILWAY 1840–1841

The B&G's Act of Incorporation of 1836, in common with those of other early railways, took for granted that it would be operated on a system similar to that used on canals, tramroads or turnpike roads. Any authorised party, a carrier, could run his own wagons, coaches and locomotives on the line on payment of a toll whilst those not owning their own locomotive engines could run their wagons and carriages by paying an extra fee, in addition to the toll, for the use of the railway's locomotive power. Lastly, members of the public could also use the railway to transport themselves or their goods using either carriers or the company's rolling stock on payment of the relevant toll and rate.

Whilst the company had exclusive control over the running of the railway and could prevent collision of both interests and trains, the idea soon evolved of a more convenient mode of operation whereby the company provided locomotive power and rolling stock in trains running to fixed timetable. Carriers could still use their own wagons and be allowed discount rate for doing so.

It had been learnt by experience that the complex operations of a railway required a dedicated and disciplined workforce, and since the only such bodies of men then existing were the armed forces and the police, it was natural that their organisation should be taken as a model. Their code of conduct and of discipline were adapted to suit railway needs. Former army and navy officers were the only people who, at the time, had experience of commanding and enforcing discipline on large bodies of men. This fact explains why it was that such men became prominent in the management of early railways;

but though military men were appointed to command they looked to the police code for guidance.

Apart from the staff of the Locomotive department, for which men with special skills were required, all railway staff in the early days were recruited as Special Constables. While the line was still under construction their job was to patrol the formation and protect materials and structures. Though paid by the railway it would seem that they were responsible to the civil magistrates. It was only after the opening of the line and when the by-laws of the particular railway had been approved by the BoT, that they became, as it were, railway police and responsible to the company.

Entries in the B&G Minutes indicate that as the line opened in stages, there was a fresh swearing-in of 'Old Hands', and new recruits, to the Code of Regulations drawn up by Capt. W. S. Moorsom, who had made a careful study of the police codes of neighbouring railways. The code[1] is summarised here; constables were required to bind themselves to devote their whole energies to the service of the company; to be willing to work and live wherever the company should need them; to obey orders promptly on pain of dismissal and to accept no gratuities or tips. There was to be no drunkenness or rudeness to passengers. For both of these offences they faced dismissal. Further, they were to wear their company uniform at all times when on duty, and to keep it clean and neat. Each man had to repeat and sign this form of enrolment:

'I — — — being this day engaged as — — — in the service of the Birmingham and Gloucester Railway do hereby bind myself to observe and obey the foregoing regulations.'

As far as wages went the job was quite attractive. The basic rate of 18s. per week would be riches to a farm labourer, and it was quite competitive with the wages of factory workers in the towns; but the code was strict, and though as time went on, a number either resigned or were dismissed, there was no difficulty in replacing them.

By the end of 1840 some 123 constables had been recorded as having been sworn in, though doubtless there were many others, and it was from this nucleus that the first railway staff came – switchmen, shunters, porters, brakesmen, guards, station clerks, station inspectors, and of course those who were still called policemen, whose job it was to patrol the line and regulate the traffic.

Road coach links had to be organised at various stations in order to encourage passenger traffic. The board's 'economy' in building a direct line avoiding centres of population *en route* might facilitate transport of goods from Birmingham to Gloucester and vice-versa, but it was not likely to encourage the passenger traffic which other railways had found, to their surprise, was a more profitable source of revenue than freight.

Gloucester station was reasonably situated, as was Camp Hill, and later Curzon St. in Birmingham, but the remaining stations were not. Spetchley, the station for Worcester, was the most badly sited of all. It stood 3 miles east of the city, and had to be served, at B&G expense, by road coaches which met all trains and provided a service, which as time went on, proved to be not only inefficient and a cause of complaint, but also a continual drain on the finances of the company. Tewkesbury had its branch and a station in High Street, but owing to a Parliamentary ban on locomotives, had to be worked by horse power. Cheltenham's station was a mile from the town centre and carriages were required here to transport passengers to and from the railway. Finally, until Birmingham, Camp Hill was reached in December 1840, road links were needed here too, at first from Bromsgrove then from Cofton Farm.

William Burgess was both secretary and superintendent and as such he was responsible for the day to day working of the railway. His most notable achievement was his 'General System of Management'[2] which he presented to the board in July 1840. It covered all aspects of working the Railway, but was destined to last only a short while. He planned 5 departments: general office, headed by the secretary; traffic and stores headed by the chief inspector; way and works headed by the resident engineer, Mr Wetherall; locomotive headed by the engineer of locomotives, William Creuze; and carriage and wagon headed by the foreman, Edward Lean. Each department's task and organisation is discussed in detail, and for convenience that which refers to Locomotives and Way and Works is outlined in their respective chapters.

The general office department was concerned basically with accounts and share details and was at Waterloo St., Birmingham. Traffic and stores was more complex. It dealt with the '. . . starting of trains, regulation of stations and the proper accommodation of passengers . . .', in addition to regulating and accounting for all the stores kept by the various departments. There was considerable overlap with the passenger side of the business, which for convenience, we have left to its own chapter. Since the stations were the origin and destination of the company's traffic they naturally assumed a high position in the control and regulation of the trains. At each principal or first class station, a station inspector was placed who had overall responsibility of the station staff, passengers and goods traffic. Law and order was kept by the station police. These were additional to the police who patrolled certain parts of the main line and inferior too, since their pay was nearly half that of their patrolling colleagues. At least one man was to be on duty at all times at the principal stations, to 'prevent every species of disorder, . . . direct the . . . passengers, and to see that no loose characters idle and lounge about . . .'. They were sworn in as constables which gave them powers of arrest on the property of the railway company.

Switchmen were signalmen at the stations, operating points and carrying signal flags by day and lamps by night. Their duties were based upon the code of signals to be found in the signalling chapter (see Chapter 16). Sworn-in as special constables '. . . they must be constantly at their respective places. . .', woe betide them if they were not! General patrolling of the line, at places not important enough to warrant the expense of a policeman, was entrusted to members of the platelaying gangs, usually the foreman. Again sworn-in as special constables, there were to be one per mile during daylight and one per three miles at night to discourage and prevent trespass and theft.

Government, through the BoT, found it necessary to control railway management and successive 'Regulation of the Railways' Acts were authorised in Parliament. Twentieth century bureaucracy must surely have had its roots in those early railway days, though the Government did, in most respects, have the safety of the travelling public at heart. Lord Seymour's Act was the first and became law in 1840. It empowered the BoT to make statutory inspections of any railway to be used by passengers; to receive and amend all railway by-laws, rules and regulations; to receive regular returns of traffic, locomotive and staff statistics etc; and finally to be given immediate notification of any accident causing personal injury either to employees or the public.

Notice was given to all the B&G employees in October 1840 that the management would fully enforce the Railways Act as regards safety and that the slightest infraction of the working rules would render the offender liable to dismissal and prosecution. Perhaps this was why the B&G had such a good safety record when compared with its contemporaries. Further Acts were to lay down rules for the carriage of H.M. Mails, military personnel and goods, third class travel, construction and so forth.

Management by committee was due to end in January 1841 when the GC and BC were to be abolished. Full Board meetings were to be held from then forward on a fortnightly basis to discuss policy, investment and so on, leaving the day to day management to the superintendent. It is strange to note that the BC Minute book continued to record all the board's proceedings right up to August 1842 despite the existence of a 'board' minute book since 1836.

All was soon to change, however. Capt. Constantine Richard Moorsom RN, later Admiral, and brother of William Scarth, the engineer, was elected onto the Board in January 1841 and within two weeks had been elected chairman. He proposed a revolution in the management of the railway. Before considering these changes however, let us see what had happened during the first six months of

operation as recorded in the report of the February 1841 general
meeting.

Passenger trains had all but rendered the road coach extinct, except for
feeder traffic: '. . . the season of the year at which the complete opening
took place was much against the passenger traffic . . . experience of
other railways has shown that it takes time to develop the resources of
these undertakings and the Directors see no reasons to alter the views
they . . . conveyed in the revised [traffic] estimates. . . . The Proprietors will participate in the satisfaction that more than 120,000
individuals have been conveyed along the railway since it opened,
without the slightest accident . . . earnest attention . . . has been
devoted to the adoption and enforcement of regulations for the
continued safety of travellers.' Goods traffic was in a different position:
'The arrangements of the Company have not yet allowed their
conveying goods except to a very limited extent, but applications have
been received from the principal carriers and they are prepared to
commence using the railway whenever the Company can accomodate
them . . . the Directors believe that in this branch of business the
receipts will be large. The Postmaster General having required two
night trains each way for the conveyance of the mails, they commenced
running on the 6th Inst. [Feb] . . . owing to the unseasonableness of the
hour, the number of passengers conveyed [by them] has been small.'
Receipts were £21,769 for the period July–December 1840 but operating
expenses were 'heavy, in consequence of the circumstances attendant on
the partial opening of the line'. They exceeded revenue by £611.

Capt. CR Moorsom (henceforth referred to as Capt. Moorsom or
'the chairman') was a naval officer who had been involved with the
L&B since 1833, first as joint secretary, then as director, and was thus
experienced in railway management. To understand the circumstances
under which he was invited to join the board, we must revert to August
1840. The board had been split over several issues, notably the question
of running Sunday trains. Joseph Walker, then the chairman, eventually resigned over the same issue and also because of a continued
disagreement with Charles Sturge, and left the B&G without a
chairman at a critical time in its life. The result was that things got
somewhat out of hand. Of the situation, Capt. Moorsom remarked
some years later[3] 'How was it that I became Chairman of your Board?
. . . I was solicited by your Board and by a body of Proprietors holding
nearly one quarter of the shares, and I consented as a matter of duty . . .
summoned to assist a concern which I knew to be in a tottering state,
but which turned out to be all but insolvent . . . the condition of the
engines was such that little more than half were fit for work; the trains
were . . . in danger of being stopped for lack of engines; and they were
seldom within the time appointed for their arrival. The Company's

servants were inexperienced. Many were inefficient and there was no
proper division of labour . . . and . . . with the exception of the
Resident Engineer's department, all was in a state of disorder . . .'.
Except for a few isolated instances, evidence of the 'tottering state of
the Company' does not appear in the board Minutes. It will be
remembered that the directors had referred to their finances as a matter
for congratulation in August 1840, all the loan capital having been
received. But by October, the Gloucester Banking Co. had refused to
grant a £10,000 overdraft, so the board, without a care in the world,
simply switched their dealings wholly with the Birmingham Banking
Co. who, several days later informed the board that they were £19,000
overdrawn and fixed a £20,000 limit to the overdraft they would allow.
The last call on the shares had been made in November which brought
in nearly £95,000, yet a month later the solicitors were to arrange
further loans of £20,000 to £25,000. No indication is given as to where
the money had gone to!

Capt. Constantine Moorsom was elected a director on 12 January
1841 after a requisition was received from forty eight proprietors
holding nearly 25 per cent of the shares. He warned them that he would
only accept the post if the existing system of management was replaced
by one proposed by himself, which was agreed, and on 26 January he
was elected chairman.

Capt. Moorsom explained his views on railway management and
how he proposed to apply them to the B&G to the proprietors at their
February 1841 general meeting. 'I would not', he said, 'have become a
member of another railway board under their present constitution . . .
there is neither satisfaction to the public and proprietors nor credit to
one's self to be gained by being one of so numerous and irresponsible a
body as railway boards are . . . Railways should be managed by a
system which shall make every man holding office responsible for his
acts, which is by no means the case at present'. Boards, he felt, had too
many members with too few able to give sufficient time and attention.
They were derived from the canals, whose boards often had up to 28
members, but whose task was mainly the accounting of tolls since no
canals were carriers. As applied to railways, the system gave rise to
divided responsibility where the individual had none at all while the
large board trusted one man with nothing and another with everything.
He proposed 3 to 5 directors each having responsibility for a certain
aspect: coaching & carrying; locomotives; way & works; finance; with
the chairman having general superintendence but no executive power.
'Under such a system no highly paid officers could find place . . . and
[it] would only require ordinary and steady men as heads of department
who would work contentedly for moderate remuneration . . . The
spending of money and accounting for it should never be confided

to the same persons. The auditing of accounts should be in hands independent of every authority but the Board.' Fraud and theft under the present system were rife, he said, while upwards of 30 or 40 men could be saved in the passenger train operation alone. Directors would be administrative, not executive, (a general executive officer would be in charge of executing orders, i.e. the general superintendent) and would meet weekly to examine reports and returns of every aspect of every department allowing them to 'judge by results' how matters were going on.

A system of contracts would eventually be relied upon to work possibly all railways, thereby enabling the director's duties to be less burdensome, but until then, his 'executive system' would be best. Needless to say such a masterly approach to railway management won the instant approval of the proprietors; many were delighted by his promises of reduced working expenses, and the system was adopted for a trial period. We think he would have been wise to have added that he could not change matters overnight, for this, apparently was what most proprietors expected!

Evidence of the so-called 'tottering state' of the company came to light during the meeting. To date the total capital spending had reached £1,268,000 which, the directors said, would cover all the liabilities including the Gloucester Docks branch (if approved by Parliament) but excluded the Worcester branch (also if approved). However, having had full ownership of the Cheltenham–Gloucester line thrust upon them, with its unforseen heavy expenditure, they were £60,000 short, and the Board recommended further loans be made to cover the shortfall. It would be repaid in full when the CGWU redeemed their moiety by 1845.

This proposal was adopted by the meeting but not without a fight! Mr Tartt, a principal shareholder, proposed an independent board of audit to account for all expenditure, working practises. mistakes, management and so forth. Great errors had been made in estimating the cost of the railway (50 per cent higher by that time) and the probable traffic. These had to be managerial errors, unintentional perhaps, but errors they were and should be found and corrected to ensure the future efficiency of the railway.

However, the proprietors were obviously in good humour that day. They defeated Tartt's proposal and doubtless returned home thinking Capt. Moorsom would put all to rights in a trice so that the dividends would come rolling in. An intelligent shareholder would, however, have realised that the transformation promised by the new chairman could only be the result of a long term process. What is more, no one then realised that the country was heading for a recession which was to affect all railways and cause receipts to drop and expenses to rise. There were stormy times ahead for the B&G.

CHAPTER NINE
1841 & 1842

Capt. C.R. Moorsom lost no time in tackling the problem before him. He quickly appointed his executive directors: finance, Joseph Gibbins; locomotives, Charles Sturge; way & works, A.W. Daniels; coaching & carrying, Harvey. B. Tymbs; whilst taking police and general arrangements himself. Rules and regulations had to be changed to suit the new format, but perhaps the most important task was to investigate the company's finances. The board resolved that 'Prompt and effective measures must be taken to place the finances of this Company upon a proper basis.'

In April 1841, two non-executive directors were appointed to see where the money had gone and where more was needed. A 'Special Report' was issued to all proprietors which must have added greatly to their anxieties. At their last general meeting they had been told that £60,000 extra was all that was required to put the finances in order. Now, after a more detailed enquiry, liabilities of £172,000 had been uncovered. This was for: land and engineering works, notably the Gloucester Docks branch and a junction with the BDJc at Birmingham; extra rolling stock; stations at Cheltenham, Gloucester, Bromsgrove and Birmingham (Lawley Street); and additions to Bromsgrove Locomotive Works. It was proposed to raise fresh capital of £175,000 by selling scrip at £17.10s.0d. each, which would entitle the holder to one quarter-share (worth £25) in the B&G. Parliament would be asked for permission to create additional shares which could then be exchanged for the scrip, but until the necessary Act (which would also seek additional borrowing powers) had been obtained, interest at 5 per cent would be paid to scrip holders.

A special general meeting was held in May to discuss these proposals, and the proprietors had little choice but to put their faith in Capt. Moorsom's ability and sanction the money raising. They were assured that the figure was a final one, except for some contemplated projects which could easily be met from the additional borrowing powers proposed.

Changes were made among the executive officers in July 1841 when the combined post of secretary and superintendent, held by William Burgess, were separated. Outdoor superintendent and indoor secretary seem hardly the wisest choice for a combined post but, this was the B&G!

George King came from the L&B to take up the post of secretary on the recommendation of Mr Creed, secretary of the L&B. Soon after this Burgess resigned as superintendent, following an allegation that he had been trafficking in shares: John Kidder from the traffic department was appointed as a temporary replacement. One Humphrey Brown, a self-opinioned owner of a water transport business in Tewkesbury, applied for the position. He was backed by 124 proprietors but was rejected on the recommendation of Capt. Moorsom. Brown was later to play a part in the overthrow of Moorsom's system and it would seem that the two were not the best of friends. In the end, Mr F.H. Wetherall, the resident engineer, was given the permanent appointment of outdoor superintendent; the permanent way maintenance was shortly to be put out to contract and would require only an overlooker on behalf of the company, thus posts of resident engineer and traffic superintendent were ripe for combination.

By the August 1841 general meeting trains were running through to the L&B station at Curzon St. and continuous railway communication was established between the north east, north west and the midlands to Cheltenham and Gloucester. The proprietors at the meeting were no doubt eager to hear of Capt. Moorsom's progress. Addressing the meeting he jubilantly announced that: 'The results have answered my fullest expectations, I hold in my hand a few particulars connected with the working of your railway . . . which will give you a picture of the state of things.'

Historians can be grateful for the detail which Capt. Moorsom insisted should be put into his half-yearly reports. In contrast to the management of many other railways, who were inclined to skate over unpleasant details, telling shareholders only what they wanted to hear, Capt. Moorsom concealed nothing either good or bad. His in-depth reports give a valuable picture of all aspects of B&G affairs during the time of his chairmanship. His coverage of the locomotive stock is of particular interest. Unfortunately, as we shall see later, it was this honesty which led to Capt. Moorsom's downfall.

In brief, reductions were recorded in maintenance of way expenses (soon to be put out to contract), numbers of employees (886 to 719: compare this with 271 in June 1843), and locomotive expenses (the whole department had been reorganised under the management of J. E. McConnell). Goods traffic was developing but was hindered by unsettled negotiations for through traffic with the GJR, L&B and BDJc. There was also the dilemma of having two possible modes of operating the goods traffic, either to let the established carriers keep it and then only put it on the railway when it suited them, or to undertake carrying in competition with the carriers. Sensibly, the board announced their preference to foster the traffic via the regular carriers but not to refuse goods offered directly to them by private customers. Another possible encouragement for goods traffic was the opening of a spur from the tramway to the goods depot at Gloucester by which transfer could be effected to and from the docks, albeit at some expense and inconvenience.

All told, receipts were £38,000 and a profit of £1,100 announced but no dividend would be paid as it was of the utmost importance to be prudent and establish a depreciation fund. Capt. Moorsom had to explain this one carefully! Rolling stock, however new, was liable to need repair or replacement whether from accident or fair wear and tear. If, as was the case at present, such replacements had to be paid for solely from revenue, future dividends would inevitably suffer. However, if a regular proportion of the profits were assigned each year to the depreciation fund in order to meet such contingencies then all will be well. (Except that is for those who happened to be looking for a dividend after paying into the company's coffers for nearly 5 years.)

Shares plunged to 40 per cent discount (£100 paid up £60 value); at the news Joseph Gibbins, the finance director was forced to resign. It was alleged that he had indulged in the share trafficking which had caused the share depression, an allegation which he strongly denied but he had little option but to resign. (Justice was done later when he was proved innocent and his name cleared before a future general meeting.)

Finances had at last been sorted out, so the proprietors were told. The audit had found where the money had gone and who was to blame (full details in appendix under finances). Basically they were £390,000 over their 1839 estimate of £1,068,000. Half of this overspending was accounted for by 'works', and one quarter of the works total, £55,000 to be precise, had been spent on getting the Birmingham division contracts finished ahead of schedule. This may have been justified had there been an abundance of traffic waiting for the railway, but there was not! What is more strange is that this £55,000 comes under the 'unforseen' heading and not 'mismanagement'. Had the heavier Birmingham division works been given equal preference to the Gloucester division in construction and been completed at the same pace, and had the engineer been allowed to use his judgement instead of that of the 'economy' crazed BC, then perhaps the £55,000 could have been saved. But that is to use hindsight – never a satisfactory criterion by which to judge affairs 150 years ago.

Once again Mr Tartt proposed a board of audit and control to be chosen from the proprietors, but Capt. Moorsom was ready for him. He announced a similar scheme by which non-executive directors would be appointed to audit the half-yearly accounts. This was duly accepted by the proprietors. Audit or no audit, the simple fact was that the B&G was £0.5 million overspent and this alone was going to cost £25,000 a year in interest charges. Correspondence in the *Railway Times*[1] drew attention to this. On current weekly traffic returns the railway would be able to pay 4½ per cent on the whole £1½ million of capital were it not for interest charges! Efforts were being made to increase revenue and cut expenses, which at 75 per cent of the revenue were far too high. During the latter half of 1841, passenger traffic was given a boost by the introduction of through booking facilities to London via the L&B. A number of wayside halts had been created, mainly at level crossings, which were served by carriages attached to goods trains, the object being to attract folk from the outlying villages to patronise the railway at little extra expense to the company. Through goods traffic arrangements were made with the GJR for Manchester and Liverpool traffic to Gloucester and Bristol (by road or water) at an all-in price in an attempt to coax the freight from the Severn to the railway. Experiments with coal haulage, never seriously considered before, were made to increase traffic. But for all this, the February 1842 general meeting was a sombre affair.

Addressing the proprietors, the chairman said: 'Misrepresentations . . . in the public papers, the Company's carriages, News Rooms, and Coffee Houses of the mode of management of this line and of the conduct of the Directors . . . [are] . . . beneath us to notice . . . [we have] . . . left it to take its course because . . . at this meeting we would have to render on account of our trust.' He challenged dissidents to come forward and voice their opinions at a place and time when the directors had a fair chance of reply.

Receipts were up to £50,000 for the previous half year, but working expenses swallowed a mammoth 80 per cent of this and after allotting a certain amount to the depreciation fund, a miserly 1½ per cent dividend was announced for the whole of 1841. The GJR paid 12 per cent! Working expenses were formerly estimated at 50 per cent of the receipts, yet on the B&G they were 80 per cent, of which half had been shared equally by interest and the locomotive department. However, improvement was on the way. Whereas during the period July to

December 1840 the average cost of locomotive power had been 2s.9d. per mile; the cost in the corresponding period of 1841 had been reduced to 1s.7d., to which the chairman commented: 'I am not aware of any similar instance of such a reduction in so short a space of time . . .' In saying this he agreed that the cost was still much too high, and that the B&G had still a long way to go before they could be on a par with other railways such as the Manchester and Leeds, whose locomotive costs were only 11s.5d. per mile. He could also have pointed out that the M&L had no Lickey Incline for which expensive locomotive power had to be provided, and which added some 10 per cent to the costs of the locomotive department.

Goods traffic was increasing (10,000 tons between July and December 1841), and a clear policy had emerged whereby only those goods likely to be profitable would be carried. They were opposed to engaging in a price war with the canals but would encourage carriers to use the railway instead. Working methods were still under debate with certain directors who wanted the company to set themselves up as sole carriers, whilst Capt. Moorsom insisted on keeping to the established carriers (as did the L&B) in line with his policy of contracting out as much of the business as possible, thus saving the expense of extra rolling stock and warehousing. The compromise solution was continued. Coal from Birmingham had been carried experimentally to Cheltenham but the expense of returning empty wagons made it virtually profitless. However, this did not stop the traffic, which later grew to provide much needed revenue in place of the as yet absent merchandise traffic.

Humphrey Brown told the meeting that were the goods department in the hands of a competent and qualified person (i.e. himself!), then the traffic would quickly reach the levels predicted in Parliament. It was there to be taken if only the B&G would go after it instead of sitting and waiting for it to come. He wanted the company to set up as sole carriers and compete actively with road and water transport. Merchants from Tewkesbury complained bitterly that they were originally encouraged to set up a corn and coal trade to Cheltenham from their quay, yet now the rates had been quadrupled. This was an obvious ploy by the company to prohibit Tewkesbury from using the B&G's scarce resources for what was quite unprofitable traffic.

There was better news about the passenger traffic. The numbers carried, and the receipts, had again risen; unfortunately this was only temporary. As the country sank into recession so did the B&G's passenger traffic, and there was no significant improvement until 1844 when the BrG opened. One of the major deterrents to passenger traffic was the hideously expensive and unsatisfactory omnibus service between Worcester and the main line at Spetchley. The board realised the only solution was to build a direct branch line, one which would benefit the company, the Worcester people, and the public in general. Various attempts had been made to achieve this during 1840 and 1841. These in turn led to further proposals in 1842 and agreement a year later!

What then was the situation in Worcester? It will be remembered that in spite of the B&G's attempts to placate the city, their relationship had gone sour. Worcester, as far as the B&G was concerned, was going to have an omnibus link, and it would serve them right for their intransigence. However in July 1841 the Chamber of Commerce approached the B&G with a view to settling their differences and putting their city on the railway map. Faced with the prospect of determined opposition from the town council to any future applications they might make to Parliament, the B&G agreed to set the machinery of negotiation in motion again.

Two B&G proprietors had submitted detailed proposals in support of a deviation line to serve Worcester instead of a branch.[9] The board remained unimpressed and voted in preference of a direct branch railway between Tibberton and Bredicot on the main line into the city centre. Predictably, when the Worcester factions considered the virtually unchanged B&G plan they were unchanged in their rejection of it, and insisted that a deviation line would suit Worcester the best. But if a branch were to be made, it would have to be that from Abbotswood.

All things considered, 1841 had not been a good year for B&G shareholders. Their dividend was ridiculously small, and no immediate hope could be offered for an improvement. Share prices however had risen slightly, being now quoted at £64 instead of their previous price of £60. On management's side it had been a year of slow but steady progress. Twelve months had passed under the new system introduced by Capt. Moorsom. Improvements had resulted it was true, but there were still doubts among the proprietors about its value. The board considered however that it was too soon to be able to judge the system's success or failure. They opted therefore for its continuance.

Reorganisation of working practices continued. Reductions were achieved in the way & works department by the contracting out of track maintenance, and police numbers were reduced as far as possible without sacrificing safety. Guards' rosters were tightened up and most significantly the locomotive department underwent further changes. Since August 1841 it had been run by an outdoor superintendent of locomotives (G.D. Bischopp) and a foreman of locomotives (J.E. McConnell). It had been decided to reorganise the department under one head, whose remuneration would be linked to the economical working of the locomotives. Bischopp resigned in April 1842 to join the Disc Engine Co. of Birmingham, leaving Mr McConnell as candidate for the superintendency. By mid-1842, 30 men of all trades had been laid off, drivers were paid on a mileage basis and were offered a bonus for coke saving. Quite a comprehensive shake-up, and out of it emerged a considerable drop in locomotive expenses; though at 1s.7d. per locomotive mile they were still much higher than those of other railways.

The seeds of discontent however, sown amongst the proprietors the previous year, were rapidly growing. Share prices were at a large discount and letters from their disgruntled owners appeared in the press in almost serial form.[3]

Ignorant of railway management and especially the precarious position of their railway before Capt. Moorsom's rescue operations, they were profit hungry and a group called the committee of shareholders waged a war of words to stir up discontent and oust the board. They circulated propaganda to the proprietors before the August 1842 general meeting, from which the following extract is taken: '. . . I take the liberty of addressing you . . . that some of the subjects alluded to in Capt. Moorsom's letter [circulated in defence of his system and dealt with a little later] may not mystify the true situation of the undertaking at this moment . . . the "tottering state of the concern" to which Capt. Moorsom alludes on entering office is not improved if we may judge by the subsequent reduction of 20 per cent upon the shares or the continuing advertisements in so many papers for loans or debentures. . .' Locomotive expenses were 50 per cent more than railways like the Manchester and Leeds (1s.5d. per mile against 11½d.) and were '. . . more in proportion to the mileage than any other line in England . . . In regard to the locomotives, it is no doubt a lamentable evil [in the] adoption of them.' Capt. Moorsom's system had, they said: '. . . made so much confusion and irregularity as to compel the separation of the goods from the passengers and to require two extra engines and trains each way for merchandise and with what results, a diminution . . . in the traffic revenue.' Passenger traffic was but 60 per cent of the Parliamentary estimate and goods traffic only 25 per cent and of this nearly half was heavy loading, coal and so on, never originally intended for the railway and: '. . . paying a rate scarcely equal to . . . [the] actual cost of tracking [sic].'

Hot on the heels of that letter came another from 'a shareholder' who asked his fellow proprietors whether '. . . the very disastrous state of our undertaking . . .' was caused by uncontrollable sources, such as the national slump, or the inefficiency of the management. He blamed Capt. Moorsom's system which was in '. . . the hands of 5 directors, but whose duties are divided in such a way as . . . to place all the power in the hands of the Chairman, who is, in reality, a dictator.' Moorsom's: 'education, habits and peculiarities of opinion . . . [and the] . . . injurious practical effect of his theories' were incompatible with those required to manage a concern which must compete directly and indirectly with other businesses, and what is more, Moorsom himself chose the executive directors who were thus committed to his policy and unlikely to 'condemn themselves by reporting to the shareholders his incompetencies.' Mr 'shareholder' maintained that the only altern- ative was to return to management by the whole board with the executive placed in the hands of a competent Superintendent. No one person could thus take control and if the Superintendent was incomp- etent he could easily be replaced, whereas in the present system the Proprietors were faced with the: '. . . neccessity of displacing a Chairman [who was] determined to cling to his office.'

Capt. Moorsom's version of the state of the B&G, told in a letter to the proprietors, was, as you would expect, a different tale: 'Your railway has been very economically worked and unless great care and attention had been bestowed upon it, the expenses would have been much greater than they are.' The B&G could not be compared with other railways, he went on. It had the Lickey Incline, high coke costs, scanty passenger traffic, extreme competition for the profitable mer- chandise, a large number of stations and level crossings in proportion to the length of line and expensive permanent way maintenance. He knew the railway was in a poor condition when he took over and knew a Board on the usual plan would be unfit to deal with the difficulties. Power needed to be confided in a few directors who would pledge themselves to a distinct defined individual responsibility. '. . . I state decidedly that none other system of management in my experience . . . has worked so well as this . . . '

What were the results of the first half of 1842? Receipts had fallen 20 per cent and expenses had risen and now took 95 per cent of the receipts. Interest payments of £12,000 contributed in no uncertain terms! A derisory profit of £1,600, was all they had to show and not one iota of a dividend. No wonder shares fell another 10 per cent (57 per cent discount, worth £43).

Passenger traffic had fallen heavily (though January–June figures were always less than July–December). Goods traffic had risen in spite of the recession though full development was impossible owing to the still defective arrangements for Bristol traffic and at Gloucester Docks. The board were well pleased with their system of sharing the carrying business with the general carriers; coal was now being sent regularly to Cheltenham from Birmingham.

Bristol traffic was a cause of concern. The unfinished state of the BrG could well be blamed for a great deal of the B&G's absent passengers and goods, and the Board likened their position to a railway only half opened. This is a significant change of tune. It will remembered that in 1835, Bristol could have been the other side of the universe as far as the B&G was concerned, but now it appeared to have completely ousted Gloucester as the 'southern terminus' of the B&G. In the words of the chairman: 'What would the traffic of the L&B be like without the GJR? . . . [and] of the GJR without the Liverpool and Manchester?' The locomotive department trends were at least encouraging. Costs were down to 1s. 3¾d. per mile though still one third of the whole expenses. As the report stated, the ratio to other expenses depended upon coke costs, gradients, the traffic on offer, the number and weight of trains, the number of stops and so on, and the B&G was not favourably blessed in any of those. Lickey Incline costs were about to be revolutionised by the saddletanking of the three big Norris bankers [the first recorded in English locomotive history] which would significantly reduce their working costs. Rostering of the entire engine stud had also been revised with significant increases in efficiency; Gloucester to Bromsgrove and Blackwell to Birmingham, were worked as separate sections by the smaller engines, and the Lickey Incline was worked exclusively by the Norris bankers.

Of the locomotives themselves, *Herepath's Railway Journal*[4] thought them a mixed collection of far too many different designs. Proper management of them was impossible, and it was not necessary to say: '. . . how much more convenient it would be if they were all of two classes [one for goods and one for passengers] instead of this variety.'

Proof of the divided feelings among both board and proprietors occurred during the election of Directors for the coming year. George Ellins, a member of the committee of shareholders faction, was proposed and according to the *Gloucester Journal* reporter present,[5] the vote by hand showed a definite majority for him over his competitor. However the Moorsom brigade demanded a scrutiny (a vote by the number of shares held by individuals) in which Ellins was defeated. This was allegedly illegal under the circumstances and it was rumoured that Moorsom would resign if Ellins had been successful. Subsequently Ellins did try on many occasions to take up his rightful place on the Board and was forcibly removed. Board meetings were held behind closed doors for some while after! According to a letter circulated after the general meeting by George Tate, the chairman of the committee of shareholders, the directors held a substantial number of proxy votes from their supporters and middle of the road shareholders, sufficient to block any move to overthrow the board. He implored those sharehold-ers to come forward and help swing the balance of power and to enable a better regulated system of management to be attained.

Finally at the general meeting, Chas Shaw, another 'committee' man, moved that the number of executive directors be increased to two per department. He was a leading merchant from Birmingham and felt sure that trade depression had been the major cause of the company's poor performance and was optimistic that overseas trade was reviving and would bring better times for all. This motion was rejected and was replaced by a resolution which, while expressing confidence in the board, hoped that they would reconsider the number of directors to ensure the most efficient running of the company. Before the dust had settled on the meeting, the board met to discuss reinforcements to their members and within a week there were two extra. The passenger and goods sections were separated and two directors assigned to the goods.

Further reorganisation followed rapidly. The check office which accounted for the issue and collection of passengers tickets was decimated, the secretary's office was to be examined for similar treatment, parcels and luggage rates rose and passenger fares likewise, though day return tickets were introduced to stimulate optional travel.

Locomotive and goods departments were to be fully investigated to increase efficiency and reduce overheads. The B&G had also joined the railway clearing house. This had been founded in January 1842 to act as a central accounting system for interchange traffic between the multitude of independent railway companies, and the B&G's participation emphasised their commitment to being a link in the chain of railway communications. Finally it was decided to investigate general pay levels with a view to reduction where possible.

All in all, this was to be a last ditch effort by the Moorsom brigade to prove the value of their system, but time was running out. The committee of shareholders, shrugging off their defeat at the general meeting, were planning their next battle. The struggle occupied a major part of 1843 and together with other unrelated episodes did much to change the future of the B&G.

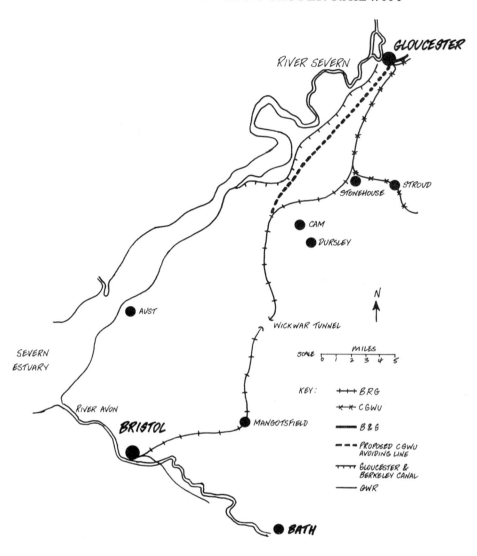

GLOUCESTER

RIVER SEVERN

STROUD

STONEHOUSE

CAM

DURSLEY

N

AUST

WICKWAR TUNNEL

SEVERN
ESTUARY

SCALE   MILES
         0 1 2 3 4 5

RIVER AVON

KEY: +++ BRG

BRISTOL   ×—× CGWU

MANGOTSFIELD   ▬▬ B & G

                 ▬ ▬ PROPOSED CGWU
                      AVOIDING LINE

                 ┬┬┬ GLOUCESTER &
                      BERKELEY CANAL

                 —— GWR

BATH

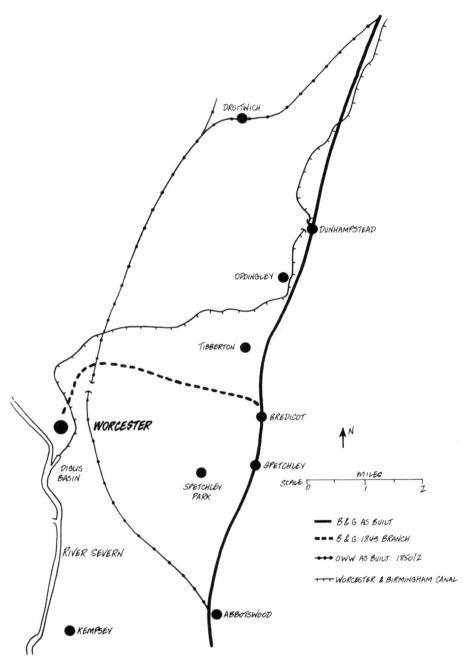

DROITWICH

DUNHAMPSTEAD

ODDINGLEY

TIBBERTON

WORCESTER

BREDICOT

DIGLIS
BASIN

SPETCHLEY

SPETCHLEY
PARK

RIVER SEVERN

N

MILES

SCALE 0   1   2

ABBOTSWOOD

KEMPSEY

B & G AS BUILT
B & G 1843 BRANCH
OWW AS BUILT 1850/2
WORCESTER & BIRMINGHAM CANAL

CHAPTER TEN
1843, COMMITTEE OF ENQUIRY

Having failed to get a representation on the board of directors, the committee of shareholders (abbreviated to 'committee' from now on) altered their tactics. It would appear that power struggles were fairly common in early railway companies. Battle took place at special general meetings called to appoint a Committee of Enquiry to examine the particular railway 'lock, stock and barrel', often with 'tumultuous scenes'! Now it was the B&G's turn to suffer. The 'committee' called a special general meeting which was held on 18 January 1843, and was 'numerously attended'![1]

The directors fired the first shot. They felt the question boiled down to one of 'no confidence', and if the meeting approved the appointment of a proprietors-only Committee of Enquiry, then they would be compelled to resign! On the other hand an enquiry comprising an equal number of directors and proprietors was likely to be of great benefit and they would co-operate with that.

Mr Tartt spoke for the requisitionists. He told the meeting that he had lost a considerable amount of money in the concern due to the depressed state of the shares (now at more than 50 per cent discount) and further he had lost the confidence of those he had encouraged to invest in the company who had likewise lost vast sums. Were it proven that on the one hand, money had been improperly spent and was recoverable by law, or on the other that the goods traffic could be trebled, would it not boost the share prices? [Does he want to sell them at a profit?] He went on to discuss the more embarrassing aspects of the B&G. The goods traffic had been proven as remunerative by Parliament, but where was it? Surely trade was not totally annihilated in the district? Railways were supposed to create traffic, but this one actually repelled it! The GJR were now putting their Bristol traffic on to the very water conveyance that the B&G was meant to supersede. Were it not for coal, repudiated and despised twelve months ago, but now a valued traffic, the whole would be much less than the present 20 per cent of the Parliamentary estimate. Reference was again made to the Tewkesbury traffic, once encouraged at 1s. 6d. per ton to Cheltenham but now 6s.; a rise in tolls impolitic compared with the 4s. per ton rate for certain goods to Cheltenham from Birmingham, and illegal in terms of the tolls authorised by Parliament. If the management of the goods department was not a fit case for enquiry then what was?

Financial estimates had risen from £950,000 to £1,270,000 by the time of opening, yet the audit of 1841 showed that nearly £1,400,000 had been spent; a sum which did not include the Worcester and Gloucester Docks branches, or stations at Gloucester and Lawley St. Birmingham. Such was the dubious nature of the expenditure that investigation was surely needed. For example, he quoted: '. . . £52,000 for expediting the opening of the line; preparing it for a traffic which had not yet been secured'. Then there was the basin at High Orchard, Gloucester, set by the canal with no connection with the main line and no prospect of one. Mr Tartt described the situation beautifully: 'I have discovered at Gloucester a work of extraordinary description. It is a vast basin near the ship canal, so ingeniously constructed as to receive a stream which is fast filling it up with mud and so admirably situated that we have no power of approaching it . . . It is a melancholy spectacle, that gloomy basin; and particularly when you consider that at the bottom of its foul waters lie some £20,000 [corrected by Moorsom to £14,000] of your money. You would suppose the buildings which surrounded this basin would be warehouses or sheds for goods. But no . . . they are 6 large coke ovens, not one of which is at work, being so badly placed that it is found we can contract for coke on better terms than than we can make it in these ovens!' Next in line was Worcester. Mr Tartt spoke of the three proposals; the Abbotswood branch for which the Worcester people pretended to have the company's bond; the branch from Spetchley (or thereabouts) endorsed by the company, then the deviation line, contended by some to be impracticable, however desirable. 'Was it therefore unreasonable', asked Mr Tartt, 'when all these conflicting statements were afloat, to ask that a committee of enquiry be appointed to investigate and ascertain . . . which was the best line?'

The basis for a working arrangement between the B&G and BrG had been discussed for some months and Mr Tartt thought the arrangements were a matter for continued negotiation, while the subject should also be discussed by the committee of enquiry. He likened the

BrG to 'a lady between two lovers, the B&G and GWR, and he feared that the latter would convince the object of his addresses that a union with him was much the better thing'. The Bristol representative, Mr Fripp, believed that 'the B&G would never see its natural and proper traffic until it was connected with the BrG, a union which was essential to complete the chain of communications.' In conclusion, Mr Tartt emphasised that the 'committee' wished change for the sake of improvement and not from any personal dislike of the directors but: 'If they persist in acting the 'Road to Ruin' instead of the 'School for Reform' they must expect to find a discontented public and an empty treasury.'

Formal resolutions were proposed and much debate followed, the result of which was a Committee of Enquiry to consist of four proprietors and three directors. This was seen as a victory for both sides but of the four proprietors, two, Messrs Shaw and Tate, were later to become directors, so you may judge just who won the war.

After the special meeting, February's general meeting was an anti-climax. Pledging their efforts towards increasing the traffic and profits, the directors outlined their investigations formulated during the previous year but suspended in favour of the CofE. (hereafter used for Committee of Enquiry) and which formed the basis of the CofE. Mr Tartt pointed out, much to the amusement of all, that if the CofE could not improve the position of the company then: '. . . they would jeopardise their characters as men of talent and . . . of business'!

A little progress had been made in the fortunes of the company; receipts were up and expenses constant but still at 80 per cent of revenue. Goods and passenger traffic had increased, and locomotive expenses were reduced to 1s. per mile as against 2s.10d. in 1840. A profit was announced, enabling a dividend of 1¼ per cent to be paid to the unfortunate proprietors. They had now received 2¾ per cent in two years! With the GWR soon to become legal owners of the CGWU and pressing to gain control of the BrG, Joseph Sturge (brother of director Charles) spoke openly about amalgamations.[2] 'Much has been discussed privately as to the practicability both to the public and the shareholders of the Company of joining this railway to some of the larger branches connected with it.' One third more capital was expended, he continued, on small schemes like the B&G, BrG and so on, for the want of 'guided men' to plan and run the railways under one management. The B&G, he felt, would pay 'at least 6 per cent' when the connection to Bristol was established, and even more if worked as a whole. With this in mind, and with the impartial view of the two or three directors of the company who shared their time with the L&B Board (C. Moorsom and C. Sturge), he hoped the meeting would consider the following resolution: '. . . that in the event of overtures being made upon an equitable basis for lease or purchase of the B&G by any other Company, the meeting recommends the Directors to entertain it.' A brave and intelligent proposal; the empire created by George Hudson goes to prove it [even allowing for his misdeeds!], as does the later creation of the LNWR. Unfortunately, the majority of proprietors shuddered at the effects that this might have on their already precarious share values, and besides, they hoped that their optimistic CofE would soon secure for them more traffic and profits than they would know what to do with. With lightning reactions the resolution was withdrawn! Shortly, a correspondent to the *Railway Times* endorsed Joseph Sturge's proposal.[3] A short line like the B&G could never pay high dividends, especially one with no connections at its southern end; it could work twice the distance of line from Birmingham to Bristol with the same machinery and same number of men that worked the Birmingham to Gloucester route.

Mention has been made above of the B&G's forthcoming application to Parliament during the 1843 session, so the events leading to this need to be outlined. Determined to put an end to the expensive and unsatisfactory omnibus link between Worcester and Spetchley, the Board began another series of proposals with the Worcester committees. These culminated in a proposal by the B&G in August 1842 to form a branch from Bredicot to Sansome Fields near the centre of the city. Their argument as ever was the need for a central terminus and a junction which favoured north and south equally. Yet, as before, when put before a public meeting, their old adversary Mr Pierpoint rejected their branch in favour of a deviation line or the Abbotswood branch and succeeded in getting the meeting, allegedly composed of bribed 'working class' people, to outvote the B&G scheme again. Of this latest debacle, the *Worcester Herald*[4] concluded that the city was determined to oppose whatever the B&G offered them.

Persevere they did; in fact they decided to put their branch before Parliament in the next session come what may. Capt. W.S. Moorsom was called in to survey the route, almost identical to the 1835 plan with a branch to the gas works and to the river Severn. With all the predictability of clockwork Mr Berkeley, the Worcester town council and Chamber of Commerce registered their dissent. The *Railway Times* suggested that had the city authorities to pay the legal costs from their own pockets they would have had a railway years ago![5]

Another attempt was also made to obtain the branch line from Gloucester Docks, and together these made up the 'Branches Bill', lodged separately from the 'Money Bill'. This latter was primarily to authorise capital and convert the scrip issue of May 1841 into quarter shares.

Both Bills were dealt with in March, and as part of the new Standing Orders procedure, a special general meeting was required to gain the proprietors' sanction. The Money Bill's main purpose was to legalise the raising of £175,000 by scrip and £60,000 by loan vote as authorised by the proprietors in May 1841 (the amounts realised were £143,000 and £41,000 respectively). 10,000 quarter shares would need to be created, exchanging these for scrip and mortgages or bonds for the loan notes. Proprietors were told that liabilities over and above the present £1,440,000 capital cost were still £150,000 although half of this was contingent upon certain events (such as £50,000 pledged for rolling stock to work the BrG section, about which more later). Opposition from the proprietors was vigorous but they were told that the CofE endorsed the bill, and they were morally bound to exchange the scrip for shares to rid the company of the interest payments (about £12,000 since their issue). Henry Killick, a proprietor and chairman of the CofE emphasised the need to put money into the railway to enable it to pay a fair return, he and his business associates were so confident that they had been buying up shares and scrip. He added: 'A few words about our much abused line which I was led to believe was one of the worst in England. . . . I found the road equal to any I was ever on, and I have been over the line several times with gentlemen competent to give an opinion and they were much pleased with the road, the attendants and the working . . . I do not think the present line would be adopted if it had to be made again, but this cannot be altered now . . . the Proprietors have a good prospect and no other road in the country can show much less to complain of.' As for past management, Samuel Baker, an ex-chairman, admitted: 'In the early days of railways no man was thought unfit for the business of a railway director; no one was incompetent to lay out millions of money. This had been the cause of great errors.' Finally, Mr Fripp, the Bristol representative, warned the proprietors to: 'Pause before you fetter your Directors in the cares of economy upon which they have entered and before you paralyse the vigour and confidence which is essential for the support of the Directors in their negotiations with our companies.' A direct reference no doubt to the BrG, he feared that the GWR would take over that company and he wanted to keep it independent as a link between the west and the north of the country.

As for the Branches Bill, both branches were endorsed by the CofE. £50,000 spent on the Worcester branch would yield an instant profit since the omnibus link, itself a deterrent to trade, could be scrapped, and in the (certain!) event of disagreement with the Worcester people, the company was ready to submit to arbitration by the BoT. Gloucester Docks spoke for itself. £14,000 had already been invested there and only £5,000 extra was needed to complete the link, with the prospect of an impressive rise in goods traffic. Voting was very close. 2,300 and 2,100 against.

The Branches Bill didn't stand a chance, Mr Berkeley and the Worcester town council saw to that. However the Money Bill, though it had a rough ride being opposed by both Worcester and the GWR, did eventually receive the Royal Assent on 27 June 1843, the same day that the CofE published its findings. The clauses relevant to the finances are outlined in the appendix, but of interest here is that pertaining to Worcester. Both sides in the fiasco had agreed in March that if Parliament did not settle the route of the branch they would refer their differences to the BoT and abide by their findings. The town council petitioned for a clause to this effect in the Money Bill and this was duly included. A committee of the BoT was to fix the point of junction, terminus, and intermediate route, with due regard to convenience, cost, private rights, public interests and agreements already entered into. Once this had been done the B&G would have to get an Act and build it. No penalty was fixed for default, it being felt that recourse to common law would remedy any breach of the agreement.

So, at last, the differences between Worcester and the B&G were settled, but in spite of all the argument and ill-feeling of the past eight or nine years and the eventual reconciliation, the B&G never built either branch or deviation line, though it was not for want of trying!

Before seeing what the CofE had been doing, no small revolution was in prospect on the BrG. For some time the B&G directors had realised that the true traffic potential of their line would only be realised when a continuous line of railway was open to Bristol, and the profit would be even higher were they to come to some working arrangements with the BrG. (It will be remembered that earlier plans for amalgamation in 1840 had failed.) With this object in mind, Capt. Moorsom visited George Jones, the BrG chairman, in September 1842. He proposed a system whereby the B&G worked the BrG's trains at cost price using B&G locomotives, rolling stock and crews. The BrG would undertake the remaining tasks. This, thought the B&G, would not only suit both companies but also prevent the broad gauge of the GWR from infiltrating the narrow gauge South Midlands.

The GWR intended to do just that! They had been courting the BrG with precisely that aim in view and in the eyes of most of the BrG Board, they were a more soundly based company than the nearly bankrupt B&G. In December 1842 therefore, George Jones wrote to Capt. Moorsom warning him that in spite of their original intention to adopt the narrow gauge, if it came to a vote it was likely that the majority of his board and proprietors would opt for the GWR broad gauge for their line to Gloucester.

This did not deter the B&G. A railway whose earthworks and tunnels were only designed for the narrow gauge would not, they thought, be so mad as to lay wide gauge. They therefore persisted in their proposition and were prepared to lay out £50,000 in additional stock to work the BrG section.

However, in April 1843 the proprietors of the BrG formally accepted a working agreement with the GWR. Mr Fripp, a Bristol and Exeter railway director and B&G shareholder, tried in vain to show the proprietors the folly of treating with the GWR. He reminded them: 'In 1840, the Directors, considering the question of gauge to be adopted said "the most important feature in this line is its immediate connection with the railways leading to Birmingham and the manufacturing districts of the North, and there can be no doubt that its traffic both in goods and passengers will consist of such as will be required to pass the whole distance between Birmingham and Bristol. The shifting of this traffic at any point betwen these 2 places . . . could not fail to be of serious inconvenience to the public and, in consequence, of prejudice to this undertaking".' He went on to ridicule the directors' fear that if they did not bow to the GWR, who hemmed them in at both ends of their line, then all their traffic would be taken by the GWR via Swindon. 'What nonsense', he said, 'the distance via Swindon was twice that of their railway so how could the GWR possibly compete with us without making a huge loss?' Mr Daniel, director of the B&G and shareholder in the BrG supported Mr Fripp; pointing out that agreement with GWR was one sided and protected the GWR interests only: 'We are to pay a very heavy price for the use of the stations [Cheltenham, Gloucester and Bristol]. From the moment we sign that agreement we cease to exist as an independent Company and place ourselves entirely in the power of the GWR . . . The Directors of the B&G have offered to find locomotives for both Companies charging pro-rata for the amount of duty done and making no charge for the interest on capital.' In spite of these warnings, the proprietors accepted the GWR agreement. Thus was conceived the notorious gauge break at Gloucester, a folly which proved to be the beginning of the end for the broad gauge.

To return now to the CofE which sat from January to June 1843.[6] In the matter of staff and wages they were quite unimaginative, merely following blindly the general practice of the time. To obtain economies, wholesale cuts were to be made in the numbers of staff. The CofE thought highly of these measures; but in reality they were counter productive not only on the B&G but on other railways whose example the B&G had followed.

Small wonder that they aroused the anger of a columnist in the *Railway Times* and *Record* who wrote under the pen-name of 'Veritas Vincit',[7] and who had the plight of railway servants very much at heart.

Of the B&G he wrote in March 1843 that eleven switchmen were to be discharged, and their duties taken over by the train fireman. Those that were kept were: 'to be screwed down to the starving point of 11s. to 16s. per week . . . fatal consequences will ensue.' Police were to be dispensed with at certain danger points, including the dangerous 'Coffin Tunnel' (his delightful nickname for Grovely or Cofton tunnel); Ashchurch, where lookout men were of the 'utmost importance' in stopping smashes; the Lickey, where safety was paramount; and Spetchley, where five pairs of points were to be worked by the firemen. Now what would be the consequences if the fireman fell whilst changing points, he wondered? 'The B&G requires very steady and experienced men with a thorough knowledge . . . to work it in safety . . . One director . . . admitted the reduction would be hard on the men . . . Is there no other way to be found to retrieve the extravagant and ruinous expenditure of a railway but by endangering the public safety and screwing down the wages of enginemen, firemen and policemen to starvation point?'

In due course the wages and numbers of the locomotive department were to be cut, and 'Veritas Vincit' made sure the full story appeared before the public (see Chapters 17 and 18). He pointed out the ridiculous paradox of cutting pay, sacking those who complained and replacing them with 'Northern and Cheap' drivers who then caused more expense through accident damage than their low wages ever saved in working expenses. Add to this the fact that McConnell, the locomotive chief, had his salary linked to working expenses and received £50 extra for every 1d. per mile cut in expenses. No wonder 'Veritas Vincit' spoke so strongly against McConnell, whose salary rose whilst his underlings' numbers and wages decreased. (This shows however, that 'Veritas Vincit' was misinformed. As related elsewhere, McConnell's salary increases were not based upon reductions in labour or fuel costs, only efficiency.) Publication of the CofE report came in June 1843 and its findings make interesting reading.[8] Future prospects were bright! 'Time is gradually removing the principal obstacles to the prosperity of the line', and when the railway's resources were fully developed by the opening of the BrG and CGWU, the results would be satisfactory to all proprietors. Looking briefly at the contents of the report, the biggest shake up occurred with the staff pruning scheme. In all 54 men were sacked and the wages of the remaining 271 (there had been 719 in August 1841) were cut, saving £4,000 per annum. The reductions in wages were not, states the report, unreasonable compared to the general level of wages elsewhere but salaries of the principal officers were not to be reduced considering their responsibilities and abilities. An increase should be made to certain officers; '. . . on whose vigilance and efficiency so much of the company's success must ultimately depend.' With the Bristol connection now in the hands of the GWR, certain proprietors (including Joseph Sturge?) had requested the CofE to consider and report upon the desirability of coming to a similar agreement with the GWR. But having considered the benefits and disadvantages, they felt it best to leave the directors to decide. Finance, as ever, was an embarrassment. The latest estimate of capital expenditure was just over £1.5 millions. This did not include the branches to Worcester and Gloucester Docks, but the return of the moiety of the Cheltenham–Gloucester line from the GWR in 1845 would, they expected, more than pay for these. 'Injudicious outlay of the Company's money' had occurred in several places, notably the £14,000 at High Orchard dock, Gloucester, which the committee: 'can only hope that as the situation had certain advantages it may at some future time be available property.' Extension of the railway to the quay at Tewkesbury, authorised yet never completed, was recommended, as was the reduction of the excessive goods rates from that town to Cheltenham. Further waste had occurred on the maintenance contract for the permanent way. It had been let for seven years, and now, when they found it could be re-let for much less, they were bound to the previous contract.

Passenger traffic was but two thirds of the Parliamentary estimate, but the CofE felt sure that once the BrG and CGWU were open, and the countrywide depression lifted, the traffic would rise dramatically. The line was much visited by travellers for pleasure, especially to Cheltenham, and their numbers had fallen during those troubled times. As might be expected, goods traffic took considerable space in the report, (see Chapter 14). However, they were optimistic of better times when the BrG was opened: 'Although very great discrepancies exist in the several estimates . . . your committee are satisfied that a very large amount of merchandise must ultimately come upon the line, from which the Company have hitherto derived no benefit; and that when the communication by railway to Bristol is completed, the receipts . . . will be at least doubled.' Locomotive costs were set to fall again mainly due to: 'the Company's intelligent Superintendent Mr McConnell'. His judicious arrangements in carrying out reductions had saved £1,500 per annum and were highly praised by the committee. But not by 'Veritas Vincit' or the eighteen men dismissed or those whose wages had been cut. In conclusion the committee felt that: 'relationships with other railways must be fostered and maintained in a most amicable and frank way since this line is connected with three Companies at the North end and two at the South.'

The CofE had set out, confidently assured that through their findings they would be able to set the railway on the path to prosperity, but in fact their findings were unimaginative and commonplace. It was obvious that by reducing staff and wages economy of a sort could be obtained; but they failed to realise, as did all the others who ruthlessly pursued the same course, that economies achieved in this way would be got at the expense of safety and efficiency. The *Gloucester Journal* agreed. They said that the Report was:[9] '. . . somewhat of a namby-pamby description and objectionable . . . in as much as while it recommends an increase rather than a diminuation of the larger salaries it advocates the wretched parsimony of starving the half paid under-lings.' The only useful thing to emerge, continued the *Gloucester Journal*, was that with capital twice the estimates and traffic less than half, the public would know how much faith to put in railway prospectuses in future.

'Veritas Vincit'[10] naturally had a strong word about the pay of those superiors. 'For the duty they have to perform they are overpaid. I know well . . . what their duty is; . . . and there are too many of them. Is it not shameful to see those gentlemen straining every nerve not only in the reduction of their subordinate's wages but at the same decreasing their numbers thereby lessening their own labours; and while they are inculcating contentment on the labourers under reduction, they are drawing on the beggared finances of their Company for greater pay for themselves!' Considerable disagreement between members of the CofE came to light during July. George Tate told the *Railway Times* that whatever the findings of the CofE they did not all give their testimony to the fitness of the present directors to govern the company, often quite the opposite.[11] Tate also produced his own minority report which met with further hostile comments from the *Railway Times*[12] when they reviewed it. It suggested that Tate 'the would-be Director' and his friend Humphrey Brown 'the would be Traffic Manager' were in league to destroy Moorsom's system. As for Tate's report, they suggested he could have saved the expense for all its contents were worth!

At their August meeting, proprietors were told that the findings of the CofE were receiving attention, especially in the goods department. A revision and cut in rates, together with the employment of a goods traffic manager, were seen as a proper foundation for future prosperity. Tonnage was up in the first six months of 1843, but receipts were down as a greater proportion was in the hands of the carriers. Passenger journeys were down but an increase in fares had kept receipts constant. Through carriages to destinations on the BDJc were soon to start.

A profit of £5,500 was announced, with a dividend of 0.6 per cent! Working expenses were an incredible 90 per cent of the revenue despite reductions in locomotive and way and works costs. The elections to the Board were accompanied by heated exchanges bandied over the floor. The four directors who, though due to retire in rotation, were nevertheless eligible for re-election were replaced by four directly opposed to Capt. Moorsom, two of whom were Charles Shaw and George Tate. As leading members of the CofE they were pledged to implement the findings of the report to many of which Capt. Moorsom was firmly opposed. It appeared therefore that the CofE had won their 12 months battle and that Capt. Moorsom would, as a result, have to resign his chairmanship. This however he resolutely refused to do claiming that the proceedings had been out of order.

The *Railway Times*[13] expressed grave doubts about the way in which the chairman had been flouted, and other irregularities which had occurred at the meeting; and asked pointed questions as to how it was that Tate had managed to obtain enough proxy votes to enable him to oust those loyal to the chairman, and concluded: 'What need did the Birmingham and Gloucester Railway have for Directors when men like Joseph Sturge repeatedly volunteer to sell the Company to the Great Western Railway over the heads of the Board?'

The GWR had approached the B&G in July 1843 concerning the redemption of their rights at the Gloucester station and also about a lease of the line. Rumours circulated for the rest of the year about a takeover by the GWR which brought anxious enquiries from both companies proprietors. Both companies denied these allegations but whilst these denials may have been true in August they certainly were not in November when the Board resolved to negotiate with the GWR. They would offer the GWR their Cheltenham–Gloucester line for £400,000 and the Cheltenham–Worcester section for £900,000. It is hard to say whether or not the B&G had decided to give in. One wonders just what they hoped to gain from selling the Worcester to Gloucester half of their line, other than cash to clear their debts. The GWR too thought the offer was pointless, declined it and instead proceeded to plan for their redemption of the Cheltenham and Gloucester areas.

Cheltenham was to have a central station (later St James) connected to the joint line and to the B&G. Gloucester was to have a central station and a link to the docks, all of which required an Act of Parliament, and application was planned for the 1844 session. In addition the GWR looked into their future working of the Cheltenham–Gloucester line and to settling the long overdue accounts of construction.

The B&G's mood had however changed again when deputations from both companies met to work out an agreement on the joint line. The GWR proposed that the B&G's Cheltenham depot should be the point of gauge break for all traffic to and from the north, and that they should work all traffic between Cheltenham and Gloucester themselves. When the B&G demurred at this the GWR spokesman protested with an air of pained innocence that they were only trying to help the

B&G out of their difficulties, and had made their proposals in the best interests of both companies and the economic working of the joint line. This was too much for the B&G to swallow. They recognised it for what it was – a thinly diguised attempt at a take-over. They broke off negotiations, and joined in the successful opposition to the GWR Bill.

Capt. Moorsom resigned his chairmanship in December 1843. George Tate, Moorsom's arch-enemy on the B&G board, proposed that as the three month experimental trial of the goods traffic system proposed by the CofE had been a failure, a committee should be formed to make alterations as soon as possible. The board voted and Tate won, whereupon Capt. Moorsom vacated the chair, never to return. A few days later he wrote a letter of explanation which accused the Tate contingent of conspiring to take over the board. Three months trial of the new style of goods working could not possibly hope to reflect its success or failure, he wrote. The appointment of another committee of investigation was irresponsible and he wanted no part of it.

In the space of the next few weeks Samuel Bowley, a veteran B&G man, took over the chair, the company became the sole carrier of goods traffic on the railway and Humphrey Brown talked himself into the appointment of traffic manager. So self-assured was he that he said that he would work without salary until his plans had brought the proprietors a dividend of 3 per cent. As for Capt. Moorsom, he would neither resign his seat on the board nor attend the board meetings. The *Railway Times* advised that the sooner he: '. . . or any other honourable man cuts the connection, the better for himself.'[14] George King, the company secretary, had already done so in disgust at the treatment given to his chairman.

At the February 1844 general meeting Samuel Bowley paid tribute to Capt. Moorsom and also to those directors loyal to Moorsom's system but who were now willing to work with and accept the new. 'The meetings [of the Board] had become increasingly harmonious and he hoped that that . . . would be followed by the Proprietors at large.' Such harmony seemed unlikely amidst the calls for Capt. Moorsom to resign, while others attempted to defend him. All was settled however, when it appeared that his seat on the board was up for re-election in August so he could be replaced and harmlessly forgotten. Continuing, Bowley reassured the meeting that: 'The prospects are better now than they have ever been . . . I think that the policy on which we are now acting will . . . become the system adopted by all railway companies . . . namely that of becoming carriers on their own lines . . . In another half year the results . . . will be more clearly apparent.' A profit of nearly £14,000 was announced for the second half of 1843, enabling a dividend of 1½ per cent to be paid. Working expenses were down to 75 per cent of revenue as opposed to 90 per cent before, and shares reached £65 on the market, their best for two years. Increases in the passenger business were noted and also in goods tonnage, but receipts had fallen slightly owing to the reduction in rates. Since the company had become prime carrier in February 1844, the results were more than satisfactory. Receipts and profits were twice the weekly total of February 1843. More through traffic would be carried as a result of arrangements with the GJR, BDJC and Manchester and Birmingham railways.

Locomotive costs had fallen again, down to 10½d. per mile and now took only 10 per cent of the entire working expenses, compared to 30 or 40 per cent previously. Elsewhere on the line, the Tewkesbury branch was now worked by locomotive power and the horse coach used only for the night mail; further, the long standing anomalies regarding goods traffic on the branch were removed. Further north, arrangements relative to Worcester were in the hands of an: '. . . eminent and disinterested engineer', Mr Robert Stephenson no less, who was surveying a branch line under the BoT agreement.

For the B&G, 1843 had been a year of mixed fortunes. Another system of management was in operation, the third in as many years. There were prospects of considerable expansion in goods and passenger traffic with the Midlands and the north. There was still no rail link to Gloucester Docks or to Worcester, while the defection of the BrG, its southern ally, to the broad gauge had nearly led to despair and a sellout to the GWR. Fortunately, in their arrogance, the GWR had demanded too much, and the B&G, preferring a troubled independence to subjection, had drawn back at the last minute. But it is doubtful if the B&G or the GWR had even an inkling of the troubles that lay in store for them in the next year or two.

CHAPTER ELEVEN

1844, A BETTER YEAR

With its new working practice now established, the B&G's fortunes began to improve in the New Year. *Herepath* notes in March that B&G shares have risen to £83 and comments: 'Whether it be improved management, or what, we do not undertake to say, but certainly the B&G receipts in goods have shown a wonderful increase . . . if it continues, the railway will benefit by about a clear £14,000 to £18,000 a year. We have no partialities . . . no paid praises to sing, but facts like these cannot be gainsaid.'[1]

'Cocker' suggested in a later issue that: 'Surely there is something in railway management . . . and this has never more been exemplarised than on this line. By an alternative of management, the goods traffic has been increased from £246 [June 1843] to £1,056 [June 1844] per week. There has been no increase of distance, no new feeding lines, and yet a legitimate increase of traffic of nearly £1,000 per week . . . That this will be . . . increased by the opening through from Gloucester to Bristol . . . sufficient [evidence] is given by other railways and must soon cause shares to be at 20 per cent premium because they really are worth it.'[2] Proprietors heard their share of the good news at their August general meeting, though they only received a dividend of 1¼ per cent. Those holding quarter shares were included in the share of profits for the first time, naturally decreasing the slice each proprietor could expect.

The new chairman, Samuel Bowley, insisted that affairs were improving and the outlook promising; shares were now quoted at £114 and he said that he would be looking to increase his own holding. Perhaps he should have worried about the continuing high ratio of

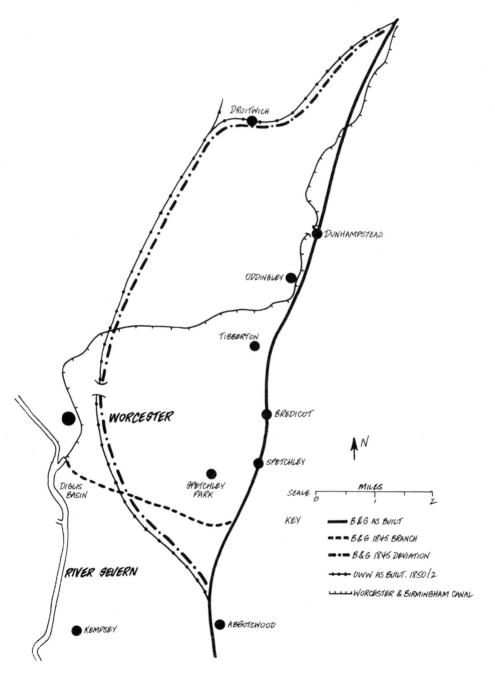

DROITWICH

DUNHAMPSTEAD

ODDINGLEY

TIBBERTON

BREDICOT

WORCESTER

SPETCHLEY

N

DIGLIS
BASIN

SPETCHLEY
PARK

SCALE | MILES
0   1   2

KEY

━━━━━ B&G AS BUILT

━ ━ ━ B&G 1845 BRANCH

━·━·━ B&G 1845 DEVIATION

━•━•━ OWW AS BUILT. 1850/2

⊥⊥⊥⊥⊥ WORCESTER & BIRMINGHAM CANAL

RIVER SEVERN

KEMPSEY

ABBOTSWOOD

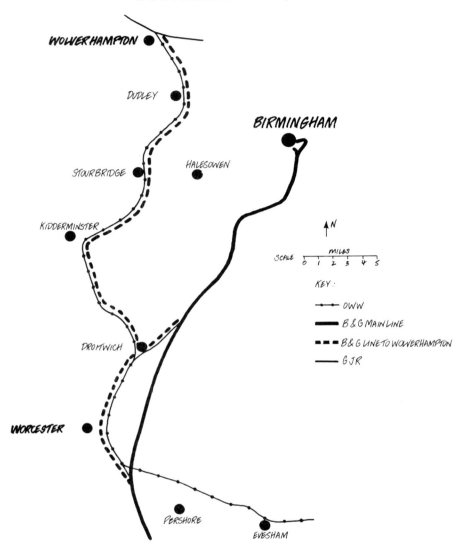

working expenses to revenue. This was 75 per cent for the first half of 1844. Interest payments (at £10,000) on loans accounted for 25 per cent of the entire working expenses.

Under Capt. Moorsom's chairmanship the half-yearly reports always gave detailed accounts of the expenditure in each department. There was no attempt at a cover-up however unpalatable the details may have been. Many proprietors complained that they were boring and unnecessary, but they are of great value to historians. The new regime, bowing to popular pressure, made their report in general terms and it is possible that thereby awkward facts were glossed over. It is therefore difficult to make an accurate assessment of the railway's real position. In particular we miss the facts and figures about locomotives and about the numbers and condition of the carriage and wagon stock. Permanent way costs were due to be cut since the contract had been re-let for £3,500 less per year. A breach of contract by the original maintenance crew had enabled the B&G to rid themselves of their expensive seven-year contract.

Alluding to the improved traffic performance, a further facility had been provided. Gloucester Docks had at last a 4ft. 8½in. gauge rail link, albeit a temporary one. Rails had been laid astride the tramway route and wagons had an unbroken journey, horse hauled, to the dockside, theoretically increasing the railway's competitive advantage over water transport.

Mr Bowley went on to say that July would see the opening of the BrG and immediate increases in traffic were hoped for. Amicable working arrangements had been made for the interchange of traffic at Gloucester (see Chapter 25).

Important developments in the Worcester area were afoot. A multitude of plans were growing, promoted in the interests of both broad and narrow gauge by various parties to open up the Black Country by linking Wolverhampton, Worcester and the south using similar routes to the ill-fated GCR. According to the Board: 'These schemes . . . appear to have originated in jealousy of existing railways . . . rather than from any sincere attempt to meet . . . the wants of the public . . . there is every reason to suppose they will . . . be abandoned.' They referred to the start of the Gauge War. The GWR was attempting via the Oxford, Worcester & Wolverhampton (OWW) to push north and west from Oxford to Wolverhampton in direct competition with the L&B, who naturally had to pursue a similar scheme (The Worcester and Tring Railway) to protect their territory.

Worcester, it will be remembered, had successfully inserted a clause in the 1843 B&G 'Money Act' empowering them to make a branch line, the route of which was to be determined by the BoT. In August 1843 the B&G was formally requested to comply with this clause and so the wheels of the of the Worcester branch had once again been set in motion.

Major General Pasley of the BoT duly arrived and began the arduous task of hearing the evidence of both sides. He appointed Robert Stephenson to survey several routes for comparison and from which the most suitable could be chosen. In January 1844, Stephenson opted for a branch line from near Spetchley to a terminus near the Albion Inn (on the Bath Road, now the A38), where there was good access for the public and from where access to the docks could be arranged via a short spur. As this was based upon the principle agreed by the B&G, they readily accepted it, and so did Worcester after some argument.

Enthusiasm for the branch line, was however soon overshadowed by events on a much larger scale. As mentioned above, plans for developing a rail network in the Black Country were afoot and the B&G had every intention of being involved. In March 1844, Bayliss, the resident engineer, was ordered to survey a branch line from Bromsgrove through Kidderminster, Stourbridge and on to the GJR at Wolverhampton. It was however evident to Bayliss that a better overall strategy would be to abandon a branch to Worcester in favour of deviating the mainline via Droitwich and Worcester (the OWW planned an identical deviation line). This was agreed to by the board. During the summer and autumn the B&G's plans matured, influenced mainly by the OWW whose route through the Black Country to Wolverhampton diverged from the Worcester deviation line at Droitwich. Local newspapers carried this advertisement:[3]

WORCESTER & WOLVERHAMPTON RAILWAY:
£500,000 CAPITAL : 10,000 SHARES

The Board desire to extend the railway to Worcester and North thereof and subsequent to a meeting with the BoT on 9th October it is proposed to divert the present line at Abbotswood, pass close to the City of Worcester and north through the town and saltworks of Droitwich, through Kidderminster, Stourbridge, Dudley and Wolverhampton. The Directors feel this is the best way to rectify an unfortunate mistake in the original formation of the line. 4 per cent guaranteed. R. Stephenson, consulting engineer.

At the end of October, a special general meeting of the B&G proprietors was called to ask for their approval of the scheme. They were told that the railway would ensure the quickest transit between Gloucester, the west Midlands and Liverpool and would enable the salt export traffic from Droitwich to Gloucester to go by rail. With a return traffic of Forest of Dean coal, this would prove highly profitable. Overwhelming approval was given (except for the guaranteed return of 4 per cent) and the application to Parliament sanctioned.

Public meetings were held at various Black Country towns where representatives of various railway companies tried to win support for their schemes in the 'build-up' to the ensuing Parliamentary session. Dudley and Worcester favoured the OWW while Droitwich preferred the B&G.

Herbert Spencer was re-engaged for the detail surveys, and records:[4] '. . . and so here I am back for a months hard work surveying and levelling. I am to be paid at the usual rate . . . a guinea [21s.] a day . . . the country traversed was the worst imaginable, . . . a jumble of coal pits, iron works, cinder heaps, tramways, canals, lanes, streets, ground which had subsided and houses which had cracked in consequence of the abstraction of coal from beneath. The levels had to be taken in more or less smoke. I helped to carry on the process of preparing the plans to be deposited at the end of the month [November] . . . a good deal of unceasing work, the day being eked out by many hours of the night.'

Plans for the Worcester and Wolverhampton railway, Worcester deviation and branch (to comply with the BoT requirement of the 1843 Act) were submitted on time at the end of November. All 10,000 shares in the venture were taken by the end of January 1845 but all was not well on the Parliamentary front. The BoT submitted a report to Parliament on railway development in the Black Country which approved of the Worcester deviation but preferred the L&B scheme to join Wolverhampton to Worcester and the south. Broad gauge hopes were thus dealt a temporary blow by the BoT's preference for the narrow gauge schemes of the B&G and L&B.

Parliament began digesting these bills in April, when remarkably the BoT recommendations were reversed and the OWW scheme in its entirety was favoured. In a very short time the Gauge Commission was to recommend against any further expansion of the broad gauge network! Through the authorisation of the OWW, the B&G lost out completely in its ambitious plans, and a mass return of deposits to the prospective shareholders followed. Traffic interchange at Worcester was catered for, however. Having lost their deviation line, the B&G were awarded running powers over the identical OWW line which was to be mixed gauge; as was that from Worcester through to Wolverhampton. The narrow gauge exchange traffic between the B&G and GJR could thus flow as originally planned. Incidently the branch into Worcester was withdrawn with the consent of all parties, early in the Parliamentary proceeding.

The Worcester story is now virtually at an end! Those familiar with OWW will know that its stern legal battles over the narrow gauge had severely depleted its finances and it was not until October 1850 that their first section, between Abbotswood and Worcester, could be opened. It was immediately leased to the MR (owners of the B&G by then). Trains ran from Worcester to Spetchley at first, since the exchange station at Abbotswood was incomplete. According to the press:[5] '. . . trains from Worcester to Spetchley occupy exactly a quarter of an hour in the transit . . . the trains run up to the junction in about ten minutes and a brief delay is occasioned here by the shunting of the train on to the mainline, but this accomplished, the run up to Spetchley is made in five minutes. There further delay is occasioned so that at present there is little saving of time by the opening of the branch, though the improvement as regards comfort is unquestionable. There is no huddling of fifteen persons in one lumbering conveyance for an hour's tedious jolting.' It was a strange twist of fate that Worcester's first taste of railway communications should be by a branch from Abbotswood, the very same ridiculed and refused by the B&G yet strongly favoured by the people of Worcester, undoubtedly with a view to a similar extension through to Wolverhampton.

Continuation of the line north towards Stoke to complete the deviation line was completed in February 1852. MR passenger services eventually all ran via Worcester until 1880 when a reversal of policy was made which has continued to the present day, when all through services over the B&G route avoid Worcester (true for 1984–5 timetable). For all the trials and tribulations of those early days, that fine cathedral city is not on the Intercity network between Bristol and Birmingham while Cheltenham and Gloucester enjoy a wide selection of services. If by some magical means the clocks could go back 150 years, we have no doubt that Worcester would enjoy a position on the main line, but history, once made, cannot be altered!

Preparations for the opening of the BrG, the B&G's southern feeder railway, were in full swing during the early part of 1844. Arrangements for the interchange of traffic at Gloucester were made. A platform was added to the north of the B&G station for passenger exchange pending completion of the GWR's station which the BrG had powers to use under its working agreement. A small shed was erected for the transfer of goods traffic, and the scene was set for the remarkable spectacular of railway history; the Break of Gauge at Gloucester. A premonition of the scenes of confusion experienced in later years occurred at the farcical opening ceremony on 6 July, two days before the public opening. The inaugural train carrying dignitaries from Bristol to Gloucester came off the rails on the severe curve between Millstream and Tramway Junctions. I.K. Brunel and the BoT Inspector spent a laborious and humiliating day repairing the damage whilst the remainder of the party enjoyed a banquet held on the platforms of the B&G station.

An inglorious start, but all the same typical of the BrG's somewhat haphazard arrangements; a characteristic of theirs which all too soon became abundantly apparent when their inadequate goods transfer shed came into use. It was so small that it hindered rather than facilitated the transhipment of loads from wagons of one gauge to those of the other.

For passengers the gauge break meant a change of trains with porters carrying their luggage. This was an inconvenience not peculiar to Gloucester but the inadequte arrangements there ensured that whatever could go wrong did go wrong! (see Chapter 25).

Negotiations between the B&G and GWR over the use and finances of the Cheltenham–Gloucester line began again at the end of July. Once more the GWR made agreement impossible by claiming the Cheltenham–Gloucester traffic exclusively for themselves. Broad gauge plans for a central terminus in Cheltenham went ahead and this became the familiar St. James station, opened in 1847. The settlement of the accounts for the joint line was an immensely difficult task. This was because the CGWU had built the earthworks and left the B&G to lay the permanent way. Balancing these two costs was the major point of disagreement between the two companies. William Burgess, who had been secretary of the B&G during the construction period, was pursuaded to return on a temporary basis to help solve the problems. Shortly after this, he was coaxed into the superintendent's chair as well until a replacement could be found for Humphrey Brown, who had had to resign because of his rudeness to one of the B&G's customers. Returning to the accounts, it was early in 1846 before they were agreed, and then only with the aid of independent arbitors. They put the true cost of the Cheltenham–Gloucester line at £200,000. The B&G paid a small sum to the GWR to complete their payment for taking over the line in 1840 (it will be remembered that they had paid £80,000). The GWR then paid back £100,000 for the repurchase of their moiety, thus settling the whole complicated transaction.

In due course, a working arrangement for the line was agreed, each company working their own trains with a mutual regard for the other's interests. There was still the problem of how the mixed gauge was to be achieved, together with the junctions at either end. Brunel and Stephenson applied themselves to the subject in October 1846 and agreed their plan of action, but it was twelve months before this, that the first dual gauge joint line was completed and inspected by Capt. I.L.A. Simmons of the BoT (see Way & Works, Chapter 15).

It was during the autumn of 1844 that the full effects of the gauge break at Gloucester began to be widely felt. Traffic, mainly goods, suffered damage, loss and mis-direction in course of transfer between the two railways. The B&G board thought it likely that a narrow gauge line would have to be laid to Bristol. Meanwhile, merchants in Birmingham and Bristol vociferously petitioned the BoT about their grievances at Gloucester and the B&G and BrG nearly came to blows over who was to blame and who was to bear the expense of compensating traders for damages and loss. The stage was set for the final act!

CHAPTER TWELVE
THE MIDLAND
TAKE-OVER

Gloucester's Break of Gauge soon became notorious throughout the land. It was not only a liability to both B&G and BrG, but a trouble spot for traders.

The BrG soon realised that their arrangement with the GWR had been a disaster. Little goods traffic was exchanged with the GWR at Bristol. The bulk of their traffic was to and from Birmingham, but its free flow was interrupted by the gauge break. Both companies realised that they must amalgamate and solve the problem together, as a united company.

On a national scale, the gauge break and parallel gauge war in the south and west Midlands emphasised the need for standardisation. The period known as the 'railway mania' had begun. With new railway schemes proliferating, the Government and the BoT realised that it was in the national interest that these should be of uniform gauge and as a first step appointed a Gauge Commission to visit Gloucester and study the problem at first hand.

December of 1844 saw rapid progress towards the amalgamation of the Gloucester railways and a formal agreement was signed on 14 January 1845 to form the Bristol and Birmingham Railway (B&B) and to apply immediately to Parliament to legalise the union. Until this Act was obtained, they would work the lines jointly and pool receipts on a pro-rata basis (see appendix for full details). Having agreed to amalgamate the two companies now felt strong enough to negotiate with the GWR. They proposed to offer their lines to the GWR exchanging their £100 shares for not less than £65 worth of GWR stock. At their meeting on 24 January however, the GWR would offer only

£60 of stock (worth £123) in exchange for each £100 B&B share (worth by then £109). The B&B held out for £65 and both sides agreed to meet again.

Two versions of the second meeting exist. That by MacDermott[1] was based upon GWR material and is the widely accepted and much published version. That in the B&G minute book differs in terms of names and dates, and since this is a history of the B&G, based upon B&G minute books, we shall adopt this latter version.

On 29 January, Joseph Gibbins and Edmund Sturge, members of the B&G deputation of the B&B, set out on their journey to London for the meeting next day with the GWR. At Rugby, whether by accident or design, John Ellis, vice-chairman of the newly formed Midland Railway Company, entered their compartment. On hearing the reason for their journey, he asked them to come back to him if the GWR refused to meet their terms. He assured them that he would, on his own responsibility, pledge his company to take a lease of the B&B at a rent of 6 per cent of their combined capital, and would in addition, undertake responsibility for the B&B's debts.

The following day Charles Saunders, secretary of the GWR declined to increase his company's offer by the £5 per share asked for, and the B&B deputation accordingly turned to Ellis. Ellis confirmed his offer, and informed the BoT of what he had done.

This was a diplomatic coup of far reaching importance and speaking of it later Mr Ellis said:'When I leased the line I had not the opportunity of consulting my colleagues and I took the bold step to secure the interests of the Company I represented . . . I had heard so much of inconvenience and loss of packages . . . etc . . . that when this thing was offered to me I considered it better to run the risk of losing a few thousand pounds than admit the plague of the Broad gauge to Birmingham.' The MR had snatched the B&B from under the nose of the GWR and when the news reached the press, the *Gloucester Journal* said:[3] '. . . it is indeed a contest between the gauges and in this one . . . the men of sharp practice who manage the affairs of the GWR have not evinced their usual far-seeing tact.' They had tried to take the line at a bargain price by giving 'depreciative offers' and paid the penalty. A correspondent to the *Railway Times* praised the MR for its acumen in getting hold of the line:[4] '. . . it kept that groping Company, the GWR, out of the North, it has already raised the value of B&B stock from £110 to £140 and no doubt it will soon be £160.' Formal agreement was made on 30 January.

The B&G solicitor, George Whately, wrote to his BrG colleague:

My dear Osborne,
The Midlands Company have agreed through Mr Ellis . . . to take all our liabilities and to take a lease of our line from Birmingham to

Bristol at 6 per cent on £1,800,000 [the combined capital] for 14 years at least. On Monday, the agreement is to be settled but these terms are finally agreed upon. The GWR were previously seen by Bowley [the B&G Chairman] and unhesitatingly refused to give £65.

Yours etc . . .

MacDermot said that Samuel Bowley and Edmund Sturge of the B&G travelled down to London on 26 January and settled with the MR the following day. A B&G minute[5] noted that a conference was held between B&G and BrG Directors after the B&G Special meeting of 29 January where it was agreed that a deputation of both companies' directors should travel down to London immediately to resume negotiations with the GWR or lease it to the L&B at 6 per cent on the £1,800,000 capital.

The outcome was none the less sensational whatever the version, but it is interesting to note the mention of the L&B. Compare it with the revelation of the L&B chairman, Glynn, at their general meeting in February 1846: 'I perfectly remember the fact of the purchase, because an honourable friend of mine who is connected with the MR, called on me to ask whether I thought the L&B would be concerned in it and I told him that I was not prepared to advise that they should.' Perhaps this previous approach by the MR suggests that their plans for the B&B were premeditated, even perhaps from the time of the MR's creation (from the Midland Counties, BDJc and North Midland Companies) the previous year.

A final agreement between the MR and B&G was signed on 8 February for a lease in perpetuity from 1 July (for details see appendix) and until then the previous B&B arrangements would stand. A bill was immediately put before Parliament to authorise the lease, in addition to the Amalgamation Bill, which was kept as an 'insurance policy' should Parliament not sanction the MR takeover.

Special meetings of B&G, BrG and MR approved the lease. At the latter, George Hudson, the company's chairman, said that his board: '. . . had come to the conclusion that it was better to incur some risk rather than that the Gloucester line should pass into other hands by means of which traffic to the North might as far as regarded the interest of the MR be affected, . . . and . . . upon proper supervision of the whole line they would ultimately find that instead of this engagement . . . providing a loss . . . it would lead to their interest.' How right Hudson was. It may have been 1848 before the lines showed a profit, but in later years it more than made up and proved every bit as valuable as the MR's other constituent lines.

Parliament accepted neither the amalgamation nor the takeover bills because they had been submitted too late to comply with standing orders. However, the BoT took a favourable view. Their report on the rival narrow and broad gauge schemes in the west Midlands embraced the B&B route and its gauge break at Gloucester. Of the B&B they said that they were: '. . . not prepared to report that we see any sufficient public reasons against allowing the proposed amalgamation of the B&G and BrG and the lease . . . to the MR, in the event of Parliament being of the opinion that the extension of the narrow gauge rather than of the wide gauge is to be desired.'

B&B and MR deputations met in May and agreed that the MR should take the lease from 7 May, on payment of £26,000 to the B&B for loss of earnings between then and the end of June. So the B&G had lost its independence to the MR, though theoretically it was possible that Parliament could refuse both takeover and amalgamation! B&B directors met periodically to endorse the MR management until the lease was legalised, and no doubt the proprietors waited eagerly for their first taste of 6 per cent dividends, if, of course, they could resist selling their shares which were now around £30 premium.

But the gauge break still remained. Giving evidence before a Select Committee hearing,[6] George Hudson stated: 'We intend to carry the narrow gauge down to Bristol and shall be coming to Parliament for a Bill for that purpose in the next session.' The following dialogue ensued:

Questioner – 'Are you aware that the BrG are under agreement with the GWR to keep broad gauge for twenty years?' [on the Gloucester–Stonehouse section]

Hudson – 'That would not be inconsistent with installing narrow gauge.'

Questioner – 'What would you do? Put a double line?'

Hudson – 'I should do it by having additional land and making another line by the side of the other.'

Questioner – 'Do you mean to say that you should not hesitate to lay down an additional line?'

Hudson – 'I think it is imperative to do so.'

Amalgamations, absorptions, gauge wars and the like have hitherto rather overshadowed day to day events on the B&G; but when we look at the traffic figures for the latter half of 1844, the effects of the BrG opening are clearly seen. Passenger traffic rose considerably. Receipts were 50 per cent higher than those for the first half of the year. Goods traffic had almost doubled in tonnage for the second successive half year, but receipts had increased less dramatically, by one third only and the BrG's contribution was more negative than positive. A considerable increase in heavy loading goods, such as coal, corn and salt, had pushed the tonnage carried up, but as this classification commanded low rates and small profits, the increase in receipts was less than hoped for. This traffic was also unlikely to have been transhipped at Gloucester in any quantity because of the obvious difficulties. Merchandise traffic, however, was profitable, attracted high rates, was carried in great quantity between Bristol and the Midlands and was the obvious target for both B&G and BrG. But in the July to December period, merchandise loadings on the B&G actually fell, due to the breakdown in through carriage to and from the Manchester and Birmingham Railway, and the deterrent of the gauge break at Gloucester.

Profits were a respectable £24,000 on a revenue of £70,000, a ratio of expense to revenue of 65 per cent – the best yet – and a dividend of 2 per cent, again better than in any previous half year, was paid. Although the major part of the B&G's Parliamentary business in 1845 had been rejected (the Worcester branch and deviation; the junctions with the GWR at Cheltenham; together with the BRG Amalgamation Bill); certain belated success had been achieved. A junction with the MR at Lawley Street (see Map 22.1), a branch into the British Alkali Saltworks at Stoke Prior, and at long last the High Orchard branch to the docks at Gloucester, had all been sanctioned. None of these were in fact completed before the MR legally absorbed the B&B. In fact the junction at Lawley Street was never started since the MR inherited the B&G's running powers into the L&B's Curzon St., and the MR were in no hurry to complete the branch to the docks at Gloucester, being satisfied at first with horse haulage of wagons over the altered tramway.

From the summer of 1845, the MR began its lengthy task of 'Midlandising' the B&B. Wages and staff levels were brought down to those of the MR and their directors gradually replaced those of the B&G, BrG and the still unofficial B&B board. Locomotives and rolling stock of the BrG came under the management of J.E. McConnell at Bromsgrove. When however he was appointed superintendent at Wolverton (LNWR) in 1847, Kirtley at Derby took over the entire MR stock. This ended Bromsgrove's short but not uneventful period as a locomotive works (see Locomotive Department, Chapter 17). Prior to the takeover, the BrG train service had been worked under contract by Stothert & Slaughter who provided engines, rolling stock and crews, and were also under contract to maintain the permanent way. Their contract was terminated to enable standardisation of train working and broad gauge locomotive facilities were provided at the then small locomotive depot at Gloucester.

The final independent half-yearly general meeting of the B&G took place in August covering the first half of the year before the MR lease of the line became officially operative but during which the line had been worked 'as one' with the BrG. In spite of their good fortune B&G proprietors still found cause for complaint. They complained that the value of their shares was derisory at only £133 each, and what was more, the MR's offer to purchase the entire stock of the B&G at £150 per £100 share (see agreement in appendix) was also derisory. What if their shares reached £200 by then? The Board did agree that a company which now guaranteed 6 per cent in a full year should attract more than just £133 per share.

Traffic statistics were not published in the report, but from BoT returns we find that the rise in freight traffic had held steady and passenger numbers had again increased. Profits enabled a dividend of approx. 1¾ per cent on the half year to be paid, the last before the 6 per cent guarantee took effect.

Railway mania was at its height in 1845–46, and following the general trend the MR and the B&B (both legally still independent) submitted a number of proposals. Priority was given to the B&B Amalgamation Bill and the MR Absorption Bill: both had a smooth ride through Parliament but the Amalgamation Bill was dropped in March 1846 and the MR Absorption Bill became law in August 1846 (details in appendix). The MR put forward four other schemes, the first three mentioned being duplicated by the B&B 'just in case' (see Map, 12.1). Great Malvern was to be reached by an ambitious loop and branch system; a line from Droitwich to Malvern then to Gloucester, with a branch to Tewkesbury from Malvern. This was soon reduced to a simple branch from Malvern to Tewkesbury, which failed to pass the standing orders committee. Another attempt was made the following year in a modified form in which the MR tried to penetrate into south Wales via Hereford; the full scheme was a line from Worcester to Hereford with branches to Ledbury, Malvern and Ashchurch but this was years ahead of its time and again failed. Malvern did eventually get its link with the MR but by the independent Tewkesbury and Malvern Railway of 1860, opened in 1864. It was taken over by the MR in 1877 but survived only until 1963.

Cheltenham's sister spa of Bath was next on the list. A 10 mile line from Mangotsfield estimated at £270,000 was proposed but met with no success in Parliament. Economic gloom in the country postponed a further attempt until 1863 when it failed again, but the MR's persistence was rewarded the following year with success. The branch was opened in 1869 and was later connected to that famous cross-country railway, the Somerset and Dorset Joint. It closed 102 years later, but we are fortunate in that the splendid MR station has been preserved, albeit for use as a car park!

The most provocative scheme was for an independent narrow gauge line from Gloucester to Standish Junction, Stonehouse to run alongside the broad gauge GWR line, together with the conversion of the broad gauge to Bristol into the narrow. This new 8½ mile section, by which running over GWR metals could be avoided, would cost £100,000, but was worth every penny to George Hudson. He fought tooth and nail to have his way, but the GWR were not to be humiliated twice and fought back with all their broad gauge might. The MR's weapon was the BoT's recommendation of any suitable measures to complete the uninterrupted chain of communication from the north of England to the south coast and the port of Bristol. In retaliation, the GWR had its agreement with the BrG, signed in 1843, which included a clause forbidding the BrG to encourage the building of any other line or from diverting traffic from the Gloucester to Stonehouse line.

Parliament approved the principle of the bill but referred the gauge question to the BoT. MR engineers protested that a mixed gauge line would be dangerous and expensive to run and they would settle only for a separate narrow gauge line from Gloucester to Stonehouse and narrow gauge onwards to Bristol. Naturally, the GWR insisted that a mixed gauge system could be easily worked and that MR opposition was simply based on their dislike of the broad gauge. The BoT mediated and recommended a mixed gauge system to suit both MR and GWR.

Parliament agreed, and gave the MR the choice of mixed gauge or nothing. They chose nothing rather than submit to the GWR and lost the bill, but the GWR had some revenge. They successfully petitioned a clause into the MR's Absorption Bill forcing them to keep and maintain broad gauge rails from Standish Junction to Bristol, and there they remained, unused, until 1872 when the Gloucester area was converted to the narrow gauge by the GWR. They still kept running powers and used them with great success from 1908 when their Honeybourne line enabled them to compete with the MR over the Birmingham to Bristol route. Not to be defeated by the GWR, fresh proposals were submitted in the following session by the MR. The Gloucester and Stonehouse Junction Railway came before Parliament in 1847 and became law in 1848. But despite the passing of the Act, the GWR flourished under the Agreement made with the BrG in 1843, and used it to obtain an injunction against the MR; so that it was not until 1854 that the MR was able to build and use their avoiding line. Even then the GWR insisted that the MR should, under the 1843 BrG Agreement, continue for another 10 years to pay tolls for running powers over the broad gauge line from Gloucester to Standish which they never used.

Finally in the 1846 session of Parliament, the MR promoted a branch from Barnt Green to Halesowen to connect the local coal mines with the MR's main lines, and provide reliable transport of upwards of 2,000 tons of coal per week to the saltworks at Droitwich, and unite the B&B

to the proposed Stour Valley extension of the L&B. This was one of the 'gauge war' lines in opposition to the GWR backed OWW, which would have given Halesowen a branch from Dudley. The OWW won this battle as well, but in 1865 the independent Halesowen and Bromsgrove Branch Railway was authorised to provide a similar outlet, with a branch to Northfield. The Bromsgrove line was abandoned and the name changed to the Halesowen Railway which opened after considerable delay in 1883. It became jointly owned by the GWR and MR and remained intact until closed by Dr Beeching. A remnant remains as the freight line from Northfield into the British Leyland plant at Longbridge.

So, the only success of the MR in the 1846 session was their Act to absorb the B&B, passed on 3 August (details in appendix). The final general meeting of the B&G, only a formality, took place later in the month. Mr Sanders, the secretary since 1843, was cordially thanked for his labours in the disposing of the company to the MR, and was given the balance of the company's funds as a testimonial. Several days later, on 31 August, the seal of the B&G was fixed to the deeds of conveyance to the MR, after which the company seal was solemnly broken. The B&G had ceased to exist.

Some may think that in ending the story here we are leaving a tale half told. That may be so, but this is a history of the Birmingham and Gloucester Railway, and to follow its development by the Midland, and how it fared under the LMS, and subsequently BR is far beyond our terms of reference.

Suffice it to say that though the B&G Company is dead, the railway they built is still vigorously alive. Though the B&G promoters were fiercely attacked in their day for their 'point to point' strategy, it can be argued that in their planning they were in reality a century and more ahead of their time; for while other meandering lines built in the area, either to supplement or compete with the B&G, have either declined or disappeared, the B&G lives on providing a direct and therefore all important link between south Wales, the west of England, the Midlands and the north.

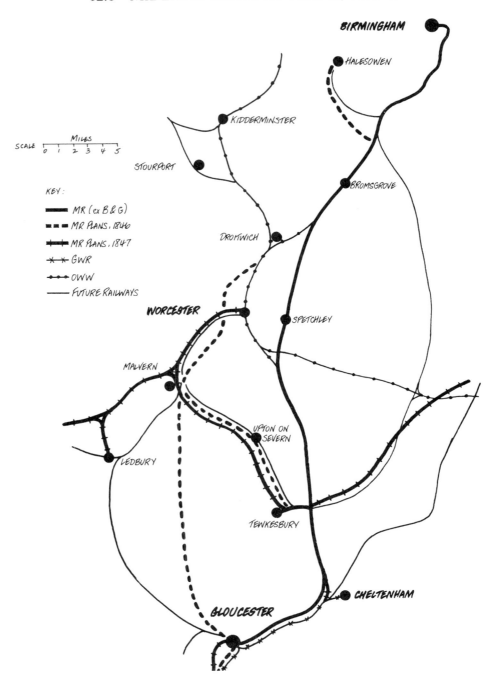

15:1 MIXED GAUGE CHELTENHAM TO GLOUCESTER, 1847 (CONJECTURAL AND NOT TO SCALE)

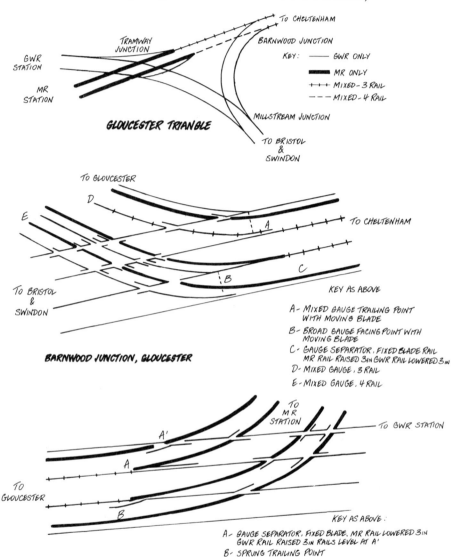

GLOUCESTER TRIANGLE

KEY: ——— GWR ONLY
▬▬▬ MR ONLY
+++ MIXED - 3 RAIL
--- MIXED - 4 RAIL

BARNWOOD JUNCTION, GLOUCESTER

KEY AS ABOVE

A - MIXED GAUGE TRAILING POINT WITH MOVING BLADE
B - BROAD GAUGE FACING POINT WITH MOVING BLADE
C - GAUGE SEPARATOR, FIXED BLADE RAIL MR RAIL RAISED 3IN GWR RAIL LOWERED 3IN
D - MIXED GAUGE, 3 RAIL
E - MIXED GAUGE, 4 RAIL

CHELTENHAM JUNCTION, CHELTENHAM

KEY AS ABOVE:

A - GAUGE SEPARATOR, FIXED BLADE, MR RAIL LOWERED 3IN GWR RAIL RAISED 3IN RAILS LEVEL AT A'
B - SPRUNG TRAILING POINT

CHAPTER THIRTEEN
GOODS DEPARTMENT

Freight prospects for the B&G seemed, on paper, to be excellent. In the mid–1830's, imports via Gloucester docks were 250,000 tons and exports 200,000 tons per annum and even more by-passed Gloucester travelling on the river Severn, between the Midlands and Bristol docks. All this traffic was there for the taking and assuming that only a fraction could be secured by the railway, considerable profits could be expected. Parliament estimated that 70,000 tons could be attracted to the railway, but in reality this amount was easier to estimate than secure, and the shortfall caused endless disharmony between management and shareholders.

Early railways, or any railway for that matter, had three courses open to them in the matter of gaining freight traffic. They could:

(a) Offer the professional haulage firms inducements to use their railway in preference to road or canal; but in order to do this they would have to demonstrate incontestably that theirs was the quickest, cheapest and most reliable method of transport.
(b) They could set themselves up as sole carriers. To do this they would have to build up their own team of freight experts capable of competing so to speak 'in the market place' with the long established professional experts at the job.
(c) They could try to make the best of both worlds by soliciting professional carriers to use their facilities, whilst at the same time accepting all traffic offered to them directly.

The promoters and most of the board of the B&G were either industrialists or merchants. Few had any experience of the transport business, they provided the product and hired carriers to transport it. The L&B had been in much the same position at first. Lacking experience they felt it best to rely on the professionals rather than incur the risk and expense of building up their own goods department as the Grand Junction Railway had done under their forceful general manager, Capt. Huish.

It was only natural therefore that William Burgess and Capt. C. Moorsom, who came to the B&G from the L&B and had to build the B&G up literally from scratch, should follow the L&B lead in adopting method (a). This was a mistake, as both L&B and B&G found to their cost; but they are not to be blamed for it, nor are the professional carriers for sticking to the routine they knew rather than incur the expense of transhipment from road wagon or barge for the, as yet, untried last 51 miles of railway to Gloucester. What the B&G management can however be blamed for was that they were so sure of the superiority of their method of transport, that they just sat back and waited for the traffic to come to them, which of course it didn't.

As the B&G opened up in stages during 1840 and 41, a mere trickle of goods traffic was carried in wagons attached to passenger trains until full arrangements and facilities for carriers had been completed in March 1841. One of their early consignments, in October 1840, proved how much staff and management had yet to learn about goods transport. A load of lace and scarlet cloth *en route* to Nottingham from Bristol was loaded into several wagons at Cheltenham and attached to the evening passenger train for Birmingham. The secretary, William Burgess, takes up the story:[1] '. . . the engineer having had at starting, a quantity of wood put on the fire, which when burnt blew out of the chimney in large flakes and one piece lodged in the tarpaulin of the Goods wagon and burnt through it . . .' The subsequent fire burnt a considerable quantity of lace and cloth for which the B&G had to pay £120 compensation. Compare this with the meagre total of £590 received for goods traffic during the first six months of operation.

Advertisements were placed in the local press during March 1841 announcing that the company was ready to convey goods on the railway while the local professional carriers, Haines & Co, Pickford & Co and H. Southam & Son, made similar announcements: 'Goods delivered to Birmingham by noon will reach Bristol next morning' announced Pickford and Co, who undertook to forward all goods from Gloucester to Bristol in Fly Waggons.[2] Capt. C. Moorsom had put the goods department under the control of H.B. Tymbs, the director in charge of the coaching and carrying department, but H.P. Edgell, goods manager at Gloucester, considered Tymbs' arrangements far from perfect.

He was brave enough to put forward a long list of his own quite advanced ideas in a letter to the directors dated June 1841.[3] Several of these were eventually adopted to the benefit of the company, but not until Capt. Moorsom had ceased to be chairman.

Carriers, said Edgell, would never put bulky goods like coal, stone, etc. on the railway, for they found it more economical to use their own water conveyance, since speed was not usually important for this class of goods. They would put some goods on the railway but they always sent the major part by water and pocketed the difference between the low water rates and the higher railway rates. Bulk transport at low prices, he urged, was the answer for the B&G. Don't sell the railway in terms of speed, charging a high rate, sell it on price and you'll get the goods!

But what price, he asked? Why does the B&G charge 8s. per ton from Birmingham to Gloucester for bulky goods when the L&B charges 6s. for a similar journey? If the price was low enough all the goods between the north and west would use the railway especially when the BrG was open. This policy, he jubilantly predicted, would knock 9 out of 10 boats off the Severn. Should the company be their own carriers as on the GJR, he then asked. Yes! 'Induce all the world to come . . .' Shareholders would much rather send their goods by rail and give the company, rather than the carrier, the profit.

High rates for goods would not pay with a carrier on the line, he continued, since carriers would always put as much traffic as they could on their own water conveyance rather than use the railway; they had large establishments and many vessels to keep. If the company were to become carriers he could personally arrange conveyance to Bristol at a low rate which, in conjunction with the GJR, could bring all the Manchester and Liverpool to Bristol traffic on to the railway instead of by water from Birmingham. Collection and delivery at large stations could easily be arranged by contract and smaller stations could use their under-employed porters' time profitably in doing so. He recommended that the present classification of goods into five categories (see appendix) should be reduced to three: manufactured valuable merchandise at the highest rate; followed by general goods requiring warehouse protection; while all bulky, heavy, non-valuable merchandise such as coal, which could be kept outside, would go for the cheapest rate. Discount should be offered for regular transit of large tonnages, for example the salt, soap and soda output of the British Alkali works at Stoke. Finally, he thought Worcester traffic could be ignored. To attract it to the railway would require rates far lower than for water conveyance and would result in huge losses for the company.

This mammoth effort was studied by the Board and was almost completely ignored. After Edgell left the company the following year, Burgess, the ex-secretary wrote to him saying: 'I am fully of the opinion that your general views as to carrying on the traffic of the B&G

were correct, and that had they been acted upon, the revenue for goods would have been much more than [it now] is . . .' But Moorsom had his own views, and would not be swayed. He announced at the general meeting of August 1841 that the B&G would continue to let goods traffic to the carriers but that they would also accept whatever was offered to them directly, thus adopting method (c) (see above).

One of Edgell's suggestions was however taken up. This was the idea of securing the Bristol traffic of the GJR with the assistance of a carrier to Bristol, by road or water depending upon the customer's requirement. Southam & Son, long established local carriers, were appointed to undertake the Gloucester–Bristol leg while at the northern end the GJR were much in favour not only of traffic to Bristol but intermediary points on the B&G, such as Worcester and the Stoke saltworks. By November 1841 a comprehensive list of rates was agreed on and advertised (see appendix).

Southam stated with great satisfaction in February 1842,[4] that a large quantity of packs, bales, etc. left Manchester by the 'luggage train of the GJR' late one Friday, reaching Gloucester, and the vessels of Southam Evans & Co. on Saturday and arriving in Bristol by canal and river on Sunday evening; 46 hours in total at only 2s. per hundredweight! Through traffic was also anticipated over the BDJc to the north and east Midlands. Opened in 1840 the BDJc traffic ran over the L&B to Curzon St. from Hampton in Arden, but a direct line was opened in February 1842 to a terminus at Lawley St.; convenient in every way except for the 40ft. difference in levels with the connecting railways! Wagon transfer was effected by an inclined plane to the GJR, but it would be another 2 years before a wagon hoist was provided for the transfer of wagons and coaches to the B&G and L&B.

In anticipation of increased traffic, a change in the working of goods traffic was made. Wagons, in general, had previously been attached to passenger trains as required and although it provided economy in locomotive power, it did nothing to help punctuality. With heavier traffic in prospect, a change was vital. From November 1841 two all-stations goods trains ran each way daily, to which passenger coaches were attached for the use of 'local' passengers, who presumably did not mind lengthy waits whilst wagons were shunted *en route*.

That same month J.D. Payne was appointed head of the goods department. His instructions were to give special priority to plans for the increase of the business of the department but in this he was not very successful. Traffic, or rather the lack of it, was not only noticed by the Board, but by a correspondent to the *Railway Times*[5] who listed 23 railways, large and small in England, most of which took one third of their receipts from goods traffic. Not the B&G, this took only one sixth. There were only 2 railways, small ones, which had a smaller ratio between merchandise and passenger receipts.

Proprietors at the February 1842 general meeting were also disturbed, if only at the lack of profits. Capt. Moorsom's system had been in operation for one year by then, yet only 17,000 tons had been carried in that period compared with the 70,000 tons hopefully estimated by Parliament. Capt. Moorsom assured them that traffic was increasing and that their system of acting as joint carrier along with other firms was paying off handsomely.

Coal traffic was being experimentally carried. Whilst coal had not been included in the Parliamentary estimates on the grounds that its long distance transport by rail could not be competitive with the canal and river carriers, nevertheless such had been the need for revenue that they had to give it a try. During 1842, four carriers–cum–coal merchants had enquired about rates for Derbyshire coal between Birmingham and Cheltenham. Cheltenham was one place likely to provide a steady trade in coal, its wealthy population and its gas works being heavy consumers (58,000 tons in 1837). Forest of Dean coal was brought cheaply by water to Gloucester and thence by the Gloucester & Cheltenham Tramroad to Cheltenham, while Staffordshire coal came via the Severn and the Coombe Hill canal to within 3 miles of the town. There was opportunity for traffic here provided that it could be carried more cheaply by rail. An earlier report (1838) had estimated that both types of coal could be brought to Cheltenham via Tewkesbury at less expense, but the short distance and small revenue would not be nearly enough to pay for the locomotive and wagon stock required for haulage. Tewkesbury had therefore been written off. Gloucester was out of the running too since there was no direct line to the docks where Forest of Dean coal was landed. It was midlands coal which could win revenue for the B&G provided it could be sent cheaply enough. But the return of empty trucks would make serious inroads into revenue. If a return load could be found then profit was assured, otherwise they would have to charge 6s. per ton from Birmingham to Cheltenham with little profit. (10,000 tons were carried in both 1843 and 1844 so the venture must be classed as a success.)

Messrs Oldham and Little in February 1842 asked permission to run their own private coal trains of 20 wagons, hauled by their own locomotives on paying a suitable toll. This arrangement was rejected by the Board as being a little too dangerous besides interfering with the normal working of the line.

One merchant who did start up a trade in coal was one Mr Williams. He rented the wharf at Alston Lane, Cheltenham and regular coal traffic began in July 1842. Later in the year he set up wharves at Spetchley, Eckington, Bredon and Ashchurch, and purchased a fleet of wagons for his exclusive use. A complicated system of 'back traffic' was arranged whereby his empty coal wagons returned north with general cargo at a discount rate, so that both he and the company profited, and he became a valued customer. Williams went too far however in 1843, when it was discovered that he had been soliciting other carriers to load their traffic into his wagons at the 'back traffic rate'. Williams was summoned before the board and reprimanded for his abuse of the special concessionary rates which the B&G had allowed him. He was however such a useful customer that he continued to work with the railway even after they had become the major carriers on their line, and so on into Midland Railway days.

Reverting to the general state of the railway's traffic in 1842, a Bristol shareholder told the *Railway Times*[6] that he was convinced that Capt. Moorsom's system was a failure. 'How is it', he asked, 'that there is half a million tons of freight available to the B&G yet out of this "enormous mass" they could scrape up but £200 worth per week?' One reason for this became apparent in April. Messrs Crowley & Co. sent a consignment of casks of porter from Bristol to Dudley. They specified that rail transport should be used between Gloucester and Birmingham. It transpired that an agent of Crowley's had seen the porter travelling from Birmingham to Dudley in one of Southam's water vessels. Thus, just as Edgell had predicted, the 'carrier' system was open to abuse and fraud.

Southam said that it was a pure mistake, and doubtless it could not be proved otherwise, but various other such 'mistakes' came to light during the next few years and it is certain that many more were never exposed. The only sure way of protecting the railway and the customer was to rid the line of carriers, but Capt. Moorsom was never quite convinced of this. One wonders just what tonnage the B&G were defrauded of. As Edgell so rightly pointed out, a carrier who had invested in a large fleet of horses, carts and boats was unlikely to scrap them all just to suit the railway. He could receive goods marked 'per railway', send them by water, charge the railway rate and pocket the difference. When the customer, in his innocence, found that his goods took just as long by 'rail' as by water, he would revert to water only!

To justify his job, Mr Payne announced a new scheme for the goods department in the summer of 1842. Carriers would operate only from the principal stations (Birmingham, Spetchley, Tewkesbury, Cheltenham and Gloucester) and they would be quoted inclusive rates between those points in four classifications (see appendix). Intermediate stations would be catered for by the company acting as sole carriers, with the public being quoted all-in rates from these stations, and from the principal ones, but at a higher rate than the carriers. This was in effect an incentive for the carriers to put more of their traffic on the railway as it represented a lowering of their rates. It worked! Tonnage sent by the carriers between July and December increased from 3,800 to 5,100. New regulations for carriers also stipulated the maximum load per wagon at 4½ tons, a gross weight of 6½ tons or so. It makes today's 100 tonners seem positively monstrous!

August of 1842 saw the formation of a Committee of Shareholders who wished to overthrow Capt. Moorsom and his system of management. The Chairman had circulated a letter to all proprietors in support of his system before the general meeting in August. This outlined the gains in the goods traffic under his rule: '. . . unsatisfactory, of course it is. Why? . . . your railway is in fact a line only partially open and on a broken line of communications . . . neither the same amount of traffic can come nor can that which does come be as well managed as when . . . communication is perfect . . . For your Manchester traffic you depend upon the GJR who exclude carriers . . . but carriers can bring their goods by water to Birmingham and why should they transfer them to your railway only to retransfer them at Gloucester?' The table below was used by Moorsom to show how little difference there was statistically between the B&G and the profitable L&B, one year after opening.

B&G Estimated Traffic 70,000 tons			L&B Estimated Traffic 175,000 tons		
Period	Tonnage	% of Estimate	Period	Tonnage	% of Estimate
1841	17146	24%	1839	44240	25%
June 41–42	20734	29.5%	June 39–40	63624	35%
Jan 41–42	27456	40%	June 39–40	77445	44%

His message was really 'be patient', but the proprietors felt they had been patient long enough. In reply, the committee of shareholders voiced their dissatisfaction with Capt. Moorsom's system of management. They claimed that the tonnage carried was only a small fraction of that on offer, and of that secured, a large proportion was bulky heavy goods like coal and iron which was barely profitable. Tolls as set by Parliament were contravened by the prohibitory rates which the company levied on local traffic (i.e. Tewkesbury). in order to concentrate their resources on the through traffic. But where was the through traffic? Profitable merchandise continued to go via the Severn and the canal to Bristol where delivery was promised in 5 days and which promise was kept. By rail, the journey was promised in 2 days, yet unpunctuality was so frequent that many customers ordering goods from the north actually specified that they should not travel by rail. Bristol traffic, as pioneered by H.P. Edgell, was sent either by land or water from Gloucester according to the merchant's wishes. However, the connection was deteriorating and a thorough shake-up was necessary to remedy the situation. Naturally the board realised that full development of the traffic was impossible until the defective communications to Gloucester Docks and to Bristol had been rectified.

Whilst reliability of the through traffic was pretty poor, the settlement of payments for the use of other companies' wagons etc. was complicated. Matters improved when the B&G joined the Railway Clearing House in November 1842. Wagons went astray with alarming regularity and a clerk was employed from September; 'to trace this Company's wagons lost on other Railway Companies' lines.' Goods went astray with equal regularity. The affair of the missing trusses was a case in point. Two of these sent by Messrs Marling of Stroud disappeared, one allegedly on the GJR, the other on the BDJc. Arguments as to who had lost them and who should pay compensation went on for months! Then 200lb. of fish belonging to a Mr Olive was lost and the B&G had to pay compensation at 6d. a pound.

In an effort to achieve reliability, goods trains were restricted to a manageable number of 16 loaded wagons with passenger accommodation for 3rd class only. These early morning and afternoon trains were to be supplemented by an extra 'goods only' train in each direction running as required for the carriage of coal, empty wagons and company stores. Further, all goods trains were to carry a travelling porter in addition to the guard. His job would be to assist the guard in braking, shunting, loading and, in light of recent events, to watch out for fire. Furthermore the travelling porter's assistance would enable the guard to expedite shunting and thus ensure reasonable time-keeping throughout the run. Freight charges were investigated, notably those for short hauls which had been criticised by the committee of shareholders. However, whilst some rates, such as those for imported grain from Gloucester Docks, and wool travelling south, were reduced, the rates for short distance traffic continued proportionately higher. A comprehensive investigation of the entire department was ordered for the new year too, but as it turned out, this was done by the CofE instead.

The CofE was to give particular attention in 1843 to the goods department because of its failure to win a reasonable proportion of the available traffic and, moreover, the high cost of handling the small amount of traffic that it did get. During April the CofE found themselves awash in a sea of technicalities. Minute 39[7] reads thus: 'Mr McConnell attended and presented a report . . . on the gradients of the line, the power of the . . . engines accompanied by tables of resistance and a diagram of the trains. The report pointed out the serious obstacles to the conveyance of heavy loads and the maintaining of a due rate of speed arising from the gradient and curves and described the engines now in use on the line for tracking [sic] . . . the trains.. . . . The average gross load . . . [that the engines could haul] . . . is estimated as 83⅓ Tons. The numerous quick [sic] curves on the line render it very desirable to confine the load to as few wagons as possible. An increase of 10 tons per load may be made to the foregoing average for the traffic between the intermediate stations with the exception of . . . Ashchurch to Cheltenham on which the train is remote from the assistance of the pilot engines.' The average train make-up at the time was 15 wagons weighing 65 tons, (41 tare, 24 net load – thus the average load was approx. 1½ tons per wagon against a maximum of 4½ tons and each train was running at only one third capacity) so in order to make up the ideal weight, the following formation was adopted: 14 loaded wagons (average net load to be increased to 2¾ tons where possible), 4 empties, 1 composite carriage, 1 third class and 1 luggage van. In total about 85 to 90 tons.

The CofE's final report was published in June 1843[8] and by then all was not going well for the B&G's freight business. British Alkali at Stoke had stopped sending salt, soap etc by rail because of a dispute over rates, while J.D. Payne could only report a steadily decreasing rail tonnage matched by an increasing tonnage carried by canal and waterway operators. With the half yearly meeting ahead, and the mood of the CofE only too apparent, Payne probably thought it was better to resign than be sacked, and gave in his notice in May 1843.

Those proprietors who expected the CofE report to contain a magic formula for increasing their traffic were to be disappointed although it did prove that the traffic was available if the company could go out and get it.

An estimate of the Severn trade in 1840 was as follows; between Gloucester and Worcester per year, 585,000 tons were carried comprising 303,000 tons of merchandise, 70,000 tons heavy loading, 168,000 tons of coal and 44,000 tons of salt. Of this total 274,000 tons per year was carried to Birmingham and the north via the Worcester and Birmingham canal; 150,000 tons of merchandise, 24,000 tons of heavy loading and 95,000 tons of coal.

Of this massive total the B&G had only 29,000 tons in 1842! About 5 per cent of all that available. The CofE acknowledged that until the defective link to Bristol could be mended by the opening of the BrG, much of their traffic would stay with the water carriers. Nevertheless decided: '. . . to compensate . . . for the usual means of transit between the West of England by offering the carriers and the public the use of the line at very moderate rates of carriage between Birmingham and Gloucester viz:– 6s. per ton 1st class, 8s. 6d. per ton 2nd class and 11s. per ton 3rd class. These rates offer a very considerable reduction . . . but the Committee believe they will leave a profit to the Company and be low enough to induce the carriers to bring a much larger proportion of their goods upon the railway.' As for being exclusive carriers: 'On the one hand . . . their establishment is equal to the management of a much larger traffic . . . ; and if the whole . . . were in their hands the full benefit of the parcels traffic could be secured and the carriage of goods . . . more economically conducted. On the other hand . . . with the present imperfect means of transport below Gloucester, the Company are not in a position to engage in that strenuous competition with the Water Carriers which must be the result of excluding the latter from the line. To undertake the sole carriage on the railway the Company must maintain an establishment at Bristol . . ., a good communication with the water at Gloucester must be obtained, and arrangements . . . made for regular conveyance by land and water from that place, as well as . . . soliciting and collecting goods at Birmingham. . . . but as so great a change will be effected within a short period by the opening of the railway between Bristol and Gloucester, the Committee think it most desirable to leave the carriage of merchandise on its present footing.' Parcel traffic was lost to the Post Office and the larger carriers who were more geared up to delivery on a national basis. Coal, while not contemplated in the Parliamentary estimate as a source of revenue, had become a very important one. As much as 90,000 to 100,000 tons per annum (1843 figure) was consumed in Cheltenham alone, from Staffordshire, Derbyshire and the Forest of Dean, and all of which could go by rail. Again the same old problem of returning empties was cited as the major cause for small profit on the traffic.

Staff in the goods department suffered less than most in the cuts made by the CofE, down 2 to 12. Payne left in July, to be replaced by one W.B. Brown at a salary of £250 per annum for the first year, £280 for the second, and £300 for the third, if he should last so long! Naturally the findings of the CofE were not unanimous but they were united in wanting a reduction in the rates charged, especially for short distance traffic and this was arranged in September. The effect of this was practically instantaneous, and reversed a steady decline. In the first half of 1843 the tonnage had dropped sharply, but of more significance, the proportion sent by the carriers rose 250 per cent which meant a drastic loss of profit to the B&G.

Offers to re-negotiate through traffic rates with the GJR and M&B were received and speedily concluded, British Alkali at Stoke announced a return to rail transport as soon as through communication to the docks at Gloucester was possible. To cope with the increase, wagons had to be sent by passenger and mail trains.

Then came the resolution that George Tate had longed for, and that H.P. Edgell had strongly advocated in 1841. Tate, elected a director in August 1843, moved that the three months trial of goods traffic since the reduction of rates had been a total failure (i.e. not doubled, as apparently was the target) and a committee of investigation should be convened immediately to rectify matters. This motion was passed, and signalled the departure of Capt. Moorsom, and the carriers, from the B&G.

Tate's committee reported on 19 December 1843. Their proposal that the railway company should be their own major carrier from 1 January 1844 was unanimously passed, and Humphrey Brown won his long sought post as traffic manager of goods and passenger departments. He was to work without salary until the profits paid a 3 per cent dividend. New rates and regulations were issued (see appendix) which although not excluding carriers gave them only 10 per cent discount on the rates offered to the public. Traffic rose to such levels that an extra goods train each way daily was needed in addition to the usual two mixed (goods and passenger) trains each way.

For the first time in their short history, the B&G could announce real improvements. Now that they were the major carrier, the weekly receipts were double that of the previous year and as the year progressed the traffic increased considerably. This brought lavish praise from the railway press who had previously poured scorn on their dismal performance.[9] They felt strong enough in May 1844 to further discourage the carriers by discontinuing their discount and with the prospect of a rail link to Bristol by mid-summer, the future looked quite promising.

Bristol traffic transfer was to be at Gloucester and the B&G arranged to manage the BrG business there when they opened to goods traffic from 2 September 1844. Both companies were exclusive carriers which made life easier from an accounting point of view; $\frac{5}{9}$ of the Birmingham Bristol rate went to the B&G and $\frac{4}{9}$ to the BrG after deducting 6d. per ton for transhipment.

Humphrey Brown could be well pleased with his first six months work. Tonnage at 35,000 and receipts at £14,500 were considerably higher than in the whole of 1843. Interchange of traffic at Birmingham with the MR, together with a joint cartage arrangement was effected in June 1844 soon after the MR's formation. The B&G could rightfully take its place in the so-called chain of communications between the north and south of the country.

That was the theory; the chain had a weak link in it at Gloucester where there was break of gauge. The effects of this are discussed in a later chapter. Suffice it to say now that neither the B&G nor the BrG had expected this to be more than a local inconvenience. Both were astounded to find that their problem had become one of national significance, and that Gloucester had become a battlefield in the gauge war. Something had to be done to secure uniformity of gauge and keep traffic moving, and that something was quite beyond the capability of the two inexperienced companies involved. They looked first to the GWR for help, but since the GWR's attitude was discouraging the Midland astutely stepped in, and by leasing the two lines secured that there should eventually be standard gauge all the way to Bristol. Although this was not possible till 1854, the Midland took steps at once to relieve the position at Gloucester by investing in proper transhipment facilities to replace the totally inadequate equipment provided by the BrG.

As a result of the gauge break at Gloucester and the prospect of repeat performances at other places under 'threat' of invasion by the broad gauge, the Government appointed a Gauge Commission to enquire into the problem at Gloucester.[10] Officers and management of both companies were called on to give evidence. J.D. Payne, goods manager of the BrG and now in charge of the B&B goods deptartment at Gloucester, complained of the misleading advice given to the BrG by I.K. Brunel. He had told them that broad gauge wagons would hold twice as much as their counterparts on the narrow gauge. In consequence the BrG had been handicapped by having only some 60 wagons to transport freight brought by the B&G's 400. Wyndham Harding, BrG traffic manager, stated that he had complained to Brunel about the inadequate transfer shed he had provided for Gloucester – a shed which would only hold three wagons of each gauge at any one time – and that Brunel had paid no attention to him. But the clearest picture of the general situation came from J. E. McConnell's evidence. By that time McConnell was not only locomotive superintendent of the B&G, he was superintendent of the line as well. His evidence can be summarised as follows: Traffic flows over the route were fairly evenly balanced but only 20 or 30 tons weekly went beyond Bristol, while 200–300 tons needed to be transhipped weekly at Gloucester. Coal was sent both ways on the B&G line; that from the Forest of Dean and South Wales went to Birmingham Gas Works via Gloucester Docks; while up to 100 tons daily was sent from Birmingham to Cheltenham. Copper, tin and iron went north from South Wales via Gloucester Docks. Linen, corn, vegetables, fruit, hops and potatoes were the commonest freight from the Birmingham direction. Livestock caused the biggest problem at Gloucester! The largest train to arrive at Gloucester was a 330t gross load of salt from Droitwich for export via the docks; there was, said McConnell, no chance of transferring that type of goods at Gloucester to the broad gauge.

As for the relative merits of broad and narrow gauge, McConnell thought the advantage lay with the narrow gauge which for goods traffic allowed a lower tare weight of wagon for a given load, and therefore lower working expenses. A narrow gauge train capable of taking 138 tons net would gross 519 tons (381 tare) whilst a broad gauge train would gross 721 tons (583 tare) for a similar load. Speeds were higher too. He related that on the BrG a train of 235 tons (load only 97t) took 4 hours 13 minutes for the 37 miles from Bristol to Gloucester, inclusive of 6 stops. At Gloucester the load was transferred together with a further 45 tons making a payload of 152 tons in 36 wagons (gross 254t). The 51 miles from Gloucester to Birmingham were covered in 3 hours 55 minutes inclusive of 6 stops. Allowing for 105 minutes spent in stops this gives an average speed (between stops) of 15 m.p.h. on the BrG and 20.4 m.p.h. on the B&G. Gauge break or not, freight traffic on the B&B line averaged 120,000 tons in 1845 and 1846 and rose steadily, but after 1848 separate traffic figures were not kept for the B&B section. Today's traffic is, as elsewhere on BR, a shadow of that carried in the heydey of the railways, but even so, to watch the evening procession of mammoth Speedlink and Freightliner trains passing at the express passenger speeds of 1910 is an exhilarating experience. Nevertheless, to have watched that 250 ton train mentioned by McConnell hurtling along at 25 m.p.h. behind the snorting, panting Jones & Potts 0-6-0 must have been an impressive sight for his contemporaries too.

Having briefly looked at the goods traffic development up to MR days, a few incidental points can be related. Parcels traffic provided a steady revenue, but competition from the Post Office and other carriers was fierce. Collection and delivery was provided only at the larger stations; presumably other stations operated a 'to-be-called-for' service only. London parcels were a valuable source of revenue, and an arrangement with the L&B for a through service, made in 1842, allowed reliable and punctual collection and delivery. Competition with the GWR (who carted by road to Swindon or Oxford) kept the prices down, for example after December 1842 the carriage of small parcels up to 12lb. between Cheltenham and London was reduced from 2s. to 1s. 6d. Small parcels of 12lb. and under were carried by passenger train in a box closely supervised by the guard; larger packages went by goods train. These latter trains were however not always noted for reliability. One Liverpool merchant who sent parcels of perishable goods complained about delays and the ruin of his wares in consequence. Now that the railways had driven the coaches off the roads, they should at least provide as reliable a service, he protested to the *Railway Times*.[11]

Salt was one of those 'heavy loading' traffics for which the railway was at first thought unsuitable because of the attractive lower rates offered by water carriers. Vast tonnages went from the Droitwich and Stoke Prior areas via canal and river to Gloucester and Bristol for export – 43,000 tons in 1840. Similar quantities went northwards. Not surprisingly, when merchandise traffic failed to materialise, the railway sought a substitute and arranged special rates in 1842 with the British Alkali Co. at Stoke to Birmingham at 4s. 6d. per ton and to Gloucester at 6s. The rate to Birmingham was competitive with water transport, since the wagons and their contents could be transferred to other railways and taken anywhere (almost) in the Midlands and the north, but it was useless to take the salt to Gloucester until a direct rail link to the dock was effected. Rates were increased, and in March 1843 the traffic stopped. When the CofE ordered a lower rate and a temporary through route to Gloucester Docks was completed the salt traffic returned (mid 1844). When the B&G submitted a revised plan for a conventional branch to the docks to Parliament in 1844–5, a branch to Stoke works was included in the Bill. But it was not until the OWW's Worcester deviation line had been completed in 1852 that Droitwich Saltworks got a rail connection with the B&G. These rail links provided cheap transport for the customer and profits for the B&G, since they could return the wagons laden with coal. In MR days the *Gloucester Journal* noted[12] that 150 ton trains of salt ran at regular intervals to the docks where the MR were supplying slips for shooting salt into waiting vessels.

Worcester traffic had been, according to H.P.Edgell, a 'dead letter' because there was no rail connection. Parcels were carried from Spetchley by road coach while heavier goods, if sent at all, went by horse and cart. Ever optimistic about the B&G's plans the *Gloucester Journal* envisaged Worcester merchants as flocking to the railway once the CofE offered reduced rates in September 1843: '. . . most of the carriers in this City will be compelled to avail themselves of this mode of conveyance'. 30 or 40 boats would certainly soon be laid up and 3 or 4 times that number of boatmen would be thrown out of work! The actual effect of the railway on Worcester traffic was, according to the *Worcester Chronicle*[13] to place it: '. . . at a distance of three days from Birmingham which under the old coach system was only a few hours journey.'

Finally the mail traffic. On completion of the railway late in 1840, negotiations with the GPO were begun relative to the costs of forwarding the mails by rail. Two trains each way would be required every night including Sundays; one serving mails to and from Bristol, Gloucester and Liverpool, Manchester, Preston, Carlisle and Edinburgh via the GJR; the other serving Derby, Sheffield, York, Hull, etc via the BDJc. These would necessitate the line being kept open all night with consequent extra expense of police, station staff, and locomotive crews, to say nothing of additional rolling stock. In addition, road connections would have to be provided at Cheltenham, Tewkesbury,

Worcester, Bromsgrove and Droitwich. It took ten months of haggling before the price was settled (at 2*s*. 7½*d*. per mile) during which time the B&G had carried the mails without pay! The mail service began on 6 February 1841 with trains leaving Gloucester at 7.15 p.m. for the north east and 9.00 p.m. for the north west, returning at 12.45 a.m. and 3.10 a.m. from Birmingham. Two and a half hours were allowed for the journey, and departure time could be delayed for 30 minutes should the Bristol mails be late arriving at Gloucester by road.

These trains ran nightly until March 1844, earning some £10,000 revenue each year. After that time a single train each way replaced the two. This left Gloucester at 8.50 p.m. and returned at 1.00 a.m.; a significant drop in revenue resulted. When the BrG opened in July 1844, rail transport replaced the road link to Bristol.

CHAPTER FOURTEEN
PASSENGER TRAFFIC

The B&G may have been conceived and born from the need for reliable and speedy goods transport but it was not long before its passenger carrying potential was realised. The majority of the population were static, having neither the need nor the means to travel, whilst those who did had to endure long hours in horse drawn stage-coaches over the extensive but largely primitive road network. A swift, smooth ride over iron rails was attractive to passengers and profitable for the railway promoters.

During the early 1830s six stage-coaches ran daily over the Birmingham, Cheltenham, Gloucester route; these connected with local services. There were many private carriages too, belonging to wealthy families, besides those of the fashionable visitors who came to take the waters at Cheltenham.

Parliament in 1836 considered that the line would have a passenger potential of 400,000 journeys per annum bringing in £90,000 revenue. By 1839 the opening of the GJR and L&B had stimulated travel so much that 22 coaches daily made the Birmingham–Gloucester trip. Previously static, travel-shy folk flocked to the railway proving beyond doubt their magnetic attraction. The B&G were sure that much of this traffic would come their way in addition to their expected freight.

As early as November 1839, a Cheltenham coach proprietor, Mr Dangerfield, had approached the company with a view to transferring all his coaches (physically) on to the railway when it opened between Cheltenham and Bromsgrove the following year. This prompted the secretary and superintendent, William Burgess, to set down on paper what he considered should be the railway's mode of working. The general travelling public, or to be precise, the 1st and 2nd class public, were to be conveyed in coaches mounted on railway wheels, prototypes for which had been under study for some time. Facilities for transporting road coaches on special wagons were also planned mostly for the benefit of the private owner.

Burgess advised the board that other railways charged the inside coach passengers at the 1st class rail fare, and the outside ones 2nd class. The coach itself was charged as a 4 wheeled carriage per the Act's list of tolls and rates. However, while some railways conveyed long distance passengers the B&G could not, neither did it go near Worcester, a great coach 'connecting place'. He decided therefore it would be best to stay aloof from coach proprietors and concentrate on carrying passengers the easy way in the company's carriages.

In December 1839, a deputation of the B&G board visited the Manchester & Leeds Railway on a fact finding mission to see it in operation. They were especially interested in the M&L's rolling stock and their system of fares for passengers. The deputation reported that the: '. . . System of Ticketing for Passengers is both more economical and a greater security against frauds on the Company than any other we have seen.' This was Thomas Edmonson's now famous system of printed, consecutively numbered tickets which he devised whilst working as a stationmaster on the Newcastle & Carlisle Railway. Since the Newcastle & Carlisle had shown no interest, he had moved on to the Manchester & Leeds, who had encouraged him to perfect the system and where it was observed by many railway officials; and the B&G were among the first to adopt it. A ticket printing machine was purchased for £60 and a further £100 paid for patent rights. With this full sets of numbered tickets covering all permutations of journeys on the B&G could be printed at the check office; kept at relevant stations; issued for passenger journeys; collected at their termination; and returned to the check office where they could be balanced against revenue from the issuing station. This was a foolproof system from which that in use today has evolved.

The question of Sunday trains was a difficult one in those days. Today they are taken for granted, but early Victorian moralists were firmly against infringing the Sabbath. The directors, many of whom were Quakers, resolved not to run any trains other than those for the mails on Sunday. A number of proprietors were against this however. Whether they thought it right and proper to offer the public a service every day of the week or just because they lost a day's profit is neither here nor there, but whatever their motives, they proposed to petition the general meeting of August 1840 on the subject. A circular was sent out to all proprietors by the directors asking for full support at the meeting to defeat the proposal on religious and moral as well as economic grounds. Few road coaches ran on Sundays. This proved that there was little demand for a service, for it was certain that if a market had been there coach proprietors would have exploited it. Any trains run would consequentially be empty and extremely expensive.

The general meeting decided against Sunday travel but the defeated party tried again the following March. This time they were opposed even more heavily. A circular pointed out: '. . . a large number of the Company's servants would be precluded from attending their religious places of worship and be compelled to work on the day appointed for rest.' The motion was once more decisively defeated and the Sabbath preserved until well into MR days. (Sunday trains are recorded in a timetable issued on 6 January 1855.)

Passenger services commenced on the B&G on 24 June 1840 with two journeys each way daily between Cheltenham and Bromsgrove with a coach link to Birmingham. These increased to five each way from 8 July (see appendix for details). The effect on the travelling public was immediate. From the pages of the *Gloucester Journal*[1] we find that: 'No very inconsiderable revolution has already taken place in the coaching departments of the neighbourhood since the partial opening of the railway: most of the Birmingham coaches from this City [Gloucester] having already altered their route so as to make use of the railway [i.e. picking up and setting down passengers from the terminal stations]. The effect will of course be more complete when the whole line is opened, but though some coach proprietors sustain considerable losses by this too formidable competition . . . the injury is in a minor degree compensated by the stimulus from those districts to which the main line does not reach; the coaches being thus feeders to the railway and participators of some of its advantages.' A later issue[2] complimented the B&G after a trip on the railway: 'For ease of motion it exceeds any railway we have yet travelled upon.' William Burgess' general system of management[3] devoted a considerable portion to the passenger business which for management purposes came under the traffic and stores department. Day to day running of the trains was under the immediate control of the superintendent whilst station business, together with the receiving and despatching of trains, was the station inspector's task. Each principal station (Gloucester, Cheltenham, Ashchurch, Tewkesbury, Spetchley, Bromsgrove and at that time, Camp Hill) had one of these, with other stations under the control of the station clerk and perhaps a porter.

Inspector's responsibilities were, in the main, the safety and comfort of the passengers and the prompt arrival, loading, unloading, signalling and departure of the trains. His task was a supervisory one ordering his staff of porters, clerks, police and switchmen, for whose actions he took overall responsibility. Porters' duties were similar to that now virtually extinct breed of railwaymen who have helped generations of the travelling public and their luggage in and out of carriages. Porters were also expected to assist in the shunting of wagons.

Wagons and carriages in those days could be moved by hand, if not by one man certainly by two. A gentleman's carriage on a flat wagon and horses in a horse box often had to be marshalled into or out of a train with as little delay as possible. This called for prompt work by the porters, who were occasionally maimed or killed in the course of this duty. Clerks had the difficult and tedious task of issuing, receiving, despatching and accounting for all fares, parcels and so on, and had to make up any deficiencies from their own pockets. Hours were long indeed, from the first train to the last followed by the balancing of the days accounts.

Having attended to the passenger's needs from entering the station to boarding their train, the train staff of (in early days) two guards and a train porter, took over. The first guard was in overall charge of the train and its passengers and received his instructions from station inspectors and the superintendent. First he had to check brakes, lamps and the cleanliness of his train before it left the originating station. Then he had to check that the passengers were in their proper seats, did not smoke and were behaving in a seemly fashion. In addition he was train brakesman, applying them on the request signal from the engine driver. The second guard had to assist him in his duties. Train porters were there to assist by providing further brake power when required and to assist station porters in speeding the passengers in and out of the trains with minimal delay and maximum safety. Needless to say the luxury of three men to a train did not last long, and train porters were discontinued, possibly under the scheme of Capt. C.R. Moorsom.

Passengers were carried on terms laid down by the company's by-laws which basically governed the booking and inspections of tickets, penalties for fraudulent travel, smoking and drinking in carriages or stations, and damage to railway property. Breach of these brought the penalty of a fine, such as £2 for smoking or £5 plus damages for vandalism. These fines were heavy when it is remembered that the average wage was £1 to £1.10s.0d. per week. By-laws had to be submitted to the BoT and they let it be known that they disapproved of the rigidity and severity of those regarding ticket abuse.

In cases of ticket loss the honest passenger was liable to be given the same treatment as the fraudulent one, namely a fine of £2 and the full Birmingham to Gloucester fare. The superintendent appeased the BoT by instructing his inspectors to show their discretion. But zeal sometimes overcame discretion! John Perkins travelled from Cheltenham to Gloucester and on being asked for his ticket he claimed that he had already given it up. The collector did not believe this and demanded the full Birmingham to Gloucester fare of 7s. 6d. He refused to pay this, whereupon he was prosecuted and fined £2 for refusing to deliver his ticket.

On the other hand, it would be interesting to know just how successful the B&G were in preventing fraudulent travel. Writing to *Herepath*[4] a traveller asked: 'What check have they against passengers taking 2nd class tickets and travelling in a 1st class carriage? I have repeatedly observed that when a train is preparing to start, the passengers rush up to take their places and take them just where they please, no enquiries being made as to whether they have paid 1st or 2nd fare; or at least the tickets are not demanded . . . either at departure or arrival until leaving the station excepting at the two Termini where the tickets are collected from the carriages at the arrival of the trains.' The only exception to fare paying was reserved for those holding free passes. These were only given to senior officials travelling on railway business; Proprietors were allowed one each for travel to the general meetings until the CofE put a stop to the privilege. Defford gardeners were allowed three per week to enable them to accompany their produce to Birmingham market (again disallowed after the CofE); whilst Mr Hicks, the surgeon of the Railway Friendly Society was refused a pass between Cheltenham and Gloucester, even when travelling on Society business.

When Capt. Melhuish of the BoT inspected the Cheltenham to Gloucester line in October 1840 his report mentioned some interesting working details: 'The times for departure and arrival of trains . . . appear to me well arranged to prevent collisions.' Clocks at stations were placed in conspicuous places and could be seen from the trains. Watches were provided for enginemen and a placard showing the working timetable of the train was placed on the engine enabling the driver to keep to time. Station inspectors were instructed to note the arrival and departure time of every train and report to the superintendent to ensure regular timekeeping. They were to allow a certain space of time between consecutive trains.

At Cheltenham, Capt. Melhuish noted that the 9.30 a.m. was 22 minutes late arriving, too great an irregularity for public safety. However he discovered that: '. . . the down trains [from Birmingham] use Birmingham time and the up trains [from Gloucester] use Cheltenham time and that the clocks of those towns frequently vary from 10 to 15 minutes.' The secretary, Burgess, agreed with him on the desirability of: '. . . establishing some particular time to be observed on all railways', which would secure punctuality and decrease accidents at junctions. He recommended to his superiors at the BoT that all lines to London and the branches thereon should: '. . . be constrained to adopt the London time under the appellation of the Railway Time.' It would inconvenience no one and make for improved safety and timekeeping. Another 'first' for the B&G, but unfortunately not to be adopted for many years.

Initial traffic was beyond the expectations of the directors, who told the proprietors in August 1840 that: '. . . when the whole line is open, traffic will be increased to an amount far exceeding any calculations . . . hitherto . . . made.'! One of the earliest journeys was recorded in the Diary of Rachel Whinyates[5] 'Got up early to see Laetitia off. We went to the train station [Cheltenham] at a little after 7 o'clock and at 8 the strange and wonderful steam conveyance set off moving slowly at first. The carriages are comfortable like armchairs for 6 people in each. At Birmingham they enter a fresh train for Liverpool. One cannot help but feel nervous. God grant a safe arrival.' She need not have worried, the B&G's safety record was really quite impressive compared with that of other lines. Only one passenger was killed in an accident whilst the line was in their ownership, though several expired from natural causes *en route*, and minor injuries were a little more regular. (Full details in Accidents! see Chapter 21.)

Browsing through the timetables issued by the B&G (see appendix), we find an impressive range of connecting services advertised from either end of the railway, but this was to be expected from a link in the 'chain of communication'. Coaches from Gloucester gave reasonably good connections to Bristol, Bath and the west, and were linked with the railway timetable; but the rail links at the Birmingham end were not so well arranged. Until the B&G's extension line to the L&B was complete in August 1841, passengers had to find their own way to Curzon St. to catch connecting trains on the L&B or GJR, but having reached Curzon St., passengers often had a lengthy wait.

One such passenger told the *Railway Times*[6] that: 'A detention of one hour and threequarters takes place at Birmingham unless you travel by night or by 2nd class train, for instance, passengers by the 9.00 and 11.15 a.m. trains from Manchester, Liverpool and Ireland are detained ¾ of an hour . . . and frequently arrive just in time to witness the departure of the train for Gloucester. Surely some arrangement might be made with the Directors of the GJR and B&G to remove this grievance. It appears to me that Manchester, Liverpool, and Ireland are better feeders to the B&G than the North Midland line.' Good arrangements had to be enforced between the B&G and L&B to prevent accidents at their junction, though mutual respect for the complementary traffic flows between Gloucester, Cheltenham, Worcester and London (via the L&B in competition with the GWR) ensured that there were good connections in that direction at least from Birmingham.

The development of passenger services between Cheltenham, Gloucester and London was much in the minds of both B&G and L&B. From September 1841 four 'up' trains from Gloucester and three 'down' trains ran in connection with the L&B and through tickets were issued for 1st class passengers. Gloucester was now within 8 hours of the capital by train! The service proved so successful that in November 1842 one through carriage (1st class only) ran each way daily between Gloucester and London.

Twelve months of passenger train operation since the opening brought great satisfaction to the Board. From Capt. Moorsom's detailed statistics, we find that the average earning per mile of the Birmingham to Gloucester trains was 7s., they were, on average, 9 minutes late and averaged 19 m.p.h. Mail trains (2 each way nightly) carried a total of 116 passengers on weekdays and 96 on Sundays.

Road traffic had been severely affected. The *Gloucester Journal*[7] noted that on the Cheltenham to Gloucester Turnpike, traffic had declined so much that receipts from tolls failed to pay the maintenance costs and these had to be met from parish highway rates.

A novel idea was introduced in November 1841 when passenger accommodation was included in the daily goods train each way. These stopped at every station anyway so it seemed sensible to add third class and composite (1st and 2nd class) carriages in an effort to attract local passengers. An attempt to attract further local custom to these trains was made by allowing them to stop at 'places besides the regular stations', such as level-crossings or police-posts where a member of staff had to be kept regardless, this again made commercial sense. At least the B&G were trying, though many contemporaries thought a general cut in fares would not come amiss!

The first advertised connection with the GJR was arranged in May 1842 when the 2 p.m. from Gloucester was timed to connect with the 5 p.m. to Liverpool. Further arrangements with the GJR followed during the summer when two 'up' trains were to be diverted into the GJR Curzon St. station, which was quite separate from that of the L&B, though there is no evidence that this actually happened.

1842 and 1843 were years of trade recession in the United Kingdom and this naturally affected the traffic of most railways. The number of passenger journeys on the B&G fell sharply and the Board had to take action to offset losses. Service levels were studied with a view to reduction and fares were increased in November 1842. To compensate in a measure for this, day-return fares were introduced between most stations over a certain distance, and season tickets appeared over similar distances at the weekly rate of six times the single fare. Goods trains now carried third class accommodation only.

While arrangements with the L&B might have been good, relations with the BDJc were poor. Two complaints reached the railway press[8] early in 1843 regarding connections between the North Midland, BDJc and B&G, which made a nonsense of the so-called countrywide chain of communications which the arrival of the BDJc at Lawley St. should have made possible. One train left York at 8.45 a.m. and arrived at Derby by 12.45 p.m.: '. . . it is there detained 45 minutes for no apparent reasons except to enable it to reach Birmingham 35 minutes after the departure of the train for Gloucester'. Similarly a train from Leeds at 7.09 p.m. arrived in Birmingham at 12.45 a.m.: '. . . exactly one minute after the train for Gloucester has left.' This would have been the first mail train and any passengers would be condemned to a 2½ hour wait for the second mail! Compare this with the statement in the Committee of Enquiry (CofE) report in June which stressed the importance of maintaining the: '. . . most frank and amicable relations with the several railways with which we are connected . . .'!

Complaints did however bring results. Arrangements made with the BDJc, York and North Midland, North Midland and Great North of England Railways were put into force in August 1843 and through carriages were exchanged with the BDJc via their wagon hoist on two trains daily each way.

1844 saw the opening of the BrG, an occasion to which the board had looked forward for a long time. Connections between most trains were possible even if a wait of 30 minutes was sometimes necessary. It was hoped that the inconvenience to passengers caused by the break of gauge would be no more than normal at any other junction station where it was necessary to change trains but the reality often proved otherwise (see elsewhere for details).

Fare levels came down during the year. That to London, for instance, from Gloucester or Cheltenham fell to 30s. 1st class and 20s. 2nd class, while 3rd class passengers could book through for 9s.5d. using the 2.30 p.m. Birmingham to London train. In connection with 3rd class, the Cheap Train Act provisions were obeyed from November 1844. This required every public railway to run at least one train each way daily for 3rd class passengers at 1d. per mile. Of course, since the B&G had catered for this class of passenger from its opening, no 'hardship' was enforced on that railway company!

Following the merger of the B&G and BrG in January 1845, and the lease by the MR, more care was taken to co-ordinate services between Bristol, Gloucester, the Midlands and the north. Express trains ran from mid-1845 and 1st class passengers were 'whisked' from Bristol to Birmingham in 3 hours, and connections made with the GJR and L&B at Birmingham. No such timetable coordination, however, existed between the MR and GWR at Gloucester or Bristol, and if by accident it did, the appalling timekeeping over the B&G section rendered it all but useless! One victim wrote to the *Railway Times*[9] from the station at Gloucester: '. . . I have just missed the mail train by the GWR to London in consequence of the B&G train arriving here 15 minutes later than the time on the table.' This was his third taste of B&G timekeeping; on the previous two occasions the trains had been 30 minutes late! He later discovered that: '. . . although there is a full ten minutes difference between the starting of the . . . trains to London . . . and the arrival of the Birmingham train, the latter only catches the former twice or thrice a week'!

Fares came in for adverse comment too in early MR days. The *Gloucester Journal*[10] produced the following table in March 1846, saying that the MR overcharged on its fares and ran the slowest trains, especially between Birmingham and Bristol!

Line	Miles	1st Class	2nd Class
Birmingham – Gloucester	53	14s.	10s. 6d.
London – Brighton	50½	10s.	7s. 6d.
Gosport – Farnborough	57	10s.	7s. 6d.
London – Wolverton	52½	9s. 6d.	6s. 6d.
Birmingham – Bristol	88	22s.	15s. 6d.
London – Gosport	88	16s.	12s.
London – Dover	88	15s.	10s.

One gentleman took his family from Spetchley to Birmingham, 27 miles, for which he paid £4.9s.0d., then from Birmingham he went to Leamington, 27 miles on the L&B for which he paid £2.12s.6d.! The railway's reputation for high fares even applied to convicts. They were conveyed, 6 or more, in a horse box at 3rd class rates!

EXCURSIONS

One part of the passenger business on the B&G which did give bargain travel was excursion traffic. Numerous trips were organised at return fares often one third of the usual, but such were the numbers conveyed on a single trip that not even the B&G could fail to make a profit!

A memorable day was had by all when the Gloucester Mechanics Institute chartered a train to Birmingham on Monday, 3 May 1841. It consisted of 5 first class coaches (7s. 6d. return), 12 second class coaches (5s.) and 6 third class (3s. 6d.) which the organisers had fitted with seats.

Departure from Gloucester was at 6.30 a.m. with 420 on board and two locomotives to provide power. After stops at Cheltenham and Ashchurch no less than 623 passengers were crammed into the train. As the first class coaches could seat 18 and the second class 24, there must have been an improbable 46 'sardines' in each third class carriage!

All went well until the cavalcade reached Bromsgrove; there the fun started! The train was divided and the first portion of 14 coaches, one train engine, and one banker started to climb the Lickey, but, in the words of the *Gloucester Journal* reporter[11]'. . . the pantings of the two engines so nearly resembled the puffing of a broken, winded horse that it was a clear sign that they were not going to be able to get up, so the [bank] engine which was to have assisted the second portion was sent ahead to charge the train, buffer up and push.' The second portion went up more easily than the first but there had been considerable delay and they did not reach Birmingham until 10.30 am. Return was at 6.30 p.m. and a splendid day had been had by all; the reporter thought that the company's officials deserved the highest credit: 'Considerable precautions were taken by the Company to ensure the safety of the travellers by which nothing occurred from first to last to damp the enjoyment of the party . . .' One less successful trip to Birmingham comprised 22 carriages, half of which were open 3rd class. It was a fairly typical summer's day, pelting down with rain, soaking the poor folk in the open carriages and so affecting the locomotive's adhesion that both legs of the journey took five hours instead of four. Misery for the excursionists, but perhaps a good day for Birmingham umbrella salesmen!

Several longer trips were recorded. A thirteen coach special left Gloucester one morning in June 1843 *en route* for Liverpool and Bangor, being joined at Birmingham by a similar train from Nottingham and Derby. The combined 34 coach special went on to Liverpool and returned 3 days later. A 'Pleasure Train to London' was run in July 1844 giving passengers four days in the capital.

Tewkesbury Races, held on the Ham, attracted passengers from Gloucester and Cheltenham in the first locomotive hauled passenger trains over the branch. One train nearly ended up in the Avon! (See Accidents, Chapter 21.) The opening of the BrG gave excursion organisers further opportunities and one of these gave rise to possibly the worst case of passenger abuse that we have found recorded. The occasion was the Gloucester Mechanics Institute excursion from Worcester, Tewkesbury, Cheltenham and Gloucester to Bristol on 15 July 1844 and the story is told by the travelling *Gloucester Journal* reporter.[12]

Two trains were run owing to the number of passengers, one for Gloucester folk and one for 'the rest'. The former train ran on time in each direction and a thoroughly good day was had by all. However, in stark contrast, the latter train was late in arriving in Bristol, late in returning and the excursionists were shabbily treated by the B&G staff at Gloucester and Cheltenham. A Worcester man complained that: 'On returning, a delay of two hours took place at the Gloucester Station and upon some parties naturally becoming a little clamourous to ascertain the cause of delay, some man in authority called out: 'If these fellows don't keep quiet keep them locked in another half hour'. Upon arrival at Cheltenham about forty 1st class passengers, who had been told by the stationmaster at Gloucester that their carriages should 'go through', were unceremoniously turned out by the superintendent there and it was not until they had been kept in the cold until nearly 1 a.m. that he provided other carriages and the only answers the passengers could obtain from him in reply to their well-founded complaints was that: "If they did not like it they should not go at all"; and instead of arriving at Worcester at 11 p.m. we did not do so until 3 a.m.!'

The largest excursion of all was run in September 1846 on the BrG section of the MR. (A little out of context but included nonetheless). Four thousand Sunday School children with 500 teachers and friends travelled from Bristol to Gloucester in two trains of 29 carriages each. Their return was, according to the local press[13] in: '. . . one enormous train consisting of 58 carriages drawn and propelled by seven engines, four of which went the whole distance'!

COACH SERVICES

Considering that the only two towns *en route* served centrally by their stations were Gloucester and Birmingham, it is not surprising that a considerable number of connecting coach services were run to cater for those less favourably situated. The cost to the company was on average £3,000 per year; another of the B&G's expensive economies. Worcester had the most (in)famous service from Spetchley. An office was rented opposite the HopPole in the city and Mr Meek provided the service with an omnibus carrying 13 people whose fare for the journey was borne by the company on a contractural basis. Connections were made to and from every passenger and mail train, with 40 minutes allowed for the journey. At first it left much to be desired but an improvement was made during the summer of 1841. The *Gloucester Chronicle* reported it as in the shape of:[14] '. . . a carriage with 2 bodies for 1st class passengers . . . such an accommodation has long been required.'

Its running expenses were a cause of much worry to the board, who tried a number of times to replace it with a branch line without success. In 1844 for example it conveyed 78,372 passengers at a cost to the company of £2,698 and the expense continued well into MR days. In fact Worcester travellers had to put up with the 'lumbering conveyance' until the first part of the OWW loop opened in 1850.

Cheltenham's station was, considering the nature and quantity of passenger traffic, ill-placed at one mile from the centre of the town. It was a prime candidate for a road coach link. The arrangements were, however, a little unpopular. The *Gloucester Journal*[15] thought that: 'An abuse exists . . . At the Lansdown Station the trains discharge Cheltenham passengers. Here each . . . can either walk or take a carriage to town; charge 6*d*., but if he has the slightest item of luggage the charge is 1*s*. This will certainly raise prejudice in favour of the old method of transport – who will pay 2*s*. 1st class fare plus 1*s*. when he gets horse vehicles door to door for 2*s*.? Before opening, a report attributed to the Company said it was their intention of keeping carriages for free travel to Cheltenham. ' Any coach owner could apply for the business and several hotel owners provided transport which conveniently terminated outside their hotel door to discharge passengers! This must have caused some degree of congestion, since early in 1841 the trade was given over to just two coach owners, Messrs Dangerfield and Haines, an arrangement which was not well received by the hotel proprietors. An advertisement appeared in the *Gloucester Journal*[16] from the Fleece and George Hotel owners who: '. . . beg to intimate to their Friends and the Public in consequence of the Directors of the B&G having deprived them of the privilege of sending omnibuses to convey passengers from the Cheltenham station, they have determined boldly to resist such an infamous monopoly and respectfully announce their omnibuses will Ply at the Gates of the yard to convey Passengers into the Town at half price, i.e. 3*d*.' After a long monopoly, the trade was again thrown open to competition in January 1844.

Bromsgrove and Droitwich omnibuses were poorly patronised and required a subsidy from the company in addition to the fare. At Gloucester, several hotel proprietors, notably the Ram Hotel and Commercial Inn, sent omnibuses to meet every train to ply for custom, whilst long distance travellers to and from the west could take a coach to Bristol and Bath in connection with the B&G trains. These started from Cheltenham and ran to Gloucester on the train and thence by road to Bristol and Bath. Those with the money could travel inside for 10*s*. to Bristol and 13*s*. to Bath, while the less well off paid 6*s*. and 8*s*. respectively to travel outside.

At various times during the B&G's history Alcester, Hereford, Malvern, Pershore, Redditch and Stourbridge had coach connections with the railway to stimulate travel from these outlying districts.

CHAPTER FIFTEEN
WAY AND WORKS

In this chapter the engineering side of the railway is expanded upon in two parts; earthworks and structures (excluding stations), and the permanent way.

Geologically speaking the B&G line lies on two quite different formations. At the northern end there is new red sandstone with heavy marl soils while the southern is oolitic with blue and yellow clays and quantities of sand and gravel. These two extremes are linked by an intermediate area of lias rock and clay.

Consequently, building materials were plentiful and relatively cheap. Sandstone and limestone provided excellent material for bridges and other structures. The clays made good ingredients for bricks while gravels, sand, burnt marl, burnt clay and stone rubble were used for ballast. These were not the best materials for the purpose as was found to the B&G's cost later, but they did provide a cheap road bed, serviceable at the time.

But it is earthworks which inevitably govern the cost of any railway's construction, and, while south of the Lickey the route was relatively free from difficulty, and was completed within the time and cost estimated by Capt. Moorsom, the northern section from Bromsgrove to Birmingham handsomely exceeded his estimates (see Chapter Six). Armed only with picks, shovels, horses and tram wagons, it was human muscle power which built through the countryside the smooth steady gradients required by the railway.

Over 4.5 million cubic yards of material was hewn from cuttings and shifted either to form adjacent embankments or if no embankment was near enough, it was piled onto temporary spoil heaps beside the line for use elsewhere. At Defford the cutting slipped under the great weight of one of these heaps, derailing a passenger train. Moseley cutting was the biggest according to Whishaw,[1] over a mile in length and with a maximum depth of 85ft. Those at Bredon, Barnt Green, Grovely and Longbridge were almost as long. Sir Frederick Smith of the BoT found these latter three in a dangerous and unfinished state when he inspected the Cofton to Camp Hill section in December 1840, and he warned that they were likely to slip. He described Grovely as 'rugged and precipitous' and felt unable to pass the line as safe. But the B&G opened it all the same, though police were kept on duty at Grovely in case of accident. The cutting sides were eased to a gentler batter shortly after opening. Embankments on this section of line were also particularly heavy, the highest being some 62ft. and here again Sir Frederick found cause for concern. He remarked that those at Wychall, Northfield and in the Rea Valley were very lofty and appeared to be insufficiently consolidated.

Tunnels were cut at Moseley and Grovely (which later came to be known as Cofton). Moseley tunnel was forced on the company by local opponents in Parliament. A tunnel 150 yards long was considered neccessary to protect Moseley Chapel from the noise and vibration of the railway. The directors were, however, unconvinced of its necessity, and in 1837 resolved to disregard that clause in the Act and save some £1,500 by digging an open cutting instead; but before work had commenced their intentions became known, and their opponents obtained an injunction in the Court of Chancery which compelled them to comply with the stipulations of their Act.

The portals (illustrated) are of a most unusual but very satisfying design, which Capt. W.S. Moorsom used again later in his career at Southampton. Grovely tunnel was however really necessary at the time. It was 440 yards long and was continually troublesome until finally opened out by the LMS in the late 1920s. Trial borings found its quartose sandstone very wet and soft in places and considerable drainage had to be done before excavations could start. Tenders for construction were not completed until February 1840 and Messrs W & J Noel's estimate of £15,500 (with completion by 31 July) was accepted.

Progress was slow; the instability of the rock made it necessary for the whole tunnel to be bricklined and water continually threatened to flood the permanent way. Policemen stationed in the cutting at each end of the tunnel had the unenviable task of keeping a special watch on it. A report by an independent authority was commissioned in December 1841 which recommended trussing the lining throughout. This may have strengthened the structure but it didn't stop the water. In May 1843 Mr Wetherall, the resident engineer, reported that the tunnel continued to be very wet and acted as a drain for the whole of the adjoining land.

Moseley Tunnel (south portal), Birmingham. Collection of D. Ibbotson (Historical Model Railway Society).

Bridge 72 over the road from Shernal Green to Goose Green (W.V. Awdry).

Bridge 57. Farm overpass (W.V. Awdry).

Ornamental bridge over unclassified road near Cofton. Collection of D. Ibbotson (Historical Model Railway Society).

Bridge 70 between Dunhamstead and Shernal Green (W.V. Awdry).

Farm access underpass at Bredon's Norton (W.V. Awdry).

Being a continual source of trouble, it soon became a favourite subject for vituperation by 'Veritas Vincit' in his letters to the *Railway Times*.[2] During the CofE purge of 1843 when many men lost their jobs, he wrote: 'At Coffin tunnel [his delightful nickname for Cofton] . . . they have already discharged 2 policemen, one from each end. This tunnel has never been properly finished at either end, and the consequence is that . . . often . . . wagonloads of loose rock fall down and obstruct the line. Now suppose only a small piece of rock were to fall down and no-one were there to remove it from off the rails . . . The consequence would be that the engine and tender would be thrown off the line and the passengers dashed against the sides of the tunnel; in fact this tunnel all through is far from being perfect; it is propped up in places and there is no-one placed there to watch it.' He was soon pleased to report that: '. . . men are now employed in finishing the tunnel in a proper manner. . .' Though not 'proper' enough since a Board minute in August 1843 reported a brick fall from the vent shaft. As an insurance policy against delays which might be caused by future repairs, the two lines of track were moved together so that the adjacent rails of up and down lines were 4ft. 8½in. apart which would allow, in case of neccessity, a train to run along a central path.

Bridgework on the railway was of great variety (see illustrations). There were 162 over- and under-bridges of stone, brick, cast iron and wood while another 127 culverts were built. The majority have been rebuilt though some of the lightly used occupation under-bridges remain showing the graceful horseshoe arch.

Lack of adequate clearance in Capt. Moorsom's design for a bridge near Kings Norton came in for criticism. This was responsible for the death of a footplate man (see Accidents, Chapter 21). Several were built in violation of the Incorporating Acts provisions for minimum dimensions and had to be rebuilt at considerable extra cost. One, just north of Bromsgrove station, is a case in point. Herbert Spencer[3] was involved in the redesign of this bridge and he tells us that the extra cost was 'between one and two thousand pounds.' Others needed repairs to stonework and drainage, possibly because Moorsom had had to build them 'on the cheap' owing to the Board's unceasing financial constraints. The incessant rains of 1839 and 1840 may have contributed in more or less proportion as well. 'Veritas Vincit'[4] describes the state of some in the Birmingham area: 'The first bridge below Camp Hill within 50 yards and right opposite the house of Mr Wetherall [Resident Engineer] . . . is supported by brickwork and with all is in a very rickety condition . . . so much so that they have been obliged to remove the gravel from the top of it and have recourse to two longtitudinal beams supported at each end to carry the rails. . . . The third bridge below is in an almost equally bad state. The brick walls which support the embankments and the abutments . . . are off-the-plumb and bulged out to a considerable extent so that wooden props are resorted to to keep the bridge from falling. If one stands under these bridges and leans his back against the brickwork when a train passes over, it will make him tremble . . . !'

By far the biggest bridge was that designed by Moorsom to cross the river Avon between Defford and Eckington. It was of cast-iron construction 275ft. long consisting of three segmental arches of 73ft. span. These were supported on two lines of cast iron columns resting on caissons filled with concrete. Moorsom was awarded the Telford Medal by the Institute of Civil Engineers for his design of the river-bed foundations of the bridge. It was the first practical example of iron caissons being sunk into the river bed to form a chamber, which, once the water had been pumped out, were filled with concrete and masonry. This bridge at first gave trouble too! Shortly after the opening in June 1840 the wing walls began to bulge and several stones in the abutments became displaced. Herbert Spencer[5] was again involved in the repair and blamed the damage on 'imperfect construction' as a result of Moorsom's efforts to keep construction costs within the original estimates. Moorsom, in a report to the Board, claimed that the shrinkage then expansion of the material used for the extensive embankments either side (40,000 cubic yards) was the cause, but wherever the blame lay there was no alternative but to rebuild them. According to Spencer: 'Pulling down and rebuilding of this had to be achieved without interruption of traffic; one of the . . . lines being closed and the trains diverted onto the other. A large gap in the embankment was necessitated and the available line of rails was shored up. The proceeding was . . . risky and entailed in me considerable anxiety. No accident happened however.'

Level-crossings of the railway by roads were plentiful, though only south of Bromsgrove. They were not allowed to cross turnpike roads on the level but there were sixteen highway crossings,[6] forty occupation and ten footpath crossings.[7] All the highway crossings had gates which were kept shut across the roads and were attended by gate-keepers whose wages were between 7s. and 18s. per week after payment of rent for their houses, and were kept constantly on duty! Several of the keepers' cottages (see illustrations) still survive, albeit with an upper storey added in MR days. The absence of windows at the rear of these cottages bears witness to the company's desire to avoid attracting window tax.

Capt. Moorsom had worked out his plan for laying the permanent way by the end of 1836. He based it upon the principle adopted by Brunel for his broad gauge, but met with considerably more success! A continuous bearing of timber baulks (7ft. 6in. length) was to be laid down for each rail on a base of ballast 16in. thick and interconnected by transoms embedded in the ballast at intervals of 5 or 7ft. 6in. rails, which were to be 56lb. or so, per yard and in 15ft. lengths, would be firmly secured in chairs or pedestals every 15ft. and spiked every 5ft. In Moorsom's opinion, the timber to be used was immaterial, but had to be treated with Kyan's Anti Corrosion process or similar.

When Mr Locke of the GJR investigated Moorsom's designs for the railway the following autumn (1837) he recommended an increase in the weight of rail to 75lb. per yard using a conventional sleeper system instead of the longitudinal design. But Capt. Moorsom took little notice of this advice and without untoward results. He simply changed his plan slightly; chairs holding the rails would be fixed at 5ft. intervals while intermediate saddles would give all the support required. This allowed the use of much lighter rails without risk of breakage. In loose earth, such as on embankments over 5ft. high, rails would be laid on cross-sleepers at 2ft. 6in. intervals in what was to become the conventional manner.

Herbert Spencer[8] was also critical of Moorsom's track design but from a different angle. He thought the system of chairs and saddles would give vertical but not lateral support and the oscillation of the engine would cause bulging in the intervals between them. This prophecy proved well founded he said, but there is no evidence in the minutes to support this.

Sir Fredrick Smith found no faults when he inspected the Cofton–Camp Hill section in December 1840, though he questioned the use of cross-sleepered track on embankments which he felt unsafe. He would have preferred to have seen the longitudinal system!

When J.E. McConnell gave evidence at the Gauge Commission[9] he reported that the cross-sleepered track was being replaced with longitudinals, for the embankments had now consolidated and the sleepers, insufficiently treated, had mostly rotted! He preferred the longitudinal system; the triangular baulks allowed ballast to be packed firmly either side, though for a mixed gauge system he admitted that sleepered track would present fewer difficulties. The rails on the B&G were too light from the start, he added, and should have been 75lb. per yard, as Locke had recommended.

A different approach to Moorsom's standard system was needed for the Cheltenham–Gloucester line which had to be laid to accommodate mixed gauge eventually. Brunel and Moorsom agreed in July 1840 to modify the longitudinal system for a three rail line, the common rail being the right hand one according to the direction of travel. To cater for the increased weight of broad gauge trains, their rails would be held in chairs laid every 2ft. as opposed to 2ft. 6in. for the narrow gauge, and the baulks would be wider to give more support.

When Capt. Melhuish of the BoT arrived to inspect the line in October 1840 (then of course, without the broad gauge rail) he found that it: '. . . differs materially from any I have yet seen.' He went on to say that the way is formed by laying large baulks of pine 16ft. to 36ft. long end to end joined by dowells and 'strong oaken pins'. Pairs of baulks, he continued, are coupled at 4ft. 8in. centres by transverse timber ties. Cast iron chairs are bolted to the baulks at intervals of not less than 2ft. 2in.; rails are then secured in with beech wedges and the whole assembly brought to the correct height and ballasted up.

By the time the GWR's third rail was laid and ready for inspection the B&G had ceased to exist. It was 11 October 1847 when Capt. Simmons arrived to give the the BoT's seal of approval, or otherwise, to the novel three rail system with monstrous junctions at Cheltenham and Gloucester. Track was laid wholly on transverse sleepers in contrast to the Brunel–Moorsom plan of 1840. Much heavier rail, 83lb. per yard, was used. While the three rail system was perfectly simple in all respects, the junctions were not! At Cheltenham the narrow met the broad and joined it, requiring no moving pointwork in the accepted sense. At Gloucester (Barnwood Junction) broad gauge lines diverged requiring moving pointblades, whilst the narrow gauge line, as at Cheltenham, merely had to cross the broad gauge lines.

Pictures speak louder than words, so please study the drawings and draw your own conclusions! They were constructed from a study of the text of Capt. Simmon's report, for the drawings he made are unfortunately missing. He was unhappy about the number of rail gaps needed to accomplish the mixed gauge junctions, especially at Gloucester; but since he was assured that the expected speed of the trains over them was to be low, and that the drivers were ordered to take special care, he felt that the junctions could be passed for traffic without risk to public safety.

From 1844 a considerable track relaying programme was embarked upon. This was mainly due to the rotten state of the beech and larch sleepers. Longitudinal baulks, as mentioned above, replaced the transverse sleepers on embankments. 16 miles needed relaying, of which 5 were completed by April 1845, though how much more was relaid longitudinally is not stated. November 1846 saw the first replacement of longitudinal by sleepered track and no doubt this was the MR's policy from then on.

Track maintenance was done for the first twelve months by the way and works department, and charged to the capital account. But towards the end of 1841 it became the first of Capt. Moorsom's contracted-out services. The contract was drawn up to include all routine repairs to earthworks and structures besides the track and trackbed while the company was to find replacement rails, sleepers, baulks and so on.

Messrs Berwick and Lamb won the contract for a seven year term starting at a price of £174 per mile per year, but reduced to £159 for the final two years. For some reason the L&B extension line was not included.

Considerable criticism was made of the contract at the January 1843 special meeting. When the CofE published its report in June of that year, they claimed that it could be re-let at a much lower rate, and regretted the considerable length of time for which the contract had been signed. All that could be done, said the report, was to ensure that the contractors were held to perform their obligations to the letter. Under strict inspection of their work, Berwick and Lamb's maintenance was found to be unsatisfactory, thus giving opportunity to terminate the agreement on the pretext of their breach of contract. It was then re-let from January 1844 at £102 per mile per year.

Details of rails, sleepers, chairs and saddles appear in the appendix.

CHAPTER SIXTEEN
SIGNALLING

It would appear that until *c*. 1845 signalling on the B&G was only basic. Improvements were made from time to time out of necessity but these, although referred to in the minutes, are not described in any detail. Therefore, much of the information given in this chapter has had to be drawn by inference from other sources.

Both Capt. W. Moorsom, engineer in chief, and William Burgess, secretary and superintendent, had gained railway experience on the L&B so it was natural, therefore, that in drawing up a signalling code for the B&G they should rely heavily on that of the L&B. In fact Capt. Moorsom's signalling code drawn up in preparation for the opening of the Cheltenham–Bromsgrove section in June 1840, was an exact copy of the earliest code used on the L&B. Policemen stationed at intervals along the track regulated the traffic by displaying coloured flags by day and lamps of corresponding colour by night. White showed that all was clear; green warned that caution was neccessary; and red gave the order to stop.

William Burgess in his revised code of management simplified the signalling by using white and red flags and lamps only. 'No signal' indicated all clear. In this case the policeman would stand facing the train with his flags rolled up and resting on his shoulder. After the train had passed and for the space of five minutes, any following train would be shown the 'red', and then be allowed to proceed, but cautiously, when the driver was shown the white flag. Once ten minutes had gone by the line was assumed to be clear ahead, and the policeman would indicate this accordingly.

Members of staff responsible for operating the signals were

switchmen at the principal stations (under orders from the inspector) and policemen or foremen platelayers at places other than stations. Small stations had a flag staff and signal lamp, the ancestor of the fixed semaphore. This consisted of a large flagpole on which could be hoisted the red or white flag by day, and the corresponding lamp by night. Level crossings had to have a signal displayed by the gate-keepers; white when the gates were open to the railway and red when closed; whilst water cranes had a signal fixed to show white when the jib had been swung clear and red when the arm was over the rails.

At night all policemen and switchmen had to show a white beam to prove they were at their posts, and which showed all clear, but when waved meant caution. A red bulls-eye lamp was carried on the last vehicle of a train, while two such lamps indicated to station and wayside staff that an unadvertised special train was to follow shortly. By day this was indicated by affixing a black and white target board to the last vehicle.

Engine drivers communicated with their train guard via the engine's steam whistle; one short blast to call the guard to alert, three short blasts to apply the brake and one long one for all clear. In reply the guard signalled with a white flag when the train was ready to start. This was, of course, a primitive system; although quite adequate for uninterrupted stretches on a line with a low density of traffic, it was none too safe where a junction with another railway occurred.

Capt. Melhuish of the BoT reported on the B&G code of signals in October 1840: 'I found, on comparing them with those of the L&B that a very material difference existed and as I cannot but consider uniformity on all those points, which will admit of its application, as highly conducive to the regular and safe working of locomotive power, I was induced to ask the Secretary (in case of my recommending it) whether he would be disposed to adopt the code of the L&B, it being a company highly spoken of and whose road had now been of some years in full operation . . .' The secretary did agree that a common code of signals would be advantageous but as: '. . . he considered his signals more simple and consequentially better than those of the L&B, he should certainly feel disinclined to change until some code had been generally approved and authorised'. As for the junction between the L&B and B&G, Capt. Melhuish thought that a railway from Gloucester to Birmingham which would be worked by two sets of signals 'ought to be prevented'! In general, he surmised, a common code of signals should be: '. . . selected and framed under [the BoT's] authority', to be adopted by all railway companies, especially since staff moving from one railway to another might well become confused. Local signals: '. . . found requisite at certain points of a line of railway' should not be interfered with.

Gloucester Junction, as the L&B called it, was one of these 'certain points'. (see Map 16.1) It was where the B&G joined the L&B to run over L&B rails to reach Curzon Street station, Birmingham. The points at the junction were to be entirely under the control of the L&B switchman who was to signal to the Gloucester to Birmingham train driver when the line was clear. To do this he was to use what was called in the L&B rule book 'a Stationary Signal'. It was a red disc on a post which could be swivelled through 90 degrees to show either its full face (danger – stop) to the driver of an approaching train, or if turned at right-angles so that the driver could only see its edge, it gave him permission to proceed. Red and white lamps indicated the aspect of the disc by night.

To allow Birmingham to Gloucester trains to negotiate the junction in safety, the switchman, knowing their time of departure, had to block all L&B traffic in both directions, from the time they were due to leave until they had actually cleared the junction, using signals of a similar character. This was good enough in fine weather, thought Sir Frederick, but there was a potential hazard when visibility was poor. He suggested that the L&B ticket platform be removed to the London side of the junction thus providing a compulsory stop for the L&B trains into Birmingham and avoiding the danger of signals being misread. In addition, all Gloucester bound trains were to stop and check the signal before crossing to the B&G line.

Despite its utter simplicity and reliance totally upon human judgement, no accidents were attributed to the signalling in the B&G's independent days. But the B&G like the L&B before them, soon found that signalling by policemen alone was both labour intensive and unsatisfactory, and in March 1842 a Mr Curtis was invited to lay his 'scheme for signalling' before the BC, and Mr Wetherall was told to examine its possibilities. We suspect that Wetherall thought poorly of it, for Mr Curtis and his signals are not heard of again. Signalling problems remained however, and the strain of daily traffic clearly revealed the line's persistent trouble spots, of which Bromsgrove was the worst. When, in September 1842, yet another run-away had taken place, the Board summoned Mr Harrop, the way and works inspector, to attend their meeting on 4 October. They asked him if there was any signalling (other, of course, than policemen) at Bromsgrove. He replied that there never had been 'any disc or signal at Bromsgrove'. Thereupon they ordered Wetherall 'to erect posts and signals similar to those of the London & Birmingham Company'.

The Minutes give no details or specifications of the signals ordered so it is to be assumed that the signals referred to were of the type mentioned above as having been erected by the L&B at 'Gloucester Junction'. It is however evident that such signals were installed not only

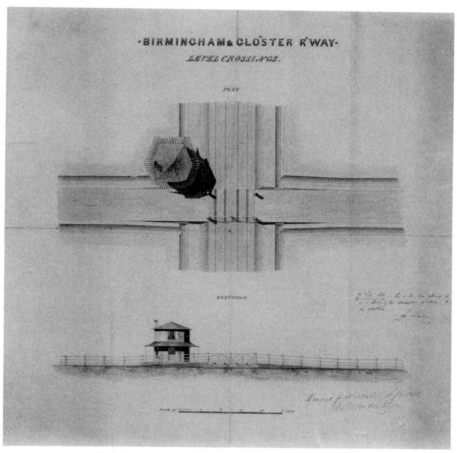

Early level crossing design (Gloucester Records Office).

B&G crossing Keepers Cottage, Alstone Lane, Cheltenham (David Lyall).

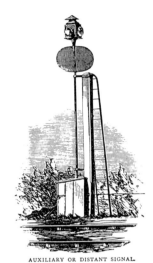

HOME SIGNAL.

AUXILIARY OR DISTANT SIGNAL.

Early signals on the B&G (David & Charles; F.S. Williams, *Our Iron Roads*).

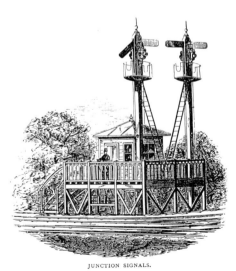

JUNCTION SIGNALS.

Junction signals as supplied by Stevens & Son (David & Charles; F.S. Willams, *Our Iron Roads*).

at Bromsgrove but at other, perhaps all, stations on the line; for in February 1843 Mr McConnell reported Driver J. Powell 'who disobeyed orders by not stopping at Stoke . . . when . . . the red disc was shown, and of having also passed Droitwich Station contrary to orders when another train was there, and the disc hoisted as well as the red flag shown.' For this flagrant breach of safety regulations Powell was dismissed.

These disc signals, when properly installed, were not unlike the tall signal in the accompanying illustration. The lower signal shown beside it has an oval shaped board painted green. This type of signal is mentioned in the London & North Western Railway Rulebook of 1847, and is referred to as a 'precautionary signal'. Such signals may or may not have been used on the L&B in 1842; but though they may have used it we have been unable to find any evidence that the B&G did so. It would seem that following the Board's instructions to Wetherall, disc signals were installed at all stations on the line, and that pending proper erection, the disc itself was issued and 'hoisted' when required up the signal flagstaff already there. It is not known if every station had them, but it is known that the disc signal posts were not always sited, nor were they always of such a height, to give the best visibility. Road overbridges often obscured the driver's view at places such as Droit-wich, Bredon, Ashchurch and above all at Defford. At Defford, the fact that the road bridge obscured the signal was a contributory cause of the accident there in August 1845. An up special freight train collided with a wagon left on the line by Dore, the stationmaster, inspite of the fact that the up mail, which had just passed through the station, had carried the two red tail lamps which indicated that another train was following close behind. The goods engine, derailed by the wagon rolled into the path of a down passenger train just entering the station.

Ward, the goods train driver, was killed, and his fireman, Baird injured, and one passenger in the down train was killed too. The first passenger death in the B&G's five years of operating. At the inquest, attended by 'Veritas Vincit', McConnell gave evidence of the type of signals used on the line:[1] '. . . they formerly used lamps on poles but that in consequence of these poles being too low, the signals were not seen on approaching the stations and that they in consequence resorted to the use of the handlamp.' When asked why the lamps on the poles could not be seen, McConnell replied that all their stations had low bridges close by, which obliterated the lamps on the poles from the driver's view.

General Pasley, the attending BoT official, recommended the erection of poles 30ft. to 40ft. high with improved lamps which could be seen over the tops of the bridges. A Board minute in September ordered McConnell to provide double signal lamps at each station between Birmingham and Gloucester. These were presumably posts with one signal at high level for distant viewing and the other at the usual height; the exact description is not given.

Writing of the accident in December, 'Veritas Vincit' reported a delay in replacing the signals although McConnell had allegedly told the BoT that improvements were in hand. 'Veritas Vincit' affirms that: '. . . all the signals he had in progress were two large ones for the Lickey Incline. All the other signals on the line are the same as when they were deprecated by the Coroner's Jury. No 30ft. posts and lamps have yet been erected. If life should again be lost in consequence, will not the Attorney General be called in . . .?'

Perhaps the directors anticipated 'Veritas Vincit's' involvement, for a month earlier they had ordered McConnell to use his best endeavour towards perfecting the signals as soon as possible. That same November they reported the adoption of the electric telegraph on the Lickey Incline, but alas, the minutes give no further details, except that in 1846 orders were given to build cottages at Blackwell to house the operators.

But we have pressed ahead too far, and must now return to December 1844. With the merger of the B&G and the BrG imminent, McConnell for the B&G, and Wyndham Harding, BrG traffic manager, had been instructed to draw up signalling regulations for the combined companies. When drawn up these were agreed by both Boards sitting separately. No details are given in the minutes of either company, but there is the strongest possible presumption that at Tramway Junction at least, B&G type signalling should prevail.

Spurred to activity by the Defford accident the MR (B&B) management committee began to set signalling improvements in hand. In mid-1846, just prior to the Midland's absorption of the B&B, the minutes state that a tour of inspection had shown the signalling system to be greatly improved; but also recommended that the number of signals be increased so that the number of policemen employed might be reduced. A further inspection in August was ordered, and following this the decision was made to erect further signals where neccessary to 'allow the proper and safe working of the traffic'.

There was one spot, however, which by 1846 had become very hazardous indeed. Under their unified signalling regulations of December 1844 the B&G and BrG had been able to conduct their Bristol and Birmingham traffic into and out of Gloucester with reasonable safety. But with the arrival of the GWR in June 1845, Tramway Junction had become a perilous place.

It will be remembered that to a GWR driver a red disc meant 'go', but to a B&B driver it meant 'stop'. It is easy to imagine the complications which ensued when drivers of the two companies met at Tramway Junction. Both, while acting correctly according to their rule books, inevitably found themselves on collision course! The problem was to find a method of signalling such trouble spots in an unmistakeable manner. When, therefore, Mr Barlow (B&B resident engineer) reported in 1846 that he had had an offer made to him by Stevens & Son, Signal Engineers, to supply some of their patent semaphore signals for use on the line between Birmingham and Gloucester, the MR (B&B) management committee accepted it with alacrity. They bought 19 signals for the sum of £383 (see illustration).

By October a pair had been installed at Tramway Junction where they were seen by a reporter from the *Gloucester Journal* who described them as: 'a very complete set of signals of the most approved description . . . as sanctioned by the Board of Trade'. Some little time later after a conference on site between the GWR and the MR (B&B), the GWR added fresh regulations to their rule book ordering that these semaphores at Tramway Junction be respectfully observed and obeyed.

Signalling in fog was assisted by Cowpers fog signals, an ancestor of the familiar railway detonator. Cowper, an L&B engineer, had in July 1843, sent or brought specimens of his fog signals to the B&G for trial. McConnell was asked to test them and gave a favourable report, he wanted to lay in a stock. However, (probably from parsimony – you remember the Purge was on at the time!), he was only allowed to buy two dozen. In 1844 Cowper made some improvements and had them tested by the BoT Inspectorate, and a report signed by General Pasley was issued in April of that year.

Pasley described the detonator as a small flat circular tin box containing a charge of gunpowder mixed with fulminate. The box had lead wings by which it could be clipped to the rail top. Pasley recommended it on grounds of reliability and suggested that all railway companies be circularised to encourage its adoption. But it was not until November 1846 that the MR adopted them as standard for use on their B&B lines.

Communications between driver and guard of a train is not a twentieth century 'hi-tech' invention! Mr McConnell reported in May 1844 that he could make a device for guards to signal to drivers at £2.10s.0d. and was told to proceed and experiment. It must have died a death, for after the Defford accident the following year, the inquest heard how the guard of the goods train had seen the red signal but was unable to pass the alarm to the footplate crew.

Two local inventors were spurred into action and their schemes were reported in the *Gloucester Journal* later in 1845.[2] In September, one James Williams of the carriage department at Bromsgrove had invented a guard's alarm signal which consisted of a large bell and a visible warning attached to the outside of the first vehicle of the train. It was activated by the guard pulling a long rope which passed along the carriages to the guard's van, and the inventor hoped that a trial would be allowed by Mr Hudson. Mr Banfield, an organ builder from Birmingham, had invented a: '. . . new railway whistle . . . enabling conductors of trains to communicate with each other in a far more effective manner than by the system now in use.[?] . . . An experimental train of 8 carriages was fitted with small airtight tubes which communicate with a very powerful whistle attached to one corner of the engine tender, and by a very simple arrangement, the Guard was able to give a signal instantly, and, if neccessary, to vary it, so that he could be perfectly understood by the engine driver.' The experiment is stated to have been completely successful, but yet again no more was heard of it.

CHAPTER SEVENTEEN
LOCOMOTIVE DEPARTMENT

by Rev. W.V. Awdry

Edward Bury was one of the great authorities on locomotive affairs in the 1830s. He was, moreover, locomotive superintendent of the L&B. It was therefore only natural that the B&G should consult him. He agreed in 1838 to be their agent and adviser for locomotives, workshop equipment and design and also for the stationary engine power needed for the Lickey.

Bury wasted no time. He ordered four locomotives from Forrester of Liverpool at £1,660 each. These were for future delivery, but for immediate needs for line construction he obtained two secondhand engines, a 0-4-0 Stephenson *Planet* from the Leicester and Swannington Railway, and a 0-4-2 from the London and Southampton Railway. These were named *Leicester* and *Southampton* respectively.

Two "Forresters" arrived in November 1838 and were set to work on the southern part of the line, while delivery of the remaining two was promised midway through 1839. The board were delighted and it was proposed to give Bury £100 by way of a gratuity in addition to his 5 per cent commission. When it came to the point, however, they somewhat characteristically reduced the gratuity to a mere £50.

Having insisted that Captain Moorsom take their line straight up the Lickey under the mistaken impression that this reduction in mileage would prove economical, the Board had intended to follow contemporary practice and work the incline with stationary engine power as the L&B did at Camden. Bury approved of this, and set to work on the design of engines for the job. Judge of Bury's annoyance, however, when Captain Moorsom rejected his advice and determined to work the incline with locomotive power just to prove that his critics Brunel,

Stephenson and Bury himself were wrong. He had seen a trade catalogue from Norris of Philadelphia which recorded the spectacular hill climbing feats of his engines, and had started negotiations with Norris for a supply of locomotives.

Bury was furious; Norris was his 'bete noir'. Between 1831 and 1837 he had exported some 20 locomotives to America. Norris had promptly pirated his basic design, and adapted it to suit American railroad conditions. Now, his crowning act of piracy was to export these imitations back to England, claiming that they could perform feats of hill climbing of which his (Bury's) engines were incapable – as indeed they were, as we shall see in Chapter 23.

The story of the B&G's entanglement with Norris is a complicated one and will be told fully in the next chapter. It reflects little credit on Norris and his agent, William Gwynn, for their 'confidence trick' salesmanship, or on the B&G and their engineer for their gullibility. In the end the B&G found that they had been jockeyed into buying 13 engines when they really only wanted three!

Norris locomotives came in three sizes. The smallest, weighing 8 tons, were the class Bs; the class As were 10 tonners, while the class A Extras were powerful 12½ ton engines. The B&G only wanted 3 A Extras to lift their trains up the Lickey, but Norris and Gwynn manoevred the BC into such a position that in order to buy the A Extras they had to buy 7 class Bs and 3 class As as well!

On the whole, though the Norrises had a large appetite for coke, they were neat looking engines with what David Joy was later to describe[1] as 'plenty of pull' and, when in running order, they invariably got away smartly with their trains. They had however a number of inbuilt weaknesses which, under British operating conditions, were likely to put them out of action within a few months. Their wheels of chilled cast iron were designed for the lightly laid resilient American railroad tracks of the period. They broke with alarming frequency on the rigid baulk laid track of the B&G. Their inner fireboxes were of iron, designed for wood fuel, in the prevailing American fashion, and their boiler tubes were of copper. With wood as fuel both could expect a reasonably long period of useful life, but with coke the fireboxes quickly burnt through, while the fierce blast, drawing coke dust and cinders through the tubes, abraded the soft copper at an alarming rate, and it was not till all the 'Americans' had been fitted, at considerable expense, with copper fireboxes, hard brass tubes, and wheels with wrought iron tyres, that they became capable of reliable running.

Thus it was that within a few months of opening the railway, Norris cripples filled the sidings at Bromsgrove Works putting on them a pressure which neither the works nor the staff were equipped to sustain.

It was fortunate therefore that when in March 1840, in view of plans for opening the line later that year, Capt. W.S. Moorsom asked the Board's permission to order fresh locomotive power, they agreed with what was, for them, surprising alacrity. He was told to obtain estimates from British builders for the construction of six engines similar to *Victoria*, a Norris class A. The Captain had neither the time nor the ability to design a locomotive for himself, so he withdrew *Victoria* from her line construction work, cleaned her up, and put her on display at Camp Hill, Birmingham.

In the end, nine locomotives were ordered – 3 from Hick of Bolton, and 6 from Nasmyth, of Manchester. The new engines were delivered between October 1840 and August 1841. Their arrival at intervals was to prove a godsend to the hard pressed locomotive department so much so that Herbert Spencer noted in February 1841[2] that: '. . . in consequence of the urgent want of train engines on the line, the new engines shall be at once handed over to Mr Creuze', (locomotive superintendent) thus, as a matter of urgency, forgoing the usual acceptance tests. It was notable that in these engines both Hick and Nasmyth had seen the Norris weaknesses mentioned above and had taken steps to rectify them.

We have, in previous chapters, referred to Mr William Burgess' 'General System of Railway Management'.[3] We have seen that it was a comprehensive work covering most aspects of railway operation including a set of rules for enginemen. These have quite clearly been adapted from the L&B rule book. It is not possible to include them all, but some extracts are of interest:

Enginemen when in motion on the road must stand where they can keep a good look-out ahead.

No engine must travel along the wrong line [i.e. the right hand road], except in case of accident or emergency. If wrong road working is unavoidable, the fireman must first run back to the nearest available shunting loop to stop oncoming trains before the wrong road working begins. During the wrong road working the driver must make constant use of his whistle.

All engines travelling in the same direction shall keep 600 yards at least from each other . . . of which circumstance the policemen, constables, platelayers and gatekeepers will give the neccessary signal.

No engineman shall at any time leave his engine or train on the line unattended.

Goods or luggage trains . . . shall always keep out of the way of coach trains, by shunting if neccessary.

No luggage train shall pass any station or stopping place whilst a
coach train has stopped, or is in the act of stopping on the other
line of road.

The driver will use the tender brakes to prevent as much as possible
the neccessity of using the carriage brakes.

In the event of the road . . . being obscured by steam, fog or smoke,
any engine or train . . . should not pass through . . . but . . .
shall stop . . . and shall ascertain that the way is clear and safe
before attempting to proceed.

There were other regulations concerning fog or thick weather in which
case 'frequent use should be made of the steam whistle' and 'should a
train stop either at a station or at any other place, a man must go back
for 400 yards to warn on-coming trains and prevent collision'. These
rules were designed to secure safety in operation, and were ordered to
be strictly observed. The company minutes show that failure to do so
brought penalties on the culprit in the shape of a fine, suspension or
even dismissal.

We mentioned above that the inbuilt weaknesses of the American
Norris design caused them, under British conditions, to get out of
order very quickly. The line from Cheltenham to Bromsgrove had
been opened in June 1840 and extended to Cofton Farm in September,
but yet in September – just three months after opening – William
Creuze reported despairingly of the conditions prevailing at Bromsgrove Works. 'The stationary engine is now complete, but delay in its
erection through Mr Bury's dilatoriness caused great inconvenience
. . . the water arrangements . . . though apparently finished, are
useless. Every pipe laid by Bramah Fox & Co must be taken up and
relaid. This is being done, but work is hampered by lack of labourers.
The Yard at Bromsgrove is choked with wagons and coaches . . .
nearly all the 'Americans' are very much out of order. This is due to the
construction of their fireboxes, and their tubes being made of copper
which our fuel does not suit . . .'[4] There they were – crippled engines –
some of which were less than three months in service, waiting and
deteriorating outside a workshop too small and too inadequately
equipped to do the job for which they had been built.

How had such an appalling situation arisen? The only possible
answer is, that it was allowed to happen through the incompetence of
the BC. They had put themselves in a position of great financial
difficulty through their 'expensive economies' as related above in
Chapter Six. As a result they lost confidence and began quarrelling
among themselves. The result was indecision and further waste of time
and money. So much money had been wasted on line construction that

structures, stations and equipment especially that for the locomotive department suffered. Sanction for expenditure on essential buildings was delayed, and these often had to be hurriedly and expensively erected in a last minute scramble.

Bromsgrove Works were a case in point. Capt. Moorsom, once the Lickey Incline had been forced on him, had seen quite rightly that the operation of the incline was the key to the successful working of the whole railway. Therefore a reserve of locomotive power would be needed at the foot of the incline. The site had been bought in good time, in May 1839.[5] In view of the fact that the opening of the first section had been fixed tentatively, for April or May 1840, this in itself was none too soon. Capt. Moorsom, with Bury's help, presented plans and estimates early in July 1839. Those for the station buildings and cottages were thought too expensive, but his plans for the works were accepted, and he at once (19 July), advertised for tenders. That of Sykes & Brookfield for £5,759 was accepted and signed in August.[6] Work began at once and Capt. Moorsom was authorised to order whatever machine tools and equipment he and Bury thought necessary.[7]

On Bury's advice there was to be stabling for some 12 engines on the east side with repair bays for as many more on the west, together with a stationary engine, turnery, brass foundry, smithy etc. on the ground floor; while a second storey was to house a drawing office, joiners' and pattern-makers' shops, with store rooms as well. Work went ahead well till October 1839 when the BC, having wildly overspent through their 'economies' in the Moseley area, decided to 'economise' yet again.

They thought it better, they said, to have the Locomotive Works at Camp Hill instead of at Bromsgrove, and to carry 'the large building only one storey high . . . making it available for all purposes during the partial working of the line.. . . .'[8] Capt. Moorsom was asked for his views on this, and was apparently so pungently forthright that the Board was called in to give a ruling, and Charles Sturge was deputed to go down and investigate. He said that he thought '. . . the Works unnecessarily large, and that only one half [i.e. the north end] of the large engine house should be erected, and that one half only of the cottages should be proceeded with'.[9] Sturge got his way and in December 1839 work was halted. Not unnaturally Sykes and Brookfield claimed £750 compensation for breach of contract. The BC, aggrieved, asked Moorsom for his opinion. Moorsom bluntly told them Sykes and Brookfield were quite justified, and said he was surprised at the moderation of their claim.[10]

With work stopped, the uncompleted buildings attracted the attentions of local vandals, and Moorsom asked to be allowed to swear in a posse of railway policemen to protect the buildings; another expense which the BC grudged, but had to accept.[11] Eventually work was re-started, and the truncated shell was finished in April 1840. This was inspected by Capt. Moorsom, a deputation from the BC and Edward Bury. Perhaps it was due to Bury's influence that the committee were induced to build a house for the locomotive superintendent on the approach road to the station; and also to build a shed near the works for locomotive coke at a cost of 'not more than £100'.[12]

As mentioned above the shell of the works was finished in April 1840, and Whishaw visited them probably in August of that year.[13] It is noticeable that he confines his description of the works to measurements and the intended use of each part of the building. Now Whishaw was interested in all kinds of machinery. After visiting Wolverton, for instance, he described most of the machine tools he saw there. He would certainly have done so at Bromsgrove if there had been any to describe; but the only mechanical contrivance he saw at Bromsgrove was 'the engine-race and turn-table'. He doesn't mention lathes in the turnery, or even the stationary engine. The inference is simple. *They just weren't there.* In spite of the fact that the building had been finished in April, and the line partially opened in June, the BC had not bothered to take whatever steps were needed to tool up the works at all and it was not for want of asking either. That this conclusion is correct is amply borne out by the despairing report by Creuze and Burgess in September 1840 and partially quoted above.[14] It went on to say: '. . . The Works and Station at Bromsgrove are in a very rough unfinished state. In this connection it is remarkable that no fatal accident has occurred since the opening of the line . . . Nearly all the American engines are very much out of order . . . Several . . . have been retubed, and will probably run for some time longer, though I have no expectation that they will run long enough to wear out those tubes . . .' [i.e. Burgess expects that their iron fireboxes will burn through very soon and need replacing with copper]. Burgess went on to say that he had made enquiries about the cost of replacing Norris iron fireboxes with copper ones from Nasmyth, Haigh Foundry and Middleton, and recommended that '. . . a contract be made with one of these . . . at a rate per engine, and that the Omnibus house at Bromsgrove be set apart for these particular repairs.'[15]

Already then in September 1840, with the line only partially open, the premises as cut down on Charles Sturge's recommendation as unnecessarily large are quite inadequate, and other premises, not built for the purpose were having to be pressed into service. Such repair equipment as there was, had had to be of the 'make-do-and-mend' variety as could be devised by William Creuze or his foreman, Rutherford. However, following Creuze and Burgess' report, quoted above, the BC had bestirred themselves slightly and a trickle of lathes and other much needed equipment had begun to come in; but a large back-log of cripples still needed repair, and it was slow work with primitive tools and an unskilled workforce. Together with this they still had the task of coaxing the least crippled engines into service to keep traffic moving. A David Joy could have done it, and indeed did do just that some 12 years later at Worcester under similar circumstances.[16] Joy did it and revelled in the doing of it because he was that sort of person. But Creuze was not a man of Joy's calibre.

Creuze had one worry less in October 1840. Sykes & Brookfield had, by then, built a bank-engine house for £400.[17] The bankers at least would no longer stand deteriorating outside in all weathers. It was something to be thankful for, but not much. As will have been realised the building airily called the engine house could not hold even half the B&G locomotives under cover. Burgess had, it will be remembered, asked for the use of the omnibus house as a shed for repairs. This request would seem to have gone unheeded as did also Capt. Moorsom's requests for a lean-to shed against the east wall of the works building. It was to be a modest affair some 90ft. × 30ft. covering two tracks into which locomotives could be put under cover for repair. He had asked for this shed repeatedly ever since June 1840, and it had just as often been refused as an 'unnecessary expense'.[18]

With this backlog of repairs, and lack of facilities to deal with them, Creuze gave up the struggle and took refuge in drink. Only Joseph Rutherford battled on, inducing reluctant locomotives to run the trains. Rutherford's death therefore in the Bromsgrove explosion of November 1840, was not only a tragedy for his family, but disaster for the locomotive department. Creuze was by then an alcoholic, and it had been Rutherford who had, in spite of all, maintained some standard of discipline and workmanship in the repair shop. Richard Walworth, foreman at Gloucester was, on Creuze's recommendation, promoted to take Rutherford's place, and in consequence things went rapidly downhill. The cripple sidings filled up while slipshod and dangerous expedients were adopted to keep some of the engines on the road. Accidents were sooner or later inevitable. The first (which put John Donahue, bank-engine driver and his fireman out of action for some 3 to 4 weeks) happened during the last week in March 1841 and was hushed up; but it was impossible to hush-up the second which occurred on the night of 7 April near 'Vigo Bridge' (No. 106) on the incline (see Chapter 21).[19] A 'blow-out' from a carelessly repaired locomotive scalded Creuze to death and seriously injured Walworth and two other unauthorised passengers on the footplate of the *Boston*, which was being used as a transport vehicle for private purposes. The inquest on Creuze's death revealed a scandalous state of affairs in the locomotive department for which the BC were partly responsible, and of which they were blissfully unaware.

Of this accident the *Railway Times*[20] commented caustically: 'A driver leaves his engine on the main line in charge of the stoker without informing the police. It was only the vigilance of the policeman which enabled him to notice an engine standing where it had no right to be, and move it away thus avoiding a collision in which the Mail could have been involved. . . . The stoker drives the engine up and down the line for some time and then takes on the footplate unauthorised passengers including a woman. Further he allows one of these to interfere with the controls. . . . The driver had no business to leave his engine on the main line. The Company's employees have no business to consume the Company's fuel and water for their own private purposes. . . . For these irregularities the Superintendent, Mr Creuze, must bear the blame for they were done entirely with his knowledge. . . . We only trust that these acts were irregularities and not the general practice.' Horrifying revelations were made at the Inquest.[21] Particularly so – indeed hair-raising in view of the high steam pressure in Norris boilers – was the evidence of Thomas Horton, a fitter at Bromsgrove. Norris engines, he said, had no mud holes through which their boilers could be washed out. It was necessary therefore to remove a boiler tube for the purpose. Removing a tube and replacing it was laborious and expensive, so it had become the usual practice to remove the tube permanently, and plug the resulting holes in front and rear tube plates. [This would have been reasonably safe had the plugs been threaded and screwed in tight, but that would have been too much trouble.] Horton calmly stated that these plugs were just turned from a piece of iron bar to a force fit size. They were then hammered in and fastened by a steel ferrule. He apparently saw nothing out of the way in this, and assured the coroner that it was perfectly safe. [And this after what had happened a fortnight before to John Donahue on the *William Gwynn*, and a day or so ago to William Creuze on the *Boston*!] Horton said too that in the case of the *Boston*, since they had no iron bar handy, they had used bits of tube instead. They had just sealed off the ends and used them as plugs. The work had been done under Mr Walworth's personal direction.

However Horton did say that he had noticed another engine so fitted with sealed off tube – the *Baltimore*, had that day had its force-fit plugs removed. This had been done on the orders of William Burgess.

Walworth was sacked; G.D. Bischopp, the chief draughtsman, was recalled from his honeymoon to take Creuze's place, and an advertisement for a foreman of locomotives was inserted in the railway press. The *Railway Times* displayed it on 1 May.

Among the short-listed applicants was a young man of Scots/Irish extraction, James Edward McConnell. On 2 July he was offered the job of foreman of locomotives at a salary of £200 per annum with house,[22] and his acceptance was reported by Charles Sturge to the BC on 6 July. Having accepted, however, he began to have second thoughts. The conditions irked him. Charles Sturge had told him that though they intended eventually to put both locomotive and running departments under one head, he would, at present, have control only of the workshops and repair and maintenance of locomotives. G.D. Bischopp, the senior officer, would be outdoor superintendent with control of traffic and engine crews.

This system of divided rule was quite common at the time. It was, for instance, the arrangement on the GJR, at Crewe, where Alexander Allan was foreman of locomotives, and Francis Trevethick the superintendent; but McConnell saw that in the present locomotive crisis on the B&G it would have grave disadvantages. He was to be responsible for the reconditioning of the B&G locomotive stock. The works were cramped and ill equipped. Like his friend David Joy[23] he welcomed the challenge to his ingenuity; but having repaired the engines he wanted control over their handling in traffic; otherwise his work might soon be undone by some drivers' inexpertise. Further, he needed reports on each engine's behaviour under steam on the road. This was vital if they were to be maintained in running order. This was why, having provisionally accepted the post, he met Charles Sturge in Birmingham on 9 July, and told him[24] that unless he was given authority over both engines and their crews, he would have to withdraw. The BC declined to give way over this, and met on 20 July expecting to have to start selection over again. They were pleasantly surprised when Sturge reported that McConnell was at Bromsgrove, and that he had reported for duty on 14 July.

Clearly, something had happened to make McConnell change his mind; but what? In the light of later events, the probability is that after meeting Charles Sturge in Birmingham on 7 July, McConnell had gone down to Bromsgrove and talked things over with Bischopp. He found Bischopp in difficulties too. Bischopp was not a natural leader. He was first and foremost a draughtsman whose skill lay in getting mechanical ideas down on paper; but the building of such machinery and getting it to work, is a very different matter. Further, if our reading of Bischopp's temperament is correct, he does not seem to have been a person endowed with sufficient self-confidence and personality to enable him to cope with problems of personnel and discipline, and in particular those arising from the slackness of the Creuze/Walworth regime.

But whatever the explanation may be, the fact is that McConnell did change his mind, and the most reasonable theory is that he and Bischopp met more than once during that week, liked each other, and decided that they could work out an arrangement which, while keeping for Bischopp his over-all status, allowed McConnell all the observation and control of locomotives and their crews in traffic which he needed. This 'who-does-what' arrangement was soon worked out between them. It was approved by the BC on 3 August, and ratified by the Board in October 1841.[25] What follows is a summary of its main points:

1. With four exceptions all engines were to work to and from Bromsgrove only. [The four exceptions were the Forrester 2-2-2s which were the only locomotives which could be relied on to run the 51 miles between Gloucester and Birmingham without breaking down on the way!] The 8 ton Norrises were to run to Birmingham and back; while the 10 ton Norrises did the Gloucester run.

2. Mr Bischopp was to have a pilot [shunting] engine at Gloucester and a bank engine [assistant engine, probably a class A, but not an A extra] at Camp Hill; and that two spare engines were always to be available for his use at Bromsgrove. [This was in addition to the three 12 ton Norrises which were the regular Lickey Bankers]

3. This policy was to ensure that every engine was inspected at least once in three days and impending trouble caught before it could happen.

4. Mr McConnell would be allowed a free hand in running repairs, with the proviso that he must always consult Mr Bischopp before making alterations or improvements.

5. Mr Bischopp would allow Mr McConnell every facility for obtaining information about the behaviour of any locomotive on the road.

It is abundantly clear that this policy paid off, for by 1 January 1842, at the half-yearly meeting, Bischopp was able to report that all arrears of maintenance in the locomotive department had been made up.

But this is to look too far ahead. We must return to July 1841. Almost the first thing which the board asked Bischopp and McConnell to do, was to prepare a report on the state of the department for possible use at the August half-yearly meeting. This report was to cover the whole department, staff, plant, and locomotives. In it they were expected to include suggestions aimed at increased efficiency and economy. They worked it out together and submitted it to the new chairman Capt. C.R. Moorsom.

In the first place since each was to be in charge of a different side of the work:

1. Each were to have a separate set of books.

2. Bischopp is to have 1 clerk, 1 storekeeper, and 2 foremen.

3. McConnell is to have 1 clerk, 1 storekeeper, 1 timekeeper, 1 foreman at Bromsgrove, and 1 foreman at Gloucester.

4. The shed at Gloucester was to be extended towards the station and partitioned off so as to serve as a shop for occasional repairs.

5. A shed for a pilot engine was to be put up at Bromsgrove nearly opposite the present shed.

6. A shed to cover two lines and pits at Bromsgrove on which engines now stand exposed, was to be built and tooled up for occasional repairs. All these proposals were approved on 3 August 1841.[26]

Note should be taken of item 6. The provision of this shed had been asked for repeatedly ever since June 1840, and as often refused as 'unneccessary expense' was obtained by McConnell within a month of his arrival. This has something to say not only about McConnell, but also about the calibre of the new chairman, Capt. C.R.Moorsom, who, in contrast to many of colleagues on the B&G Board, really knew something about railway management. The staff felt the difference too, for only a week later McConnell reported to the BC that he wished to engage Mr Hutton as clerk, and while he was prepared to continue the services of Mr Luke [timekeeper], 'he will not consent to continue the employment of Mr Whitworth as Storekeeper after what he has seen of the Stores account'.[27] Luke shortly afterwards found it expedient to resign; Whitworth's place was taken by a Mr Penn at 30s. per week, and a Mr Gee was taken on in place of Luke.

Then the locomotives had to be inspected carefully. There is, unfortunately, no information to be found in the Minutes or half-yearly meeting as to how many cripples and sound engines there were and which they were at this time. Such information as we have has had to be deduced from other sources.

The last of the English Norrises, *Lifford* (No. 30), had been delivered in August from Nasmyth, and since both Hick and Nasmyth had noted the defects in the American Norris design, and had taken steps to counter them, it could be presumed that they would be reasonably reliable in traffic.

Apart from routine maintenance the four sturdy 'Forresters' would give no trouble; but four other engines were in such a state as to be incapable of running at all. These were the Stephenson 0-4-0 *Leicester*, the John Jones 0-4-2 *Southampton* and two Norris B's *Moseley* and *Pivot*. They had all suffered fearfully at the hands of Thomas Fowler the Contractor. *England* too, was in a bad way for the same reason; but Bischopp and McConnell decided that these would have to wait for attention until the back-log on the others – all American Norrises – had been cleared up. There is no evidence as to which or how many of these were at Bromsgrove for heavy repairs in July–August 1841, but the indications are that the number was dangerously high.

Both Bischopp and McConnell knew that it would be touch-and-go whether they would be able to keep the traffic moving with their existing stock of ailing locomotives. From what the Chairman and Charles Sturge had told them, they knew that there was no chance of the B&G investing in any more engines for the present. They would have to do their best with what they had.

They took stock of them, and decided that whatever might be done in future for the out-and-out cripples these would have to be left alone for the present. The banking engines must be kept in good order for their own particular duty. Three pilot (shunting) engines were needed, one at Gloucester, another at Camp Hill, and a third at Bromsgrove. The four reliable 'Forresters' were to be rostered for the mail trains; and because of the unreliability of the remainder, four spare engines would be needed of which one was to be stationed at Gloucester, a second at Camp Hill, while two should be kept in reserve at Bromsgrove.

With four engines out of action, as mentioned previously, this left only twelve engines out of a stud of thirty to run the daily services. This should have been ample for a main line of only 51 miles, but both Bischopp and McConnell could see that most of these were in urgent need of 'shopping'. Even a few break-downs could land them in serious trouble. Accordingly they decided that the best way to meet trouble was to forestall it. That was why in their report, summarised above, they recommended that Bromsgrove should become a 'posting station' for the change of engines. This would give McConnell the opportunity he needed to examine each engine at least once in three days and so catch trouble before it happened.

Other matters had to be considered in their report, in addition to the condition of the locomotive stock. Foremost among these was their running cost. Between July and December 1840 the average cost per locomotive mile had been at the astronomical figure of 2s. 9d. This was partly because of the short life of the American fireboxes and boiler tubes and the cost of their replacement. Some of this work had been done and had produced savings in the next half year, so that the cost per locomotive mile had dropped in July 1841 to 1s. 11¾d., but this figure was still much too high. The completion of the retubing and fireboxing programme could be expected to produce further savings in the August–December period; but the real problem was the huge appetite which all Norrises had for coke. Both As and Bs were burning, on average, some 48lb. per mile. This was nearly twice the figure reported from other railways. To counter this, Bischopp proposed to introduce a 'Coke Premium Plan' as had been tried out on other railways, notably the North Midland. He would work out a norm lower than the average. Each driver and fireman would keep their own particular engine, and their fuel would be issued in bags of specified weight, and the amount left at the end of each day's work would be recorded together with the mileage covered. Then at the end of a specified period (say 3 months), each crew would qualify for a bonus on their wages for each lb. of fuel saved per mile on the norm. He had already sounded out the views of the locomotive men, and had to admit that they were less than enthusiastic, on account of all the extra work it was likely to involve, but he felt that opposition might be overcome if the Board would agree to award a bonus figure sufficiently large to make it worth their while. The proposal was 'left on the table'. The A Extras on the Lickey were more voracious even than the As and Bs. The bank-engines had to be kept in steam for 16 hours every day, and in consequence their coke consumption was 92.41lb. per mile travelled, and their operating cost was 17s. 5d. per trip of 5 miles, for only 2½ miles of which they were doing revenue earning work.[28]

Bischopp and McConnell had ideas about this and other problems but though these ideas would, and eventually did, reduce operating costs, the putting of them into practice would involve capital outlay, and this the Board as a whole was reluctant to consider. They were fortunate however in that from the start of their new regime at Bromsgrove, the B&G had a chairman who was exceptional for those days.

Capt. C.R. Moorsom, RN, had gained considerable experience in railway management on the the L&B where he had been joint secretary since 1833. This experience led to him being invited to assume the chairmanship of the B&G left vacant by the resignation of Joseph Walker in December 1840.

When Capt. Constantine took over, things were, as we have seen, at a very low ebb indeed. He admitted afterwards that had he known just how bad they were, he would never have undertaken the chairmanship;[29] but, having given his word he was bound to honour it and try, with an inexperienced staff, (he tactfully refrained from applying that adjective to the board!), to bring some order into the chaotic affairs of the company.

He, with Charles Sturge, was a member of the selection committee which appointed McConnell, and was glad to have in authority in the locomotive department, a young man who not only had ideas, but also the ability and determination to carry them out. On his side, McConnell found in Capt. Moorsom a chairman who, in contrast to many of his colleagues, was not just interested in the railway as a means of producing dividends, but who really was interested in, and knowledgeable about, the numerous and varied problems involved in running a railway. Whether he agreed with them or not, Capt. Moorsom was ready to listen to new ideas, and was often able to present them to the board or the BC in such a way as to win acceptance; whereas if put forward bluntly by Bischopp or McConnell they would probably have been dismissed as impracticable or too costly.

Bischopp's coke premium plan was a case in point. Suggested in June, it was not until October that the chairman won the BC over to offering a worthwhile premium of 20s. per 1lb. of coke saved per mile on the norm[30] and to agree to try it out for 6 months – with results, as we shall see later, which were well worth while. Later too it was with the chairman's encouragement and backing that Bischopp and McConnell were allowed to carry out experiments with the bank-engine *Philadelphia* which were to result in the cutting of the cost of the Lickey working by more than half. The chairman approved too, and gave encouragement for McConnell's plan to fit larger driving wheels to some of the Norrises to make them more useful for passenger traffic even though, as Charles Sturge gloomily pointed out, new sets of driving wheels would cost £100 per pair.

But McConnell was not only interested in locomotives. He was interested in his workmen too. He had ideas about the organisation of labour in the works so that each man had his job, knew what he was doing and why. It has been alleged that Daniel Gooch preferred his enginemen to be illiterate. That may or may not be true of Gooch, but the reverse was true of McConnell. He wanted his mechanics and enginemen to better their status among railway servants by taking a pride in themselves and their jobs. Soon after his arrival at Bromsgrove (September 1841), he called a meeting in the station house in order to launch what came to be known as the railwaymen's library. The report (*Gloucester Journal*, 18 September) says that 'above 50 of the persons present enrolled their names as subscribers'. McConnell was the right man to start that sort of thing. He, like his work force, had started at the bottom and, being largely self-taught, was himself an illustration of the scheme he proposed. This fact should be borne in mind, and should cause to be treated with a certain reserve, allegations made later by 'Veritas Vincit', about his conduct towards his work people. The railwaymen's library, once launched, continued and apparently prospered even though at first, authority in the shape of the BC looked at it somewhat askance! But there came a day in March 1844 when, choosing his moment, McConnell asked the Board for a contribution.[31] The request was 'laid on the table', but a week later McConnell was told that they had voted the library twelve guineas (£12 12s. 0d.). We get the impression however that they were still somewhat suspicious for, instead of giving McConnell the money, they deputed Messrs Bowley and Beilby to 'choose and buy such books as they shall consider suitable for Mr McConnell's railwaymen's library'! We cannot help wondering how far their ideas of suitability accorded with those of McConnell's railwaymen!

But to return to 1841–42. At the half-yearly meeting held in February 1842 the chairman was able to report[32] that, as a result of three months working of the coke premium plan, coke consumption on the main line had fallen to 36.6lb. per mile as compared with the previous 48lb., and that enginemen had earned £73 in coke premiums. By this and other means (the clearing up of the backlog of locomotive repairs, for instance), the cost per locomotive mile had been cut from 1s. 11¾d. to 1s.7d. It was still much too high however, for as yet Bischopp and McConnell had been unable to do anything about the bank-engines. Their report on the locomotives as given to the Board previous to the meeting[33] was terse and to the point, but tantalisingly gives no detail. This is all it says:

Locomotives in working order during the past 6 months	22
Average number under repair during the past 6 months	5
Locomotives not in use	3
Total	30

The locomotives not in use are described as 'two old engines and one disc'. The 'old engines' were of course *Leicester* and *Southampton* which had been bought second hand, and the 'disc' was *Moseley*, which had been fitted experimentally with a Disc engine (see Chapter 18).

Clearly their regular examination plan had paid off, and the 'under repair' figure had been reduced to that for normal routine maintenance. Bischopp and McConnell were now able to give practical expression to their plans for cutting the cost of working the Lickey; plans which they had been discussing with the chairman during the past months.

The bank-engines were expensive not only because they had to be in steam for 16 hours out of the 24, but also because they only earned revenue on half their mileage. If therefore the other half of their trip could also be made revenue earning, while cutting out mileage for other engines, costs would fall appreciably. Briefly, Bischopp and McConnell were planning to rebuild the bankers with increased adhesive weight, and consequently greater tractive effort. The trials held in August 1841 when Edward Bury visited Bromsgrove with one of his engines (see Chapter 23), had shown that the A Extras had power and to spare, if only they had the extra weight to enable their driving wheels to grip. If this could be arranged it would be possible to do away with the expense of double-heading up the Lickey.

The Class Bs were now in reasonably good condition. Apart from routine maintenance it was unneccesary to bring them to Bromsgrove for inspection after every trip. The bank engines working alone could take trains up the incline, and hand over to the class Bs at Blackwell. On the down journey the Bs would come off at Blackwell and their trains be taken over by returning bankers which would thus be in revenue earning service for the second half of their trips as well.

Bischopp made detailed plans and elevations of an A Extra as they hoped to rebuild her; but the arrangements at Blackwell outlined above would necessitate the establishment of a sub-shed there to provide shelter and servicing facilities for the Class Bs. These would have to be adequately planned, but in order not to alarm the Board or BC the cost would have to be kept as low as possible. Once a workable scheme had been evolved the chairman put it to the BC on 18 January 1842. It is doubtful however if either the committee or the secretary really grasped what it was all about. The Minute [34] was recorded obscurely thus:- 'Proposed siding on top of the Lickey. To be laid on the Down line side for the purpose of carrying out the contemplated arrangement of working the engines without ascending or descending the Lickey incline.' 'Ordered. That the above proposal be laid on the table for further consideration.' That the plan, thanks to the chairman, did secure the cautious approval of the BC, and that Bischopp and McConnell were allowed to rebuild *Philadelphia*, is shown by an entry dated 8 March 1842[35] 'read letters from Mr McConnell of 3rd, 5th, and 7th of March about water and coke tanks fitted to the bank-engine in order to run without tender, stating that the plan answered perfectly and that the coke consumed per day was reduced from 17 to 13 bags.'

This evidence of economy pleased the Committee greatly and once *Philadelphia's* final tests proved successful, it is clear that the rebuilding of the other two (*Boston* and *William Gwynn*) was authorised and went ahead quickly, for on 5 April Mr Wetherall produced a revised diagram of train working intended to come into force on 1 May; and it was ordered that '. . . the Works neccessary at the top of the Lickey to allow for the New Plan be set in hand at once'.[36] The bank-engines as rebuilt were no beauties. The harsh angular lines of their saddletanks saw to that. Clark[37] gives a diagram (illustrated here) but no more. It is a pity that no detailed drawing is available, but those prepared by G.D. Bischopp for the Institute of Civil Engineers were lost, though the paper he presented survives.[38]

Philadelphia is the locomotive he described. Her tender had been removed as an unneccessary 7 tons of dead weight. Enough coke for the 5 mile trip was carried in bunkers on each side of the footplate which was now enclosed at the rear by a protective railing. 400 gallons of water were carried in the ungainly looking saddletank. It was fabricated of sheet iron and was 8ft.9in. long and 3ft. deep at the sides. The tank's base was curved to fit the boiler on which it was bedded down on a layer of felt. Four wrought iron straps held it in position.

In addition to the normal controls on the footplate, a stop-cock linked the safety valve to a pipe which led into the water tank. The driver could thus use waste steam for feedwater heating. The Norrises were very free steamers and frequently blew off all the way up the bank. It will be remembered that in 1919 Mr Fowler used a similar device for his Lickey banker, No. 2290.

Two more points may be noted. It had been found that the boiler tubes, 8ft.11in. in length, tended to sag. A centrally fitted tube plate now prevented this and incidentally strengthened the boiler to withstand the vertical and lateral stresses imposed on it by the weight of the saddle tank and the surge of water within it. The second point was that the locomotive was now braked. This was an unusual feature on locomotives at the time, but was essential for a locomotive most of whose life was to be spent working on a 1 in 37½ gradient. The brakes were flexible steel plates the width of the driving wheel tread, and to which sectional hardwood blocks had been fitted. One end of the brake band was pivoted on a stud projecting from the main frame forward of the driving wheel. The pressure of the brake on the tread was adjusted by a screw attachment at the footplate end. It is not clear whether the engine had brakes on both driving wheels. If so, each brake would have to be adjusted separately. It was claimed however that one brake was quite capable of holding the locomotive anywhere on the incline.

That they had teething troubles was only to be expected. *Philadelphia* as rebuilt was the first saddletank engine in Britain. Even when her tank had been cut down to a capacity of 400 gallons it still fouled the water cranes at Bromsgrove which naturally had not been designed for that type of engine; so, rather than reduce the tank's capacity further it was the water cranes which had to be adapted to suit.

'Veritas Vincit'[39] expatiated on this and other troubles with glee, and called the rebuilding of the Norris bankers one of 'Mr McConnell's expensive and futile improvements'. He was wrong on three counts. The rebuilding had, from the first, been a joint affair between Bischopp and McConnell. It is beyond question that they planned and worked the project out together. However, by the time that the rebuilt bankers actually went into action on 1 May 1842, Bischopp had resigned to take up an appointment with the Disc Engine Company of Birmingham, and McConnell was left in sole charge. That error therefore may be excused, but not so the others. From 1 May the three saddletanked bankers settled into their new routine and won the approval of General Pasley, Chief Railway Inspecting Officer of the Board of Trade.

The Board and the BC were pleased too for not only had the bankers now got a reserve of power enabling them to handle single handed all but exceptional loads; but also for the first time real economy had been achieved in working the Lickey without loss of efficiency. Whereas during the six months ending 31 December 1841 the bankers had travelled 6,210 miles at a cost of £324 13s. 6d. for coke, the coke bill for the 6,600 miles the bankers travelled from July to December 1842 was £165 19s. 0d., a quite remarkable reduction and the cost of working the Lickey had fallen from 17s. 5d. to 7s. 1½d. per bank-engine trip. So much for 'expensive and futile improvements'!

As mentioned above, by the time that the saddletanked bank engines went into action McConnell was in sole charge at Bromsgrove. The agreement McConnell signed on becoming locomotive superintendent is interesting. His salary was to be £250 per annum with house so long as the running costs per locomotive mile remained at 1s.6d. Thereafter for every 1d. by which he cut running costs over a six months period he would be paid a further £50 per annum till he had reached a maximum of £500. A clause inserted into the Agreement stipulated that '. . .only those economies which resulted from Mr McConnell's own initiative would count for the purpose of calculating his salary'. Thus a fall in the price of fuel or materials would not benefit him, nor would such economies as wage cuts or staff reductions ordered by the Board. To cut a long story short, however, from 1844 to 1846 McConnell was earning maximum salary having succeeded in reducing running costs to nearly 10½d. per locomotive mile.

But to return to 1842. In this change of policy in which the whole locomotive and running departments were put under one head it is possible to see the wise hand of the chairman, Capt. C.R. Moorsom. His hand is evident too in the appointment of McConnell to this position. During the nine months or so that he had been with the company, McConnell had, with Bischopp's backing, revolutionised the department, and still had plenty of ideas for further development. That he had in fact been able to carry through such improvements as had been made was in great part due to the support given him by the chairman. The Board and the BC were, as a whole, reluctant to sanction further outlay, and the chairman often had hard work to persuade them. McConnell was fortunate that in his first two years in the locomotive department of the B&G he had a chairman who was exceptional for those days.

The report which McConnell prepared on the locomotive stock for the August 1842 half-yearly meeting is the fullest and most detailed that we have in the records of the B&G; but all the same it only tells half a tale. We found it not detailed enough, and therefore tantalising. He divided the locomotives up into classes according to their wheel arrangement. The 4-2-0s which were all Norrises were subdivided into classes according to the diameter of their driving wheels, and the dimensions of their cylinders. It is possible even with this limited information to identify some of the engines; the four 2-2-2 Forresters for instance, and the one 0-4-2, *Southampton* which had been out of use in July 1841, but which had now been restored to running order again;

but it would have helped the historian greatly if he had referred to the engines by their names or numbers. There should have been 34 of them; but whereas *Southampton* was tough enough to have been repairable even after the shocking treatment given her by the contractor, Fowler, one 0-4-0, *Leicester*, and one Norris B, *Moseley*, were 'write-offs'.

In the list we find four new locomotives. There are two 2-2-0 Burys numbered 33 and 34, and surprisingly two Norris A Extras numbered 31 and 32, and named *Niagara* and *New York*. The two Burys were named *Evesham* and *Kempsey* respectively, and had been bought early in 1842 when McConnell had suggested that there was a need for more locomotives to help out with a hoped for increase in traffic in the summer. Both McConnell and the board thought it would be tactful to order them from Edward Bury who had retired from his visit to the B&G in the previous summer in something of a huff! (see Chapter 23).

A 'sweetener' they thought, would not come amiss, and after all Edward Bury was at that time an influential man in the railway world. The 'Burys' were good little engines provided they were not over-loaded.

The acquisition of two more A Extras in May 1842 doubtless gave McConnell and the board considerable satisfaction. This time it was Norris who had been caught off balance; after some protracted bargaining he was forced to let them go for £1,000 each. They were probably saddletanked like the others, and may on occasion have been used as auxiliary bank-engines, though there is no concrete evidence for this; but there is evidence that they were used for freight and passenger service elsewhere on the line.

In his report on the locomotive department mentioned above, McConnell said that he had been experimenting with the Norrises in order to see what difference, if any, a change in the size of their driving wheels would make. Thus three Class A's had been fitted with 5ft. diameter wheels; three had been given driving wheels of 4ft.9in., while three Class Bs had driving wheels of 4ft.3in. He does not say whether he was pleased with the result; but he does say that during the last six months(Jan–June 1842), out of the whole stud of 32 engines on his 'active list' he never had more than four engines under repair at any one time. Bearing in mind the appalling situation which had prevailed a year ago, this was a splendid achievement. As far as the locomotive department was concerned, the B&G was on its feet again, and in better shape than it had been before; but this success had been a costly one, and the price was reflected in the dividends or rather the lack of them.

Mutterings of discontent were in fact heard at that August 1842 general meeting and reached full force in 1843. These were led and fomented by a certain Mr Tartt or Tate. These people neither knew nor cared about the problems involved in running a railway. Other railways, they argued, paid good dividends, and they expected the B&G to do the same. An outstanding example of their stupidity was their criticism of the chairman for having introduced a locomotive and rolling stock depreciation fund to offset the cost of repairs and replacements. This fund was, quite correctly, charged against revenue and included among operational expenses. This they claimed was a book-keeping trick to reduce the disposable balance and deprive them of the dividends to which they were entitled. It was, as we have seen in another chapter, in vain that the chairman told them the truth, namely that it was he who had been called in to rescue a mismanaged and nearly bankrupt concern, and that he was in the process of putting it on its feet again. He was howled down, and a quite unconstitutional Committee of Enquiry (CofE) was set up by share-holders led by a self-styled expert named Tate. They poked and pried into company affairs keeping the company's servants on tenterhooks. Capt. Moorsom resigned the chairmanship in protest, and the secretary, George King went with him. McConnell was minded to go too, but fortunately for the B&G, the chairman dissuaded him. In this connection it was fortunate for McConnell that he had had some 18 months under a good chairman to establish himself firmly in the locomotive department, and to prove his worth to the company. It was notable that though during the troubled year of 1843 he spoke his mind on occasion to both the Board and the CofE we have never found in the Minutes any suggestion that his services should be dispensed with, even though the heads in other departments might and did roll. Large numbers of staff were either declared redundant or had their wages cut. Pointsmen were discharged, and firemen were ordered to do their work instead. This called forth, and rightly so, caustic comments from 'Veritas Vincit'.[40] Footplate men did not escape either. On 20 April acting, as he made quite clear, under protest, McConnell issued a directive from the Board that in future a driver's pay would be reduced from 7s. to 6s. per day of 12 hours and firemen from 6s. to 5s. Mail train drivers and firemen got off more lightly with a cut of only 6d. a day.

As a result of this directive all drivers and firemen gave in their fortnight's notice, and McConnell had to search around for fresh crews. Six fitters from the works at Bromsgrove volunteered their services together, it is alleged, with his sister Elizabeth, and after work in the evenings he gave them a 'crash course' in driving and firing on the shunting engine kept there. Together with McConnell there would be some 8 people on the engine and tender. The fitters were numbered off 1 to 6. On the first outing No. 1 drove and 2 fired, watched by the remainder till it was the turn of Nos. 3 and 4 and so on. 'Veritas Vincit' held this up to ridicule. He was shocked that a woman should be allowed on the foot-plate of what he dubbed 'Mr McConnell's Amusement Engine'.

All the same, strike or no strike McConnell had to keep the trains running and prepare for the worst in the short time available. As it happened however he never had to call on the 'fitter drivers'. During the first week in May he was able to report that all drivers except Hinett wanted to keep their jobs on the directors' terms and that he had accepted them back with the exception of four whom he had previously found unreliable, and whose places he had filled with men coming from the St Helens, and the Stockton & Darlington Railways. Hinett's departure was a loss to the company. A fine driver, cool headed and reliable, he had, only a short time before been commended for bravery at a mishap at Defford. Hinett left the B&G and joined the BrG which was then in process of construction.

There is no positive evidence of how McConnell managed to persuade the others to change their minds, but a clue is provided in the CofE's final report issued in June 1843.[41] 'In the wages of engine drivers a very moderate reduction has been made as they have extra duties to perform. The committee would not reduce their wages below those paid on other railways; 'The wages of firemen have been reduced in the same proportion . . . Most of the 'old hands' have remained. Coke saving has been [re] introduced, and is continuing . . .' It is clear from this that McConnell used the coke premium scheme (at which the CofE could not cavil as it was 'in the interests of economy') to bolster enginemen's earnings as nearly as possible up to the previous level. Reading between the lines, it is clear that on the whole McConnell's relations with his enginemen and workforce must have been good, and that they felt able to trust him to get the best terms possible for them under the circumstances.

On the other hand he must have been able to impress on the committee that he knew what he was talking about. This fact is mentioned in their final report. 'The Committee must here state that they feel much indebted to the Company's intelligent Superintendent Mr McConnell for his judicious management . . . and for his zealous attention to the interests of the Company generally.' McConnell would have stressed to the committee the responsible and dangerous work performed by his enginemen and had thus secured reconsideration of the cuts originally proposed. The coke saving scheme had, it will be remembered, been introduced by Bischopp in 1841 following its success on the North Midland Railway. It had been tried for experimental periods with fair success, but had not been popular with enginemen on account of the extra work involved; but now McConnell was able to 'sell' it to them as a means of off-setting cuts in their pay. Between January and June 1843 the accounts show that footplatemen earned £197 in coke premiums, and the company's coke bill had fallen from £3,170 in December 1842 to £2,197 in June 1843.

The threatened wage cuts came into effect on 5 May that year and it was in June that the Board, having checked the accounts submitted to them by the secretary, awarded McConnell a rise in salary of £150. 'Veritas Vincit' had this information whispered to him by someone to whom McConnell had confided this news. Being 'Veritas Vincit', and having that sort of mind, he drew the inference that this was McConnell's reward for having engineered the locomotive department wage cuts, and blazoned this abroad in the *Railway Record*. He could not have been more wrong. It had nothing to do with the wage cuts to which McConnell was opposed anyway. The Minutes[42] report that the secretary had examined the accounts of the mileage of the engines and their running costs between 1 July and 31 December 1842, and had found the figures to be 306,192 miles run in revenue earning service at a cost of £18,607 12s. 8d. which worked out at an average cost of 14½d. per locomotive mile. Thus in 6 months, by good management and without the aid of wage cuts, he had reduced the locomotive mile cost from 1s. 6d. to 1s. 2½d. which, by any reckoning, was no mean achievement. Since therefore under his written contract of engagement he was entitled to a £50 rise for every 1d. saved on the average locomotive mile costs, even the dividend conscious CofE could find no excuse by which they might enable the Board to wriggle out of their obligation to pay him the £150 rise in salary which he had earned.

The CofE issued its final report in June 1843. As always happens, some of its recommendations were implemented, and some quietly forgotten as the railway shook itself together again after the upheaval. For instance in the case of staff dismissed as redundant it is noticeable in the records that names of men dismissed sooner or later begin to reappear in the wage and/or salary lists. One who did not reappear however was a driver named Sixsmith whom McConnell dismissed for, as he alleged, passing on information to the press (alias 'Veritas Vincit'). Sixsmith appealed to the Board protesting his innocence, but the Board took no action. Veritas Vincit denied that Sixsmith was his spy, and that may well have been true; 'Veritas Vincit' went on to say that he needed no informants; but when we remember that his strictures covered not only the B&G but railways wide spread all over the country – that is straining credibility a great deal too far! There is a curious twist to this story. We have in our collection a photograph of Locomotive No. 1 of the Sydney & Paramatta Railway in Australia with her driver standing alongside preparatory to the hauling of the opening train in 1854. The locomotive was one of a batch of four designed by McConnell for the S&P Company, and the driver's name is given as Sixsmith. With such an uncommon name, is it stretching credulity too far to imagine that this might be the driver Sixsmith whom McConnell had sacked from the B&G some 11 years before?

For the half yearly meeting in August 1843 Mr Reuben Heaton of Birmingham, who had been the independent inspector of B&G locomotives since 1840, reported that they were in better condition than ever before. No details are given, but McConnell in his report, said that the number on average in good running order during the past six months had been 29; four, on average were under repair at any one time, and only one was out of service and likely to remain so. She is not named, but it is beyond doubt that this locomotive was the *Leicester*.

The 29 locomotives were used in rotation to run the daily services, the average number of locomotives needed for this being 13. Further, with the good condition of the locomotive stock it had been possible to dispense with some 27 of the employees at the works; thus reducing the locomotive department staff to 110.

McConnell had been able to keep his own clerical staff mostly intact, and thus keep himself free for more important practical work. He had probably had to fight hard for this with the CofE and/or the Board, and it was fortunate both for the railway and for himself that he had won. He did not escape criticism in the railway press, notably the *Record* – but such criticism was surely somewhat naive. A locomotive superintendent is not solely responsible for the repair and upkeep of his locomotives. He must be much more than a mere works foreman. He must be forward looking and able to plan for the years ahead, and this, as events of 1844–45 show was precisely what McConnell was doing in 1843. To do this he had to be able to keep abreast of the then rapidly developing railway engineering technology, and perhaps strike out on a line of his own as he did in the case of the breakages, often alarming, in the, then used, wrought iron railway axles. These breakages, seemingly inexplicable, were causing frequent accidents. McConnell was one of the first to tackle this problem which we now call 'metal fatigue'; he began his investigations as early as 1842, and after much experimentation his improved patent hollow axles provided a reliable cure.

Valve gears were an important field for experiment too. Many different types were being evolved to enable steam to be used expansively and therefore more efficiently in the cylinders than was possible with the gab gear fitted to most, if not all of the then B&G locomotives. Having experimented and found what was best for his purpose, he took care that such gear was fitted to his next locomotives viz. *Bristol*, *Hercules*, and *Great Britain*.

The rough riding of locomotives at speed was another problem investigated by McConnell. It was not then generally understood how to counteract the thrust of rotating cranks and reciprocating motion. The effect of this was not too serious at low speed, but when higher speeds were called for, rough running resulted sometimes ending in derailment. The Heaton brothers, whom we have mentioned above in connection with the B&G locomotive inspections, were the first to take the problem up. Following their advice, McConnell experimented with weights between the spokes of the driving wheels of his locomotives to counter-balance the thrust of cranks and driving gear. In this he was no innovator; he was merely doing as an individual what other engineers were also doing to solve this pressing problem.

Engineering problems there were in plenty during this period which might be termed the adolescence of the locomotive, but other problems pressed too on a locomotive superintendent. These were not necessarily engineering problems, but nevertheless they had an important bearing on the welfare of his locomotives.

Water which was fit for locomotive consumption was a vital necessity, not only at Bromsgrove, but elsewhere along the line to Gloucester. Bromsgrove was situated, geologically speaking, at the junction between the Lickey sandstone and the Cotswold oolitic limestone. The latter produced hard water, full of salts as at Droitwich and Cheltenham. This water, however health giving it might be as spa water to humans, had the reverse effect on locomotives and caused priming, and furred up boilers. A well sunk on the works site at Bromsgrove had served for a time, but its water had, by August 1842, become unfit for locomotive consumption. Recourse was had to surface water piped from a stream some 100 yards south of Bromsgrove station, but this was not really adequate and the search went on for a reliable supply. It was not till 1844–45 when the rights were obtained for the tapping of the spring at Pike's Pool, a mile or so up the incline, that a source of good locomotive water was obtained. A well had to be sunk at Blackwell to serve the sub-shed established there. The well at Spetchley continued to give problems as also did the water supply at Eckington. It is not generally known that the roof over the pillared portico at Lansdown station was not only a pleasing arch-itectural feature, but also provided a vast tank for the collection of rainwater for the benefit of B&G locomotives. This device was Capt. W. Moorsom's idea however and dated from the very early days. At Gloucester prolonged negotiations were required with the Dean and Chapter of the Cathedral in order to be allowed to obtain an extra 1000 gallons a day from the Robins Wood spring.

Coke problems loomed large too, either from expense or irregularity of supply. The B&G had from the beginning bought coal and established ovens for coke making at Gloucester. Almost from the time of his arrival, McConnell had considered this wasteful since no attempt was made to collect and either use or sell the coal gas and other by-products of the cokemaking process. He did make an attempt to put the waste heat generated to good purpose in heating locomotive feed water, thus saving fuel; but the apparatus needed was deemed to be too expensive at the time, and the project was never revived.

In 1844 coke problems again loomed large regarding both quality and irregularity of supplies, to say nothing of increasing price. It is not surprising therefore that at McConnell's own suggestion (which of course was put forward 'in the interests of economy'), he was authorised to set up a gasworks at Bromsgrove[43] so that both works and station could be lit, and a supply of locomotive coke made. Tenders were let by January 1845 and gas was being produced some six months later. By July–August 1846 more gas was available than works and station could consume, and the surplus was piped up the Lickey to illuminate the yard at Blackwell. Gas was also sold to the Bromsgrove Gas Company.

As noted above the CofE report was issued in June 1843 and the recommendation that the railway should become 'Sole Carrier' and thus expand the goods traffic was persisted in. McConnell was quick to take advantage of this. He asked for, and got, three goods locomotives, two of which, *Bristol* and *Hercules* were built to designs carefully prepared by himself. In addition to these he planned, designed, and himself built at Bromsgrove the *Great Britain* to haul the heavy goods trains up the Lickey.

By the time however that *Great Britain* emerged from Bromsgrove in June–July 1845, the B&G and the BRG had unofficially amalgamated to form the Bristol and Birmingham Railway, and the B&B had, in its turn been leased by the Midland Railway with the prospect of complete absorption in the following year. Though McConnell remained in charge the additions made thenceforward to the locomotive stock were under Midland Railway auspices and paid for with Midland Company money. Such particulars as are known about them appear in the appendix.

Giving evidence before the Gauge Commission of 1845, McConnell aired his views on the capabilities of both broad and narrow gauge engines, and on how he worked the B&G section of the B&B. He considered that the broad gauge had no real advantage in either speed, safety or power. At the moment broad gauge engines were thought to run with greater steadiness at speed, but the narrow gauge engines could be made equally capable of such feats if required.

Three broad gauge engines were kept at Gloucester, the remaining eight being stabled at Bristol. The BrG provided a daily service of eight trains each way. The B&G shed at Gloucester housed eight engines and the B&G section ran fourteen trains daily, four of which were 'short trains' between Cheltenham and Gloucester only. If, he maintained, the narrow gauge were continued right through to Bristol, the number of engines required to work the line could be greatly reduced. He then went on to describe how he worked the B&G section of the railway, namely from the top of the Lickey to Birmingham with one set of engines, and from Bromsgrove to Gloucester with another, leaving the Lickey to be worked by the bank engines alone. If narrow gauge to Bristol could be achieved, the run from Bromsgrove to Bristol and back (151 miles) could be regarded as one day's work for an engine. There should be no difficulty about this, he said, provided the locomotives were kept in proper order.

But it was not till 1854 that this desirable state of affairs was finally obtained, and by that time McConnell had been in charge of the LNWR Works at Wolverton for some seven years. He had been offered this post and had accepted it in January 1847. On his release in February from his position at Bromsgrove the following Minute[44] was recorded: 'That intimation be given to Mr McConnell that Mr Kirtley is now in charge of the Locomotive department, and that the Secretary do assure Mr McConnell that the Directors are much gratified that his efficiency on the Birmingham & Bristol Railway has ended in his promotion to his present important position.' Once Matthew Kirtley had assumed control of the locomotive stock it was absorbed into that of the Midland, and Bromsgrove Works were closed in favour of the centralisation of all locomotive construction and repairs at Derby. In August 1847 Bromsgrove Works were let to Messrs Kinder and Johnson, Coachbuilders of Worcester, for a rent of £316 p.a. which included the occupation of McConnell's house. For some reason, however, when the lease expired Kinder and Johnson did not renew it, and Bromsgrove became one of the Midland Railway's most important wagon works, and McConnell's house the residence of the station-master. The fate of the B&G locomotive stock can be traced from information supplied in the appendix; but their replacement and the subsequent changes made by the MR are beyond the scope of the present work.

CHAPTER EIGHTEEN
LOCOMOTIVES
by Rev. W.V. Awdry

General particulars of all locomotives used by the B&G and the B&B (standard gauge) will be found in the table in the appendix. This table was researched by the late Mr Edward Craven who gave the author permission to use it. The notes which follow are mainly anecdotal in character and derive either from the B&G Minutes or the Press. They are confined to those locomotives only which were actually built for or by the Birmingham and Gloucester Company.

THE NORRISES

A feature which made the B&G unique among early British railways was their employment of American built locomotives. In 1840, their opening year, 17 out of their 23 locomotives were Norrises. It sounds very odd, but the whole thing probably arose from a streak of obstinacy on Capt. W.S. Moorsom's part. When the line had first been planned, Robert Stephenson, Brunel and others had scouted the idea of using locomotives to work the Lickey Incline, so very naturally Moorsom was determined at all costs to prove them wrong. Somehow he had obtained a copy of Norris' Trade Circular of 1838, and the hill climbing feats of Norris engines were, he felt, the answer to his problem. It was not true, as F.S. Williams alleges[1] that Moorsom had been to the United States and actually seen them at work. He had merely, very naively one feels, taken at their face value statements made in a catalogue.

The late Mr P.C. Dewhurst made an exhaustive study of Norris engines[2] and maintains that reports of their hill-climbing feats were substantially true, but he claims also that Norris got his results not by revolutionary design, but by using two 'gimmicks', one of which was mechanically sound and the other fraudulent. The first was the arrangement of the coupling bar between engine and tender. The bar on the engine was set at an angle (see the illustration of *England* later in the chapter). It rose from the level at which it met the bar on the tender up to a point where it was bolted to the underside of the footplate just behind the firebox. When therefore the engine was under load there was a downward pull at the firebox end of the drawbar causing the engine to pivot about the driving axle, thus throwing extra adhesive weight on the driving wheels in order to give the engine a high adhesion rate in relation to the load.

While the above gimmick is mechanically sound the second savoured of trickery. It lay in the safety valve and pressure gauge. J.E. McConnell soon discovered this, and mentioned it in a paper which he read before the Institute of Mechanical Engineers.[3] '. . . The pressure however on the American engines was very fallacious, for the spring balance only indicated about *⅓ of the actual pressure in the boiler . . .*' (author's italics). No wonder the Norrises were lively engines and got away smartly with their trains! No wonder also that when the first Norrises arrived in this country, and were tried out with an independent mercury pressure gauge set for a maximum of 55lb. per square inch,[4] they failed to perform what Norris had assured the B&G Board they could do.

And yet, although the engines failed their tests, the B&G bought them! The whole business sounds very odd. How was it possible for Norris, operating from the other side of the Atlantic, to jockey the B&G directors into such a position that they had to buy whatever locomotives he chose to send them, locomotives moreover which they had already rejected as inadequate?

It is an intriguing story. The facts were these. Capt. Moorsom and the directors were interested in one thing and one thing only, namely an engine which could lift traffic up the Lickey. Capt. Moorsom thought he knew more about engines than he really did. The directors knew nothing. Norris and William Gwynn, his agent, quickly sized them up and quite simply resolved to unload as many engines on them as they could.

In November 1838 Gwynn undertook that Norris would supply, for £1,750, *a 12 ton engine capable of lifting 75 tons up a gradient of 1 in 38 at 15 m.p.h.* (author's italics), and also an 8 ton engine able to take gross loads of 100 tons up 1 in 300 at 20 m.p.h.. The 8 ton locomotive would cost £1,545.[5] If these engines were approved, i.e. *if their performance matched the directors' stipulations* (authors' italics), then the B&G agreed to buy two more of the larger and 6 more of the smaller engines at the price stated. It is quite clear that while they thought the smaller engines might be useful and agreed to buy them, they did so only by way of a 'sweetener' for Norris. It was the 12 ton engine for the Lickey which they really wanted.

The agreement was duly signed and sealed by both Norris and the B&G Board; but Norris was 3,000 miles away and knew it! *England*, a small 8 ton engine, was duly shipped to Liverpool. She was off-loaded in March 1839, and reassembled under the direction of Norris' fitter/driver, Israel York. For some reason however no trials were possible till May. Capt. Moorsom's report was disappointing. In only five out of twenty one trial runs had the engine succeeded in performing her stipulated duty. The directors, accordingly, refused delivery and cancelled the order for her six sisters. But Gwynn was a silver-tongued salesman, and somehow managed not only to soothe their ruffled tempers, but also to persuade them that even though the smaller engine had failed to do the lesser task, nevertheless the *larger* engine would be capable of the harder task of lifting 75 tons gross up 1 in 38. Further, and this sounds incredible, he cajoled them into buying *England* after all! (An engine which they had stated that they did not want because it could not do the work they required from it.)

This surely was a triumph of salesmanship, but Gwynn was not yet satisfied. He gave them a week to cool off, and then, visiting the BC, he spun them a heart-rending yarn about the damage which their refusal to buy the six engines would do to Norris' reputation. If they would generously reconsider their decision, Norris would let them have the small engines at the reduced price of only £1,525 each.[6]

The committee, battered perhaps by Gwynn's eloquence, weakly gave in even though at this stage of the proceedings (May–June 1839) they still had time to break with Norris and order from English builders. Certainly, general purpose locomotives of greater power could be had at home at this time for £1,300–£1,400. Astute men of business, as they thought they were, Gwynn had nevertheless managed to beguile them.

Note that Norris had contracted in writing to supply three 12 ton engines to work the incline; but that Gwynn, at this stage, never mentioned the weight of the engine which Norris intended to send next. He merely spoke of a *heavy* or *larger* engine (author's italics). The directors, in their innocence, assumed he meant the 12 ton engine they had been promised; but the overwhelming probability is that when in 1838 Norris contracted to supply a 12 ton engine, *he hadn't even got one on the drawing board!* And though, to do him justice, Norris always had intended to supply the 12 tonners in the end, he needed time in which to design and build them. Hence his instructions to Gwynn to employ delaying tactics.

This is obvious from his next move. He did have a 'larger' engine in stock. She was a 10 ton Class A. He named her *Victoria* and sent her over. She arrived in July 1839. Gwynn ensured there were delays over the trials which took place on the Bolton and Leigh Railway's 1 in 30 incline. She showed that whatever her capabilities might be for hauling traffic on the rest of the B&G, she would be useless as a banker on the Lickey. The directors did not get Capt. Moorsom's report till November. Angrily they resolved: 'That Mr Gwynn be informed that the Company will not accept delivery, but that they will hold the engine, and return it to Mr Norris on the repayment of sums advanced by them'.[7] (These sums were £320 spent on freightage, customs and port dues, paid in order to get possession of the engine for assembly and testing.)

They also cancelled their agreement to buy the six smaller engines. Burgess was sent off to deliver this message to Gwynn. Gwynn was however quite unmoved. His delaying tactics had paid off handsomely. He had put the B&G directors just where he wanted them. He had not only given Norris time to get the 12 tonner into production, but by keeping the B&G directors preoccupied with the bait of the 'heavy' engine, he had excluded from their minds all thought of getting tenders from English builders for an alternative supply of locomotives. It was now too late for the B&G to get any English locomotives built in time for the line's opening in June 1840. This time Gwynn didn't even bother to come and see the directors himself. He sent them a message through Burgess. He still dangled the bait of a 12 ton engine in front of their noses, but now said it would only be supplied on conditions. 'The Secretary reported that he had seen Mr Gwynn who was willing to bind Mr Norris to supply a 12 ton engine . . . provided that the Company would purchase the engine *Victoria*, and carry out the agreement respecting the six 'light' engines dated July 3rd 1839'.[8] The Board argued and haggled, but they could not fail to see that they had been forced into a corner. They sent a message back saying that they were prepared to pay £1,325 for *Victoria* and her tender; £1,000 to be paid at once and the remainder on the receipt of the two small engines scheduled for delivery that month (these were *Atlantic* and *Columbia*). In paying for these however they insisted on withholding 25 per cent of the purchase price until the 12 ton engine had actually been delivered.[9]

The 12 ton engine *Philadelphia* duly arrived in May 1840, and nothing was said about her boiler pressure. She proved successful on the Lickey. An account of her trials does not appear in the Minutes, but Capt. Moorsom published some results later in the *Railway Times* though he made no mention of boiler pressure in spite of being challenged to do so by a persistent correspondent who signed himself 'C.E.' This is not surprising.[10] From a calculation based on the work done Mr Dewhurst estimated that the boiler pressure would have to have been at least 90lb. p.s.i.,[11] but a revelation of that sort in 1840 would have been most disturbing!

Capt. Moorsom was delighted with *Philadelphia*'s performance, and issued a general invitation to Members of the Institute of Civil Engineers to come and see her at work. Dolby's well known picture of the Lickey Incline purports to show *Philadelphia* in June 1840, but commits a number of errors.

In the first place the engine is shown with a sand-box dome and a lock-up safety valve on her boiler. While it is true that a sand-box was fitted, this was not done till July 1840,[12] and though a lock-up safety valve would have been a desirable feature, there is no record of one ever having been fitted to any of the American Norrises. They were however fitted to six of the English built Class As (see below). The sand-box loosely resembles that fitted by Hick to his Class As whilst the safety valve is not unlike those fitted to the front ring of the boilers of Nasmyth's second batch. The first 'Hick' had been delivered in October 1840, and the first of Nasmyth's second batch arrived in June 1841.

It is therefore probable that while Dolby's picture may have been commissioned in June 1840, and Dolby may have visited the Lickey at the time to make a preliminary sketch, the picture as such was not completed till June or July 1841 when he came to Bromsgrove for final details. Imagining from their superficial resemblance that all Norrises were alike he drew the boiler furniture from the first engine or engines he happened to see.[13] However, faults and all, Dolby's picture is, apart from the carving on Scaife's tombstone in Bromsgrove churchyard, the only representation of an A Extra that we have.

CLASS A EXTRA

Driving wheels. 4ft. diameter; cylinders 12½in. × 20in.; weight in working order 12½ tons (illustrated on front cover). In all, the B&G acquired five of these locomotives, and we append below such information as is available about each.

Philadelphia (B&G No. 13) was delivered in May 1841 accompanied by her fitter/driver, John Donahue, who stayed for some years with the B&G. *Philadelphia* came to be regarded as his engine. She successfully underwent her acceptance trials on the Lickey in June 1840, as related above, and easily beat off Edward Bury's challenge in August 1841 (see Chapter 23), after which the capability of the A Extras as banking engines was proved beyond question; but they were expensive brutes, and their operation absorbed a large slice of the B&G's meagre revenue.

It was not until Bischopp and McConnell had saddle-tanked *Philadelphia* (see above, Chapter 17), and by so doing not only reduced their fuel consumption, but increased their haulage capacity, that the cost of working the Lickey was brought down to manageable proportions. *Philadelphia* was taken into Midland Railway stock in 1847 and continued in service either on the Lickey or elsewhere until scrapped in 1856.

William Gwynn (21)   Dimensions as for *Philadelphia*. Delivered in December 1840. In March 1841, with York away on holiday, John Donahue was driving her on a banking turn when a force-fit plug, which he himself had fitted to the firebox tube plate to cure a leaking boiler tube, blew out. The resulting blow back forced open the fire door and scalded both Donahue and his fireman, who were confined as a result to their lodgings at the Vigo Alehouse for some three to four weeks. Unfortunately the warning went unheeded – with dire results (see below). *William Gwynn* was saddle-tanked in March–April 1842, and continued on the Lickey until perhaps 1846. She survived to be taken into MR locomotive stock in 1847, but was sold in May 1852 to a Mr Knox for £250.

Boston (14)   Dimensions as for *Philadelphia*. Her delivery in August 1840 as a spare bank-engine enabled the line to be opened to Cofton Farm on 17 September. On 7 April 1841 a force-fit plug (which had been inserted in her firebox tubeplate under the direction of Richard Walworth, foreman of locomotives) blew out scalding all except one of the five people who were using the locomotive as their own private means of transport. William Creuze, locomotive superintendent, was killed, and an inquest revealed a scandalous state of affairs prevailing at Bromsgrove Works at the time. Saddle-tanked in March–April 1842, on and from 1 May that year the three A Extras put in action McConnell's new system of working the Lickey whereby each bank engine alone hauled traffic up and down, doubling thereby each engine's mileage in revenue earning service, and more than halving their previous cost per mile.

It is perhaps worth mentioning that during the saddle-tanking of *Boston* McConnell tried an alternative method of feedwater heating to that which he used on *Philadelphia*. Aware of the abundant waste heat dissipated up the chimney, an attachment was fitted in the smokebox to trap some of it and divert it back to the water tank.[14] The experiment was unsuccessful, a fact on which 'Veritas Vincit' dilated with malicious glee. Both *Boston* and *William Gwynn* were, in consequence, fitted with the waste steam feedwater heating device which had been successfully employed on *Philadelphia*. We have only mentioned this experiment as it marks the beginning of McConnell's lifelong interest in making the best use possible of smokebox heat which otherwise would go to waste.

Many of his most successful patents including the first ever superheater in 1852, stem from his interest in this problem. *Boston*, like *Philadelphia* was taken into MR stock in 1847, and scrapped in 1856.

Niagara (31); *New York* (32) Dimensions as for *Philadelphia*. In February 1842 the BC received word that '. . . there were two engines of Mr Norris (similar to the Company's bank engines) now lying at Liverpool, and which Mr Norris had, through the medium of the Engineer in Chief, offered for sale to this Company.' The price which Norris would be asking was presumably the £1,750 each which he had charged for the other three. The committee were not at all anxious to buy. However, the company did need fresh locomotive stock and McConnell was sent to Liverpool to look the engines over. On his return he reported on 1 March that they would be worth having if they could be bought cheaply. Doubtless he pointed out to the committee that this time it was Norris who had been caught off balance since no other British railway had shown any interest. They would therefore be in a position to beat Norris down. This idea appealed strongly to the committee, and it was ordered that 'The Engineer in Chief be informed that the Committee will give £2,000 for the two engines.'[15] Two months of haggling followed. By 3 May Norris had dropped his price to £1,100 each, but the committee, still smarting from the events of 1839–40, remained adamant and Norris gave way on 10 May. The engines were delivered by 17 May and McConnell reported that it would cost merely £15–£20 each to put them into working order.[16] It is alleged by Clark[17] that they were saddletanked as the other A Extras had been, but if so this was not done immediately. In the locomotive list which McConnell drew up in August 1842 they were put in a different category to the bank engines. When however in 1847 they were taken over and numbered into the MR stock, they were then numbered consecutively with the A Extra bank-engines. The inference therefore is that they had been saddletanked at some date between September 1842 and August 1846, and possibly used on the Lickey as auxiliaries at busy times. It is probable that they were also used on the main line as well since *Niagara* has been named as the engine hauling the down passenger train involved in the accident at Defford in September 1845. They did not long survive the MR takeover. *Niagara* was sold in May 1851, and *New York* in April 1855. Both must have seen hard service for they only fetched £200 each.

THE CLASS Bs

Driving wheels originally 4ft. diameter (later 4ft. 3in., 4ft. 6in., 4ft. 9in., 5ft.) Cylinders 10½in., × 18in. Weight in working order 8 tons (see illustration).

England (5) was the first acquired by the B&G. She was landed at Liverpool in charge of Norris' fitter/driver Israel C. York who stayed with the B&G for many years. An account of her unsuccessful trials and the haggling which followed has been given above, but in spite of failing all tests the B&G were 'conned' into buying her. They set her to work as a ballast engine on the Moseley/Lifford section and she suffered in consequence from neglect and ill treatment. Out of sorts in 1840, she was reported out of action in August 1841 and again in February 1842. It is probable that she was sold to the Disc Engine Company with *Moseley* in 1843; but the Disc Company must themselves have disposed of her at some unspecified date, for David Joy in his diary[18] records sketching and riding on her at a Nottinghamshire colliery in 1851. 'The little thing could pull,' he wrote, 'but she was odd, plenty of cast iron in her. Even the crosshead pins . . .'

Atlantic (7), *Columbia* (8), *Birmingham* (9), *Gloucester* (10), *W.S. Moorsom* (11) and *Washington* (12) (All dimensions as for *England*), formed the batch about whose acceptance there was so much haggling. They were delivered between November 1839 and August 1840. Only two of them are mentioned by name, *W.S. Moorsom* which hauled the inaugural train on 24 June 1840, while *Gloucester* had the doubtful distinction of being reported by Burgess in September 1840 for having a badly leaking tube plate after less than three months in traffic.

Following J.E. McConnell's arrival, and the traffic arrangements agreed with Mr Bischopp, the Class Bs were rostered to haul the Birmingham–Bromsgrove traffic, while after May 1842 their run was curtailed to Blackwell only, where they handed over their trains to and picked them up from the newly saddletanked bank-engines.

Though kept in good condition it would seem that by 1845 they were found to be underpowered for the work they were expected to do, and none were taken into MR stock in 1847. *Columbia, Gloucester,* and *W.S. Moorsom* were the first to go, being sold to the Taff Vale Railway between September 1845 and January 1846 at prices ranging from £400 to £530. *Atlantic, Birmingham* and *Washington* would seem to have been in better condition for they were sold last and went to industrial concerns between April and November 1846 at a price range of £600 to £720.

Moseley (16) and *Pivot* (17) had the same leading dimensions as the Class B's and are believed to have been a pair of Norris engines shipped over to England as a speculation some time in 1838–39. They were bought by Thomas Banks of Manchester who had set up as a locomotive builder in a small way. *Moseley* was bought by the B&G at the contractor, Fowler's request. He and his drivers had, through neglect and ill treatment, put the engines already supplied to them out of action, and he needed a replacement.[19] *Moseley* arrived in February 1840 and Fowler lost no time in putting her out of action too. Predictably he blamed Banks, who took her back and put her to rights, but by October she was again out of action with a burnt out firebox. This time she was sent to the Haigh Foundry to have a copper one fitted. but she must have remained something of a lame duck, for when in May 1841 the Disc Engine Company, of Birmingham, asked permission to experiment with her the B&G raised no objection.

The agreement was that the B&G were to have the option – if the experiment was a success – of taking the engine, as converted, for a payment of £100 to the Disc Company. If on the other hand the B&G did not want her like that, the Disc Company were to have the option of either buying her outright for £1,100 or else reinstating her original cylinders and motion, paying the B&G in addition £150 compensation for the time she had been out of use. Mr Bischopp was interested in Disc engines (a primitive form of steam turbine;)[20] and it is probable that the experiment had been allowed on his recommendation. It was not a success. The Disc Company thought retubing might help, and the B&G obligingly had this done, but to no avail.

Moseley remained obstinately static, and even Bischopp had to admit in December 1841 that she was useless. She hung about for a long time, taking up valuable space, until at last a solicitor's letter to the Disc Company coupled with the threat of legal action reminded them of their responsibilities, and they bought and removed her in 1843. It is very probable that they took *England* as well.

Pivot, sister engine to *Moseley*, was brought from Banks in July 1840[21] to replace *Leicester* (see below) who by then had 'retired hurt'. Fortunately, for her, *Pivot* did not have to suffer Fowler's brutalities so long as the others; but she was nevertheless on the cripple siding at Bromsgrove when McConnell arrived. But though out of action in July 1841 she was on McConnell's 'active list' in December of that year. It would seem however that she had a reputation for contrariness, and that though some drivers could get on well with her, others could do nothing at all. McConnell therefore tried various experiments to improve her performance. For instance she was the first of all the Norrises to be fitted with 5ft. diameter driving wheels in place of their standard 4ft.,[22] and in 1844 she was reported out of action because of experiments McConnell had been making with her valve gear. 'Veritas Vincit' uses this incident as an excuse for one of his spiteful 'digs' at McConnell in the *Railway Record*. At least one attempt was made to sell her, probably more; but there were no takers, and she survived to be taken into MR stock in 1847, but was withdrawn and scrapped shortly afterwards.

THE CLASS As

The B&G had only three American built locomotives of this class-ification. They were: *Victoria* (6), *Baltimore* (15), and *President* (20).

They had driving wheels 4ft. diameter; Cylinders 11½in. × 20in., and weighed 10 tons in working order.

Victoria, on her arrival in July 1839 was a dreadful disappointment to Capt. Moorsom. In his innocence he had expected that Gwynn's 'larger' engine would be the promised 12 tonner which he desperately needed, but instead he had to write sadly to the BC, 'I have to report that an engine called *Victoria* . . . has been delivered at Liverpool, and brought up on the Bolton Line. This engine however is lighter, being only about 10 tons in weight, than I should have contemplated under the provisions of the Agreement . . . The performance made by this engine is . . . not equal . . . to that which was stipulated for. The fair [presumably – 'average'] amount performed being 39.5 tons gross load carried 13 m.p.h. up an incline of 1 in 30, which is about 15 tons less than an equivalent to the stipulated performance'.[22] As we mentioned above, the directors cancelled the deal, but in vain. They were well and truly caught and had to buy *Victoria*, haggle as they might. Having got *Victoria* they put her to ballast engine work to earn her keep. She seems to have performed reasonably well, for when in March 1840 the directors decided that they needed more 'general-purpose' engines, *Victoria* was withdrawn from line construction, cleaned up and dis-played at Camp Hill as a model for English builders to copy.

Having served as a model, *Victoria* was set to work again and was reported as being under repair at Middleton's Works in June 1840 with Reuben Heaton (the B&G locomotive inspector) noting the cost of the work which the BC insisted should be charged to Thomas Fowler. *Victoria* is not mentioned again in the Minutes. She was entered in the 1847 MR stock list, but was scrapped soon afterwards.

Both *Baltimore* (15) and *President* (20) would appear to have led uneventful lives mainly, it is to be presumed, on the Gloucester–Bromsgrove run. They are each mentioned once and once only. In April 1841 following the 'Boston Explosion' William Burgess made an inspection at Bromsgrove and found that *Baltimore* had been given a 'force-fit' tubeplate plug similar to that which had blown on the *Boston*. He at once ordered that it should be removed and a proper repair made. *President*'s mention came in February 1842 when McConnell announced that she, with some others, had been fitted with 5ft. diameter driving wheels. Both engines were entered in the MR stocklist, but were subsequently sold to a Mr Pickering for £100 each.

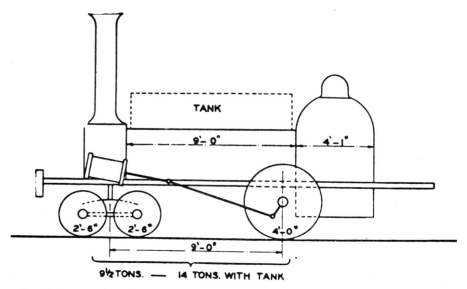

Class A Extra, as later fitted with saddle tank (From *Railway Machinery*, D.K. Clark, 1855).

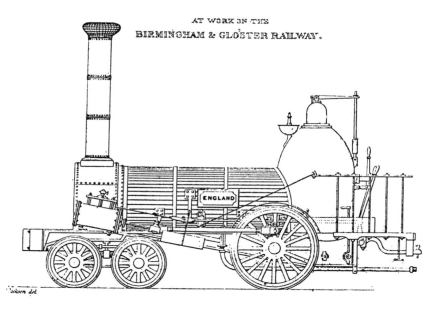

Norris Class B, *England* for B&G Railway (David & Charles; *Railways of Great Britain and Ireland*, Whishaw, 1840).

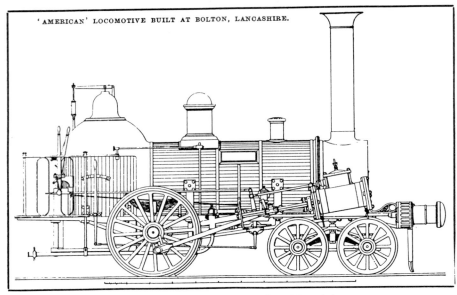

Hick Norris Type A (*The Railway Magazine*).

Nasmyth Norris Type A MK I (The Science Museum).

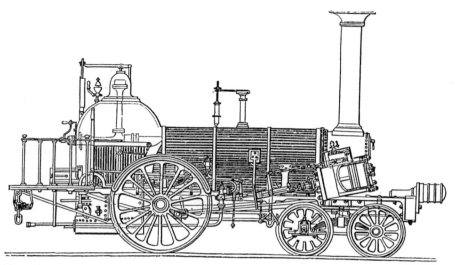

Nasmyth Norris Type A, MK II (Kingsmead Reprints; Drysdale Dempsey, *Treatise on the Railway Locomotive*).

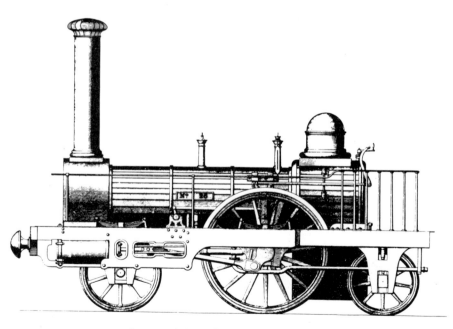

Forrester 2–2–2 (The Science Museum).

Leicester, seen here as Leicester & Swannington Railway's *Comet* (The Science Museum).

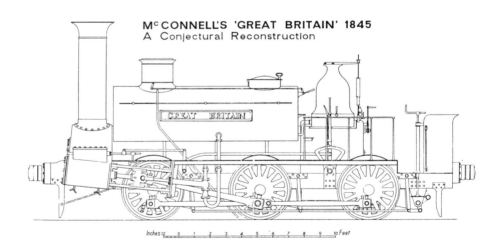

McCONNELL'S 'GREAT BRITAIN' 1845
A Conjectural Reconstruction

Great Britain (Historical Model Railway Society).

English Norrises

As mentioned above, the high spot in *Victoria*'s career must have been when she was cleaned up and exhibited at Camp Hill as a pattern for English locomotive builders. In spite of her failure at hill climbing there must have been something about her behaviour, both then and since, which had given Capt. Moorsom the impression that she was a good general purpose type. His action, however, put a number of noses out of joint, notably Edward Bury's. Five out of the fourteen firms, to whom Capt. Moorsom wrote, flatly refused to tender. Forrester said that he only built to his own designs, Bury wrote a letter full of offended dignity, while Stephenson, Sharp Roberts and Mather Dixon all said they were much too busy. Seven others, however, submitted estimates. Their prices ranged from John Jones' £1,320 to Benjamin Hick's £1,150. Hick therefore got an order for three engines. Later Stothert tendered and so did Nasmyth. Nasmyth's price was lowest of all at £1,100, so he got an order for three engines too. Delivery was to be four months from the date of placing the order, and one engine per month after that. In August, Nasmyth said that if the B&G were to increase their order to six he would drop his price from £1,100 to £1,050. This offer was accepted.[23]

Bredon (18), the first 'Hick', arrived in October (see illustration, courtesy *Railway Magazine*). She was, as far as general dimensions were concerned, an almost exact copy of *Victoria*, but she also featured important improvements. For instance her valve gear was of the same four-eccentric type with down facing gabs, and reversal was still effected by the use of two levers on the footplate but '. . . the Hick engines had an arrangement for maintaining the rear ends of the vibrating rods clear of the handles so that though the four rods . . . vibrated, the hand levers on the footplate did not.'[24] The boiler mounted sand box was a useful feature, and so was the lock–up safety valve on the front boiler ring. In addition to these, the spring balance connected to the safety valve over the firebox dome was calibrated to show the correct boiler pressure. The centrally placed bogie pivot was an improvement on the 'off-set' Norris one, and the copper inner firebox would give lower, because less frequent, replacement costs.

Spetchley (24) and *Eckington* (25), the other two 'Hicks', were delivered in February and March 1841 respectively, and went into traffic immediately. We have been unable to find any adverse comment on these engines, and are therefore led to assume that McConnell found them generally reliable and economical. *Eckington* was in fact sold, after five years service with the B&G, to B&N Sherwood for £1,300, which considering she cost only £1,150 in the first place, speaks well not only for Hick's workmanship, but for McConnell's maintenance.[25] *Spetchley* fetched £1,000 from Wykes & Porter in 1847, while *Bredon* was the only 'Hick' which the MR withdrew and scrapped.

NASMYTH NORRISES

The first batch of 'Nasmyths' on the other hand had 'teething troubles' and there were loud complaints as soon as *Defford* (19) was delivered in November 1840. The dispute waxed so furious that Nasmyth himself came to Bromsgrove in February 1841. He agreed that any repairs due to faulty workmanship should be charged to him. He defended himself vigorously however, against Moorsom's criticisms of his departures from the strict Norris design.[26] The variations which he had introduced were, he maintained, improvements. He had kept to the same general dimensions and outline as *Victoria* (See illustration from the Lane Collection – Courtesy of the Science Museum), but *Defford* herself had important variations for the better. Her cross-heads were held by four steel bars instead of the two cast-iron ones used by Norris, and these slide-bars were arranged, not in the Norris diamond fashion, but in the flat. The valve motion too was an advance on the Norris type. It was of the 'opposed gab' arrangement. This meant that the reversing lever (one only was required), could pull instead of push the valves into position. The vibrating rods were done away with, and there was no movement of the lever on the footplate while the engine was in motion. The regulator was of the 'sliding quadrant' type, much easier to operate than the 'pull out' Norris variety. The single safety valve had a spring balance correctly calibrated, and all wheels had cast iron centres and spokes with wrought iron tyres shrunk on, turned and riveted.[27]

Ashchurch (26) and *Droitwich* (27) arrived in January 1841 accompanied by Archie Torrey, Nasmyth's foreman, to see them through their trial period. This 'running in' period must have been a long one, for Torrey was certainly at Bromsgrove during the first week in April 1841. On 7 April he was one of the unauthorised passengers in *Boston*'s tender when she blew a force-fit plug and scalded Creuze to death.

The first batch of 'Nasmyths' would seem to have been variable in quality. We have already remarked on the complaints about *Defford*, and it would appear that the pair delivered in January (*Ashchurch* and *Droitwich*) had their 'teething troubles' too. Herbert Spencer had the job of trying them out and writes in his diary for 18 January: 'I have been twice to Lancashire . . . the first trip terminated in a most complete catalogue of disasters. We were detained about four hours on the coldest day of the whole month, first in the middle of Chat Moss in consequence of a trifling accident to the engine boiler, and on the next day shortly after leaving Warrington, the engine burst a tube which terminated the second day's adventures.' This was probably *Droitwich*, for *Ashchurch* would seem to have been a useful engine. She was sold in 1846 for £1,300 – a profit of £250 after five years service. *Droitwich* found no buyers and was scrapped in 1848. She would appear to have had her 'quirks' as Herbert Spencer has already indicated. She was also the subject of another of 'Veritas Vincit's' snide comments in the *Railway Record*.[28] '. . . Again there is No. 27 [Droitwich] made by Nesbit [sic]. A better engine . . . was never run, but Mr McConnell must dabble with her . . . his alterations were such that what he ordered to be done today, was undone tomorrow, and she has been not fewer than eleven times under repair this year.' These remarks, however, raise an element of doubt. If 'Veritas Vincit', who claims to be so knowledgeable about railway matters, shows himself misinformed about the name of an, even then, well known engineering firm, we cannot escape the conclusion that he may also have been misinformed about other matters.

Pershore (28), *Upton* (29) and *Lifford* (30) were the second batch of 'Nasmyths'. They were being delivered at the time of McConnell's arrival, and such was the dearth of runnable locomotives they were taken straight into stock without the usual acceptance tests, but they seem to have proved themselves reliable.

In addition to the other Nasmyth improvements, each had a copper inner firebox, brass boiler tubes, and a lock–up safety valve on the front ring of the boiler.[29] The illustration shown is the only one known to be extant and comes from Drysdale Dempsey's 'Treatise on the Locomotive Engine' of 1857. It is a sectional drawing which has often been mistaken for one of the American engines. We have found no complaint about these engines, and it would seem that they went straight into traffic without trouble. Their quality is shown by the fact that *Pershore* was sold in 1846 for £1,200, while *Upton* fetched £1,000 a year later.

THE FORRESTERS

In July 1841, at the time of McConnell's arrival, there were only 6 non-Norris locomotives in a stud of 30. Four of these were sturdy 2-2-2's built by Forrester of Liverpool. *Bromsgrove* (1) *Tewkesbury* (2) *Worcester* (3) and *Cheltenham* (4). They had been bought through the agency of Edward Bury during 1838–39, and had been set to work on line construction in the southern half. After the opening they are rarely mentioned, never by name, and then only as 'the mail engines'. The inference is that they caused so little trouble and were so reliable that they were taken for granted and, reading between the lines, it is possible to feel that Bischopp and McConnell had an affection for them. With their double wrought iron frames, they had sufficient strength and flexibility to stand up to the battering of the B&G's non-resilient baulk road in contrast to the more lightly framed Norris types.

When, in December 1840, the locomotive stock was in such a parlous state that more than half the engines were out of action,[30] the 'Forresters' were among the few which still kept going. Since they were the most reliable, and indeed with their 5ft. 6in. driving wheels, the only expressly passenger engines the B&G had, it is not surprising that Bischopp and McConnell rostered them exclusively for the mail trains.

They survived the misuse and neglect of the construction period, but they were not a success at this kind of work. The complaint generally made was that they were too light. This sounds odd when it is remembered that they weighed 12 tons 5 cwt in working order – only a little less than the Norris A Extras. The problem was however a matter of weight available for adhesion. Whereas when starting under load much of the A Extra's weight was transferred to its rear, and therefore driving wheels, the rear wheels of the 'Forresters' were 'idlers', valuable to correct 'shouldering', but which, on starting tended to reduce the adhesive weight available on the Forresters' driving wheels. (It will be remembered that the Gresley pacifics had the same problem as compared with the 'sure-footedness' of the GWR 4-6-0's).

An illustration of the 1838–39 Forrester type is shown here by courtesy of the Science Museum, and an illustration of their 1840 model will be found in Fig. 11 of 'Clark's Locomotive Machinery, 1850'. It is however clear from the known dates of delivery of these engines that the B&G Forresters were of the 1838–39 type. Their outside cylinders 13in. × 18in., were bolted between the inner and outer frames, and drove the 5ft. 6in. driving wheels. The leading wheels were 3ft.6in. in diameter, and the trailing wheels 3ft. The axleguards and frames were solid, and not bolted together. The valves were worked by an arrangement of vertical rods directly above the driving axle and behind the driving wheel, so it is not possible to see from the drawing exactly how the motion was conveyed to the slide valves. The engines cost £1,660 each, had copper inner fireboxes, and 130 brass boiler tubes of 1⅝in. outside diameter.

THE 'OLD ENGINES'

The Forresters had survived the construction period, and had, so to speak, come up smiling. Others were not so fortunate. Pushed out of the way on a cripple siding at Bromsgrove were the two remaining non-Norrises. They were the 'two old engines' mentioned by Bischopp in his report of December 1841.

The first 'old engine' was *Leicester* (22). She was a 0-4-0 Stephenson *Planet* with 5ft. wheels and 12in. × 18in. cylinders. She had been built by Stephenson for the Leicester and Swannington Railway and delivered by sea from Newcastle up the Humber and Trent, and finally by canal to Leicester where steam was raised in her on 12 July 1832. She hauled the opening train on 17 July with George Stephenson on her footplate, but came to grief when her chimney fouled the roof of Glenfield tunnel. This, however, was only a small setback, and she continued to work the line till increasing traffic outclassed her and she was sold to the B&G for £500 in 1838.

The L&S had called her *Comet*, and the illustration, (courtesy Science Museum), shows her thus; but the B&G named her *Leicester*, and set her to work on the Moseley–Lifford section (Thomas Fowler, contractor). By March 1840 she was in a very poor way. Retubing and other repairs unspecified were badly needed. These were done, but Fowler's incompetent drivers soon had her out of order again, and she was out of action both in July and December 1841, waiting for someone to do something for her. Various attempts were made to sell and/or repair her, but nothing came of them, and she stayed out of use until replaced in 1846.

It was another story with the other 'old engine'.

Southampton (23), was a 0-4-2 with 5ft. driving wheels and cylinders 12in. × 18in. She had been built by John Jones for the London & Southampton Railway in 1837 and the B&G bought her for construction work in 1839 and paid £900 for her. They put her on the Moseley Hill excavation. She had to be withdrawn for repairs and retubing between January and March 1840. Her firebox wore out in October of that year, and she was given a new one of copper, but again had to be withdrawn in December for repairs unspecified. In view of other urgent work on hand at the time these repairs had not been done; but in contrast with *Leicester*, McConnell must have seen that her case was not hopeless. He treated her as a 'stand-by job', and by August 1842 he was able to report that she was now on the 'active list'. She was still in such good order in 1847 that Thomas Hale paid £1,000 for her.

THE BURYS

In December 1841 Bischopp reported to the BC that since both *Leicester* and *Moseley* were out of action, and *England* was in poor shape, it would be advisable to procure replacements ready for an anticipated increase of traffic in the summer. It would seem from the discussion which followed that both he and McConnell were anxious to get reinforcements for the five Class Bs then working the Bromsgrove–Birmingham section. It is interesting to note that Charles Sturge must, in the last six months as director in charge of locomotives, have learnt something about their foibles, for he raised no objection, as he had done a year ago, on the grounds of 'unnecessary expense'.

The secretary was ordered to write to Mr Bury, Mr Stephenson and Messrs Sharp Roberts asking for their advice about engines most suitable for the purpose, bearing in mind the 1 in 84 gradient on the Camp Hill Curzon Street line. Their preference would be for an engine with cylinders not exceeding 13in. diameter, and of the smallest gross weight in accordance with that size. [We are led to infer from this that the trackwork in this section, considerable lengths of which had been laid with Reynold's Rail, was not in the best of condition!] The engine and tender should be ready for delivery on or before 1 May.

Replies from all three firms were received by return. That from Sharp Roberts was referred to the chairman. Stephenson favoured 14in. diameter cylinders with 5ft. driving wheels; but Bury, perhaps still smarting from his defeat on the Lickey 6 months before, adopted an uncompromising attitude, probably based on his own standard production methods. 'They could have', he wrote, 'either an engine with 13in. cylinders, and 5ft. driving wheels, or with 14in. cylinders and 5ft. 6in. wheels.' Take it or leave it! In the end they opted for the the smaller size, and ordered two, which, with copper firebox extra, would cost £1,355 each, and one tender at £200. They probably felt that since Bury was still not only their locomotive adviser, but also prominent in L&B affairs, that it would be politic to keep on the right side of him.

The two little 'Burys' weighing presumably between 8 and 9 tons each, were both delivered in June and were named: *Evesham* (33) and *Kempsey* (34). They went into service with the Norris B's on the newly constituted Blackwell–Birmingham run. Of *Evesham* McConnell reported in the Minutes soon after her arrival under the heading 'Detention of Train. The 2.45 down was delayed because the fusible plug in the new engine *Evesham*, lately delivered from Bury, had fallen out. The plug is now screwed in in the same way as on all the other engines.'[31] Apart from this lapse, their service must have been adequate as it is unremarked; but we cannot help wondering how those little 'featherweight' engines managed on the 1 in 84 between Garrison Lane and the L&B Junction.

FREIGHT ENGINES

1843 was the 'Year of the Committee of Enquiry', when no expenditure was allowed unless 'it was in the interests of economy', and no fresh locomotives were added to stock. McConnell was however quick to take advantage of the CofE's findings with regard to freight traffic.

He pointed out that existing stock both of locomotives and wagons, was inadequate to manage the hoped for increase in 1844 and, 'in the interests of economy', asked in December 1843, for two 0-6-0 engines capable of tackling gross loads of 200 tons. Having expected that his request would be put on one side for future consideration, he was pleasantly surprised to be told to go ahead.[32] Orders for two 'long boiler' goods engines were placed with Jones & Potts of Newton, at £1,357 each, to be delivered in June and July respectively, and to be built to his own design.

While these two were in building, McConnell was allowed to buy a third engine from Sharp Roberts of Manchester.

Wadborough (35) was a 0-4-2 and came for the bargain price of £1,050 together with five new wagons for which Sharp's accepted a reduced price of £160 for the lot. '*Wadborough*' had 4ft. 6in. driving wheels and cylinders 14in. × 20in. She was delivered in February 1844, and though not outstanding, she would seem to have performed adequately for she was taken into MR stock in 1847 and not replaced till 1852.

The 'Potts' engines were, with the possible exception of the 'Forresters', the best 'buy' the B&G ever made.

Bristol (36) and *Hercules* (37) were 'long boiler' 0-6-0's with driving wheels 4ft.6in. diameter and 15in. x 24in. cylinders. They arrived on time, and went into traffic immediately giving no trouble. Until the MR take-over of 1846, and possibly beyond, they tackled all loads they were offered in a capable manner. For instance McConnell, in his evidence before the Gauge Commission of 1845, related how a goods train hauled by a broad gauge 0-6-0 had taken 4 hours 13 minutes to travel the 37½ miles from Bristol to Gloucester with a gross load of 235 tons and a payload of only 97½ tons.

After the 97½ tons had been transfered to the B&G, together with extra freight offering at Gloucester for Birmingham, the gross load for the narrow gauge run had become 254¼ tons and the pay-load had risen to 152½ tons in 36 wagons.

The 51 miles to Birmingham was covered in 3 hours 55 minutes including 6 stops. It is quite clear from the description he gives (4ft.6in. driving wheels, 15in. × 24in. cylinders), that either *Bristol* or *Hercules* had powered this run, which was very creditable indeed for the time; though in reading it, one gets the feeling that in this case McConnell had put on a special Exhibition Run! Later, when the MR had brought in other freight engines to work the traffic, *Bristol* and *Hercules* were rostered to join *Great Britain* on the Lickey in replacing the ageing and outclassed A Extras. Matthew Kirtley rebuilt them as well tanks for that very purpose, and as MR 222 and 223 they soldiered up and down the incline till scrapped respectively in 1860 and 1862. We have, unfortunately, no illustration of the 'Potts' engines in their original state, but there is a photograph of *Bristol* as No. 222, a well-tank bank-engine at Bromsgrove in the late 1850's.[33]

Great Britain (38) 0-6-0ST; driving wheels 3ft.10in.; cylinders 18in. × 26in.

Among the Minutes of the Board Meeting held on 18 March 1844 there is this terse entry:– 'Resolved that Mr McConnell be instructed to make an engine of the power named in his letter.' In his report on locomotive power for the half-yearly meeting in January 1844, McConnell had pointed out that the A Extras were becoming outclassed. It was true they now had five, but the loads offered were increasing and some trains were having to be divided or double-headed with consequent expense and delay. He therefore asked permission to design and build at Bromsgrove, a locomotive of sufficient power to tackle the problem. That permission was given in the Minute quoted above.

There is no record of her in building. She was probably, for obvious reasons, kept strictly secret. All the same, 'Veritas Vincit's' spy network got wind of her and he made one of his customary derogatory references to what was going on behind the closed doors of the works. When, however, she was completed in June–July 1845, and was found to be able to do all and more than was expected of her, he wisely held his tongue. She caused a sensation in locomotive engineering circles and was hailed as the largest and most powerful locomotive in the country. She was a 0-6-0 outside cylindered saddle-tank, and proved herself capable of tackling loads of 1000 tons on the level, and of lifting 135–140 tons gross up 1 in 37 at a speed of 8–10 m.p.h.[34]

Her main dimensions were fairly well publicised in engineering journals of the time, but no picture or photograph is extant. Accordingly the author asked the late Col. M. Whitcombe, a fellow member of the Historical Model Railway Society, to use those dimensions to draw a conjectural picture of her. We published it in the *Journal of the HMRS*[35] and it appears here with the Editor's permission.

Though most particulars about her were made public, we were intrigued and tantalised to find that nothing was ever said about her boiler pressure. The author asked an engineering friend to work out, on the basis of work done, what steam pressure would be required. He calculated that a steam-chest pressure of at least 70lb. p.s.i. would be needed, and, allowing for back-pressure, a boiler pressure of from 90 to 100lb. p.s.i. could be expected – and this when, in 1845, 65lb. p.s.i. was considered the absolute limit for safe working. No wonder McConnell didn't let it out! But he did some 20 years later. He was giving evidence at an enquiry in 1865, and was asked 'What is the biggest load you ever saw taken up the Lickey Incline?' McConnell replied: '150 tons without the engine. The engine would weigh about 35 tons. I may explain however, that it is now some 19 years ago since I had the working of the Lickey Incline, and *at the time we were only working about 100lb. to the square inch, and now the engines are always made 150lb. to the square inch.'* (author's italics)[36]

Great Britain tackled all loads offered with great success, and prominent engineers from all parts came to watch her at work, and chat with her designer.

This 'flood of pilgrims' continued through 1845 and beyond. They came to enjoy the sight and sound of Great Britain doing, with loud voiced efficiency, the job she had been built to do – lifting loads single handed of which no other contemporary locomotive was capable. Thus it was that, in 1846, she was indirectly responsible for an important development in the engineering world.

A history of the Institute of Mechanical Engineers was published in 1947 to mark the centenary of its inauguration. The author, Mr R.H. Parsons, relates how, during the 1830–1840 period, mechanical engineering had become a profession of great importance, and that one afternoon in the summer of 1846 a group of engineers were watching locomotive work on the Lickey – or was it just *Great Britain?* – when a rainstorm drove them to shelter in a platelayers' hut. Here the discussion turned to the Institute of Civil Engineers and their dissatisfaction with it. (We can discount Mr Parsons' story, borrowed from Smiles, about the off-hand way in which the 'Civils' had treated George Stephenson. Research has shown that it had no foundation in fact.)

The ICE was then the only society in the country which catered for engineers. Most engineers belonged to it, but it did not provide a satisfactory forum for airing the problems peculiar to mechanical engineers. After the work they had come to see was over, those who could stay continued the discussion in McConnell's house at the foot of the incline. All agreed that the time had come for mechanical engineers to have an institute of their own. McConnell offered his house as a venue for another meeting at which this proposal should be the main item on the agenda. This was done, and the Institute of Mechanical Engineers was born. The inaugural meeting was held in January 1847 at the Queens Hotel, Birmingham, at which George Stephenson was elected president, and J.E. McConnell, chairman.

It was in January 1847 that McConnell left Bromsgrove to take up the important appointment of locomotive superintendent at Wolverton, a position which *Great Britain* too, had helped him to attain. She herself soldiered on up and down the Lickey till 1852 when Kirtley withdrew her for rebuilding. It was probable that her saddletank had been giving trouble, for she appeared as a well-tank in January 1853. According to official records she was withdrawn in October 1861, and scrapped in July the following year, but there is a persistent legend[37] that her boiler only was scrapped, and that her frames and motion had a prolonged existence in the No. 221 which Kirtley built to replace her, and that thus rebuilt, *Great Britain* continued on the Lickey for many more years.

Fresh locomotives were acquired after her, and ran over B&G metals (particulars that are known about these will be found in the appendix), but these were B&B or Midland locomotives. Therefore, since *Great Britain* was the last locomotive planned, built and paid for by the B&G, it is with her that the B&G locomotive story must come to an end.

CHAPTER NINETEEN
ROLLING STOCK

Today's Birmingham to Gloucester Inter City passenger seated in his air-conditioned, double glazed, 125 m.p.h. coach has luxury unimagined by his ancestors 150 years ago. We hear some complaints about the riding of present day coaching stock but they are nothing to what 'Commercial' had to say in *Herepath*:[1] '. . . The B&G is proverbially the most uneasy of all in the U.K. and anything to be "well shaken before taken" may be well accommodated in their carriages either 1st or 2nd class; and . . . I can easily discover . . . that the fault is in the springs and I think that if the maker has not yet obtained a patent, the sooner he applies for one the better, or perhaps some unfortunate who has experienced a good shaking may tell such tales as will prevent his obtaining one if he neglects too long. Indeed I think it would be advisable to have a few leg straps to hold passengers to the seats for I should not be surprised to hear of some light body taking an aerial trip . . . some of these days. But to be serious, I hope the public will not always be subject to such unpleasant travelling, let the cause be what it may.' The development of the railway passenger carriage is a fascinating study in its own right, but the B&G provides only a brief glimpse of the story. Prototypes were ordered from established road coachbuilders early in 1839 but these were quickly discarded when a deputation of the Board visited the Manchester and Leeds in December 1839.

They were impressed with that railway's composite 1st and 2nd class carriages which held eight passengers in a central 1st class body with eight 2nd class at either end. It would, they thought, save considerable expenditure to have one standard design for 1st and 2nd class combined, with the additional advantage of packing 1st class passengers in at the same density as 2nd class! They also recommended the adoption of 3rd class carriages: '. . . which being without seats will be available for luggage and other purposes and will enable the Company to carry that class of passenger at low fares without interfering with the fares of the other carriages.' When put to the full Board, it was decided to order six composites and six 3rd class for a start, but the chairman, Joseph Walker, thought that the purchase of composite carriages in bulk was preposterous. He broke the constitutional rules and recorded his personal dissent in the Minute book[2] for the following reasons:

1. Because he has great doubts as to the propriety of constructing carriages with bodies 7 feet wide on wheels only 4 feet 8 inches wide thereby projecting 14 inches over the wheels on each side
2. Because he thinks it very objectionable to oblige 8 1st class Passengers to ride in one body while charged a full and fair price for proper accommodation.
3. Because this kind of carriage does not enable us to increase or diminish the demand for first or second class accomodation so conveniently as by separate carriages of the two kinds.
4. Because while 3 of these Carriages are only just equal to one first and two 2nd class of the kinds almost universally running on other and more experienced lines, no enquiry has been made into the Comparative Weight of 3 such Carriages as compared with one first and two 2nd class of the ordinary kinds, by which any advantage might be ascertained to exist.
5. Because until such saving in Weight or Cost, or both, has been ascertained, it appears very inexpedient to come to any final conclusion on a point involving so large an expenditure.

These objections were, in the main, sound. When firm orders were placed in January 1840 the chairman's thoughts were borne in mind, and a mixture of 1st, 2nd and composites were ordered, but there was no mention of third class. Whishaw[3] provides us with illustrations of 1st and 2nd class but does not mention the composites; he describes the 3rd class as open without seats, but with covered protection for luggage.

Journalists had their chance for inspection when the line opened, the following comments are representative: '. . . extremely handsome and of the best construction . . . the comfort, ease and steadiness of motion was remarked by all.[4] . . . remarkably handsome and commodious.[5] . . . of an excellent construction for the comfort of passengers.'[6] Perhaps 'Commercial' should have travelled three years earlier when both the springs and the track were in good condition.

Looking at some of their finer details as noted by Capt. Melhuish in a report to the BoT in October 1840:[7] '. . .the wheels and axles are of the most approved construction . . . since the line has been opened there has been no case of fracture either of an axle or cylinder of a wheel. In consequence of the [Lickey] incline . . . all the carriages and wagons are much better supplied with buffers and brakes . . . than upon any . . . I have yet visited. The brake . . . is of a novel and strong construction. It is worked by a single or double winch fixed on a spindle at the top of the carriage . . . and by turning the winch . . . the brake is applied to all four wheels . . . at the same time; and I should think the power nearly sufficient, if applied by a tolerably strong brakesman, to arrest almost entirely the rotation of the wheels. I am of the opinion it would tend greatly the safety of the public if the use of this description of brake were introduced on all lines of railway . . .'

Third class accommodation got its first descriptive mention when a correspondent to the *Railway Times* in September 1843 wrote that they were: '. . . the only ones I have yet seen affording to the passengers that protection from wind and weather they have the right to expect. They are large covered wagons closed at the front and with the door behind. They have seats round and passengers can either stand up or sit down. The same company have also separate 3rd class carriages with like accommodation for women and children.' Clearly, improvements had been made since Whishaw called them open trucks without seats.

Facilities for luggage were limited inside the carriage and it was at first necessary to run a luggage truck for this purpose; later, however roof-racks were attached for the storage of luggage. Several of these luggage trucks were converted to 2nd class and composite 2nd and 3rd class carriages in 1843. Her Majesty's Mails were carried in carriages similar in design to those of the 1st class but with large covered roof-racks or Imperials.

McConnell compared his narrow gauge carriages to broad gauge ones at the Gauge Commission in 1845. The latter were too short in proportion to their width, he said, they rock from side to side more than narrow gauge coaches and were more likely to leave the rails. We think that Brunel might just have disagreed!

Comparing the ballast and goods wagons (the latter were 2–2¾ tons tare, maximum load 4½t) with today's standard 40 and 50 ton two-axle wagons, we can appreciate the process in rolling stock design.

The first wagons used on the B&G were ballast wagons, in large numbers, for use during construction of the railway between 1838 and 1840. These were subsequently converted into various other types as traffic developed. Other types in early use were general goods wagons, luggage trucks running in passenger trains, horse boxes and carriage trucks. By August 1842, 133 of these various types were in service but these, the proprietors were warned, were barely sufficient to cope with the traffic on offer. It is probable that the wandering habits of some wagons were to blame for this comment. Shortly afterwards they employed a clerk to trace '. . . this Company's wagons lost on other Company's lines', having in 1842 joined the railway clearing house for this reason. Poor maintenance cost the company dearly in compensation for damaged goods; horseboxes for instance were ordered to have their roofs fixed to stop horses slipping and injuring themselves.

With an increase in goods traffic in the latter part of 1843 and into 1844, significant increases were made in wagon numbers to meet demand. Ballast wagons were converted, second-hand coal trucks purchased, and during 1844 and 1845 nearly 300 new wagons of various shapes and sizes were ordered.

Repair and maintenance was carried out at Camp Hill by the carriage and wagon department under the leadership of Edward Lean until consolidated with the locomotive department when the MR took over in 1845.

CHAPTER TWENTY
PEOPLE

The human element of history, especially of railways, is that which provides life, interest and entertainment; without them and their personalities it is simply an inanimate collection of facts and figures. It is a great pity that so little is known about the ordinary people who worked on the B&G compared with those involved in its management. Details of who was what and when, together with samples of pay of various grades at different times can be found in the appendix.

Navvies will forever be associated with railways; drink and brute strength, not necessarily in that order! Some of their less fortunate exploits are recorded under Accidents and Incidents, but they were not all bad! Through the efforts of devoted disciples of the Church, welfare and temperance organisations, some were put on the 'straight and narrow'. The *Gloucester Journal* records that:[1] 'On Sunday 7th July [1839] the Reverend F. Close preached in a wooden temple near the B&G depot [at Cheltenham], the object of which was to induce the men employed on these railway lines to attend and hear the Word of God on Sunday afternoon. On this occasion several hundred persons were present chiefly of the class for the benefit of whom these buildings were designed. The Reverend Gent said it was his intention to preach every Sunday afternoon.' Some good was instilled, as recorded by the *Gloucester Journal*.[2] One navvy boasted of working from 6 a.m. to 7 p.m., walking 2 miles to and from work every day without recourse to drink! A group of navvies who had adopted the total abstinence principle held a meeting and, according to the reporter: '. . . illustrated the good effects of their own experience of health and morality'!

The 'labouring classes' employed during the construction of the B&G were indeed fortunate in having Capt. William Scarth Moorsom as their chief. From Herbert Spencer's autobiography[3] we learn a good deal. On taking up his position in the engineering department, a colleague spoke of Capt. Moorsom as: '. . . one of the nicest men he knows, a real gentleman, and a benevolent and good hearted man . . .' Spencer found him a kindly natured man, interested in the welfare of his subordinates. A club for the engineering staff was formed and for the labourers he founded a benefit society, later the Friendly Society, with the consent of the directors. Through this the workmen paid a small subscription into a fund from which sickness benefit and medical fees would be paid. Assistance with the funds came every six months when the proceeds of all the fines imposed on the company's servants were donated; in December 1841 this was £8.6s. 2d. for the past six months. Spencer continues: 'Capt. Moorsom is treating me very kindly in every respect . . . He takes every opportunity of pointing out what he thinks may be useful to me and invites me to come and sit with them [Moorsom and his wife] in the evening . . . He is in fact the best specimen of a perfect gentleman that I have ever come near . . .' What an epitaph that sentence would make. Born in 1804 he entered Sandhurst in 1819 specialising in surveying and on being commissioned in 1822 put this to good use during ten years of peace time soldiering. On his mother's death in 1832 he sold out of the army and he and his wife came to live with his father near Birmingham, close to the proposed L&B line. He did surveys on the L&B line and, following his father's death in 1835, he visited canal and railway works all over the country besides surveying the B&G line for the brothers Sturge. He won the Telford Medal in 1845 for his bridge over the Avon at Eckington, and surveyed many railways in Great Britain and Ireland. The Institute of Civil Engineers (ICE) said in his obituary[4] that he: '. . . was a forthright and courteous man. Integrity and honour marked all his public and private dealings. He died on June 3rd 1863 after a long illness courageously borne.'

Fines, as mentioned above, were a source of income to the Friendly Society. Their imposition was made for any deviation from the company's rulebook, but they were punishment only to a certain level. If a man were caught pocketing money or drunk on duty then he got short shrift indeed.

Two guards got their marching orders, for taking money from passengers on the Birmingham–Bromsgrove coach link before the railway had reached Camp Hill. The coach fare was included in the rail fare, but these two saw a chance of lining their pockets by telling gullible passengers otherwise. Gullible they were not, for they reported the men to the authorities as soon as they left the coach!

Failure to do a proper job got many the sack. Burgess reported that it was necessary to: '. . . remove Botterill, one of the head guards, he appears to have lost the faculty of conducting business properly . . .'! Alcohol abuse cost many men an arm or a leg, as well as their jobs (see Accidents). But it did once do the B&G a favour, when fate caught up with their locomotive superintendent, William Creuze and their works foreman Richard Walworth. Creuze was replaced by G.D. Bischopp, and Walworth by James Edward McConnell, one of the best appointments the B&G ever made.

Extensive reference has been made to McConnell elsewhere in this book for his name is inseparable from the B&G's story. He was born in 1815, son of a millwright at Fermoy, County Cork. On losing his father at the age of 4 he was taken to Scotland and brought up in Dailly, Ayrshire by his uncle Alexander. At the age of 13 he was apprenticed to Claude Girdwood & Co, Engineers, of Glasgow where he gained the reputation of a steady, reliable workman. Moving south to Liverpool in 1836, he rose to be foreman in Edward Bury's Clarence Foundry, but following a disagreement with Bury he left Liverpool for Manchester where he became manager of a machine shop. He was 26 when appointed foreman of locomotives at Bromsgrove, and when Bischopp resigned a year later McConnell was appointed locomotive superintendent in his place. His career at Bromsgrove was among other achievements marked by the building of the first saddle-tank engine, the first purpose built and successful Lickey banker, and the foundation of the Institute of Mechanical Engineers of which he was the first chairman. He left Bromsgrove in 1847, and was for 15 years locomotive superintendent of the LNWR southern division at Wolverton. He resigned in 1862 and set up as a consulting engineer with an office in Dean's Yard Westminster, and his clientele grew to be world wide. He died in 1883 at his home at Woodlands Park, Great Missenden, Bucks.

The *Engineer* wrote in his obituary:[5] 'Mr McConnell's name is inseparably connected with the history of the locomotive and his loss has deprived us of another of those men to whom the world owes a great deal . . .'

Drink was not the only way for folk to take leave of their senses, in September 1845 the stationmaster at Cheltenham was removed due to 'mental derangement'! Temptation proved too great for one or two employees faced daily with amounts of money comparable to a year's wages. A clerk from Cheltenham station, Mr Caviller, was a case in point. He made off with £35.10s. which he 'blew' before being arrested in Birmingham a week later (full details Chapter 24. Cheltenham). Precautionary measures had been taken from the start to guard against such crimes. The honesty of prospective employees had to be vouched for by two sponsors and, in the case of those seeking positions with financial responsibility, security had to be guaranteed by another sponsor. During the enlistment of staff in 1840 the security was usually one year's salary, often more, and the guarantor's solvency had to be checked before the applicant could be accepted. A Mr Haynes, for instance, was employed as a pay clerk at £100 salary and he had to find security of £200. In November 1842, the Guarantee Society was formed to which the B&G paid annual premiums to insure themselves against possible loss.

Railwaymen and uniforms are inseparable. Derived no doubt from the strong military influence behind the first managers and superintendents, they must, apart from the police, have been among the first non-military uniformed organisations, and a grand sight too, we imagine! Only those in the public eye were clothed by the company; police, porters, station inspectors, guards and ticket collectors are mentioned in the Minute books. A full policeman's uniform cost £6.8s.3d. in 1839, about one months pay for him. (Say, £600 at today's prices!) The police were, however, an exception, for their uniform was distinctive. Top hat, tail coat, tight trousers and truncheon!

Directors and chairmen were sometimes in a difficult situation as the intermediaries between the proprietors and their property. When things went well and dividends were forthcoming, the directors were praised and re-elected. When they did not there were impatient cries for enquiries and replacements. To quote again the comment of Samuel Baker, one time B&G chairman: '. . . In the early days of Railways no man was thought unfit for the business of a Railway Director; no one was incompetent to lay out millions of money.' Unfit and incompetent they were, however, especially on the B&G! Their deeds form the backbone of this story, and only a few words are necessary. The most famous member of the Board was, no doubt, Capt., later Admiral, Constantine Moorsom, RN (see illustration), brother of William Scarth. His methodical approach to railway management gained from his experience as joint secretary, then director of the L&B, transformed the B&G from the 'tottering state' in which he found it, to the resemblance of a railway by the time he resigned after three years in office. Were it not for the recession of 1842 and 1843, the appalling debt left behind by the 'expensive economies' of his predecessors, the absence of a direct link to Gloucester Docks, and so on, he would unquestionably have fulfilled his aim of turning the B&G into profitability. One wonders whether the line would have joined forces with the L&B and GJR instead of the MR had he still been in office. After resigning in December 1843, he became chairman of the Chester & Holyhead Railway, and reached the pinnacle of his career as chairman of the LNWR in 1861, shortly before he died.

Among other names on the long list of one time directors were the Sturge brothers[6], Charles and Joseph (and later Edmund). They were corn merchants of Birmingham and Gloucester, Quakers, founder members of the B&G and prominent public figures in their home town of Birmingham. Samuel Baker and Samuel Bowley were public figures and businessmen from Gloucester. Baker was involved in the development of High Orchard dock and no doubt influenced the B&G's fruitless investment of £14,000 there. Bowley was, amongst other things, chairman of the Anti-Dry Rot Company whose premises at High Orchard were purchased for the B&G's depot. It is not beyond the realms of possibility that suspicious circumstances surrounded these developments, but that is not for us to say!

Directors too were open to temptation, or so the proprietors thought. On more than one occasion the sharp drops in share values were blamed upon the directors trafficking in shares. One, Joseph Gibbins, was forced to resign after these allegations. As one ex-director said of their duties: '. . . they were far more arduous than many imagined. . .'

We now turn to the 'rank and file'. Early railways, and among them the B&G, were highly labour intensive. We can however only obtain a partial record of their labour force from the company Minute books. We have been able to list 390 names in all. These are the names of men who are mentioned at least twice, and for a variety of reasons – praise, blame, promotion, dismissal or resignation. Others are mentioned only once, either on appointment, dismissal or death; but it would not be safe to assume that all the 'oncers' speedily left B&G service. John Hughes comes to mind in this connection. In July 1847 the superintendent reported his death to the Board saying that he had been 'a porter for many years at Cheltenham'. This would imply that Hughes was an 'old hand' recruited perhaps in 1840–1, though there is no record of it.

Another such was J.H. Collett. He was a clerk of the company at Worcester throughout the years of its independent existence, and in June 1840 he became booking clerk at the B&G's office in Foregate Street. He stayed there at a salary of £80 per annum till the road coach service between Worcester and Spetchley came to an end with the opening of Shrub Hill Station. All through that time nothing is heard of him whatever, either good or bad. The only sign the Minutes give of his existence is his name and quarterly salary of £20 in the accounts.

We have seen above in Chapter 8 that apart from the staff of the locomotive department who required special skills, the basic grade was that of special constable, and that these men were recruited by Capt. W.S. Moorsom in 1838–40 while the line was under construction to patrol the formation, and protect materials and structures. Though recruited and paid by the railway company they were at first responsible to the civil magistrates. It was only after the line had been opened, and the company's by-laws had been approved by the BoT that they became responsible to the company.

The complex operations of a railway demanded a disciplined work force, and the constables were sworn in to observe a strict code of rules adapted from the police code of the time, and it was from this basic nucleus that the staff of the railway was at first appointed: signalmen, switchmen, shunters, brakesmen, guards, travelling porters, porters, and, according to ability and literacy, station inspectors and station clerks.

For the really important stations such as Spetchley (for Worcester), Cheltenham, and Gloucester, special appointments were made of men considered capable of doing the job, and though the form of enrolments was at first the same, the salary was much higher at £120. George Thomas at Gloucester was allowed an assistant clerk, Moreton, at £60; Mr Martin's assistant at Cheltenham (see Chapter 24) was named Jewsbury, while Richard Lowe at Spetchley (see Chapter 27) had an assistant too. George Thomas was officially appointed in January 1841, presumably after a probationary period. He became quite a popular local character, and stayed there till his resignation in 1848.

The strictness of the police code might, on the face of it, provoke the comment 'Breathe out of turn and you're out!' But there is evidence that though this was the case in matters of theft or embezzlement, a second chance was offered in the case of other misdemeanours and the Board's sentence of dismissal transmuted to a fine or suspension. Time after time we find that employees who have in a previous Minute been dismissed are mentioned as back in the same job again or transferred to another, elsewhere.

George Stainton had been sworn-in during May 1840 and had become a 2nd class passenger guard employed on the 'short' (i.e. local) trains between Cheltenham and Gloucester. One day, in between train departure times he was reported by a passenger for being out of his van on the platform at Cheltenham hob-nobbing with his crony, driver Fox, contrary to official regulations. Since the passenger was a prominent shareholder whom it would be impolitic to ignore, sentence of dismissal was served on both; but quietly afterwards when McConnell had pointed out that Fox had left his fireman on the engine, and that Stainton was within sight of and easy reach of his van, the sentence was transmuted to a fortnight's suspension, and the next time we hear of Stainton is in December 1846 when he was promoted to 1st class guard with consequent increase in wages on account of his long and loyal service.

Thomas Enoch is another case in point. An early recruit to B&G service, he was sworn in at Bromsgrove in August 1840, and was transferred to Curzon St. in 1841 where he was given the sack for alleged rudeness to a passenger. He is next heard of at Spetchley where, having served a probationary period of some three months he is now Richard Lowe's assistant station clerk, at 25s. per week. Moreover when in 1845 Richard Lowe resigned as stationmaster to concentrate on his haulage business Thomas Enoch got the job. His salary was increased to £75 at the end of the year. He remained in command at Spetchley till his resignation in 1847 (see also Joseph Morris at Stoke, Chapter 27). But except for minor misdemeanors a second chance is all you were given, and you had to take it or else!

Anthony Foreman was sworn in at Cheltenham as special constable in June 1840, and apparently gave satisfaction till August 1842 when he was reported as having been too drunk to report for duty. He was dimissed as a special constable, but the superintendent Mr Wetherall was allowed to find him a job as a porter first at Tewkesbury and later at Spetchley. In both places the drink caught up with him and he disappeared finally from the B&G annals.

In the years of the B&G's life there are a number of success stories worthy of note. (See Timothy Suffolk, Birmingham, Chapter 22). Thomas Saunders began as a constable at Bromsgrove in April 1841. With his colleagues Adie and Clark he regulated (signalled) the traffic through the station and at the incline foot. This was a notoriously difficult post, and although he did not escape blame for accidents which happened he eventually applied for the post of station clerk and got it. He evidently proved his worth for in 1843 – the year of the purge – his wage was raised to 25s. per week. With the station clerkship it would seem he took over the management of the station and did so well that he was made station inspector at Gloucester, a post which he held till his resignation in 1847, having been offered a more remunerative job elsewhere.

But the most remarkable story is that of William Wynn, who was recruited during the construction period in August 1839 and was first employed patrolling the formation. He stayed with the way and works department and must have made the most of his opportunities for, by December 1843, he had not only survived the CofE's purge but had been appointed overlooker of the 25 miles of line from Spetchley to Gloucester at a salary of £80 p.a. His salary rose to £100 in December 1845, and in March 1846 he became inspector of permanent way on the BrG side of the B&B. His last mention in the B&B Minutes comes in April 1848 when he is referred to as chief assistant to S.H. Barlow, then the B&B's resident engineer.

CHAPTER TWENTY ONE
ACCIDENTS AND
INCIDENTS

Accidents occurred at an alarming rate on the early railways. Not all had fatal consequences but major disasters did occur causing much loss of life. Happily, on the whole B&G passengers travelled in relative safety. They had one death only in nearly two million journeys between 1840 and 1846. Death, however, by natural causes and passengers' own negligence was a little more frequent.

Most accidents happened to the railway's employees and many of these occurred because of their own stupidity, ignorance and lack of responsibility. No health and safety executive could have prevented the apparent ease with which the labour force surrendered life or limb. As there is only limited space here for what could possibly fill a volume, we have included only a cross-section of accidents as recorded in the contemporary press and the company Minute Books.

The navvy along with auxiliary labour frequently succumbed to injury. Boys were employed to drive the horse drawn trams which carted 'muck' from excavations to spoil heaps or embankments. When full, the horse and tram got up speed, the horse was detached and the tram rolled on to the tip where its contents were unloaded by a controlled derailment. William Clifford aged 13, Frederick Edwin and Augustus Holland, both 14, were killed in 1839 by falling into the paths of those trams. Holland's parents, the *Gloucester Journal*[1] tells us: '. . . lost not only a son but their chief means of living through his 14s. a week wages.'

Various degrees of injury, from minor to mortal, befell the mature labourer; embankment collapse, collisions with trams and locomotives and so on. George Davis, 19, fell from the Avon bridge and was drowned: '. . . his duty was to attend to fires kept going for drying cork used in the permanent way.' At Churchdown on the Cheltenham–Gloucester section, a temporary bridge was being rebuilt in brick when it collapsed burying six men in brick and rubble but miraculously they all walked away with no more than bruises.

The first serious accident involving a train occurred on the Tewkesbury branch on May Day 1840 only weeks before it was opened to passengers. Shortly before noon, the engine *Worcester* left Tewkesbury with a train of ballast wagons laden with rails and after depositing them at Bredon the train, under the control of Joseph Howden, returned to Tewkesbury to reload. When the train was within one third of a mile from the terminus, the driver: '. . . ran off the whole of the steam and let a quantity of water in to the boiler, calculating the impetus which had already been given to the train would carry them safely into the depot.'[2] But, unknown to him, a wagon had been placed on the line near the terminus and as the train approached it; '. . . a policeman gave the usual signal to reduce speed, upon which the engine was reversed and the brake applied, but as no steam was available, the engine could not stop. The locomotive tender conveying six to eight people and an empty wagon conveying two men were propelled in front of the engine and whilst still travelling at ten m.p.h. an awful collision took place and two men in the front wagon were crushed [to death] by the stationary wagon laden with rails; those on the tender were unhurt.'[3] The driver was found to be drunk and subsequently charged with manslaughter.

Once the line was open to passengers and regular trains ran, there were frequent mishaps, though these were fortunately not serious. Proprietors heard at their general meeting of February 1841 that: '. . . more than 120,000 individuals have been conveyed along the railway since it was opened, without the slightest accident to a single passenger', despite rumours otherwise circulated by the anti-rail newspaper, the *Globe*. But as you will discover the B&G found plenty of more entertaining subjects than passengers!

Now that the 'iron horse' was here to stay, woe betide trespassers, human or otherwise. The secretary reported a derailment in August 1840 caused by: '. . . a cow jumping over the railway fence . . . just as the Train was passing. The Engine came into contact with her and killed her and the train ran over her. Four carriages and trucks were thrown off the line but none were broken nor any person injured.'[4] In a later incident no less than nine hares were killed on the railway near Oddingly in the space of a fortnight![5]

Alcohol abuse sent many to an early grave, especially those who attempted to sleep it off on the railway! William Foster of Kings Norton did so to his regret, and Humphrey Willis met the night mail whilst '. . . expired on the line through drink'.[6] John Killcash, the porter from Stoke station took a short cut home along the railway after a drop too much and was mown down by the night mail.

The first passenger casualty on the B&G occurred on the coach link from Cofton to Birmingham prior to that section's opening. It was usual for the coach to stop at 'The Bell' at Northfield to change horses, and on this occasion the passengers took the opportunity of stretching their legs. One female passenger was standing close to the coach when something startled the horses, which took off at great speed running her over in the process. She died two days later. The verdict at the inquest was accidental death. Shortly afterwards a gentleman's servant was to travel from Bromsgrove, with two horses, to Cheltenham. It was getting dark by the time the horses were loaded into the waiting horsebox, which was then pushed (by hand presumably), from the siding towards the station, when a light engine collided with it at slow speed causing it to rapidly reverse its direction of travel. This was all too sudden for the servant, who was run down, dying three days later. Again the verdict was accidental death.[7]

Getting in and out of carriages proved too difficult for some passengers. Thomas Man lost a leg at Defford in his attempt to board a departing train. Drink got the better of one passenger's judgement as his train approached Spetchley. He got out before the train reached the platform, disappeared beneath the carriage and was dragged along for several yards. Certain death was feared but, reported the *Gloucester Journal*, '. . . he was removed when the train stopped with just a few fingers missing'![8]

Injuries to staff in the execution of their duty were frequent and mostly through their own fault. An infrequent exception was the case of John Howell, a labourer, who lost his life attempting to remove a large hammer from the path of an approaching train. A brave but fatal deed.

In contrast, the *Gloucester Journal* tells the tale of James Dudley[9] He was a guard, who: '. . . with the temerity which too frequently attaches to persons employed on railways, proceeded from the last carriage [where it seems he was often in the habit of sitting] to his proper seat on the outside of one of the carriages while the train was still in motion just before it stopped at . . . Eckington.' He slipped, fell under the train and was killed instantly. The *Journal* found it extraordinary that so many accidents had occurred on the B&G to employees, yet none to any passenger.

Two examples of drinking on the job were recorded on successive nights in June 1842[10] both at Eckington. George Musto the 'pointsman' fell asleep through drink beside the railway line whilst awaiting the mail train. His 'morning call' came when the mail train lopped off one of his legs. The following night Musto's replacement, James Playdon, repeated the performance at exactly the same spot. When the mail train arrived at 2.30 a.m., no pointsman could be found. 'The steam whistle was used most vociferously and the men with the engine hallowed most lustily but none appeared.' Playdon was eventually found, and received two months hard labour for his crime. Musto paid for his offence concluded the *Journal* but: 'Playdon must have been quite heedless of the melancholy warning to allow himself to have been surprised in so precisely similar a manner.'

A bridge near Kings Norton killed William Murraywood in November 1844. In dense fog, he leant from his engine and was struck by one of the pillars of High House bridge. He died instantly. The bridge in question came in for considerable criticism. It had: '. . . long been considered too narrow and is supported by upright iron pillars between which and the train there is scarcely more space than will admit the carriage steps.'[11] At the inquest, McConnell for the B&G said the bridge was: '. . . supported in the centre by seven pillars of cast iron . . . there was not sufficient space between the carriage and pillar.'

Another bridge accident befell William Stock, a guard. One day he was sitting on the roof of a carriage talking to a labourer who was travelling thereon. On approaching Barnt Green station, the engine crew whistled and Stock leapt up to return to his post at the brakes at precisely the same instant as the train passed under a bridge. He died in hospital.

Not all accidents happened to the 'lower class' of employee. William Westley, a pupil to the resident engineer, hitched a footplate ride on a train between Camp Hill and Lawley Street in Birmingham. He: '. . . was in the act of leaping down when the propelling wheel caught him . . . and swung him round several times,' depositing him, minus legs, on the rails.[12]

The final example, almost comical, perhaps summarises all the accidents to employees. A labourer on the permanent way sat down near the line to eat his lunch and take a nap. A train passed and he was feared killed but the train wheels had passed along his side and legs, cutting the material of his clothes, but only grazing him. It will teach him, said the reporter:[13] '. . . that a rail road is rather a dangerous place on which to enjoy a noonday nap.'

Capt. Moorsom's Lickey Incline was hailed as a death trap from the time his plans were published. However, the expected catastrophies never materialised, but many minor incidents did, which was to be expected, because it was a focal point of activity on the B&G. At Bromsgrove too, with the station, goods depot, locomotive works and bank engine manoeuvres there was plenty of opportunity for accident (see Chapter 23.)

Runaways were feared on all inclines, and all the more so on the Lickey. During February 1841, the *Gloucester Journal* reported that men at Bromsgrove had: '. . . perceived a wagon laden with quarry stones coming down the incline at such a frightful rate that they had hardly time to consider what they better do . . . before it dashed past them at 100 m.p.h. They wisely determined to let it pursue its wild career for fear that they should not have time to clear the line before the Birmingham train arrived . . .'. It was found three miles down the line from Bromsgrove.[14] Another runaway occurred during the summer:[15] '. . . a train of wagons was carelessly left near the top of the . . . Incline, and as even railway directors cannot control that venerable old gent, Gravity, they began to descend . . . the first person who saw them was a child only 9 years old . . . he jumped upon the wagons and put on the break [sic] . . . and only then did he roar out like a Trojan for more help. Who comes next? Why . . . his mother, she jumped likewise on the train . . . they brought the train to a standstill and thus prevented a smash which must surely have included themselves.' The Lickey provides the situation for two major incidents concerning locomotive failures. Mishaps with locomotives were as regular as accidents and derailments, but were mainly caused more by poor maintenance and building techniques than serious design faults. Perhaps one of the most famous of B&G disasters – as recorded by the Bromsgrove tombstones – was the boiler explosion of 10 November 1840. It happened to an engine with the tragically apt name of *Surprise*.[16]

In 1837 or so an American, Dr Church designed what was probably the first tank-engine and persuaded a Mr Goddard of Birmingham to put up the money to enable John Inshaw, also of Birmingham, to build her. She was a queer looking beast even for those days and was a vertical boilered 0-2-2 with her firebox and engineman's footplate in front. She was tried on the L&B, but being a shy steamer the L&B declined to buy her. Goddard had her firebox altered and offered her to the GJR. They showed no interest either, and she stood for some time on a siding at their Vauxhall station in all weathers. She was unsheeted, *and no one thought to put a cap on her chimney to keep out the rain.* (author's italics) In that, lay the main cause of her disaster.

At last Church and Goddard offered her at a cut price to the B&G, and she came to Bromsgrove for trial. William Burgess, the B&G secretary, reported as follows: '. . . steam was got up for trial, preparatory to putting it with a train . . . several short trips were made with the engine on two different days but on the evening of Tuesday last having been tried and when standing still, the boiler burst while several people were on the engine.' Thomas Scaife, a bank engine driver and Joseph Rutherford, foreman of locomotives at Bromsgrove, had strolled over to join John Inshaw and his son, Paul, on the footplate. The *Worcester Chronicle* reporter resumes the story.[17] '. . .in front of the furnace or firebox stood Scarf [sic]. Immediately behind him was a circular aperture about 2ft. diameter, made we believe for allowing the fireman or stoker to get in or out of the engine. Rutherford was standing at his side a little distant from him and on one side of the firebox with his back to some brass railings . . . Henshaw [sic] and Paul were alongside Rutherford and the witness Luke and others were near the same place a little further back . . . Scaife was blown backwards through the hole . . . his remains presented a hideous mess scarcely recognisable as a human being. Rutherford was projected through the Brass rails and thrown a distance of many yards. The others were thrown in the air over the rails and should all recover. . .' Rutherford died next day and was buried alongside Scaife, who was shortly to have been married. The funeral service was well attended. The tombstones do not show Dr Church's engine, but those of the Norris type. This fact has led many historians astray. Scaife was a bank-engine driver and it is appropriate therefore that his stone shows an 'A Extra' (this engine can be seen on the book jacket). Rutherford's stone shows a 'Class B' in recognition of his loyal service to the company.

His men, who '. . . almost idolised him . . .' launched an appeal for the support of his widow Martha and their three children. There was '. . . a spirited subscription . . . in which some of the Officers . . . joined.' This enabled Martha Rutherford to support herself and her family by setting up as a shopkeeper, and she was still allowed to live in one of the Company cottages at the station.

The epitaph on Scaife's tombstone is worth quoting:

> My engine now is cold and still,
> No water does my boiler fill:
> My coke affords its flame no more,
> My days of usefulness are o'er.
> My wheels deny their noted speed,
> No more my guiding hand they heed:
> My whistle too has lost its tone,
> Its shrill and thrilling sounds are gone.
> My valves are now thrown open wide;
> My flanges all refuse to guide.
> My clacks also, though once so strong
> Refuse to aid the busy throng.
> No more I feel each urging breath,
> My steam is now condensed in death.
> Life's railway's o'er, each station's past,
> In death I'm stopped and rest at last.
> Farewell dear friends and cease to weep,
> In Christ I'm safe, in Him I sleep.

Of the others involved, all recovered, with the exception of Williams, a brakesman on the Lickey. He was given light duty as a policeman at Camp Hill, but died in 1844 having been in and out of hospital ever since the accident. His wife was given a gratuity of £5 by the Board.

The inquest judged that the explosion was '. . . occasioned by the boiler being constructed of iron plates which in evidence appear of insufficient thickness, and we attach a Deodand of £60 upon the engine.'

This was probably the best they could do with their imperfect understanding of the report made by Mr R.E. Prosser MICE who examined the engine's remains. We quote extracts from his report.

> 'This engine . . . was left on the side of the railway at Vauxhall station . . . where it lay for many months exposed to the weather . . .'
>
> The internal or fire tube being a reservoir for water [entering through the uncapped chimney], this exposure no doubt diminished the thickness of the iron plate by . . . rusting away . . .
>
> Up to the time of the engine being taken to the Grand Junction . . . it was deficient in evaporative power . . .
>
> To increase evaporative power Mr Inshaw lowered the back end of the firebars by 10 in.', and by this he increased the quantity of steam . . .
>
> The explosion . . . was . . . owing to the action of intense fire upon the [rusted] plate which burst. The heat first driving out the water from between the internal and external cylinders forming the boiler [i.e. the firebox water jacket], the plate became overheated and, of necessity burst; the space for water circulation being only 1½in. at this part . . .'

Further evidence showed that there was an accumulation of bits of screws, plugs and rivet heads in that 1½in. waterspace which restricted circulation adjacent to the point of failure. With that evidence in mind of faulty design and workmanship it is not surprising that the boiler exploded as it did.

An accident occurred on the Lickey near Bridge 106 (near Vigo) during the night of 7/8 April 1841 when, according to the secretary in his report to the Board:[18] '. . . a melancholy accident [has occurred] which has deprived you of one of your chief officers under circumstances of an unusually painful nature.' The cast is as follows; William Creuze, locomotive superintendent; William Walworth, locomotive foreman; Israel York, a driver, an American; Mr Torrey, foreman of Nasmyth Gaskell Ltd; Edward Shaw Carter, a fireman.

Now there was a cover-up! Two versions of the events were told, one by the secretary to the Board, and another by the fireman at the inquest. The two American drivers on the B&G, York and Donahue, lodged at a public house at Vigo Bank about two thirds the way up the incline. Donahue had been injured in a previous accident and he was confined to bed.

In the secretary's version Creuze and Walworth were in charge of banking duty on Tuesday evening, 7 April, along with driver York and fireman Carter. Having banked the first up mail, Creuze and Walworth left their locomotive, *Boston*, at Vigo Bridge, ostensibly to visit Donahue but in reality for a drinking bout. They left the fireman in charge with orders to drive the engine back to Bromsgrove.

At Bromsgrove he was joined on the footplate by York who had just returned from a holiday. Together, they banked the second up mail which was due in Camp Hill at 11.30 p.m.

On the way down York, the driver, stopped *Boston* at Vigo Bridge, announced that he was going to bed, and ordered the fireman to wait with the engine for Creuze and Walworth. Some two hours later the night duty policeman came down from Blackwell to say that the down mail would be due shortly. It was now 1.15 a.m. and still there was no sign of Creuze and Walworth. The fireman therefore had to drive down to Bromsgrove and cross over to the up line at the station where Mrs Walworth was waiting. She demanded to know where her husband had got to. When the fireman told her, she insisted on joining him on the footplate and they set off for Vigo bridge. Once there, Mrs Walworth marched off to fetch her husband, leaving the fireman to wait for her return with the party. This turned out to consist of Creuze, the Walworths and Archibald Torrey who was Nasmyth's foreman. (He had come to Bromsgrove in connection with some locomotives recently delivered from his firm.) They scrambled on to the engine and set off down the Incline. Soon afterwards a plug in the firebox backplate blew out, spewing the boiler's contents over footplate and tender. The fireman was badly scalded but managed to jump clear as did Walworth who was only slightly scalded. Torrey somehow escaped unhurt, but Creuze and Mrs Walworth were blown back into the tender. Creuze took the full blast perhaps because he was too drunk to move, but his body shielded Mrs Walworth from injury. Once the boiler had blown itself out Torrey stopped the engine with the handbrake, the others climbed on and they rolled down to Bromsgrove by gravity. A doctor was called and their hurts were attended to; but Creuze died at 6 a.m. that morning. The jury at the inquest blamed the accident on the improper fitting of a boiler plug. They fixed a deodand of £25 on the *Boston*.

At the inquest the story told by the fireman was heard. (This story sounds suspiciously as if it had been concocted by Walworth to minimise any blame which might be attributed to him.) According to this version driver York and fireman Carter were on banking duty that evening. Creuze was with them. After taking the second mail up to Blackwell, Creuze and York alighted at Vigo bridge to go to the alehouse, and ordered the fireman to await Creuze's return. After two hours however, he was told by the watchman to make way for the down mail, so he drove to Bromsgrove where he took on water and, having crossed to the up line, he was hailed by Walworth who demanded a lift for himself and his wife to Vigo bridge. (This sounds odd at 1.30 a.m.!) Accordingly he drove the engine back to the bridge where he dropped both Walworth and his wife; then, noticing that the water level was low he drove up to Blackwell and back with his pumps on to fill the boiler. After 20 minutes Creuze, the Walworths and Torrey arrived. Subsequent events were very much as described in the secretary's version as related above.

The scandalous state of affairs in the locomotive department revealed by the enquiry into this accident have been discussed fully in Chapter 17. Suffice it to say that Creuze was found to have been a drunkard which '. . . rendered him totally unfit for his situation, and to hide the consequences he was obliged to descend to the meanest subterfuges.'

Collisions and derailments were quite common as on most early railways. Thirty or so were of sufficient proportions to have been recorded in either the Minute books, local press or by 'Veritas Vincit' between 1840 and 1846. A selection of the more interesting follows.

In its early years, the railway still bore the scars of construction. Plant growth on the cuttings and embankments would have been slow especially where the soil was poor and spoil banks remained along the banks and cuttings for years. At Bredon, the cutting had quite steep, gravelly sides with spoil banks above. One night during the winter of 1841 a slip occurred. Frost action had loosened the gravel and clay mixture. This was set in motion by the vibration of an approaching train, which ploughed into 18in. to 24in. of gravel. The engine was derailed and the pressure of the coaches forced the tender to jack-knife against the engine. Joseph Billingham, the fireman, slipped from his footplate and was crushed between the engine and tender. He died in hospital. The policeman had passed the spot only minutes before the tragedy and had seen no sign of impending danger. By then the light had failed and the driver had no chance.[19] Accidental death was the verdict at the inquest, with a deodand of £20 placed on the engine and a rider that the cuttings be made safe and spoil banks removed.

'Veritas Vincit'[20] provides some insight into the cause and effect of some notable accidents. Whether his accusations are always true is open to doubt but his descriptions are humorous and are quoted verbatim. In a letter to the *Railway Record* he records how, in July 1843, McConnell and two other officers of the company took charge of an excursion train from Gloucester to the Tewkesbury Races. As it approached the terminus at Tewkesbury the train got the better of them. This, we suggest, was probably a case of priming. Any driver will tell you that once an engine has 'got the water', it can become virtually uncontrollable. 'At the top end [of the station] there is a gateway and beyond that a line of rails which crosses a public street and leads down to the river . . . There was some scaffolding erected inside this gateway which would not admit of an engine to pass under it but on this occasion the engine proceeded at full speed under the gateway . . . , the scaffolding catching the chimney, down it came . . . and the engine getting into the street, a pig that was passing at the time was run over and killed . . . The engine and train kept bending their way to the River Avon and had it not been from chance . . . , those most perfect of enginemen and their superior officer would have had a cooling dip in the river. You may picture . . . the state of the passengers . . . Would you believe that orders were issued by these gents to all servants who witnessed the occurrence not to say a word about it . . . and threats were very fully held out . . . Because the two engine drivers were locomotive superintendents they will not be dismissed, but if any two enginemen . . . had fallen into the same blunder every one of those superintendents would have joined in the cry . . . 'Discharge them'. How will they make . . . expenses of this disaster appear on the ledgers?' A similar incident was recorded by the *Tewkesbury Examiner*:[21] 'The Engine Driver, through . . . an error in applying the brake . . . suffered the passenger carriage . . . to get disengaged from the engine and it was propelled through the station house doors which . . . it shivered to pieces, the carriage then proceeded across the High St. and down Quay Lane but was luckily stopped before it reached the Avon. [Some] . . . passengers . . . alarmed . . . jumped out of the carriage but none was seriously injured, though several sustained inconvenience from falling into the mire of Quay Lane.' McConnell's alleged employment of substandard, inexperienced, ill-trained drivers is mentioned frequently by 'Veritas Vincit'. One such driver, turned (according to 'Veritas Vincit') from labourer to driver, lost control on the downgrade approach to Gloucester station:[22] 'There were two empty carriages in the station into which the engine pitched, turning the first over on top of the other . . . the other . . . broke down a part of the platform. This was another cause of 'merriment' to the passengers. To talk of alarm or destruction . . . is it seems . . . absurd and slanderous.' One of McConnell's 'Northern and Cheap' drivers was taking two crippled locomotives for repair at Bromsgrove. Near Dunhampstead he was signalled to caution as the goods train was just ahead. 'Disregarding his instruction . . . the driver proceeded on at the top of his speed slap into the train, smashing two of the wagons to pieces, damaging others, straining the leading axle of his engine and otherwise injuring it. The breaksman . . . was pitched over the smashed wagons into one that did not break . . .'

The worst accident of all occurred at Defford just after 10 p.m. on 30 August 1845. A special goods train was to run from Gloucester to

Birmingham that night. It was to follow the up mail (the last regular train of the day). When the 'special' reached Defford it collided with an empty wagon, spilling wreckage in the path of an approaching down train.[23] The *Gloucester Journal* reported that: 'The rails were torn up, the engines were shattered and carriages were lying in broken confusion one upon the other and the fire of the engines having communicated with them they were burning and seemed likely to become a general blaze.' Joseph Ward, the driver of the goods train was found beneath his engine and 'had ceased to exist'. Another man, Miles, a carpenter who had been working on the railway and was returning as a passenger to Cheltenham died shortly after, becoming the first and only passenger killed in an accident on the B&G. Damage was said, by the *Tewkesbury Examiner*, to be £3,000. The inquest held that the driver, Ward, was to blame for excessive speed and ignoring signals, but 'Veritas Vincit' attended to see fair play on behalf of the deceased driver. He came to a different conclusion, and accused certain officials in the Company of trying to cover up gross mismanagement.

In accordance with regulations, the up mail had carried two red lamps at the rear to indicate that a special train was to follow. James Dore, the Defford stationmaster and John Murphy, the porter had noticed the signal; Edward Shaw, an employee of the permanent way contractors, was sent to act as signalman south of the station and to stop all trains there. Ward, the driver of the special, had a powerful engine, MR No. 75, and it was alleged that he was a speed merchant. At Defford, an empty truck was waiting on a siding adjoining the up-line. It was to be sent south by the last down train, yet although Dore knew a special was due, he decided that Murphy should push the truck from a siding onto the up line where it could be quickly attached via the crossover to the down train thus causing minimal delay. This was the usual procedure since only two staff were kept at the station. Dore stood on the up platform holding a red lamp to stop the up special. Murphy carried a red lamp as he shunted the wagon. The contractor's man held a red lamp to the south of the station, yet the goods train driver, Ward, ignored all three signals and smashed into the wagon.

'Veritas Vincit' noted the presence of a great many company officials at the inquest, who were there, he alleged, to: '. . . prevent the truth from coming out . . . because the inferior servants of the company are afraid to state all they know.'

During the inquest, contradictory evidence came from the guard of the goods train and from Dore the stationmaster; concocted by the latter to blame Ward, who being dead could not defend himself. Baird, the stoker, was bullied by the foreman of the jury into giving misleading evidence, based on guesswork, implicating Ward of driving the train at 30 m.p.h. through red signals, which 'Veritas Vincit' found impossible to believe. Baird described how water-pump trouble had occupied both him and Ward until nearly a mile and a quarter from Defford, by which time the fire, steam pressure and speed were low. How could 30 m.p.h. be attained under such circumstances in a mile and a quarter with twenty laden wagons? 'Veritas Vincit' also pointed out the bad position of the signal lamps which were difficult to see from a distance owing to the bridge south of the station and also the scandalous misconduct of Dore for allowing a wagon to be put on the up line when he knew very well that a train was due, regardless of how many red signals protected it. Dore also contradicted himself when he denied seeing the twin red light on the Mail train which indicated that a special train was following shortly. He also refused to assist the badly injured fireman after the smash and had left Ward's body two days covered with a few empty coke sacks. Further, when Ward's widow had been present, Dore was alleged to have said; 'There he is, the villain, if he had lived he would have been hung'. 'Veritas Vincit' proclaimed Ward innocent and Dore guilty; the dead man could not defend himself against Dore's allegations and so posthumously received the blame. The inquest implicated Ward but pointed out the poor signalling arrangements, the poor layout at Defford, the lack of staff at stations and the breaking of the company's rules and regulations. A deodand of £1,500 was awarded against the engine 'No. 75'.

At the end of the day, whatever the accident, whoever the guilty party, further seeds of railway safety were sown. The Regulation of Railways Acts of the 1840s, the efforts of the BoT, the development of signalling and working procedures, and the increased training and awareness of staff all played a part in making the railways one of the safest modes of transport.

Accidents are incidents, but not all incidents are accidents! So, here are some of the more interesting and sometimes humorous ones. Navvies, as we have already seen, were magnets for incident. Many are the tales of drunkeness and theft. Theft of boots was common, many a navvy saved the price of a new pair by taking those of a sleeping or drunken colleague. But would anyone commit murder for a pair of shoes? At the back end of 1838 a young man was drinking at the Malt Shovel at Burcott in company with 'Railway Workers'. He was later found without shoes, 'senseless', his skull having been smashed.

Vandalism is certainly not a twentieth century evil. The secretary reported in August 1840,[24] '. . . a mischievous and diabolical attempt . . . to throw the train off the rails by . . . placing . . . iron and wood across them.' Fortunately, the obstruction was discovered before disaster occurred, and the culprit was caught and punished. A similar act the next year was interrupted by a watchman who discovered two men placing large pieces of clinker 'upwards of 1 cwt' on the line.

We have met the cow who lost her life under the wheels of a B&G train. Later, some of her cousins had a narrow escape. The driver of a Birmingham train near Spetchley saw two cows on the line ahead. He slackened his speed and on approach, instead of getting off the line, they immediately started off at full gallop continuing the same pace for nearly one and a half miles, the train keeping close behind, until eventually turning to one side they allowed the train to pass.[25]

'Cops and Robbers' was played in May 1841 in a lively railway chase. George Comely, a petty forger, attempted to flee from Gloucester to America via Liverpool. His victim, Mr Gillman of North Nibley, set off in pursuit but arrived 20 minutes after Comely had caught a train at Gloucester [the 11.30 a.m.]. He managed to convince police superintendent Walker of his bona fides and chartered an engine for £10 on which he and the superintendent set off in hot pursuit, or as the *Journal* reporter quaintly put it, in 'high pressure steam'! They sighted the train at Ashchurch and caught up with it at Spetchley where the pursuers crept on board and were able to arrest Comely as he left the train at Camp Hill.[26]

We end this chapter on a more humourous note.[27] '. . . two colliers . . . were returning from Cheltenham [to Gloucester] . . . both . . . tolerably 'fresh' . . . when one of them . . . knocked off his companion's hat with an umbrella by way of a frolic. Without an instant's hesitation, the hatless 'Forester' endeavoured to open one of the doors of the carriage in order to follow his property; but being unable to open it . . . rushed to the other side, opened the door and sprang out . . . At the same instant an up train passed on the other side, so . . . had [he] . . . succeeded in opening the first door he must have been . . . knocked to atoms. As it was, he fell on his head amidst a quantity of cinders but was able to immediately get on his feet . . . on finding that he was liable to prosecution for what he had done, he ran off, having recovered his hat and made a wide berth of the station.'

CHAPTER TWENTY TWO
BIRMINGHAM

Birmingham was the target first for canals, and then for railways during the Industrial Revolution. In the 1840s it was second only to London in its importance as a railway centre, and as such it still continues.

Prior to the B&G's Act of 1836, Birmingham already had links authorised with Liverpool, Manchester and London while the BDJc, incorporated in the same year as the B&G provided rail connection with the north and east Midlands by running over L&B metals to Curzon St. from Hampton-in-Arden.

The advantages to be gained by interchange of traffic with these lines at Birmingham were paramount in the minds of the B&G's BC, so much so that against the wishes of the GC they pressed for and obtained authorisation for a junction with the L&B and the use of the L&B's station. The GC begged them to save expense and establish only a depôt in south Birmingham so that the B&G would have dealings with Gloucester only and not with railways to the ports of London and Liverpool.

Plans submitted to Parliament in 1836 allowed for a junction with the L&B, a depôt for the B&G at Camp Hill and a spur to the BDJc's proposed Birmingham terminus. The latter was not authorised. Camp Hill was to be the local passenger and goods depôt. Facilities for locomotive and stock stabling were to be provided here too though its permanent use for any of these purposes became very much in doubt towards the end of 1839. Plans were mooted for a large terminus at Lawley St. adjacent to the BDJc's proposed depôt and reasonably close to the L&B and GJR at Curzon St. Of course, this all happened after the

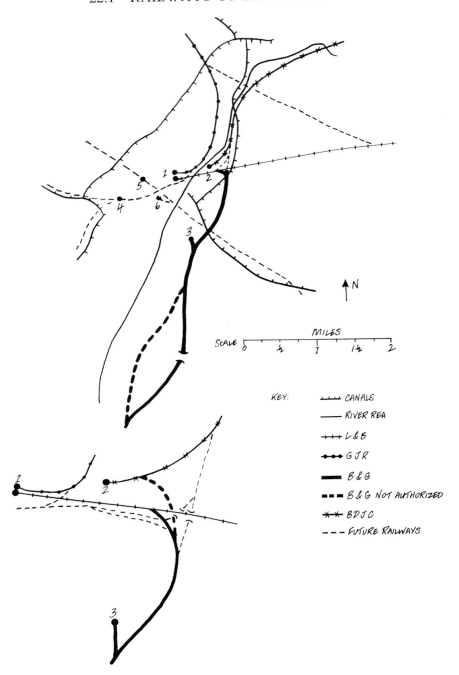

KEY:

+++ CANALS

— RIVER REA

+++ L & B

•—•—• G J R

━━━ B & G

▬ ▬ ▬ B & G NOT AUTHORIZED

✶✶ BDJC

– – – FUTURE RAILWAYS

MILES

SCALE 0   ½   1   1½   2

N

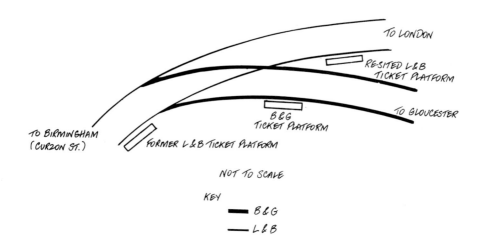

TO LONDON

RE-SITED L&B
TICKET PLATFORM

TO GLOUCESTER

B&G
TICKET PLATFORM

TO BIRMINGHAM
(CURZON ST.)

FORMER L&B TICKET PLATFORM

NOT TO SCALE

KEY

━━ B&G

── L&B

Camp Hill site had been purchased. So to find a use for it, it was proposed firstly to establish a temporary repair and maintenance depôt there and then to make it the main locomotive works even though work on the locomotive shops at Bromsgrove was already in progress.

These plans did not eventuate and all was left as it was except for the decision that the Camp Hill passenger depôt would close when junction with the L&B had been made, and the station at Lawley St. built.

Sheds for the maintenance of carriages and wagons, minimal locomotive cover and goods sheds were erected here in addition to the passenger station. Work on the latter was far from satisfactory in the eyes of Sir Frederick Smith, the BoT inspector who visited Camp Hill in December 1840. The station was less than half finished, rails had not been laid and no signal lamps were fitted. An immediate flurry of activity from the B&G engineer allowed him to report completion of the station except for the portion which had been in place before the inspection.

It was opened for traffic on 17 December 1840; but when the L&B junction opened in August 1841, it was downgraded and used for goods traffic, carriage and wagon maintenance and for the station pilot engines only. Passenger traffic returned briefly between November 1841 and November 1844 when carriages were run with goods trains for local traffic and 3rd class passengers.

Subsequently the carriage and wagon department was moved to Bromsgrove and by the time the MR took over in 1846, Camp Hill had become a depôt mainly for fruit and vegetable traffic. The MR later built a passenger station on the main line leaving the spur to serve the goods depôt.

The B&G's Act of Incorporation not only allowed them to build a junction with the L&B but to have running powers into the Curzon St. terminus and to '. . . any future terminus of that Company in or near Birmingham.' It was this inherited clause which enabled the MR to gain access to New St. some 20 years later.

The B&G directors had been undecided whether to build their own main station at Lawley St., or to form a junction with the L&B or BDJc, or both. This indecision delayed the construction of the extension from Camp Hill until late in 1840 when plans for the Lawley St. station were dropped on the grounds of expense and the original plan to use Curzon St. was re-adopted. By taking this wise course they not only saved the expense of a new station but brought their trains within easy reach of the L&B and GJR at Curzon St. – whose terminii were adjacent but not connected physically – with ideal connectional possibilities.

Passenger trains ran into Curzon St. from 17 August 1841 and the B&G were charged an annual rent of £1,000 for this facility. Goods traffic, the greater part of which was to be exchange traffic with the GJR, was to be carried over L&B metals on a toll basis.

Trains from Gloucester stopped 70 yards short of the junction at a ticket platform where passengers' tickets were examined. Timothy Suffolk served here for three years as ticket collector. No passengers ever used the platform, so no shelter was provided, yet, in spite of working out in all weathers under bleak conditions he seems, from comments made here and there about him in the minutes, to have been a cheerful obliging soul. He collected tickets only from passengers in up trains (i.e. to Birmingham), so his work, though occasional, always had to be done at a rush to avoid delay, and as traffic increased he had to be given an assistant and an increase in salary from his former 18s. a week. In between trains he began to take an interest in the number of 'foreign vehicles' (wagons and coaches from other railways L&B, GJR, BDJc etc.) which passed on to B&G metals, and the B&G vehicles which went through to other railways. His notes were passed on to Joseph Edmondson at the B&G check office and were of great value when in 1842 the B&G joined the railway clearing house. Timothy Suffolk thus became the B&G's first 'Mileage Inspector', and as such was by September 1842 earning some 30s. a week.

In 1844 he was offered and accepted a change of occupation as a 1st class passenger guard with a wage rise to 37s. per week. His final promotion came some five years later when in 1849 he was appointed stationmaster of Yate.

The operation of the junction between L&B and B&G at Garrison Lane has already been explained (Signalling, Chapter 16). No collisions were reported but during the CofE purge of 1843, 'Veritas Vincit' kept one eye on the junction, just in case passenger safety was put at risk.[1] 'At the curve leading to the London junction it is . . . proposed to remove the switchmen. At this curve there are five pairs of points [for switching bank engines from up to down lines and so on]. Suppose the bank engine were crossing the line at these points and the fireman off the engine to turn them, and a passenger train coming down the heavy [sic] incline at the same time, by reason of the curve, the engineman of the passenger could not see the bank engine crossing. Coming down at full speed [he exaggerates here, there was a limit of 20 m.p.h.] he could seldom observe it until he went right over it and perhaps the whole train would be thrown right over the embankment.' B&G, and subsequently MR passenger trains continued to use Curzon St. station until the LNWR opened New St. in 1854. They continued to use this line until 1885 when they transferred to their present route over the Birmingham West Suburban Railway. The original Camp Hill line is however still in use, but for freight and diversionary traffic only.

The use of the L&B terminus had also been extended to the BDJc, incorporated in the same year as the B&G, which reached Birmingham via a junction at Stechford; a branch to Hampton-in-Arden was authorised for London traffic and this was built first and opened in August 1839. But high tolls charged for using the L&B line between Hampton and Birmingham together with unreasonable delays inflicted on their trains by the L&B, determined the BDJc to pursue their independent line into the city via the Rea Valley. This opened in February 1842 and terminated at Lawley St.

A junction between the B&G and BDJc had been authorised by the latter's 1840 Extension Act, but the restricted space, within the angle of the convergence of the L&B and GJR lines at Curzon St. did not allow room enough for the B&G to build their depôt. This prevented a satisfactory agreement, and the junction was never built.

As completion of their Birmingham line approached, the BDJc still found themselves without connections with adjacent railways. An inclined spur to the GJR, opened in April 1842, enabled them to transfer, in a roundabout way, traffic with the B&G. However the spur was unreliable and frequently out of commission.

Accordingly, in January 1842 the BDJc proposed a wagon lift instead of a conventional link. The top of this sat close to the junction of the B&G and L&B thus enabling the transfer of vehicles to both lines with a single outlay. Completion was delayed until July 1843 and no sooner had it entered regular use, initially for wagons but eventually for coaches, moves for a junction were re-started. This either bears testimony to the uselessness of the hoist, or its success in the development of through traffic. When authorised in 1845 the junction was already redundant. The BDJc had become part of the MR in 1844, who took over the B&G the following year, along with their right to use the L&B terminus. A junction which would allow through north–south transfer was authorised (from Saltley to the ex-B&G line). It was opened in 1851 and replaced in 1897 following major reconstruction of the lines into New St., and of the station itself. For their part in the massive rebuilding scheme the MR were rewarded with joint ownership of New St. with the LNWR.

CHAPTER TWENTY THREE
THE LICKEY INCLINE

by Rev. W.V. Awdry

In contrast to the somewhat haphazard operating methods often permitted, or at least condoned elsewhere, the Lickey being an obvious danger spot, was worked from the first strictly to rule, and with almost military discipline.[1]

In July 1840 Capt. W.S. Moorsom drew the directors' attention to this when he demanded the provision of stronger coupling chains and more reliable brakes for wagons and coaches than were then usual on other railways. He emphasised that this was to guard against break-aways, and to provide adequate brake power for every train. The Board agreed, and resolved that brakesmen be employed who, together with the train guards and enginemen, should be drilled into strict observance of the regulations drawn up by the engineer and secretary for the working of the Lickey.

To allay any nervousness which might be felt by the public, Capt. Moorsom assured those present at the August 1840 general meeting that: '. . . In descending the Plane, the trains are under the most perfect command, and I have no doubt that by combining proper caution with ordinary skill and practise, you may . . . work the Incline . . . by . . . Mr Norris' engines with security and efficiency and I believe also with greater economy than by any other means. . .'

The set of rules had been drawn up by September 1840. They are quoted in full in the appendix, but the main points are given here. Drivers of all southbound trains had to shut off steam at Bridge 109 at Lindhurst, (half mile north of Blackwell). It was then a timber structure and painted white so as to be unmistakable. Having done this the driver was to give warning of his approach by whistling, while the guard and fireman were to man their brakes so as to be ready to stop dead at the white post set up alongside the down line some 300 yards from the top of the plane. (This post, or its successor was still there in 1986, having at some unknown date been moved from its lineside position and into the fence.)

Once the train had stopped, the Lickey brakesmen took complete charge. The first, or chief brakesman was the 'Captain' commanding the train on its 'voyage' down the bank. He directed operations from his 'bridge' on the middle coach. His 'Mate', the second brakesman, had to see that the brakes on every vehicle were in working order and manned by guards or travelling porters. He then took his seat on the leading coach. When all was ready the 'Captain', with one blast of his whistle ordered the driver to open his regulator just enough to start the train, while the fireman stood to his tender brake. Once on the move two whistle blasts meant 'Shut off steam and let her roll'; while three was a call for a general brake application. This was to be made gradually, taking the greatest care not to lock the wheels. Speeds allowed were 20 m.p.h. for passenger trains in dry weather, but on slippery days this maximum was cut to 16. Goods trains were limited to 10 m.p.h. whatever the weather.

During the actual descent, one blast from the whistle meant 'Ease all brakes', while five blasts warned of 'Obstruction – Danger'. The brakesmen had nothing to do with ascending trains, nor, officially were they allowed to ride on them. It is only to be expected however, that they often did so, especially at night.

On sighting an up train, the Bromsgrove policeman, Thomas Saunders or James Adie, whichever happened to be on duty, would ring the station handbell. This was the signal for the bank-engine to cross over the down and on to the centre line in the station and take up position on the up line under the bridge. The up train would draw in behind the bank-engine, and the banker's fireman would couple up. Meanwhile the policeman had to inspect the train. All vehicles had to be coupled with both centre and side chains, and the rear vehicle had to have its brakes manned and ready for instant use. Only when satisfied about this could the policeman allow the guard to give the 'Right-away'.

An amusing incident occurred in May 1841 (see above Passenger-traffic, Chapter 14). The Gloucester Mechanics Institute had organised an excursion to Birmingham, and members from Cheltenham and Tewkesbury came along too. The train finally left Ashchurch with 623 passengers aboard 23 coaches, the whole being hauled by two engines (Norris Class As we presume). At Bromsgrove the train was divided and the first portion (14 coaches), headed by one of the train engines and a banker, began the ascent. But the two engines were no match for the load. They stalled some way up the incline and the engine which was to have assisted the second portion was sent ahead to push!

This was, of course, an exceptional case. The B&G, except in such emergencies, never banked from the rear. They always used a pilot. It is much to be regretted that no-one, so far as the author has been able to discover, ever described the manoeuvres performed at the top, 'when dropping the pilot'. They would give any modern railwayman heart attacks! Let the rules speak for themselves:– Nos. 7 & 8 (Ascending) 'As soon as the tail of the train reaches the summit of the Plane, the fireman of the bank-engine will throw [sic] his engine from the train, and at the same moment the train engine is to slacken speed by shutting off steam, and thus allow the banking engine to go at least 30 yards ahead and turn into the siding prepared for the purpose. When the train has passed on, the bank-engine will descend the Plane on the east line at a speed not exceeding 12 miles per hour.' The hazards of this operation were frightful. Four separate people were involved in a complicated oper- ation which demanded split second timing. This timing depended on a number of variables – length and speed of train, condition of the rails, time of day and the light conditions prevailing, to say nothing of the vagaries of the weather. The fireman had to clamber over the rear of his tender, then, standing on a buffer shank, he had to hold on with one hand while lifting the heavy coupling with the other. Having done that he had to hold on like grim death while his driver sprinted for the refuge siding. The pointsman was not mentioned at all, yet he was the king-pin of the whole and had to act with unfailing promptitude in order to switch the banker into the spur and the train following it safely on its way to Birmingham.

G.P. Neele in his *Railway Reminiscences*,[2] says that such an operation was performed by trusted switchmen many times daily for years at the top of Camden Bank and '. . . so far as I remember, no accident to the running train ever occurred; a singular fact in connection with so risky a performance . . .', but he does mention that a number of pilot engines came to grief at the buffers of the refuge siding.

There is no mention in the official records of any accident happening either to bank-engines or trains during the two years that this method was in operation at Blackwell; but it is highly unlikely that everything always went according to plan. Anyway, from 1 May 1842 McConnell had it abolished in favour of a safer procedure, and McConnell's method lasted till changed at some unknown date in Matthew Kirtley's time; but that is to anticipate.

From time to time the rules were changed as the result of experience. One such alteration was made in June 1841. On 19 May the approach of an up goods train was heralded as usual by the policeman's bell at Bromsgrove. As usual the banker moved forward to the up line and stood ready and waiting under the bridge; but, contrary to regulations, the goods train failed to stop. Its speed was not great, but the bank-engine's tender and the train engine's front end both suffered. At the enquiry, the guard blamed his brakes, and said they were out of order. Mr Edward Lean, the carriage and wagon superintendent, examined them and found that, though stiff, they were not inoperable. The guard was, very properly, reprimanded and fined for neglecting to check and oil his brakes before leaving Gloucester. Repetitions however could not be ruled out, so in the interests of safety rule 3 (Ascending) was altered to read thus:– 'No engine is to be allowed to stand on the main line at Bromsgrove station'.[3] This meant that in future the bank-engine would have to wait on the centre road until the arriving up train had actually stopped.

Changes were made at summit too. As first laid out the line climbed at 1 in 300 from Blackwell for another mile and six chains before reaching line summit at a point just north of what is now bridge 111 near Barnt Green. Capt. Moorsom had foreseen the possibility of having to divide exceptionally heavy trains prior to their descent, and had laid in sidings for the purpose. These evidently had taken their grade from that of the main line (viz.1 in 300). Capt. Moorsom had probably tested them out with wagons and coaches in new condition, and found that their tendency to roll was slight. He therefore considered it could be ignored. But once in traffic their bearings had become 'run in'. The result was that if inadequately braked or chocked vehicles were left in those sidings, anything from a rough shunt to a gust of wind could set them off. After several such tearaways had thundered through Bromsgrove fortunately without damage to stock or life, a 'near miss' in March 1841 was sufficiently alarming to induce the BC to spend money on preventing a recurrence. Wetherall was ordered to lengthen the 1 in 37½ at Summit to a point at which enough height had been gained to enable 240ft. of 'dead level track to be laid before coming on to the Plane'.[4]

The next change in the rules occurred in October 1841. Referring again to the BC, Minute 523 of that date, it will be remembered that this Minute ordered that while the Class B Norrises ran the Bromsgrove to Birmingham section; the Class As were to operate to and from Gloucester. This was to allow locomotives of both classes to be brought into shops regularly for examination. The drill at Bromsgrove for both ascending and descending trains had therefore to be changed. The impending arrival of a down train would be announced by the duty policeman's bell, and the waiting Class A would prepare for action. For up trains the policeman's bell brought out the Class A Extra bank-engine with a Class B coupled on behind. They stood in the centre road till the Class A had uncoupled, run over the trailing crossover to the down line and thence to shops. The banker and the Class B drew forward and took the train away. This arrangement lasted from October 1841 to 30 April 1842. It was never intended to be permanent. Once McConnell had cleared up the backlog of maintenance which he had inherited, he proposed to substitute for the perilous manoeuvre at the top something safer and less complicated, and there is evidence, albeit not conclusive, that a month or two after his arrival he had eased the bank-engine firemen's lot by installing, experimentally, a 'trip-hook' by means of which the banker could be coupled to the train engine, and released at summit by the pressing of a treadle on the footplate. This device we find referred to in subsequent Minutes as 'Mr McConnell's Connecting Catch'.

In August 1841 the B&G had a self-invited visitor. Edward Bury invited himself to Bromsgrove to demonstrate the prowess of a locomotive of his manufacture on the Lickey. We can only guess at his motives. First of all, Bury was and had been since 1838, locomotive adviser to the company. He strongly disapproved of their connection with Norris and in consequence had for some time held himself aloof from their affairs; but now he felt that with McConnell's arrival at Bromsgrove the situation had changed. Bury had been McConnell's employer and had thought well of him. We have no direct evidence, but it is nevertheless highly probable that Bury had given McConnell a testimonial when he applied for the job at Bromsgrove.

Further, Bury believed, quite sincerely and very properly, that his engines were the best that could be found anywhere; but he made the mistake of assuming that anyone, such as McConnell, who had had a hand in their manufacture could not help but believe this too.

Finally, Bury was above all else, a business man. He wanted orders for his firm. With McConnell now in the B&G locomotive department he felt that the time was ripe to make a push to get business from the B&G. McConnell would naturally, so Bury thought, advise the company to buy Bury locomotives. Bury therefore planned his visit with the object of impressing the directors with a demonstration of the superiority of Bury locomotives. Reading between the lines it is possible to discern that Bury was a man of some conceit, and this, as far as these particular trials were concerned, was the cause of his undoing.

He arrived at approximately 10.20 a.m. on 23 August. He brought one of his own locomotives as nearly as possible in weight and dimensions similar to *Philadelphia*. This fact is important in view of Bury's remarks afterwards. The locomotive he brought with him was the L&B's No. 65, and one of his own manufacture. She was a 0-4-0 with coupled wheels 5ft. in diameter, and her cylinders were 13in. diameter with 18in. stroke. No. 65 weighed with tender in working order some 19 tons. This, it will be remembered was the weight in working order of *Philadelphia*. She had 4ft. diameter driving wheels and her cylinders were 12½in. in diameter with 20in. stroke. So, on paper, the two locomotives were fairly evenly matched.

With his engine Bury brought a test train of seven wagons and one coach. Each wagon was loaded with rail, and weighed on average with load 6¾ tons. The coach carried 15 people and its gross weight was 4½ tons. The coach was included in every test train so we need not mention it again. The full details are given in the appendix, so we need do no more than summarise the story here. No. 65 refused to move with 6 wagons (45 tons), and stalled after 270 yards with 4 wagons (31½ tons). Only when a further wagon had been removed reducing the load to 24 tons could No. 65 climb the bank at all, and this at an average speed of 8.7 m.p.h.. *Philadelphia* pulled this load up with the greatest of ease, blowing off steam all the way, and reaching a speed of 15.2 m.p.h.. The other results with lighter loadings are unimportant. The unfortunate part of the whole affair was the unsportsmanlike way in which Bury behaved. He complained about *Philadelphia*'s boiler pressure, and the unfairness of comparing locomotives of different dimensions.[5] In his chagrin it quite slipped Bury's mind that *he had issued the challenge himself, and that he had himself chosen No.65 as the locomotive best fitted to compete.* (author's italics).

His rage can hardly have been mollified by the realisation which, alas for Bury, came much too late, that he would have to face the humiliating prospect of having to ask for assistance to get his test train up the Lickey and back to Birmingham. This, Donahue, *Philadelphia*'s driver, was doubtless delighted to give, and perhaps fortunately for Bury's blood-pressure *Philadelphia* had to be coupled on in front so he would be unable to see the smile of triumph which doubtless wreathed Donahue's face!

In view of what we have said in previous chapters about the Norris's higher than normal boiler pressure it is interesting to note a further comment by Mr P.C. Dewhurst on the affair. We quote '. . . taking the figures for the heavier load – the others are of no interest – it is clear it [the Bury] developed little more than the 2231lb. of its calculated Rail Tractive Force at 80 per cent and 55lb. p.s.i. boiler pressure.' The most interesting disclosure is that the *Philadelphia* which must be presumed to have been doing its best to show well against its rival – and considering again the heaviest load – merely performed a duty equivalent to about 2944lb. tractive effort, which is significantly equal to a boiler pressure of just under 55lb. p.s.i. which is the pressure limit current at the period. This incidentally was a calculation which Bury, in a calmer moment, should have been perfectly capable of working out for himself.

Bury locomotives, as far as workmanship and materials were concerned, were far and away superior to the Norrises. The Burys were built to last. The Norrises (according to what would appear to have been the American philosophy both then and since) were built to do a job, wear out and be replaced. No. 65 was doubtless a good performer on the easy grades of the L&B, but her performance on the Lickey leads us to conclude that she suffered from inability either to make steam fast enough or to get it away freely enough; perhaps a bit of both. She was thus unable to develop the power of which she ought to have been capable.

Philadelphia's victory was decisive, and for some four years the supremacy of the Norris A Extras on the Lickey was unchallenged; but they were expensive brutes, and it was only through 'saddle-tanking' them – as described in a previous chapter – and thus reducing their operating costs to manageable proportions, that the next stage in the operation of the Lickey was evolved. We get the first hint of this in a somewhat obscure Minute of the BC dated 18 January 1842. It seems clear that Bischopp and McConnell had been discussing their ideas with the chairman who did his best to explain them to the committee, but it is doubtful if either the committee or their secretary had really grasped what it was all about, for it is entered in the Minute Book thus:– 'Proposed sidings on top of the Lickey. To be laid on the Down side for the purpose of carrying out the contemplated arrangement of working the engines without ascending and descending the Incline'. 'Resolved. That the above proposal be laid on the table for further consideration'.[6]

However, all soon became clear. The experimental saddletanking of *Philadelphia* showed that her haulage capacity had been increased to 80–90 tons gross; and this was power enough for any loadings offered at the time. If the other two A Extras were saddletanked as well it would be possible, apart from other savings, to do away with the expense of double-heading up the Lickey.

The class Bs on the Birmingham run were now in reasonably good condition. The bank engines, working alone, could take trains up the Incline and hand over to them at Blackwell. On the down journey the Class Bs would come off at Blackwell leaving their trains to be taken over by the returning bankers, which would now for the first time be in revenue earning service for the second half of their trip.

All this had to be planned carefully. The new arrangements at Blackwell would involve the permanent way department, and the traffic department as well, so Wetherall, superintendent and resident engineer had to be brought in. Operating rules at the top of the Lickey would have to be revised together with alterations in the time-table to ensure that bank-engines wasted as little time as possible at Blackwell between up and down trains. Sidings as well as locomotive servicing facilities would be needed up there too. These would have to be carefully planned and their cost kept as low as possible so as not to alarm the directors.

Thanks to the chairman's backing, the project was steered safely through, and the new system of working the Lickey began on 1 May 1842. The bank-engines, as rebuilt, were no beauties, the harsh angular lines of their saddletanks saw to that; but they and their crews soon settled into their new routine, and their economical working delighted the directors.

The new pattern would seem to have been as follows: on the sighting of an up train, the policeman's bell would bring out a big Norris to stand on the centre road at the station till the Gloucester engine had uncoupled and gone to shed. The banker drew forward and coupled up then lifted the train up the Incline alone. On reaching summit the banker's fireman would 'slip' his train by using the 'connecting catch'. The banker then sprinted for the refuge siding, there to wait for a down train. The pointsman quickly reset his switch for the main line on which, some distance away, the locomotive rostered for Birmingham was waiting. The guards braked the coaches to a standstill and the locomotive backed down and was coupled up.

It is curious that while no accident is recorded at Blackwell during the extremely dangerous process of dropping the pilot formerly employed, yet an accident followed the introduction of the safer method. 'Veritas Vincit' pounced on it gleefully. On 26 May the 11.30 ex-Gloucester, with a consist of three coaches, reached summit at Blackwell. The banker slipped the train, and ran safely ahead. The pointsman adroitly did his part, and the crew of the Birmingham engine backed her gently towards the coaches, expecting that they would stop within the usual braking distance. They did not. A brake rod on one of the coaches snapped. They rolled on and collided with the engine. The impact was slight; neither engine nor coaches were moving at any great speed, and no real damage was done to passengers, staff or stock; but the shaking they received prompted some passengers to complain, and McConnell was ordered to investigate and report. This he did on 31 May and the following directive was issued: 'Ordered that . . . Mr McConnell should renew his orders to the drivers . . . to be . . . on the alert to move the engine forward in case of the train coming at more than ordinary speed, and not to move back to attach to the train until it is completely stopped'.[7] Incidentally this extract from the Minutes is the first indication that the new plan for the Lickey had actually been put into effect as ordered.

Although from that date bankers worked all service traffic up and down the Incline, there was a certain amount of gravity working too. This increased when Blackwell became a locomotive depot. Engines were fuelled and watered there and coke was brought up from Bromsgrove in wagons coupled to any convenient train. The empties usually went down by gravity. Permanent way contractors sent their empty ballast wagons down by gravity too. Heavy goods trains were divided at Blackwell, the first portion being sent down with the engine, while the second part, after a suitable interval, followed by gravity – sometimes with spectacular results at Bromsgrove. For instance on 18 June 1842 the second part of a goods train collided with the first part just south of the station and spread itself over both roads. The chief brakeman, Wells, was given a reprimand and fined, but when a similar run-away occured in August he was sacked, and W.H. Goodwin, from the Cromford and High Peak Railway, was given the job. Following these two accidents the dividing of goods trains at Blackwell was forbidden. They were to be held there until enough brakesmen or travelling porters were available to man the brakes on every third wagon.

Gravity working for empty coke and ballast wagons continued till it too was prohibited after an accident at dusk on 23 November 1842. Mrs Woodward, a washerwoman who was employed at a house near the Incline, had asked for, and obtained, permission to use the line as a short cut, between train times, on her way home. Without telling anyone, some members of a P.W. gang used that slack time to get into a ballast wagon and career downhill on their way home. Their wagon had no lights. Mrs Woodward did not see them, nor did they see her. They felt the impact, but were quite unable to stop. Goodwin had some explaining to do when called before the board on 3 January, and the result was an order abolishing all gravity working on and from 10 January 1843, which goes on to say '. . . three wagons or less are to be attached to a returning bank-engine, and any greater number must be taken down in the same way, but in charge of a brakesman'.[8]

This rather suggests that it had not after all been possible to devise a timetable which balanced all Lickey workings, and that occasionally the bankers had to return 'light engine'.

Goodwin's interview with the Board would appear to have shaken him considerably as he resigned shortly afterwards, and an advertisement for his successor was sent out on 18 February to the railway press.

Birmingham and Gloucester Railway.
'Wanted as Head Breaksman [sic], or Bank-Rider, a person who has been used to the management of trains down inclined planes, and who is also qualified to take charge [as Overlooker] of the Permanent Way on that part of the line.
Salary £80 a year with a residence.
Testimonials . . . to the Secretary, Waterloo Street, Birmingham on or before the 13th March.

George King. Secretary.

There was a long list of applicants, but finally, in April, Thomas Russell was appointed.[9] Russell had joined the B&G as a constable at

Cheltenham in 1841, but had soon afterwards become a Lickey brakesman.

That the post of head brakesman should be combined with that of overlooker of permanent way seems a little odd, but the answer may lie in the fact that as overlooker he would be responsible for the inspection rather than the actual doing of P.W. maintenance. In the advertisement it was expressly stated that the particular stretch for which he was to be responsible was the inclined plane. He, as Bank-rider, would know – who better – by traversing it repeatedly, the position of every rough spot which was in need of attention. Safety required that this stretch, above all others on the line, needed first class maintenance.

The second consideration which comes to mind is that as overlooker he would have control of the P.W. gang and thus have authority to penalise any for such irresponsibilities as had caused trouble in the past. It was now his job to to stop all gravity working and ensure that all wagons went down the Incline under proper control. This of course is speculation, but it does offer a reasonable explanation for this odd sounding combination of jobs. Further it not only saved the B&G some money in wages (a prime consideration with them), but it also put some extra money into Russell's pocket, of which no doubt he was able to make good use.

Russell seems to have done well in the job. His predecessors, Wells, and Goodwin had come to grief in a year or even less. He was 'carpeted' once in 1845 after a run-away for which, on enquiry, he was cleared of blame, and his name occurs again in 1848 after a derailment for which he was also held to be blameless.

In 1843 he was working under difficulties. This was the year during which the CofE with its swingeing staff and wage cuts, laid a blight on the Lickey as well as every other department of the line. Of the brakemen, hitherto a team of four, one was dismissed, leaving Russell, Charles Wells, and Richard Sky to manage on their own. Strict observance of the rules demanded the presence of all three on any descending train of four or more coaches; nor could they be expected (according to rule) to trudge up the 2½ miles of incline and reach Blackwell in time for their next descending train. It is quite clear that this rule, at least, had to be quietly forgotten when, to the benefit of the bank-enginemen and brakesmen, McConnell announced that he and the superintendent had managed, in the new time-table, to balance up and down trains better than ever before.[10] Thus a bank-engine would bring a train up with the brakesmen 'riding on the cushions', and within a short while could expect a train ex-Birmingham to arrive for them to take down. This of course eased life for the brakesmen, but there were never really enough of them, and inevitably short cuts had to be taken to keep the traffic moving; sometimes 'near misses' resulted but fortunately with no damage or loss of life.

It was this aspect which 'Veritas Vincit'[11] siezed on in his letters to the *Railway Record*. In April 1843 he wrote:– 'The Lickey Incline I believe to be one of the most dangerous in the Kingdom; and what may happen with a whole new set of drivers put on, and a brakesman discharged?' Illustrations of what he meant appear in the Accidents chapter, but he particularly refers to a driver whom he names as George Dunn who, he alleged, '. . . laboured the greater part of an afternoon to take a train of salt up the Lickey without effect until his day's work was at an end . . . The driver . . . who relieved him for the night attached his engine to the train and ascended . . . with the greatest ease.' That George Dunn had had, together with many better men both before and after him, the humiliating experience of stalling on the Lickey when perhaps he had boasted that he could 'go it alone' – that we can readily believe – but what we cannot believe is that he was left with his train fouling the main line until the evening shift came on. The time-table had to be worked; otherwise there would have been a 'tail-back' of trains and no end of a row featuring in the Minutes under the heading of 'Detention of Trains'. This would certainly have attracted notice in *Berrow's Worcester Journal'* to say nothing of other newspapers; but we have not found any mention at all of such an occurrence. The likelihood is that 'Veritas Vincit's' spy at Bromsgrove added the embellishment himself and that 'Veritas Vincit' accepted it without question. He was apt to do this with any stories calculated to ridicule either the B&G or McConnell.

All the same, tall story or no, 'Veritas Vincit' had a point. Traffic was increasing, and trains, especially goods, were getting longer and heavier. Further, since the A Extras were ageing; by mid-1843 longer refuge sidings were asked for and provided both at Bromsgrove and at Blackwell, to accommodate divided trains.

The incline staff, though depleted, would be blamed if the traffic failed to get through; but in order to secure this, rules of safety were having to be 'bent', sometimes to a reckless extent. 'Veritas Vincit' was quick to comment on this. 'I cannot conclude,' he wrote, 'without calling on General Pasley to go down to Bromsgrove and watch the dangerous way in which the public are conveyed on the Birmingham and Gloucester line. It is true they have been lucky in not having fatal accidents, but it is also true that hair-breadth escapes have been numerous and, should a fatal accident occur, the Board of Trade can have no excuse in not putting a stop to the danger.'

It was with this in mind that McConnell obtained permission in January 1844 to buy the two Jones and Potts 0-6-0s each capable, at need, of lifting heavy loads up the Lickey by themselves; and to supplement the A Extras by a powerful bank-engine of his own design built specially for the job. 'Resolved. That Mr McConnell be instructed to make an engine of the power named in his letter.'[12] This was followed in May by his appointment as '. . . Manager of the Incline, and Superintendent of the Company's servants working thereon'. Almost his first act[13] was to have the lip of the incline shaved off at Blackwell in order to make the change of gradient at the top (from 1 in 37½ to level) less abrupt. Extra siding space was required too, and better water and coking facilities at Blackwell. In connection with the former, water supply suitable for locomotive use had always been difficult at Bromsgrove. Hitherto they had had to rely on the stream a few hundred yards south of the station. Now McConnell proposed, with the Board's permission, to obtain the rights to tap the spring at Pike's Pool, half way up the Incline, and pipe water down to Bromsgrove. This was successfully accomplished. The water from Pike's Pool was good and remained the station's water supply for very many years.

In October, further Lickey brakemen were sworn in. The Minute[14] does not say how many, and McConnell asked that a shelter be provided for their use while waiting for their turns of duty at Summit. Somewhat characteristically Charles Sturge said that rather than spend money on a new one they could make use of a 'box' now disused at the closed Kempsey [Pirton] station. This would serve, he said, if transported to Blackwell.[15]

In 1846, as related in Chapter 17, the yard at Blackwell was lit by gas as well as being linked to Bromsgrove by electric telegraph. The proposal to do so had first been made in November 1845, and the work was completed in 1846 with the erection of two cottages for telegraph clerks by Messrs W.A. Watson at a cost of £123.10s. each.

The B&G was now coming to the end of its independent existence. But though its career had been, in the main, undistinguished, it did for a short while in 1845–6 achieve a gleam of glory in the engineering world. It was in July 1845 that *Great Britain* rolled out of Bromsgrove Works and immediately caused a sensation. *The Times*[15] said she was '. . . the largest locomotive that had yet been made . . .', but engineers saw more in her than that. They were impressed by her power and, as we have seen above, flocked to Bromsgrove to watch her at work and chat with her designer.

Strangely, there was no mention of her made in the Minutes, but it seems clear that apart from the fact that she was more powerful and could tackle heavier loads than any other engine, she was used to operate the Lickey under a similar system to that begun by McConnell in May 1842.

The evidence he gave before the Gauge Commission on 11 August 1845 bears this out. What follows are some paraphrased extracts.

McConnell told them that he had had four years experience of working the Incline, and that this experience had shown him that the American engines, though still in use, were much too light for the work now required of them. He had therefore designed and built an engine specially for the work. It was a six coupled saddletank engine with large cylinders and small diameter driving wheels and which weighed some 30 tons in working order.

The normal average speed of trains on the Lickey, he went on, was 12 m.p.h.. The speed which his engine had attained on passenger work was 12 to 15 m.p.h.. This was because of the greater power of his engine. His engine, he told the Commissioners, could lift a gross load of 135 to 148 tons up the 1 in 37½ gradient at a speed of 8 to 10 m.p.h. This was a load far beyond the capability of the American engines. His engine, too, could haul a load of 1,000 tons on level track at a speed of 10 to 12 m.p.h.. McConnell claimed that it was speed rather than weight which caused most injury to track. He then went on to tell them how, for the past four years, he had worked the Lickey. He told them that he had found that injury was done to engines descending the incline with steam shut off. This caused a drop in temperature under the effects of which boiler tubes contracted causing leakage. It was his policy therefore to work that portion of the line from the top of the Incline to Birmingham with one set of engines, and from Bromsgrove to Gloucester with another, leaving traffic up and down the incline to the bank-engines alone.

It would be interesting to know when it was that the simpler and less time-consuming method of banking by buffering up in rear was adopted; but this, we doubt, we shall ever know with certainty. It could never have taken place until (a) sprung instead of padded buffers had become the normal practice, and (b) until the different railways whose vehicles passed over the B&G section of the Midland Railway had agreed on a standard height above rail level for their buffing gear.

The routing of their line up the Lickey had been one of the B&G's most 'expensive economies'. It was this 'economy' which helped to keep that company in debt throughout its independent existence. The Lickey remained as an expensive operating problem to both the Midland and the LMS companies, and still, on occasion, provides problems for BR. It should never be forgotten however that a great and world-wide institution owes its inception to an attempted and, for the time, a successful solution to the problem. It was J.E. McConnell's *Great Britain* which drew engineers to the Lickey, and led to the formation of the Institute of Mechanical Engineers, with McConnell as their first chairman in January 1847.

CHAPTER TWENTY FOUR
CHELTENHAM

We have already traced the early development of the railway in the Cheltenham area by the B&G, who threatened first to leave the town three miles from the railway and after several subsequent changes of plan arrived at the present route and station.

At first the main line avoided Cheltenham by several miles and had an independent line to Gloucester. It was then moved to within a mile of the town centre with a station at Mauds Elm but the planned station there was soon abandoned in favour of a central branch line. However, by agreement with the CGWU, the Act of Incorporation authorised the B&G main line only to Cheltenham. Here a junction would be made to a joint line to Gloucester with the CGWU. The present route was finally adopted in May 1837 by an Amendment Act and in December 1838 plans for the joint station were dropped by mutual consent of both Companies.

The junction with the joint line to Gloucester was to be almost directly beneath the new Cheltenham to Gloucester turnpike road bridge, and the site for the B&G's depôt would be very nearly at the point of junction of the Gloucester and Cheltenham Tramroad's branch to Leckhampton. Some historians allege that the B&G chose that site to make use of a large country house which could be converted into a station building. However, no such house is mentioned in the Minutes at any time, and contemporary maps show only one building, the tollhouse of the tramroad which was far too small and indeed is recorded as having been removed by the B&G to make way for their depôt.

A grand approach road was planned to link the station from the

Gloucester Turnpike at Lansdown Gate, and alongside the tramroad branch to Leckhampton. After eighteen months use as a private approach road, and an illegal short cut for many other journeys, its state of repair had deteriorated considerably and the board took steps to hand it over to the Cheltenham Road Trustees for the use of the general public. As such it is still known as the Queen's Road, home of the late Arthur Negus.

Work commenced on the depôt early in 1839, Thomas Newton was awarded an initial contract worth £3,125 with more following for works at platform level. As the railway approached completion the *Gloucester Journal* remarked on the extensive range of buildings which were rapidly nearing completion and which, when viewed from the Gloucester Road bridge presented a '. . . particularly neat and substantial appearance . . .' For a description we quote from a contemporary guide.[1] 'The principal building consists of the Company's booking and other offices and the refreshment and waiting rooms for the reception and general accommodation of the public. These all open immediately on the railway which passes at a level much lower [15ft.] than that of the carriage road and leading down to which are several broad flights of steps, descending from the booking office platforms. Fronting the entrance gates a neat colonnade is thrown out from the building under cover of which the carriages and other vehicles set down their passengers [this played a dual role by also supporting a large tank to collect rainwater for use by locomotives]; to the right is a range of sheds beneath which the omnibuses are while waiting the arrival of the trains and extending a considerable distance to the left are offices and warehouses appropriated to the goods and traffic of the line . . . [there is an] iron bridge which crosses the line forming a covered way from the station to the platform upon which the passengers from Gloucester and to Birmingham assemble, the down trains discharging their traffic on the broad pavement under the embankment wall immediately above which the station and offices of the Company are situated.' In addition, stables for the omnibus horses were provided. Cast iron piers supported the wooden roof over the platform, and their capitals (several of which still survive) are fine examples of early Victorian ornamental ironwork. Capt. Melhuish of the BoT thought the station was: '. . . very well arranged and provided with sheds, offices and waiting rooms sufficiently large for the accommodation of the public and of a very neat and ornamental appearance.' Despite these comments, the station was apparently unfinished, for additional works were estimated for in May 1841 and March 1843 though no details are given. A luggage lift was planned but never installed while increased accommodation for goods traffic was planned and a siding put in. It may well be that a certain amount of the liabilities mentioned above were for the coal depôts at Alstone and Tewkesbury Road and the goods yard at the latter place, of which more later.

Being a large building the station house had more room than was required by the railway, so a portion was leased to a Mr Churchill at £200 per annum. He had his fingers in several B&G pies, running the post horses and the refreshment rooms. When he asked for a lower rent for the refreshment rooms, the Board told him this was impossible; they had already had complaints of high charges and of smoking being allowed which was strictly against the rules.

Perhaps the only, and certainly the biggest, disadvantage of the station was its distance from the town centre. The CofE reported that they: '. . . do not think much judgement was shown in placing the station.' Apart from the obvious disadvantage to travellers, for whom an omnibus service was provided at extra charge, anyone wishing to make enquiries, book a ticket, send a parcel or whatever, had to make the long journey. To solve that problem they took over a room at the Old Post Office in the High Street early in 1842, then after a while moved to share Mr William's (the coal and goods carrier) offices.

Cheltenham's importance as a passenger station warranted a large staff. In 1841 for instance there was a chief clerk, assistant clerk, station inspector, five policemen and five porters. The chief clerk was Henry Jewsbury who had been promoted from the post of assistant clerk.

There is an interesting point about Henry Jewsbury. Whereas, in the Minutes, most station officials are referred to by their christian names or surnames alone, Jewsbury is always spoken of as 'Mr', a distinction otherwise reserved for heads of departments; Mr Lean (carriage and wagon); Mr McConnell (locomotive superintendent); Mr Edgell (goods); Mr Burgess (secretary) etc. There would seem to have been a strength of character about Henry Jewsbury which inspired respect, and discouraged the taking of liberties. He was certainly listened to and was able to get things done. For instance during the winter of 1841–42 he complained of draughts and coldness in the booking office. Complaints of that sort were made by other clerks at other stations and little, if anything, was done, and that after much delay. Mr Jewsbury's complaint brought the chairman (Capt. C. Moorsom) to the station to investigate, and the matter was attended to at once.

From his first appointment as assistant in May 1840, Mr Jewsbury had lived out of Cheltenham, travelling to and from work by train, and had claimed free passes for doing so from Mr Edmondson at the check or 'ticketing' office. The B&G had, from the first, been very grudging in their allowance of free travel for their employees, but Henry Jewsbury got away with it till an investigation from an 'economy drive' revealed his vouchers in the check office, and he was ordered by the Board to move house to Cheltenham. This he did in April 1842, and presented them with his removal bill for £36. It was met in full without argument!

In September 1842 Mr Jewsbury's assistant, Edward Waterfall, resigned and a young man named Caviller was appointed at £30 per annum (exactly half Waterfall's salary). Caviller was allowed to live in rooms at the station rent free, but even so Caviller's was a starvation wage and inevitably, in a place like Cheltenham, Caviller fell into debt. Jewsbury knew about this and kept urging Caviller to write to the Board about his trouble. The Board received Caviller's letter in January 1843, but did nothing about it except to pass it on to the police committee. There is no record that they gave Caviller any answer or acknowledgement. Meanwhile Caviller was continually being 'dunned' and getting more and more desperate. At last his nerve broke, and in May he absconded with some £35.10s. being a day's takings and part of the booking office float.

The Board promptly made Jewsbury responsible, and a Committee of Enquiry was mounted. A week later Caviller was arrested in Birmingham. The Board wanted to prosecute, but found on taking legal advice, that having made Jewsbury responsible they could not do so as he was now the 'injured party'. They urged him to prosecute, but he refused, and Caviller was accordingly discharged. They (especially Shaw and Tate) were furious at this but could do nothing. Eventually Sam Bowley (deputy chairman) brought them, or at least a majority round to see Mr Jewsbury's point of view and respect it; for when in October 1843 he wrote saying that he had repaid £26 of the debt, the Board agreed to remit the remaining £9.10s.

Henry Jewsbury stayed on at Cheltenham for one more year. In June 1844 he gave in his notice, saying that he had been offered a post in London, and wished to leave as soon as it was conveniently possible. His successor William Turnbull, was appointed within a week, and Henry Jewsbury then asked the B&G to pay for his furniture removal. The company resolved, 'That Mr Jewsbury's furniture be taken to London at as low a rate as possible, so that the Birmingham & Gloucester Company do not lose.' We get the feeling that they were somewhat relieved to be rid of a man whom they could neither fault nor intimidate!

Meanwhile, what of the CGWU? In March 1843 they announced that their station was to be on Jessop's Nursery Garden in St James Square. By this time they had become a puppet company to the GWR, who shortly afterwards bought them out at a bargain price and began a lengthy and determined effort to take over the railways in the Cheltenham and Gloucester area, which they considered to be their rightful territory.

By building a series of connecting lines (see map) to their central station the GWR hoped to confine the narrow gauge of the B&G to the

Birmingham–Cheltenham section with a gauge break at the B&G Cheltenham station. As may be imagined, the B&G did not take kindly to this idea, though the junctions giving access to the town centre did appeal. They had the power to run into the GWR's depôt, and to build an independent depôt for themselves, so they took the proposed junctions to Parliament. However, both the GWR and B&G's applications were refused. When the MR took full control of the B&G in August 1846 they proposed and applied to Parliament for a deviation line from Brockhampton (2 miles to the north) connecting with the GWR's branch roughly where the GWR's Honeybourne line joined; again it was rejected.

Throughout MR, LMS, and into BR days, the ex-B&G station (Lansdown in BR jargon) was an operating problem. Its short platforms forced long expresses to draw up twice, whilst through trains were handicapped by the sharp curve on which the station was built. It was not until 1964 that the platforms were lengthened when both up and down bay sidings were removed.

Lansdown station remains unchanged in many respects, a B&G 'period piece'. The colonnade has gone, but the basic shell of the station house remains, as do several examples of original B&G iron-work. It remains to be seen how long it can escape redevelopment.

Cheltenham's affluence in the early nineteenth century gave it one of the country's earliest gas works, which together with its wealthy inhabitants, gave the town a healthy appetite for coal. In 1837 for instance 56,000 tons were consumed; half each from the Forest of Dean and the Midlands. Forest coal had the best reputation and commanded 21s. per ton whilst Midlands (Staffordshire mainly) was a little cheaper but of inferior quality.

It is not surprising that the B&G planned to take advantage of this demand by bringing Midlands coal in competition with the existing water transport via the river Severn, the Coombe Hill canal, thence by road. A strip of land to the north of the Tewkesbury Road was purchased in May 1839 but no progress had been made twelve months later when mention was made of developing a site to the south of that road for coal wharves and a second class passenger station.

In September 1840, the engineer was ordered to investigate which would be the best site for a coal and goods depôt. A goods yard was set up on the south side of the Tewkesbury Road in 1841, but the provision of coal facilities at Alstone Wharf (nearer to the passenger station) was deferred until the following year. The railway was until then not competitive with the tramway, which could bring Forest coal into the centre of Cheltenham much more cheaply than the B&G could bring either Forest or Midlands coal. In fact it was not until

1848, when the Gloucester Docks branch had been built, that the railway gained traffic from the tramroad.

Several requests were received by the B&G from merchants wishing to use the land to the north of the Tewkesbury Road as a coal wharf, but it was left to the MR to develop this. It remained a coal wharf until the early 1960s when the site was cleared and facilities transferred to the south side of the road where the B&G goods yard was. This yard flourished and grew to large proportions in MR days with a private siding to the gas works, but all that now remains are a few sidings to the coal depôt, Cheltenham's sole contribution to BR's railfreight business. The sidings at Alstone spread providing carriage accommodation, a turntable, a siding to the Central Ironworks in addition to the coal wharves. All but the most basic carriage stabling now remains.

THE GLOUCESTER AND BIRMINGHAM RAILWAY STATION.

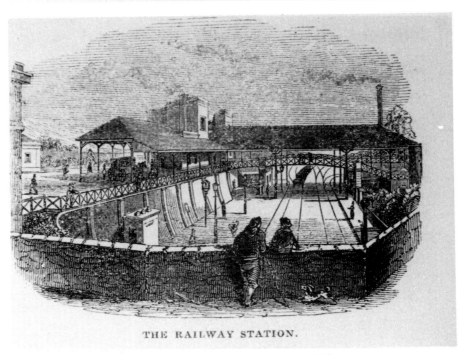

THE RAILWAY STATION.

Cheltenham Station (Gloucester Records Office).

Gloucester Station, 1849. 'Queen Victoria Changing trains' (*The Illustrated London News*).

Gauge break at Gloucester – 'Transhipment of Goods' (*The Illustrated London News*).

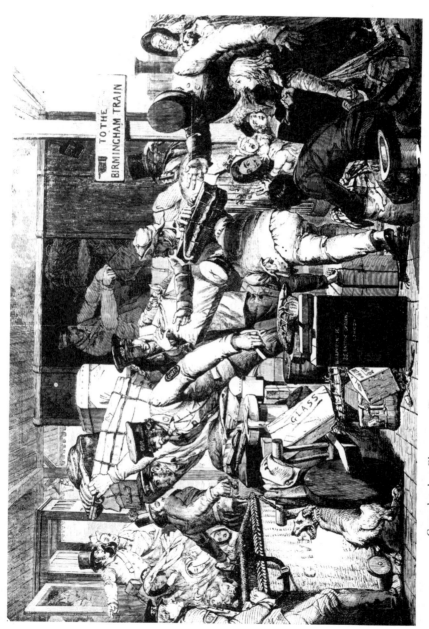

Gauge break at Gloucester – 'Passengers and Luggage being Shifted' (*The Illustrated London News*).

CHAPTER TWENTY FIVE
GLOUCESTER

by Rev. W.V. Awdry

[PART ONE]
THE STATION

Time was when there was no such place as Tramway Junction. It is interesting to reflect that it was a certain Daniel Trinder who in 1809 unwittingly decided where that bottleneck of traffic should be. (Map 25.1)

Daniel Trinder was engineer to the Cheltenham and Gloucester Railway – hereinafter called the tramway. A 3ft.6in. gauge plateway, it had been authorised by Parliament in 1809, and opened for traffic in 1810. Of the three routes which had been surveyed, that finally chosen was Trinder's. Instead of reaching the docks circuitously from north or south, as others had planned, Trinder's route was more direct. It left the Cheltenham–Gloucester Turnpike at Longevens, and struck south along what is now Elmbridge Road. Crossing the Barnwood Road at right angles it entered what is now the Elmscroft Estate and swung westward on its own right of way to cross Horton Road (then Asylum Lane) obliquely on the level. Then skirting the premises of Puff Mill (now buried with Eastgate Station under ASDA), it joined what is now Bruton Way at a point nearly opposite Cambridge Street, and having crossed Barton Street proceeded via Park Road over Brunswick Road to curve round behind Brunswick Square and enter the Docks through the main gates in Southgate Street.

Had the B&G been left to their own devices they would not have crossed the tramway on the level. Their plan (Map 25.3) shows that by the time they had reached the tramway in Park Road their line would

224

have gained sufficient height for clearance by an overbridge. Capt. Moorsom had planned the location of his depots with great care before submitting them to Parliament in 1835. The centrally sited passenger station, albeit at high level, was to be in or rather above Southgate Street approximately where the New County Hotel is now. From thence an incline was to descend to the dock basin.

Capt. Moorsom was aware of course that a line on arches through the city might provoke opposition, and had therefore prepared an alternative. This skirting the then city boundary, reached the Gloucester and Sharpness Canal at High Orchard, and a site was provided for a passenger station at or near the crossing of the Bristol Road.

Somewhat to Capt. Moorsom's surprise his high level plan was approved and authorised but with the proviso that should the CGWU's application to Parliament be successful their route was to be adopted for joint use by both railways between joint stations at both Cheltenham and Gloucester. That at Gloucester was to be near the Cattle Market and built by the B&G at their own expense on a site of their choosing which was to be bought and paid for by the CGWU and leased to the B&G in perpetuity for a peppercorn rent. Further, the CGWU were bound by their Act to build the Cheltenham–Gloucester line and have it ready for traffic (Maps 25.2 and 3) by the time the B&G was ready to open throughout in 1840 or before. But when, as we have seen above, after a year of argumentative inactivity, the CGWU showed no signs of honouring their obligations, but rather the reverse; a certain coolness developed between the two companies since for their own protection the B&G had insisted on inserting penalty clauses into the CGWU's Amendment Acts. By this means the B&G had been able to ensure that the track bed at least had been laid by mid 1840 even though they had to lay the rails hurriedly themselves (Map 25.2). Further they were empowered to buy up not only the CGWU's moiety in the joint line but also that of the tramway as well. This involved them in considerable expense so there was little money to spare when it came to building Gloucester station.

Capt. Moorsom's original high level approach to the docks had however gone beyond recall, and though plans for a joint station were now abandoned, he was bound to follow the CGWU's route as far as Horton Road (Map 25.3). Once over the crossing however he was free to choose his own path and headed away from the CGWU's alignment for some 715 yards [the distance from the crossing gates to the buffers is 716 yards on Causton's map; but on the MR(1852) track plan it is 714. We have therefore taken the average] to a spot east of the Cattle Market and just within the city boundary where he decided that his 'temporary station' was to be. In the absence of any plans the nature and site of his intended permanent station is a matter for speculation. His line rose at 1 in 180 from ground level at Tramway Crossing and the station area itself was built on arches some 6ft. above the surrounding land. It has been argued from this that he still hankered for a high level approach to the docks and if this was really so, the necessary viaduct would have straddled the city diagonally, crossing Northgate and Westgate Streets and many others as well. The cost would have been huge and quite beyond the meagre B&G finances. Our own view (arrived at from a study of Causton's map of Gloucester 1843), is that he was aiming for a station frontage on Northgate Street approximately at its junction with Worcester Street. This would have been a good central position and would have established the B&G firmly in the city; but this 'might have been', though it would only have involved a quarter mile extension, was never financially possible for the B&G, and the 'temporary station' remained on its constricted site for 56 years until replaced by Gloucester 'Midland', latterly known as 'Eastgate', opened in March 1896.

Temporary or not, the B&G Gloucester station should have been made a worthy one. It was not, and fared little better than others on the line. With all it had been the same story; too few funds allotted and orders to proceed given much too late. Though plans had been ready by October 1839 they were subject to constant countermanding and indecision by both the GC and the Board. Work was delayed till August 1840 in spite of the fact that this section of line was scheduled for opening in November.

Capt. Melhuish of the BoT thought poorly of it when he made his inspection in October, and gave only very guarded approval. He reported the station as being 'a large shed 200ft. × 70ft. with offices and waiting rooms under construction at the city end'. He noted that it was only a temporary station, and added that '. . . should it be ultimately decided to make this point the terminus, the directors would, no doubt, order such additions and alterations as may be required for the convenience of the public'.

Information about the station layout and its development is scanty. Little help is available from the company Minutes, so deductions have to be made from such track plans as are available. We have four in our collection, Causton's map of Gloucester 1843; the OS map of Gloucester 1851; the MR track plan of the station 1852; and the GWR track plan of 1855.

Causton's map is to a scale of 1in. to 3 chains (66ft.). He shows the B&G double line swinging westward from Barnwood Bridge to cross the tramway and Horton Road on the level. Gates were installed some 37ft. apart and a lodge on the south side with bow windows facing east and west provided for Michael Moseley, the crossing keeper. Soon after the crossing the B&G's two tracks became four. The main line was paralleled north and south by two sidings. That on the north, with its stop block adjacent to the road, came from the engine shed while the southern siding with stop block some 200 yards from the gates led to the goods depot west of which had been laid, in 1841, some 5 chains of plateway and edge rail track alongside each other to facilitate the transference of loads from rail to tramway and vice versa. The plateway spur then ran along what was then Barton Lane (It became Station Road and is now Bruton Way) to join the tramway opposite Cambridge Street on the way to the Docks. (Map 25.4)

The passenger station was approximately 80 yards long and 30 yards wide. It had two platforms each 60 yards in length while offices and concourse took up the remaining area. An unpretentious train shed of the type widely used at the time, covered platforms and trackage. A drawing of part of it appeared in the *The Illustrated London News* for 6 October 1849 showing Queen Victoria changing trains at Gloucester on her way home to Windsor. This of course was after the Midland take-over, and they had decorated it for the occasion, but their efforts could not disguise what must have been a bleak and uninviting structure. The shed covered platforms and trackage which consisted of four roads – two of which, the middle ones – served as engine release roads and/or carriage sidings. All four tracks were linked, in the then customary manner, by turnplates at each end of the station. A number of points are shown leading to engine shed and sidings, but these would have been of the 'stub' or, as they were then called, 'sliding rail' type. It was not till 1843–44 that these were phased out of the B&G as dangerous. The vacant area to the north reserved for the CGWU is clearly shown, also the extent of the somewhat cramped looking locomotive shed which had two roads and was some 30 yards long by 8½ yards in width. Its size in the early years was reasonably adequate. The number of engines kept here varied from time to time, but the average number was four or five which included a pilot (yard shunter), a spare engine or two, and those stabled here in between trips.

Causton's map gives no indication of how the rooms in the station building were used, but we get some help from the O.S. survey of Gloucester (1851) which was drawn to the larger scale of 1in. to 45ft. At platform level there were three rooms; a ladies' waiting room, a refreshment room, and booking office which latter had by 1851 become a telegraph office as well. It is to be presumed that the building had more than one floor and that George Thomas, chief station clerk, and George Walker, station inspector, and their respective staffs could be accommodated. Even so the building was a small one and the porters room and parcels office was outside in the yard. So also was the Railway Post Office building.

In his book *Railway Station Postmarks*[1] Mr D.P. Gowen includes a reproduction of a number of Gloucester Station postmarks. These are distinctive and show that, to the GPO, the Railway Station Post Office (RPO) was a place of considerable importance. Mr Gowen explains that in mail coach days the GPO established sorting offices every 100 miles or so along their routes. It was the business of these offices to circulate and deliver letters to places in their area. These were called forward offices. With the coming of railways the GPO saw the advantage of adapting to the pattern of the rail routes to which they proposed to transfer their mail.

Older forwarding offices, such as Chester, retained their mail coach status; but new offices, such as Crewe and Swindon, were opened. Gloucester was one of the most important of these, since by 1839–40 four different railways going north, south, east and west had been authorised to meet there.

The first Gloucester station post-mark used was a large (29mm diam.) circular one with serif type lettering. This type had been introduced in 1828 and used all over the United Kingdom; but the only other railway station offices known to have been issued with this type were Berwick on Tweed and Swindon. Having recognised that Gloucester was a key place for mail distribution the GPO was anxious to establish a railway forward office here, but the station was designated as temporary only, and since the office accommodation provided was limited, the GPO built a temporary structure too in the station yard, and there it remained until, with the abolition of the BrG broad gauge, space was available in the station concourse for a mail sorting and forwarding office adjacent to both MR and GWR stations.

To return to 1844. The BrG arrived in July of that year. They used, as they were entitled to do, the CGWU line laid for them between Standish and Millstream Bridge; but they had to lay their own track round the Millstream curve (Map 25.5). Following Brunel's survey (Brunel of course had his eye on south Wales), they crossed both the B&G and the tramway on the level at Horton Road, and came to rest on the north side of the B&G station on land originally reserved for the CGWU. The BrG were a somewhat jimcrack, penny-pinching company, and not above acquiring and laying second hand rail on their line to save the expense of buying new. Nor was their track building above reproach. The directors and shareholders found this out in an embarrassing manner when their pre-opening Special on 6 July came to a jarring halt on the Millstream curve. One of the locomotives had slidden down between the rails and embedded its wheels in the ballast because a tie-bar (or bars) had been carelessly bolted!

Indignant passengers had to walk some three quarters of a mile over rough ballast to reach their luncheon at the B&G station. Brunel and

General Pasley (BoT inspector) got no lunch at all. They had to direct the re-railing of the engine and coaches as well as repairs to the track.

The BrG provided a service of 6 trains a day each way, commencing on 8 July, but as the days passed both McConnell and Bayliss became increasingly concerned at deterioration manifest in the BrG track at Tramway Crossing. By the end of the month the crossing was becoming dangerous for B&G trains. On reporting this to the Board, McConnell was on 6 August directed to inform the BrG engineer that he was to relay the crossing to B&G satisfaction within a week. Failing this the B&G would pull it up and relay it themselves at BrG expense.[2]

The OS 1851 map shows the B&G station layout – turnplates and all – much as it was in 1843, but east of the station throat there were differences. On the south side there was a ticket collection platform. This did not appear on Causton's map, but it had all the same been provided at a very early date as a precaution against fraud. Trains stopped here before entering the station proper, and passengers' tickets were collected by one of George Thomas' assistant clerks until passenger numbers warranted the appointment of a full-time ticket inspector named Tilley who by July 1844 had been given an assistant named George Street.

Eastward again lay 'docks junction' where a standard gauge line (Map 25.5) curved away southward astride the plateway spur of 1843. It joined the tramway proper opposite Cambridge Street *en route* for the docks. This line, as we shall see below, was completed in May–June 1844 in the teeth of fierce GWR opposition and gave the B&G at last an improved access to the Docks on which their own wagons could run.

The BrG station had three roads, arrival and departure with a central road between them, all three being connected at the throat end by turnplates. Curiously no method is shown for engine release at the terminal end by turnplates or traversers. Traversers (no less than three of them) appear in the 1852 track plan – perhaps they had not yet been installed in 1851 and shunting engines were still being used, or it may be that the OS surveyors saw the traversers but did not understand their significance. An engine shed and carriage shed were provided on the north side and fuel and water facilities common to both railways on the other. Further northwestward, and extremely awkwardly sited, is shown a small transfer goods shed. The bad siting, and inadequate size of this together with the trouble arising therefrom is detailed in the Break of Gauge section of this chapter.

As one would expect in an 1851 map, the improvements which the Midland Railway put in to combat the break of gauge are shown. The MR turned Wheeler's Nursery into a goods yard. These improvements will be noticed below in part 2. The 1851 map is tantalising in that the OS, bound as they were by their terms of reference, stopped short of the then city boundary which lay a few chains east of the station throat. Light is thrown however on this area by the MR track plan of 1852 drawn to a scale of 1in. to 40ft. Interesting developments have taken place. (Map 25.6) On the south side of the B&G, land had been bought for the erection in 1850, or thereabouts, of a roundhouse 150ft. in diameter centred by a 35ft. diameter turntable which gave access to 13 radial roads each some 50ft. in length. Six were narrow, and seven of mixed gauge; by one of the latter the roundhouse was entered, and another led out to repair shops.

East of the roundhouse a standard gauge line curved southwest from Tramway Junction to join just north of Barton Street, a spur coming from Wheeler's Nursery. The line from the Junction was the branch authorised in 1845 and built in 1848 (see Docks) which gave the B&G at long last rail access to their dock basin at High Orchard. East again the plan shows trackwork both broad and narrow for some 250 yards beyond Tramway Junction and gives information about peculiarities there. The tramway has been slewed to cross both road and railway diagonally in a south westerly direction. The BrG's broad gauge line sweeps round in a north westerly curve from Millstream Bridge and crosses the tramway and the B&G both at the same spot. The level crossing gates have now been pushed some 85ft. apart instead of the 37ft. shown by Causton in 1843. The gatekeeper's lodge is still there but is now islanded in the midst of trackwork much of which was put in by the MR subsequently to 1845 in their efforts to beat the Break of Gauge.

In 1845 the GWR(CGWU) having settled their differences with the B&B(B&G), and payment, or agreement to pay, moneys owing in respect of their moiety of the Cheltenham–Gloucester line having been reached, the B&B allowed them to run into the B&B (BrG) broad gauge station over the Millstream curve; a permission of which the GWR availed themselves for some two years, thus giving Gloucester people for the first time a choice of routes to London (i.e. via Swindon or Birmingham).

It was not till 1847 however, that the GWR took steps to implement their share in the Cheltenham line and further developments began to take place east of Tramway Junction (Map 25.6). Broad gauge was laid in round the Barnwood curve, and the 1852 track plan shows partly how this was done, but for the rest and the dual gauge point work at Barnwood, we have to rely on MacDermott's *History of the GWR* who himself obtained this information from the report of the BoT inspector, Capt. Simmons.[4] (Map 15.1) Starting from Tramway Junction the broad gauge line to Cheltenham made an independent crossing of Horton Road and the tramway north of the B&G's and after about 10 yards joined up with it three rail fashion, the common rail being in the unusual position of the inside of the double track all the way to Lansdown Junction, Cheltenham. The joint line from Cheltenham was three rail too (common rail inside) as far Barnwood Junction but then, according to MacDermott and the inspector, it began to do odd things. It became four rail for several hundred yards before it finally shook free of the B&B(B&G) and then struck out on its own towards the BrG curve from Millstream Bridge which it joined some 40 yards east of Tramway Junction. This is clearly shown on the Midland's trackplan of 1852 but is not so clear on the diagram Map 25.6. However, Map 15.1, though not to scale should illustrate the arrangement adequately. The MR track plan shows another junction on the Millstream curve some 50 yards east of the above. This was where the line from the 'T Station' came in. (Map 25.6) In 1847, having adapted the joint line to take trains of broad as well as narrow gauge to and from Cheltenham, the GWR found it inconvenient to take their Paddington–Cheltenham trains into Gloucester (BrG) and out again. Accordingly, while their 'short trains' (Gloucester–Cheltenham local traffic) used the Barnwood curve, the GWR, for their own convenience, laid a line along the base of the triangle of which the Millstream and Barnwood curves formed the two sides, and called it 'The Cheltenham Loop'. Midway along the loop they established their 'T Station' at the spot where the line from the BrG station crossed the loop and terminated in a locomotive lay-by on its eastern side. This 'T Station' was an oddity to end all oddities! Where the line from Gloucester crossed the 'loop' coach-length turnplates were provided in both up and down lines. A train for Cheltenham would stop here and the rear coach (reserved for Gloucester passengers) would be detached and either horse or hand shunted to the turnplate, angled for Gloucester and then shuttled to the BrG station by the waiting tank-engine. A similar process was gone through for passengers from Gloucester in which case, of course, the coach was coupled to the train instead of being detached from it.[5]

The 'T' station remained in use for some four years until in fact the Gloucester and Dean Forest (later South Wales Railway, SWR) arrived in Gloucester in September 1851 to which the GWR made end-on junction and established an M.P.D. near Horton Road. Once this was done the 'T Station' fell into disuse and the loop was abandoned until re-opened for freight in 1901 and for passenger traffic in 1908. But again we are running ahead. Though both B&G and BrG ceased, officially, to exist in 1846 the problems the BrG had created still lived on, and to close the story here would be most unsatisfactory. Much had to happen before the problems were solved, and evidence of this comes from a GWR trackplan of Gloucester stations dated 1855 (scale 1in. to 40ft.),(Map 25.7).

Whereas the Midland track plan of 1852 showed the SWR station as a small two platformed affair standing somewhat aloof and to the north west of that of the Midland, this plan shows striking differences (Map

25.7). The up SWR platform had been demolished to make way for goods sheds and sidings, while the down platform on the south side had been extended eastwards for some 280 yards, a diamond crossover having been provided midway to enable the one platform to accommodate trains coming from both directions. The station complex was to all intents and purposes a joint one, for the eastern half of the GWR platform lay alongside the Midland station, and direct access had been provided from the one to the other.

The BrG broad gauge station was no more, all traffic being concentrated on the B&G side which still had four tracks, turnplates and all, but great alterations had been made in the trackage at the station throat, while both arrival and departure platforms had been doubled in length. The area formerly occupied by the broad gauge station had been partly filled by carriage sidings, and partly by ancillary buildings – refreshment and waiting rooms etc. – thus freeing space in the original buildings for purposes of administration, but as yet the parcels office, porters' and railway Post Office buildings were still shown outside in their 1851–2 position in the station yard. Given the new layout however, and the extra space available it was not long before a new RPO room was provided on a site on the former BrG side and easily accessible from both GWR and MR stations. That this was so is shown on another MR track plan in our collection but one whose date puts it some years beyond our present terms of reference.

It must be emphasised that the GWR 1855 track plan shows arrangements at the Gloucester stations as they were at that time, and, as we have noted above, considerable alteration had taken place since 1852. There was however one alteration which, although of great importance to the MR, the GWR did not deign to notice. This was the Gloucester & Stonehouse Junction Railway shown on Map 25.7 as the Passenger Curve. It had been authorised in August 1848, and opened for traffic in May 1854. Narrow gauge to Bristol was no new idea. It had been envisaged by the B&G, recommended by the BoT in May 1845 and also in the report of the Gauge Commission which had been issued in 1846. Giving evidence before a House of Commons Select Committee in June 1845 George Hudson, MR chairman, had expressed his company's firm intention of obtaining powers to extend narrow gauge to Bristol by building if necessary, their own independent line.[6]

The Act had not been obtained without a struggle, for the GWR insisted that the MR, being the successors of the BrG, were bound by that company's agreement of 1843 to remain broad gauge for 20 years. Eventually a compromise was reached whereby though the MR could, if they wished, build their independent line they would not be entitled to use it till 10 years had elapsed from the date of the agreement; and that further they must continue for another 10 years to pay the tolls due for running powers over the GWR Gloucester–Standish line regardless of whether or not they intended to use them. In addition the MR were to bind themselves to maintain in good order the mixed gauge between Standish and Bristol so that the GWR could exercise their running powers over that part of the line if they so desired.

The G&SJ loop line swung south at a spot which became known as Gloucester Passenger Junction some 317 yards west of Tramway Crossing. It curved sharply to pass west of the Roundhouse, over the site of Puff Mill which had been bought and demolished for the purpose, and joined the 'High Orchard' or goods branch just about five chains north of the Barton Street level crossing. The two lines diverged again at the California Crossing. Here the goods line swung south west over Park End Road on its way to the docks. The passenger line continued over Farm Street and Painswick (now Tredworth) Road crossings to Tuffley and ran thence parallel with the GWR to Standish Junction. Here the GWR swung eastward for Stroud and Swindon, while the MR joined the former BrG line and ran thence (mixed gauge) to Bristol.

At Gloucester, Bristol–Birmingham trains had to reverse into or out of the station but the break of gauge was now beaten and the same train could be used for the whole journey. This basic arrangement was to prevail at Gloucester for the next forty years.

[PART TWO]
THE BREAK OF GAUGE

Following the report of the Gauge Commission, *The Illustrated London News* wrote on 6 June 1846: 'No public question at first sight ever seemed so inept for pictorial illustration as that of the railway gauges, being nothing more than parallel lines essentially still, mechanical and monotonous; yet no-one has yielded better pictures than those which we publish today. It is another proof that the commonest everyday incidents present good subjects for pictures if we will but seek them.. . .

As universal chroniclers, we could not give the question the go-by, uninviting as it appeared; and so we despatched our artist to Gloucester where the strongest evidence on this subject is said to be made palpable every day and hour. . .

At Gloucester two different railways unite . . . The first has a width of 4ft. 8½in. between the rails; the last 7ft. ¼in. The gauge. . . is broken or interrupted; hence the term we now hear so much of . . . Gentle reader, you have now a theory of what the Break of Gauge is. If you chance to travel yourself between Birmingham or Cheltenham and Bristol you seriously feel it. The gauge being thus broken, your journey is brought to a dead halt. With all your baggage and rattletraps whatever they may be in number and size, you are obliged to shift from one carriage to another . . . . . . You will hear the Railway Policeman bawling into the deaf passenger's ear that he must dismount; you will see the anxious mamma hasten her family in its transit from carriage to carriage dreading the penalty of being late . . .' It will be recalled that when the BrG was first mooted, it had been agreed with the B&G, first in 1839 and again in 1840, that in the cause of mutual interest both lines should be of the same gauge. By April 1843 however, I.K. Brunel, had so brainwashed the BrG Board as to lead them to imagine that it would be in their best interests to be subservient to the GWR and therefore to adopt their 7ft.¼in. gauge. Very foolishly they complied and still more foolishly bound themselves to remain broad gauge for 20 years quite regardless of the fact that their livelihood as a railway depended on traffic to and from the Midlands, where narrow gauge reigned supreme. In their innocence they imagined that it would be a simple matter for passengers and goods to be transferred at Gloucester. At Gloucester, Brunel had airily told them, would happen what occurred at other places where different railways met. 'It would', he said, 'be merely a matter of stepping over a platform from one train to another.'

However, on and from 8 July 1844, when the BrG opened to Gloucester, they discovered their mistake, and what is more they discovered it the hard way! Passengers were the chief complainants at first; but by December 1844 angry traders from Birmingham, Bristol and indeed from all over the country were protesting at '. . .irregularities, losses and delays . . .' The Board of Trade investigated and issued a Report in January 1845.

The B&G admitted partial liability, and hoped that their proposed amalgamation with the BrG would assist in producing an improvement and '. . . assist in the regular and speedy transit of merchandise . . . but . . . so long as there was a deficiency of gauge it would be . . . vain to expect . . . delivery of goods along the entire line within the short period occupied by lines where there was only one gauge.'

For their part the BrG, who were after all the main culprits in this imbroglio, refused to admit liability at all except in so far as it might lie in the shortage of 'broad wagons' which they had provided. They had, they claimed, been misled by Brunel about the extra capacity of 'broad wagons'. He had assured them that only a few would be needed in comparison with the large numbers provided by the B&G. It was this shortage, caused by wrong advice which was causing the delays in goods transfer. The rest of the problem was the fault of the B&G for, had they not undertaken the management of goods and passenger transfer at Gloucester, and were not the BrG paying them as much as £500 a year to do it?

It did not take the BoT long to decide that the Break of Gauge caused by the BrG, was the real trouble and that it should be done away with. It was at Gloucester that the impact of this problem was being felt for the first time; but the BoT saw clearly that unless something was done at once the trouble would spread, for railway schemes for both gauges were proliferating rapidly.

In the west Midlands the GWR-sponsored Oxford, Worcester & Wolverhampton Railway was competing with the L&B-sponsored Oxford & Rugby Railway for powers to link the Black Country, Worcester and the Vale of Evesham with London via the GWR and the L&B respectively. It was inevitable that broad gauge intrusion into these areas would create more 'Gloucesters', and it behoved Parliament and the BoT to step in and legislate in the national interest. Accordingly the Gauge Commission was set up in July 1845 to enquire into the matter but issued its findings too late to stop the authorisation of the OWW.

Evidence given before both the Commission and the Parliamentary Enquiry into the OWW and the O&R bills give some sort of a picture of what was happening at Gloucester, though we shall have to probe deeper to find out exactly why things happened as they did.

Wyndham Harding, traffic manager BrG, in his evidence at the OWW and O&R Parliamentary Enquiry said:– 'We experience the greatest possible inconvenience both as regards passengers and goods.' He would, he said, favour Bristol as the exchange point because there, only some 40 tons per week needed to be transferred, whereas at Gloucester the weekly figure was 500 tons or more.

J. E. McConnell giving his evidence before the Gauge Commission laid great emphasis on the fact that both expense and inconvenience would be saved if the gauge of the two railways was made uniform. Numbers of staff (clerical, porters, officers), sums paid out in liability for loss, damage or delay, duplicate buildings and sidings, extra locomotives and rolling stock, these could all be cut and expenses thereby halved. Passengers, he continued, were greatly inconvenienced. 'We have tried to lessen this inconvenience . . . passengers leave their carriage of either gauge and walk round under the shed to the other side where a 'broad' . . . or 'narrow' train stands. The luggage is put into little barrows and conveyed round with them. Delays are, of course, inevitable, but passengers are under cover all the time. We must admit there is great inconvenience to invalids . . . Delay is never less than fifteen minutes and often more if carriages and horses have to be transhipped; then the delay is as much as half an hour for an eight coach train . . . ' Wyndham Harding added: 'The result of a delay with the Mail trains for instance . . . is sometimes just sufficient . . . to miss the Manchester, or other train from Birmingham, or the Exeter or Bath train from Bristol; annoyance to the the passengers who were anxious about their parcels and packages; risk and expense, as a large body of porters have to be retained who are not fully occupied, [being only required at train times], in order that no more time than is necessary should be lost in the change of trains . . .' Punch caricatured the goings-on at Gloucester in a skit entitled 'Jeames on the Gauge Question' part of which we quote:

'We took our places in the carriage in the dark, both of us covered in a pile of packages, and Mary Hann so sulky that she would not speak for some minutes. At last she spoke out:-
"Have you all the small parcels?"
"Twentythree in all," says I.
"Then give me the baby."
"Give you what?" says I.
"Give me the baby."
"What! Haven't y y y yeoooo got him?" says I.
"Oh Mussy you should have heard her squeal! We'd left him on the ledge at Gloucester! It all came of the Break of Gage [sic]".'

Brunel had airily assured the BrG that, at Gloucester, passengers would suffer no more inconvenience than having to step across the platform from one train to another. He was right of course for travellers from Bristol to Birmingham, but very badly wrong in the case of passengers coming the other way.

There were four things at least which made changing trains a nightmare for passengers at Gloucester and these can be summed up under four heads (a) Bad Planning; (b) 'All Change'; (c) Time, and (d) BrG Unpredictability.

(a) Bad Planning. The OS 1851 map and the 1852 MR trackplan show that the joint station was basically of E-shape. Both stations were, it was freely admitted, intended to be temporary only. They had been built as cheaply as possible, and little thought, if any, had been given to the necessity of allowing free circulation of large numbers of people at any one time. The B&G station was bad enough in this respect, but the BrG side was worse. It was crammed into the narrow space available between the already existing B&G station and land reserved for the GWR. It too had been built cheaply, and no thought had been given to the need for free movement of passengers either. This is the basic requirement of any mainline junction station.

Lacking this facility it could not possibly cope with the next factor b) 'All Change'. The main traffic flow, was, as we have seen, from Birmingham to Bristol and vice versa. When a train arrived from

Birmingham at Gloucester it was a case of 'All Change'. The whole trainload, together with their baggage – (and people travelled with more luggage then than now) – had to alight *en masse* on to an inadequate platform little more than 12ft. wide, and each group had to compete with others in attracting the attention of porters to unload their trunks and baggage, pile them on one of the 'little barrows' and then lead the way pushing through the milling crowd to where the Bristol train stood. It has been noted above that the joint B&G and BrG station was in the shape of an E with its platforms as extended horizontals. Trains from Birmingham arrived and were unloaded at the B&G arrival platform which was the 'south' horizontal, and of quite inadequate width. Having obtained the services of a porter, our family would have to follow him closely making sure that none of their party or belongings got lost in the crowd. The porter would lead the way to the 'vertical' on the west of the 'E'. Here, for some 46 yards, the walkway between station offices and buffers varied in width from 10 to 16ft. and would inevitably be blocked either by people standing about or trying to pass along the other way. However our resolute passengers for Bristol having forced their way through, perhaps by weight of numbers or baggage would at last reach the north horizontal, a narrow platform some 10 or 11ft. wide from which the Bristol trains were scheduled to depart. Here at last, having secured a compartment, our family could take stock and assure themselves that nothing, not even the baby, was missing.

We noted above that Brunel was right in one respect about ease of changing trains at Gloucester. This was the case in theory for passengers to Birmingham from Bristol. The BrG trains drew in on the north side of the platform which formed the middle horizontal of the 'E', while the connecting train to Birmingham was, hopefully, waiting on its southern side. This platform's width had been increased from 12 to some 22ft. in 1844 in preparation for the BrG's arrival. No problem need have been experienced here in changing trains in this direction, except for the most inexperienced of travellers; but the third factor (c) 'Time' must have caused problems to all and sundry. It was noted by a young man, George Adeney, who with his wife was, in August 1845, visiting the west of England. On 22 August they travelled from Bristol by the BrG, changed at Gloucester and caught a B&G train to Cheltenham which enabled them to spend the morning there and returned by the 12.45 train to Gloucester. At Gloucester they caught a GWR train at 1.30 for Swindon [It will be remembered that the GWR had completed their line down the Stroud Valley in May 1845 and, as a temporary measure, the B&G and BrG had allowed them to use the BrG station]. While waiting for their GWR train the Adeney's looked about them, and George noted in his diary:– 'As three several railways meet at the Gloucester Station we observed the three several clocks labelled accordingly, one indicating Birmingham time, another London and the third, Bristol time, the different lines being regulated by them . . .'[7]

It is strange that none of the railwaymen giving evidence at the enquiries we have quoted referred to this. Probably they took it so much for granted that they did not think it worth mentioning; but for inexperienced travellers it must have made the catching of connections at Gloucester a very chancy business! G.P. Neele in his *Railway Reminiscences*[8] remarks that both London and local time was given in timetables in the 1840's and on page 75 of his book gives a specimen. We have not, so far, found one for Gloucester; but perhaps the complications arising from three different railways all working to different time norms were too great to be set down in a simple manner for the average passenger.

(*d*) We have called the fourth factor 'BrG Unpredictability'. This is perhaps unfair to the BrG so we will call it Broad Gauge Unpredictability instead. An entry in the Gloucester Station complaints book dated 12 January 1846 recorded this tale of woe:

'At Gloucester Station,
          Two gentlemen are this morning put to the greatest inconvenience . . . by the departure of the Bristol train without them.
They were standing, according to the printed notice, at the Bristol Station, but the Bristol train went without them on the other side. This is considered by us, the gentlemen in question, a ground of serious complaint, clearly actionable.'
W.H. Park; G. Escott.

In other words while standing on the proper departure platform, they saw their train steaming away from that properly used for arrivals. This we understand was by no means an isolated occurence; but at this distance in time we can only speculate about the reason.

It will be remembered that the BrG Station was cramped having only two platform roads with one release road or siding between them. Further, if the OS 1851 map is correct, there were, as yet, no traversers linking them. The marshalling of trains must therefore have been time consuming and laborious, especially when, from 1845 to 1847 two separate railways were using its meagre facilities. They would each be operating to timetables which, in the manner of those times, had probably been drawn up without mutual consultation. Conflicts were inevitable, but since the GWR had a stranglehold over the BrG (the Millstream Bridge–Standish Junction line), they would be quite capable of some high handed behaviour.

It is not unlikely that the BrG got the worst of the deal, and had to fit in their trains as best they could, using from time to time whichever platforms were available for arrivals and departures. It was perhaps these irregular and unpredictable lapses from normality which provided yet another reason for Gloucester's unpopularity.

If break of gauge complications made Gloucester unpopular with passengers, they made it still more so with merchants and traders. Mutterings in the press and elsewhere became full throated grumbling and reached crescendo by December 1844 with a deputation to the BoT.

Though published in June 1846, 'An Old Carrier's Petition' was very much the burden of their complaint.[9] '. . . the bricks are miscounted, the slates chipped . . . the cheeses cracked; ripe fruit and vegetables crushed and spoilt; chairs, furniture and oilcake, cast iron pots, grates and ovens all more or less broken; the coals turned into slack, the salt short of weight, sundry bottles of wine deficient, and fish too late for the market . . .' The BoT had already become concerned and had, in response to complaints, written to Wyndham Harding, traffic manager of the BrG, who replied on 4 December: '. . . The Goods Station, [he wrote] consists of a narrow gauge line running through . . . the shed, and a platform interposed between it and the wide gauge line . . . The goods premises are insufficient for the traffic . . . up to this day a great number of wagons laden with goods . . . have been lying at Gloucester which we have been unable to remove . . . during last week . . . We keep an establishment of clerks and porters to superintend and effect the transhipment, but in the hurry of business, mistakes will occur . . . in invoicing the goods; a Carrier lays hold of a package which he thinks is his and takes it. . . . The other day a bale for Bristol was . . . taken to Brecon; a claim for some 30s. being instantly made upon us, and there is nothing that . . . senders of goods dread so much as this; it is always the cause of some mischief and a pretext for more. The expense of clerks employed in invoicing and inspecting goods, the expense of shrinking [sic] the wagons, the waste of premises, the additional carrying stock it obliges the Company of each gauge to maintain, and above all the loss of trade which is sure to result from the delay and risk attending the change . . . [from one gauge to another at Gloucester.]' J.E. McConnell, giving evidence before the Gauge Commissioners in August 1845, described the situation thus: '. . . Wagons with loads for Bristol run into a shed in which there is a platform on the opposite side of which . . . are wide gauge wagons. The sheets are taken off and the lighter goods taken out by hand, invoiced and laid on one side. The heavy goods below are then removed by crane, and loaded at the bottom of the wide gauge wagon. The lighter goods are then repacked on top. This requires great care and takes, in total, about five hours . . .' Both Harding and McConnell gave other particulars about the transhipment process at the OWW and O&R Parliamentary Enquiry in June 1845.

Speaking of the first provision made for transhipment at Gloucester Harding said, '. . . A small shed was erected capable of holding six trucks . . . not more. I said at the time . . . to Mr Brunel that it would be quite insufficient; but Mr Brunel was of a contrary opinion.' Harding went on to say that the whole length of the shed was not more than 15 ft. McConnell said that with the provision, in May 1845, of a larger shed in addition to the small one the situation had been to a certain extent improved, and that a team of 12 porters could tranship a 30 wagon train in the better part of a day.

J.D. Payne, B&G goods manager, giving his evidence at the same Enquiry said that: '. . . In the first place there was an old shed into which 3 wide wagons could be put . . . There has been a new shed built, where 5 wide wagons can be brought into juxtaposition to the narrow gauge. . . . The accommodation for the extra . . . wagons has been made since the 1st of May. This however is still very inadequate, and some transfers have to be made out in the open wherever wide and narrow gauge wagons can be run alongside each other. Where this is so transfer has to be done entirely by hand, for there are only cranes in the shed itself. In the shed there are cranes which enable goods to be lifted from wagon to wagon. The cranes rotate, but even so the design is bad and they cannot be used with facility, for the cranes are not high enough placed to lift goods over the tilts of the wagons.' McConnell's description above, of the system of wagon loading used at the time may sound odd to present day readers, but we have two reasons to believe that it was then the general practice. The first was the fact that apart from horse boxes and sheep or other livestock wagons few, if any, of the early railway companies went to the expense of building other than general purpose open wagons which could be sheeted over if necessary. It was considered far more economical to use these, as and when required, than to build wagons for special purposes, and possibly find that they were only occasionally used.

The second factor in the situation was the limited haulage power of locomotives in the 1840s before the general adoption of valve gear capable of using steam expansively. This, of neccessity, limited the length and tare weight of goods trains. If therefore, for a given tare weight, it was possible to squeeze in the highest possible 'pay-load', it could make a difference between running at a profit or a loss. Hence the careful loading of wagons with 'heavies' at the bottom and lighter goods on top. This had the disadvantage of causing difficulty at the tranship point; but it is notable that this method of loading wagons was not queried at the time either by the Commissioners or by the experienced railwaymen called before them to give evidence. Thus, in the author's opinion, it seems to show that this was the accepted method used in then contemporary practice.

An interesting query was raised however at these enquiries about the possibility of 'containerisation'. Would it be possible to devise some method by which the loaded bodies of wagons could be lifted up from one chassis and transferred to another of different gauge? This was attractively simple in theory, but had regretfully to be discarded. Wagons from railways all over the country passed through Gloucester, and to make the 'container system' work it would be necessary to get all these diverse and often quarrelling companies to agree on standard sizes and strength for the bodies and chasses of all future wagons. Commissioners, Parliament and railway experts were forced to agree that this ideal was, at any rate in the forseeable future, beyond the sphere of practical politics.

Another question which comes to mind is why had such poor provision been made for through goods traffic at Gloucester? The answer must lie squarely on the incompetence of the BrG board who can have had no conception of the volume of traffic which a rail-route from Birmingham to Bristol would generate. Wyndham Harding quoted an average figure of 500 tons per week during the first 6 months, and by the time J.D. Payne gave his evidence in June 1845 the weekly average was some 700 tons. This may not seem much to twentieth century readers, but in the 1840s it was a colossal figure and had taken the BrG quite unawares. This, it is important to add, was not the case with the B&G. Urged on by McConnell, they had prepared adequately by investing in a fleet of some 400 to 500 wagons. In sharp contrast the BrG, probably misled by Brunel's views on the capacity of broad gauge wagons, had only provided themselves with 60, to say nothing of their ridiculously small and awkwardly sited tranship shed. It was built on the end of a spur and no release roads were provided. Thus all transhipped wagons had to be hauled away before others could be pushed in, and this from the start made transhipment laborious and slow. We have no direct information as to its exact site, but the OS (1851) map of Gloucester gives a clue (Map 27.5). This map does not show the original shed of 1844 but it does show the larger one added in May 1845. By 1851 it had been adapted for a different use, but it had been built on the same spur as the other, and stood a short distance west of the BrG station. When in use as a tranship shed it had been approached like the other, by two lines of rail – broad and narrow; and, possibly because there was little space available, no release roads had been provided for it either. Once their loads had been transferred the wagons would need to be drawn away before others could be pushed into the shed in their place. No wonder, as J.D. Payne complained, it was quite the normal thing to have to make load transfers out in the open at any place in the yard where wide and narrow wagons could be run alongside each other. No wonder too that extra locomotive and carrying stock were needed, and that goods had to remain in narrow gauge wagons for lack of broad gauge into which to transfer them.

Better things however, were on the way. The OS (1851) map shows improvements made by the Midland subsequent to 1846, but these are best noted in Map 25.6 which is based on the MR trackplan of 1852. This shows that the 'improved' Brunel goods shed of May 1845 had been scrapped, and that interesting developments had taken place to the south in Wheeler's Nursery. The plan shows them in considerable detail. They were all designed to beat the Break of Gauge.

From east to west we have an Import/Export Transit Shed 70ft. × 90ft. built as far as we can judge on the site of the former B&G goods shed, and served by a spur from the High Orchard Branch to the docks. In the shed both broad and narrow gauge facilities were provided. Westward, opposite the entrance to the yard from Station Road (now Bruton Way), was a shed for local goods traffic 30ft. × 90ft. in size and served by both gauges. West of this was a carriage and wagon repair shop for vehicles both broad and narrow. North of these a large transfer shed had been built for through consignments. This was of a really useful size, and measured 60ft. × 150ft. It had four roads (two narrow and two broad) and could, if our calculations are correct, be capable of accommodating 20 wagons of each gauge laid alongside each other at any one time. What is more, plenty of release roads and siding space were provided, making it a simple matter to shunt away transhipped wagons to make room for more. Thus by 1851–52 the Midland were in a fair way towards getting the Break of Gauge problem under control.

We have however, strayed too far ahead, and must return to 1845. The Gauge Commissioners sat in London to hear evidence both for and against broad gauge, given by the experts of the day. But since the problem had first arisen in Gloucester, their enquiry could not be complete without seeing affairs there for themselves. J.D. Payne, having been warned of their proposed visit, decided that something striking and dramatic was called for and, no doubt, with the delighted connivance of the station staff, staged a performance for their benefit. He arranged that two previously transhipped trains should be unloaded and the process gone through again with maximum noise and confusion.

Once B&B affairs had been consolidated with Derby, Payne left the Midland to become general manager of the South Staffordshire Railway where he met and told the story to a young man named G.P. Neele who was then his clerk, but who rose later to become a superintendent of the L&NWR. In his *Reminiscences*[10] Neele told the story of Payne's part in the Gloucester affair: '. . . When the Members [of the Commission] came to the scene, they were appalled at the clamour arising from the well arranged confusion of shouting out addresses of consignments, the chucking of packages across from truck to truck, the enquiries for missing articles, the loading , unloading and reloading, which his clever device had brought into operation.' Put up job or not, Payne's performance convinced the Commissioners that the Midland (B&B Division) had a serious problem on their hands incapable of easy solution. Various schemes had been proposed; one of these, 'containerisation' and its rejection we have already mentioned. Mixed gauge track had its attractions by way of compromise, for it offered 'status quo' to both parties, but when it came down to practicalities the idea of running trains of mixed gauge vehicles over three or four rail track though, as was later proved, not impossible, was felt at the time to be too risky to be allowed as a matter of general practice. Other devices such as that of Daniel Gooch's adjustable wheels sliding on their axle, and which could be forced inward or outward to suit the gauge required were proposed only to be abandoned, the latter in particular because, as Gooch himself admitted, he had no real faith in it.

In the end the Commissioners were forced to the conclusion:– '. . . That in order to complete the general chain of narrow gauge communications from the North of England to the South Coasts and the Port of Bristol, any suitable measures should be promoted to form a narrow gauge link from Gloucester to Bristol.' This conclusion was endorsed by Parliament and it was on the basis of this endorsement that the Midland, inspite of furious GWR opposition, were authorised to build their own standard gauge Gloucester & Stonehouse Junction Railway (The Tuffley Loop. Map 25.7). It was an oddity, and an expensive one, born of the gauge war, and paralleled the GWR for some 7½ miles to Standish Junction; but nevertheless, oddity though it was, it remained continuously in use for well over a hundred years.

[PART THREE]
THE DOCKS

The B&G had from the first declared their interest in Gloucester Docks. We have seen (Map 25.2&3) that their Act had authorised a high level rail link to the Basin while rejecting their alternative line to High Orchard, but that the CGWU's Act had in its turn cancelled this part of the B&G's plans altogether. It is a little hard to understand why it was that the B&G allowed their important access to the docks to slip away

so easily. No clue is provided in the lengthy B&G/CGWU negotiations, but some possibilities emerge:
(a) either the B&G did not want to share dock facilities with the
CGWU or;
(b) it may have been that the B&G preferred to bide their time until
they were in position to secure an independent link for themselves or;
(c) since the B&G and CGWU had become joint owners of the
tramway which already ran to the docks, and had, by their Act been
given powers to extend it, the B&G had decided to use it for their own
purposes at a convenient time, which indeed they did.

The B&G's motives became clearer in 1838. In February of that year
Samuel Baker, chairman of the town council and a B&G director laid
the foundation stone of what was to be some 1,000ft. of extra wharfage
capable of docking ships of the largest size at the time. Following his
advice the B&G decided to take a share in this development by
purchasing land at High Orchard and building their own basin off the
canal together with a branch line to it from their city depôt.

Capt. Moorsom recommended that this should be horse worked,
running first along the tramway and thence along the line of the
Sudbrook to the canal in preference to the alternative plan of altering
the tramway and extending it to High Orchard alongside the canal.
Both plans would require an Act of Parliament, but he was of the
opinion that alteration of the tramway, though cheaper would present
difficulties as it used curves too sharp for railway vehicles to negotiate.

The general meeting of February 1839, authorised an application to
Parliament, the shareholders being told that their line could never be
considered complete until connected with the docks by rail, since other
forms of transport thither were laborious and costly. The sad fact was
however that in the event the B&G had to remain 'incomplete' for
another eleven years because this bill and its successors had to be
withdrawn owing to the implacable opposition of Worcester, which
city, as we have already seen, could not bear to allow Gloucester to
have rail facilities at their docks while they themselves had none.

But the B&G board, and in particular the GC, did not allow
themselves to be unduly disturbed by this defeat, and continued with
the development of High Orchard. Land there had already been
purchased, and a start made on the gradual acquisition of such land as
would be required for the branch. They also excavated a barge basin
360ft. × 40ft. × 6ft. deep, erecting six coke ovens nearby for the
production of locomotive fuel from Forest of Dean coal and surrounding the premises with a boundary wall.

Undaunted by the loss of their bill they assured shareholders in
August 1839 that a fresh attempt would be made in the ensuing Session,
and that if this failed '. . .arrangements are in progress by which the

extension to the canal may be attained without the intervention of Parliament.' Brave words, but in actual fact no fresh application to Parliament was made; though the 'other arrangements' were put in hand. These were to be either (a) straddling the 3ft.6in. tramway with 4ft.8½in. edge rails so that B&G wagons could be horse hauled to the Basin, or (b) if the curves encountered proved to be too sharp for standard wheelbased wagons, some with a specially short wheelbase would be built. Accordingly in March 1841 experiments were made at the Gloucester depôt using a length of track with similar radiused curves to those on the tramway and it was found that wagons of normal wheelbase were capable of negotiating all curves except one and that this particular curve could be eased quite simply.

The major obstacle to this plan was that though the B&G had by this time bought up the CGWU'S moiety in the tramway, the CGWU still claimed 'rights' in it and, backed by the GWR, they had already blocked a similar plan at Cheltenham. The B&G being unsure of their exact legal position, and being unwilling, at this time, to go to the expense of testing it in the Courts, temporarily abandoned their 'Rails along the Tramway plan' in favour of a simpler and cheaper one. This was to build a short plateway spur from the B&G goods yard southward to join the tramway where it reached the road nearly opposite Cambridge Street. This is the spur shown in Causton's map of 1842–43 and is indicated in Map 25.4. As noted above, a line of 3ft.6in. gauge plateway was laid alongside a line of 4ft.8½in. edge rail with, doubtless a platform between, so that rail borne goods could be transhipped into tramway wagons for transport to the docks and vice versa.

Completed in 1841, this arrangement appeared reasonably satisfactory to J.D. Payne except, as he noted, for the transport of bulky goods such as bales of wool which tended to foul the tramway's loading gauge. A wharf at the basin was rented by the B&G from August 1842 specially for the Bristol traffic to and from Liverpool and Manchester.

Meanwhile what of High Orchard? Investment in this property had been high, and the GC found themselves having to answer awkward questions about it, for it was isolated and appeared to be quite useless and an embarrassment to the company. Low returns recorded for goods traffic were embarrassing too, and the Board was only able, rather lamely, to account for this by blaming them on their lack of a proper connection with the canal, and their continued uncertainty about the intentions of both BrG and CGWU. In the end they had to confess that they were really as far away as ever from finding a solution to the problem.

Sharp criticism from the floor in August 1842 however forced them into action. Capt. Moorsom was re-engaged to produce estimates yet again for building a branch to High Orchard, and for laying 4ft. 8½in. gauge edge rails astride the tramway all the way to the Canal Basin. This time they took legal advice and, though Counsel's opinion is not recorded, it would appear to have been favourable in that neither did they need an Act nor were they accountable to the CGWU whose moiety of the tramway they had purchased.

The plans for the High Orchard branch were submitted to Parliament in 1843. Costing £5,000, it would straddle the tramway for part of the distance to High Orchard. The use of locomotives was not asked for since there were a number of level crossings on the route. Once again the bill was lost thanks to opposition from CGWU, GWR and of course Worcester. In 1843 whilst the Bill was waiting to be heard further trouble arose for the board in the shape of the CofE, which as we have seen above was a self constituted, self opinionated and dividend hungry body, who issued their report in June 1843. That part of it which referred to the docks asserted: '. . . the sum of £14,000 expended in the purchase of this property [High Orchard], and in the construction of the works and buildings thereon was a very injudicious outlay of the company's money; and they can now only hope that as the situation has certain advantages, it may at some future time be available property . . .'

It was indeed, but that 'time' was still some way ahead in the future! In July 1843, seven years after incorporation, and in spite of the firm intention stated in their prospectus, the B&G had not yet achieved rail connection with Gloucester Docks. The directors were on the horns of a dilemma. If, given the present mood of the proprietors, they did not secure an increase in goods traffic and therefore dividend, they were liable to be voted off the Board. Improvement in goods traffic depended on unbroken rail connection to the docks, but any further application to Parliament for the High Orchard Branch would fail as before under the combined attacks of the CGWU, the GWR, and the city of Worcester. There was a further consideration too. In another year the BrG would have opened to Gloucester and provided a rail link which could by-pass both canal and river, a route which would probably be preferable and more convenient to merchants and traders than Gloucester Docks and canal could ever be. If this happened, any money spent on the High Orchard Branch would join the 'injudicious' £14,000 already spent there of which the CofE had reported so critically.

They did however have another option which they took, and about which they had already taken legal advice. This was 'Rails along the tramway' (Map 25.5). They set to work on this at once with the approval both of the canal company and the Gloucester Chamber of Commerce. James Bayliss, resident engineer, costed the project at

£1,018, but said that since most of the materials required were already in stock, the actual cost would be in the region of £371 only. The canal company readily gave permission for trackwork on their land, and the tramway trustees were promised indemnity against traffic loss and other costs together with a toll of 6*d*. per ton on all goods carried. Then the GWR stepped in. They had purchased the CGWU in June 1843 and now claimed the CGWU's rights as 'joint owner' of the tramway. They demanded that if the tramway was to be straddled with edge rail it should be straddled at joint expense by those of broad as well as narrow gauge. As usual the GWR was somewhat high handed, and in consequence negotiations broke down. This time the B&G, on the strength of the legal advice they had taken, pressed ahead. Work began early in March 1844, and continued at high speed until the GWR obtained an injunction ordering them to stop the works, which by that time, according to the *Railway Times*, '. . . were nearly finished, and upon which nearly 160 were employed . . .' This was on Sunday 24 March, and such was the workmen's enthusiasm that on the following day they carried on as usual and refused to stop until some of the directors arrived to halt work and thus avoid a 'Contempt of Court' charge.

In the hearing that ensued however the GWR claims were set aside and their injunction quashed, so that the work could be completed. In April an advertisment was inserted in the Gloucester papers asking for tenders for the working of the altered tramroad by horsepower.

On 21 May, James Bayliss reported to the Board that the work was going on well and would be completed to schedule. This was probably the middle of June, for it was on and from 21 June 1844 that the B&G leased, from the canal company, the yard formerly used by the tramway at a rent of £26.18*s*. per year.

This was to be Gloucester's only rail connection with the docks for the next few years. It was certainly still in use in 1847, for Hunt's Directory of Gloucester for that year writes: '. . . A branch connecting (the stations) with the Docks is at present worked by horsepower, but such is the immense increase of imports and exports at the harbour, that lococmotives will shortly be used.'

Back to 1844 however. The Gloucester Chamber of Commerce were delighted, and congratulated the B&G on making the rail connection, and hoped that their rails would soon be extended to every quay. This rail link, they said, had been completed during an upsurge in canal traffic at a time when the level of the Severn was low through drought. It had, they went on, brought about over the last two months a most efficient and convenient mode of transport to the Midlands giving a 30 per cent reduction in transit time to Birmingham and which should promote fresh trade to the docks. Salt could be conveyed from

Droitwich for export with a return traffic in coal and corn. At long last the B&G had done something for which it was being applauded!

Shareholders were doubtless pleased too. They heard at the August meeting that goods traffic had shown a substantial increase. This was all the more welcome since it will be remembered that the BrG had arrived in July of that year bringing break of gauge troubles in its train. It was a measure of comfort for the B&G board to remember that in view of gauge difficulties they still had an alternative route and port. Further, it provided them with an incentive to press ahead with the High Orchard branch especially as, at long last, their arch enemy Worcester, had been pacified. Sanction for the branch should therefore be forthcoming from Parliament without undue difficulty.

Accordingly a comprehensive bill was prepared for submission to the 1845 Parliamentary Session. In addition to the High Orchard line planned in 1843, a rail link to the basin was asked for together with tramway and rail extensions along the quay to High Orchard. This latter scheme by no means meant that the line straddling the tramway had not been a success, but that horse haulage did not satisfy the B&G who wanted a locomotive worked line with easier curvature. Parliamentary sanction was needed for this.

The Royal Assent for the High Orchard line was given in August 1845 together with that for quay-side extensions and permission for locomotive haulage. By this time however the B&G had been leased by the Midland who, having plenty of other urgent commitments at Gloucester, were in no hurry to build the branch even though they had possession of most of the land.

Gloucester people thought otherwise. An irate *Gloucester Journal*[11] fulminated about almost every other port in the country getting investment from railways except Gloucester. Were the people of Gloucester, it thundered, to see their dock expansion rendered useless by the opening of other railway sponsored docks? '. . . we feel that moderate investment at the Dock basin coupled with direct interchange to the railway would pay hearty dividends, since Gloucester's position as regards proximity to markets is unrivalled . . .'

On and on, through 1845–46, the Gloucester Chamber of Commerce maintained a barrage of criticism directed at the Midland's lack of enterprise in neglecting to complete the rail link with High Orchard. In October 1846 a meeting of delegates accused the Midland of desiring '. . . to interpose delay, inconvenience and confusion and costly trouble between themselves and their best customers . . . by refusing to lay the High Orchard branch and continuing to work the Dock traffic along the tramway route by horse power.

In addition the *Gloucester Journal* remarked that with the failure of the Midland's first bill to gain narrow gauge communication with Bristol they should establish Gloucester as the main port for goods flow to the Midlands instead of Bristol. But the Midland refused to allow themselves to be stampeded. They already had rail communication of a sort with the docks, and the most they did in that area in 1846 was to put in slips at the basin for shooting export salt into waiting vessels below. For them the most important problem was the break of gauge, and it was not till 1847, when most of the improvements towards that end in Wheeler's Nursery had been completed that the construction of the High Orchard Branch could begin. (Map 25.6) It swept south in a wide curve from Tramway Junction crossed Barton Street on the level then turned westward obliquely over Park End Road at California, and following the line of the Sudbrook skirted the Park and the Spa Pleasure Grounds to a level crossing over the Bristol Road and thence to High Orchard and the quays. Once started, the work went on rapidly. The branch was opened in 1848.

With the opening of the High Orchard line giving access to the Docks for locomotive hauled trains, the B&G's lifelong ambition had been achieved, and its story, properly, comes to an end. An outline of subsequent happenings however may not come amiss. For the next hundred years or so a rail network spread throughout the dock area; from the Midland at High Orchard and Hempsted, the GWR at Llanthony, and the Dock Authority's lines connecting them both. Numerous private sidings were laid serving a wide range of industries; the Gloucester Carriage and Wagon Works, England's Glory Matches, timber importers, corn merchants, flour mills, coal merchants and a host of others.

Sadly, this former bustle of activity is no more. Apart from the GWR sidings at Llanthony which survive but in a very attenuated form, all rail connection has gone. Use of the port for freight has dwindled almost to nothing though its use for leisure activities is on the increase both on the canal and in the preserved and refurbished Victorian warehouses some of which had stood for many years empty and forlorn.

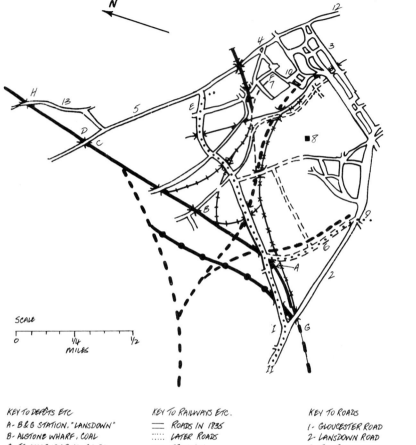

N

SCALE

0   1/4   1/2
MILES

KEY TO DEPÔTS ETC	KEY TO RAILWAYS ETC.	KEY TO ROADS
A- B&G STATION. "LANSDOWN"	═══ ROADS IN 1835	1- GLOUCESTER ROAD
B- ALSTONE WHARF, COAL	⋯⋯ LATER ROADS	2- LANSDOWN ROAD
C- TEWKESBURY ROAD, GOODS	····· TRAMWAY	3- THE PROMANADE
D- TEWKESBURY ROAD, COAL	━━━ B&G AS BUILT	4- HIGH STREET
E - GAS WORKS	▪▪▪ B&G, 1836 PLAN	5- TEWKESBURY ROAD
F - GWR STATION, "ST. JAMES"	▪ ▪ ▪ "JOINT" LINE TO GLOUCESTER, AS BUILT	6- QUEENS ROAD
G - C&GWUR STATION, 1838 PLAN	** C&GWUR, 1836 PLAN	7- ST. JAMES SQUARE, JESSOP'S NURSERY
H - B&G STATION, 1835 PLAN	- - - GWR, AS BUILT	8- BAYSHILL HOUSE
	●━●━● B&G NEW JUNCTION, 1836 PLAN	9- WESTHALL GREEN
	+++ B&G AND GWR PLAN, 1845	10 - ST. GEORGES TERRACE
	▬▬ MR PLAN 1845 & 1846	11 - A40, GLOUCESTER ROAD
	─── RIVER CHELT.	12- A40, LONDON ROAD
		13 - SWINDON ROAD

25:1 GLOUCESTER 1838–39

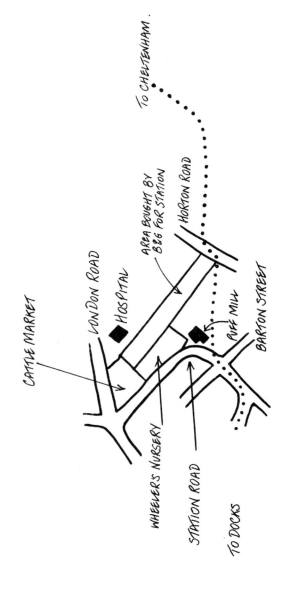

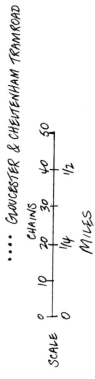

CATTLE MARKET

LONDON ROAD

HOSPITAL

AREA BOUGHT BY
B&G FOR STATION

HORTON ROAD

To CHELTENHAM.

WHEELER'S NURSERY

STATION ROAD

To DOCKS

PUFF MILL

BARTON STREET

KEY:

••••• GLOUCESTER & CHELTENHAM TRAMROAD

SCALE

CHAINS

0   10   20   30   40   50

0   ¼   ½

MILES

N

25:2   RAILWAYS BETWEEN CHELTENHAM AND GLOUCESTER

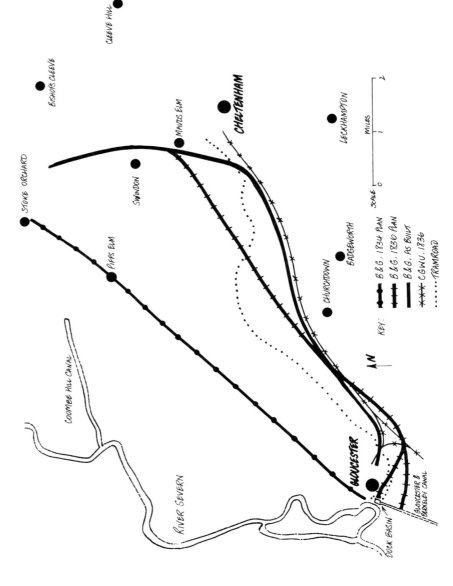

CLEEVE HILL

BISHOPS CLEEVE

STOKE ORCHARD

PIFFS ELM

SWINDON

MAUDS ELM

CHELTENHAM

LECKHAMPTON

CHURCHDOWN

BADGEWORTH

COOMBE HILL CANAL

RIVER SEVERN

GLOUCESTER

DOCK BASIN

GLOUCESTER & BERKELEY CANAL

KEY:
B&G. 1834 PLAN
B&G. 1836 PLAN
B&G. AS BUILT
C.G.W.U. 1836
TRAMROAD

SCALE   0   1   2
                MILES

N

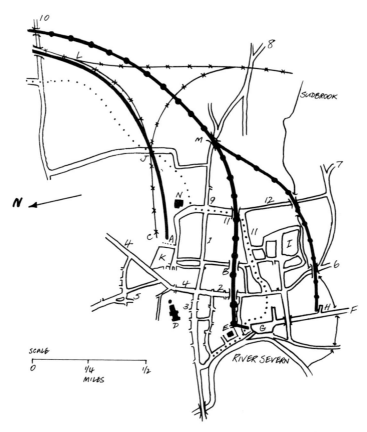

SUDBROOK

RIVER SEVERN

SCALE

0   1/4   1/2

MILES

N

KEY TO ROADS
1 - EASTGATE ST.
2 - SOUTHGATE ST.
3 - WESTGATE ST.
4 - NORTHGATE ST.
5 - WORCESTER ST.
6 - BRISTOL ROAD, A 38
7 - STROUD ROAD
8 - PAINSWICK ROAD
9 - BARTON ST.
10 - CIRENCESTER RD.
11 - PARK RD
12 - PARKEND RD.

KEY TO BUILDINGS ETC.
A - B&G STATION
B - B&G PROPOSED STATION, 1835
C - HOSPITAL, LATER GWR STATION
D - CATHEDRAL
E - COUNTRY GAOL
F - GLOUCESTER & BERKELEY CANAL
G - DOCK BASIN
H - HIGH ORCHARD DOCK
I - THE SPA
J - TRAMWAY CROSSING & JUNCTION
K - CATTLE MARKET
L - BARNWOOD JUNCTION
M - INDIA HOUSE
N - FUFF MILL

KEY TO RAILWAYS

━━━ B&G AS BUILT

●━●━● B&G, 1836 PROPOSAL

✕✕✕ CGWUR, 1836, AS BUILT

· · · · · TRAMROAD

25:4   GLOUCESTER 1841

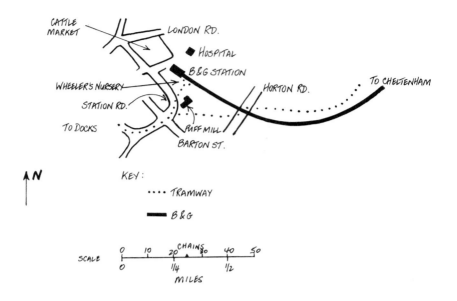

CATTLE MARKET
LONDON RD.
HOSPITAL
B&G STATION
WHEELER'S NURSERY
HORTON RD.
TO CHELTENHAM
STATION RD.
TO DOCKS
PUFF MILL
BARTON ST.

N

KEY :

•••• TRAMWAY

▬▬ B&G

SCALE

0   10   20   CHAINS 30   40   50

0   1/4   1/2

MILES

25:5   GLOUCESTER 1844–47

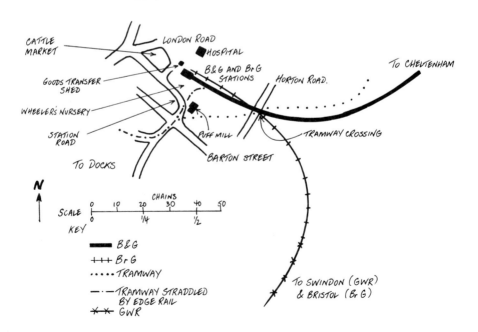

CATTLE MARKET
LONDON ROAD
HOSPITAL
B&G AND BrG STATIONS
GOODS TRANSFER SHED
HORTON ROAD.
TO CHELTENHAM
WHEELER'S NURSERY
STATION ROAD
PUFF MILL
TRAMWAY CROSSING
TO DOCKS
BARTON STREET

N

SCALE

0   10   20   CHAINS 30   40   50

0   1/4   1/2

KEY

▬▬ B&G
+++ BrG
•••• TRAMWAY
—•—• TRAMWAY STRADDLED BY EDGE RAIL
✕✕ GWR

TO SWINDON (GWR) & BRISTOL (BrG)

25:6 GLOUCESTER 1848

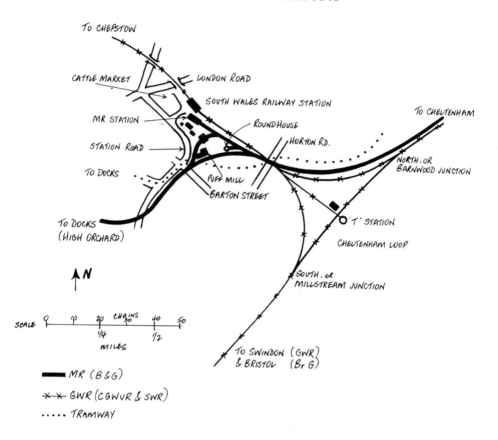

TO CHEPSTOW

CATTLE MARKET

LONDON ROAD

SOUTH WALES RAILWAY STATION

MR STATION

ROUND HOUSE

TO CHELTENHAM

STATION ROAD

HORTON RD.

TO DOCKS

NORTH, OR
BARNWOOD JUNCTION

PUFF MILL

BARTON STREET

TO DOCKS
(HIGH ORCHARD)

"T" STATION

CHELTENHAM LOOP

SOUTH, OR
MILLSTREAM JUNCTION

↑ N

SCALE 0   10   20 CHAINS 40   50
                      30
              1/4   1/2
           MILES

TO SWINDON (GWR)
& BRISTOL (Br G)

━━━ MR (B&G)

✕✕ GWR (CGWUR & SWR)

····· TRAMWAY

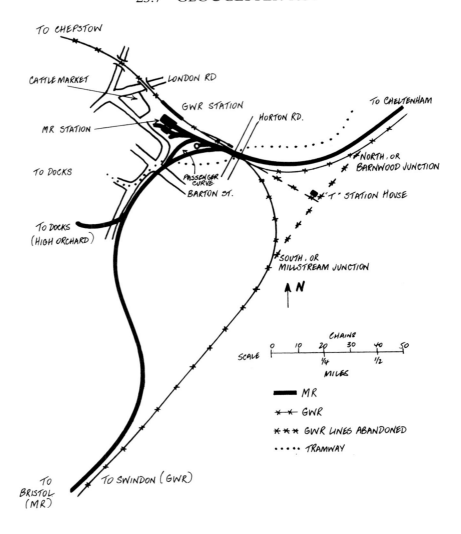

TO CHEPSTOW

CATTLE MARKET

LONDON RD

GWR STATION

MR STATION

HORTON RD.

TO CHELTENHAM

NORTH, OR
BARNWOOD JUNCTION

TO DOCKS

PASSENGER
CURVE

BARTON ST.

"T" STATION HOUSE

TO DOCKS
(HIGH ORCHARD)

SOUTH, OR
MILLSTREAM JUNCTION

N

CHAINS

SCALE 0   10   20   30   40   50
              ¼   ½
            MILES

━━━ MR

✶ ✶ GWR

✶ ✶ ✶ GWR LINES ABANDONED

• • • • • TRAMWAY

TO
BRISTOL
(MR)

TO SWINDON (GWR)

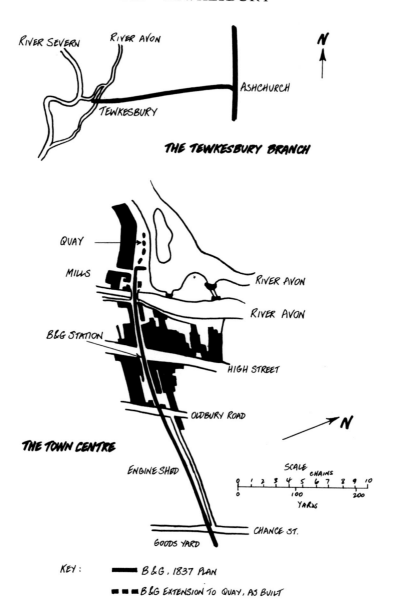

RIVER SEVERN   RIVER AVON

ASHCHURCH

TEWKESBURY

N

THE TEWKESBURY BRANCH

QUAY

MILLS

RIVER AVON

RIVER AVON

B&G STATION

HIGH STREET

OLDBURY ROAD

THE TOWN CENTRE

N

ENGINE SHED

SCALE
CHAINS
0 1 2 3 4 5 6 7 8 9 10
0   100   200
YARDS

CHANCE ST.

GOODS YARD

KEY : ━━━━ B &G , 1837 PLAN

▪▪▪ B&G EXTENSION TO QUAY, AS BUILT

CHAPTER TWENTY SIX

TEWKESBURY

Tewkesbury is as far from the railway today as it was in 1835 when Capt. Moorsom's line was to pass two miles from the town. In retrospect, this decision has actually benefitted the town regarding the preservation of its splendid architecture, also aided by the M5 taking most of the through traffic.

Tewkesbury's prosperity in the early nineteenth century was derived from its situation at the crossing of the Birmingham to Bristol and Hereford to Stow roads. It was a celebrated coaching town with up to thirty coaches daily in its heyday. When the railways killed the coach traffic they killed Tewkesbury's development; development which would have resulted in the destruction of much of what we prize now as its rich architectural heritage. The new shopping centre in the High Street is an example of the sort of thing that could have happened, only more so.

Naturally the inhabitants were annoyed by the B&G's plans to pass them by and determined to oppose their bill in Parliament. A petition '. . . 7 yards long with double rows of names' was to be presented. Fearing this opposition the B&G came to an agreement with the town and promised to build a branch line to the town with a fine station and a link to the quay on the river Avon. The latter would, thought local tradesmen, offset the loss of coach passengers by assisting the development of a small port especially for Midlands or Forest coal and its delivery by train to Cheltenham.

A bill for a branch line was submitted in the next session of Parliament and authorised in May 1837. It gave rise to a curious feature of operation not bargained for by the B&G or the Tewkesbury folk.

Since there were no less than four level crossings, three of which were in the town centre, the use of locomotives was forbidden on the branch to protect the public on these crossings. Tewkesbury had not lost its horses yet!

Contracts for the branch's construction were prepared in February 1838 and caused immediate uproar in the town. A meeting of 'influential and interested inhabitants' heard with fury that although, to their minds, the quay extension was the most important part of their agreement, nevertheless, the B&G had no intention of proceeding with it just yet.

Later in 1838 an investigation into the possible traffic was undertaken to see whether the expense of the quay extension could be justified. Coal for Cheltenham was the most likely traffic, 58,000 tons had been carried to the town in 1837, half from the Forest of Dean via Gloucester Docks and the tramroad, the other half from the Midlands (mainly Staffordshire) via the Severn, Coombe Hill Canal and the Tewkesbury Road. Bearing in mind that Gloucester had no authorised railway to its docks, the whole of this traffic might be put on the Tewkesbury branch if the price was right. Calculation proved that the railway could carry coal from the Forest more cheaply by 9d. a ton (present transport charge 3s.9d. per ton); from Staffordshire 1s. more cheaply (present transport charge 4s.6d.). Of general goods no accurate figure could be given.[1] The Board were unimpressed by these figures. They resolved to extend the railway to the quay only if willing parties in Tewkesbury would lease the whole branch for 21 years at 5 per cent on the building cost! Naturally no one took their offer up.

Local observers wondered why the link had not been made and used to transport building materials, which could be delivered by water to the quay. It is, however, certain that Tewkesbury was used as a distribution point for materials delivered by water. An accident involving a train which was ferrying rails to Bredon (see Chapter 21) bears this out. Meanwhile, construction of the branch and station was proceeding apace. Earthworks on the branch were light and progress rapid. The station, facing the High Street, was described by the *Tewkesbury Examiner*.[2] It was: '. . . built of Postlip Freestone . . . 38ft. in length and 34ft. in height. It has a fine Gothic screenwork front with oriel windows and battlements. In the centre of the building are two well proportioned gateways each 12ft. high and 12½ft. wide, one of which is designed for railway passengers and the other for carriages and goods. [The extension to the quay would pass through these.] There are suitable offices on the ground floor with cellaring underneath and four airy upper rooms forming a comfortable residence. Stone stairs lead to a light and spacious Booking office and there is a long paved platform for passengers beneath a substantial roof which is surmounted by an exterior . . . roof of 40ft. span and upwards of 160ft. long. The engine house is placed beyond the first level crossing in the Oldbury and in the yard which adjoins it are capacious sheds, coke store, weighing machines, offices etc. [which indicates the Company's intention to use locomotive power at some stage]. . . . it is calculated that the depot, station house and offices . . . cost the railway . . . little less than £10,000.' The *Railway Times*[3] found that the station: '. . . adds much as an ornamental building to the High Street and reflects great credit on the builder, Mr F.P. Holder.'

As the southern portion of the B&G neared completion in the early months of 1840, the secretary made arrangements for working the branch. Only light traffic was expected and Mr Trotman, a local carrier, was approached to work the branch with horse and carriage which was to meet every passenger and mail train. In 1842, for instance, the total cost of operating this conveyance was £280, though it varied from year to year according to the number of main line trains. Presumably what small goods and parcels there were were delivered by Mr Trotman's horse and cart in between passenger turns.

The branch did not open in June with the Cheltenham to Bromsgrove main line, but an 'illegal' (?) locomotive hauled train conveyed spectators to Ashchurch to see the inaugural train. Regular trains commenced on the branch on 21 July 1840. The *Tewkesbury Examiner* describes the mode of working:[4] 'Steam carriages have not yet been generally used on this branch; passengers are conveyed . . . in a handsome and convenient carriage drawn by one horse at a good speed; the body of the carriage is divided into compartments for 1st and 2nd class passengers, the 3rd class riding on the outside and it is so constructed as to run on the rails with perfect steadiness and security.' However, it must have been a particularly anticlimatic journey for passengers from Tewkesbury, who, entering the splendid town station, were shown into a glorified stage coach.

The secretary's estimate of only light traffic is borne out by the number of staff employed at the station – a chief clerk and (on average) three constables who, we assume, acted as porters as well. Four different men held the post of chief clerk in B&G days, and all were 'characters'. William Pengelly was appointed in June 1840 at £70 per annum and appeared in the 'Minute Books' on several occasions. He was reprimanded for rudeness to Mr Willett, a passenger; he failed to tell Mr Palfrey that the train had arrived and consequently Mr Palfrey missed it; and once he started a train before time causing much inconvenience to the prospective passengers. He was transferred to Eckington! Daniel Heath was a more responsible man judging by the fact that no complaints were recorded during his two year stint at Tewkesbury. The pressure of the job combined with looking after his

Bredon station house. An original B&G building photographed in 1969. Top – from the south; bottom – from the north-west (W.V. Awdry).

Eckington station house. An original B&G building photographed in 1969. Top – from the north-west; bottom – from the west (W.V. Awdry).

invalid wife proved too much for him however, and the Board
arranged an exchange with Defford. His replacement was J. Dore,
who, it will be remembered, was responsible for the fatal collision at
Defford in 1845 and had tried to cover himself by blaming driver Ward.
Ever since the accident Dore had had a rough time from other
railwaymen (see Accidents and also Other Stations) and the board felt it
would be best to transfer him away from the main line. However, he
found no safe refuge at Tewkesbury. His quarrels with the local driver
became notorious, and it was decided to move both as soon as possible.
A Mr Middleton replaced Dore in March 1846 but he soon incurred the
wrath of the directors. He had no head for figures and couldn't keep the
accounts 'for toffee'. He was given notice to leave, but in the short time
he had been at the station he had become so well liked that the
Tewkesbury people petitioned the board for his retention. The board
compromised and he was transferred to Eckington.

But to return to 1840, Tewkesbury suffered greatly once the B&G
main line was open: 'Whatever may be the ultimate effect of railroads,
it is evident that their introduction has been one of almost unmixed evil
to the inhabitants of Tewkesbury.'[5] All road coaches bar the Cheltenham to Hereford mail and a two-horse carriage to Malvern had
ceased to run. This was fatal for the town's inn and coach house trade
upon which many inhabitants depended for their daily bread.

Compensation was, however, in sight. A deal had been reached
between the B&G and the Quay Commissioners about the extension to
the river. Entrance was to be along Quay Street but as this was a very
narrow lane the entire row of buildings on the south side had to be
demolished to make room for rail and road, and a bridge erected
alongside the existing one. It was this expense that had deterred the
B&G initially, but the new agreement stipulated that costs were to be
shared between the company and the Quay Bridge Trustees.

Demolition commenced in September 1840 and work on the
proposed depôt proceeded. Not all the townsfolk agreed with the plans
however. Those whose livelihoods depended upon the quay apparently
did not want the B&G to interfere. They called a public meeting for 4
January 1842 to: '. . . take into consideration the encroachments that
are being made by the B&G at the quay,' and to adopt measures for
protecting the rights and interests of the town. By then, however, a
group of protestors had taken the law into their own hands, and on 30
December 1841:[6] '. . . the Company's Works had been obstructed . . .
by a riotous assemblage of Boatmen and others . . . .the earth which
had been dug out by the Company had been filled in again, . . . the
Workmen had been assaulted, their tools taken from them and a
determination expressed that the Works should not be proceeded
with . . .' The protestors successfully made their point, though it cost

barge owners Richard and William Rice a 20s. fine each for obstruction. All work was suspended pending reports and the use of Lifford as an offloading point for coal instead of Tewkesbury was contemplated. Works recommenced in February 1841 to a revised plan whereby the extension to the quay would terminate at the end of Quay Street, and the depot on the quay between the Avon's two cuts was abandoned. This was confirmed in a letter to the Board from Mr E.G. Edgell (brother of H.P. Edgell, the one-time goods manager at Gloucester) prior to the general meeting in February 1842. He was a local businessman and public figure and much concerned about the plight of Tewkesbury.[7] 'The line abruptly terminates with a wall, the landing [from the water] to which would be on average 12ft. to 14ft. high, whereas if a bridge was thrown across the river and the line extended to a piece of ground [by] the public house called the Severn . . . [name illegible], a wharf might be had exclusively for the use of this Company . . . Many persons were commencing their arrangements to form a regular coal and corn trade between Cheltenham and Tewkesbury, and there is no doubt if this line was finished to the wharf above proposed that there would be a traffic . . .' The B&G, he said, had at first encouraged goods traffic from Tewkesbury to Cheltenham. They offered a low charge of 1s.6d. per ton which was seen in Tewkesbury as compensation by the B&G for not completing the line to the quay. But now, the charge had been quadrupled and was in effect a direct deterrent to trade from Tewkesbury. He continued; 'The town of Tewkesbury had just reason to be dissatisfied if faith is not kept by the Directors. Through the town a constant and great passing of travellers took place, this the railroad has deprived it of, therefore they had hope and great reason to expect that they should have the advantage their actual position gives them with easy access to the Rivers Severn and Avon. The town of Tewkesbury through its MPs rendered considerable and effective aid . . . in the House of Commons and as this Company will again have occasion for Parliamentary assistance it might well be considered desirable to conciliate the people who will of course use their just influence . . . as they may think well. I have been told that even now with its disadvantages the traffic return from Tewkesbury bears nearly a proportionate return with other stations, the quantity of coal and grain . . . could be very great.' All the chairman could do at the general meeting was to agree with Edgell's comments, but the expense of buying and working more wagons and engines for the bulky, low profit, coal and grain could not be justified by the returns; the funds of the B&G were very low. In addition the horse-power system in use was more expensive to run than a steam engine, hence the higher rates charged. Surely not 4s.6d. a ton though? Justice was eventually done. In June the CofE reported that the: '. . .

close approach of the Railway to the waterside . . . [has] not been taken advantage of although a considerable expenditure has been incurred for that purpose at the station'.[8] They recommended that the line be completed to the quay immediately, that certain rates be reduced and that increased facilities for traffic to and from the town be made. This latter comment no doubt refers to making the necessary moves to get locomotives on the branch. McConnell was ordered to work a light engine on the branch at a 'moderate speed' to convey passengers to and from the inaugural Tewkesbury races on 18 and 19 July 1843. Now, whether the Board simply decided quietly to contravene the Act of Parliament forbidding locomotives, or whether an agreement with the Local Road Trustees was made, is not stated. No legal proceedings arose so it must have been by general consent.

Thus the *Tewkesbury Examiner* recorded:[9] 'An immense number of persons from Cheltenham were present . . . facilities [were] accorded by the Railway Company who had special trains carrying any number of passengers for a shilling each way, and it was calculated that at least 2000 availed themselves of this cheap mode of transit . . . the Ascot 'Grand Stand'. . . . had been conveyed by rail for the occasion . . .' A near disaster on one of these trains was recorded by 'Veritas Vincit' when a train allegedly driven by McConnell himself got out of control and nearly landed in the Avon! (see Accidents, Chapter 21)

Locomotives were obviously successful on the branch. In January 1844 Mr Trotman was given notice to terminate his horse and carriage except for meeting the night Mail, and on 18 February, regular steam powered trains commenced. Journey time was cut to 6 minutes, junction to terminus.

More progress was on the way. The extension over the Avon to the quay was proceeded with at a total cost of £730. A wooden bridge was erected beside the (still present) iron bridge over the Avon at the bottom of Quay Street and considerable earthworks were necessary to raise the level of the quay itself.

High Street station closed in May 1864 when the MR extended the railway on to Malvern. Decline set in during the 1950s and Tewkesbury's rail link with Ashchurch was finally severed in 1964.

CHAPTER TWENTY SEVEN
OTHER STATIONS

Brief notes on the as yet unmentioned stations follow. (Full details of opening and closing dates and mileage appear in the appendix. Where no mention is made, insufficient information exists.)

Lifford gained a 3rd class station when the Camp Hill extension was completed, but it was not a success. Recommended for closure in 1842 and 1843 it finally lost its service in 1844. With access to the Birmingham and Worcester canal the Board had in 1840 considered landing Staffordshire coal there for transfer by rail to Cheltenham, but it was left to Mr Williams, the line's leading coal merchant, to set up the trade there in 1843.

Cofton has the claim to fame of being a terminus of the B&G for a few months! Built near Cofton Church, the temporary station cost £300 though this was not money wasted. It was literally moved, 'lock, stock and barrel', and incorporated into the station at Camp Hill.

Barnt Green was a latecomer to the B&G timetable, added in 1844 as a result of local pressure. A local dignitary, the Hon. Mr Robert Clive MP, offered to give land for a station and goods shed in 1842 but in the opinion of the Board the sparse population and close proximity of both Blackwell and Lifford stations would not justify the expense. Further requests were made from the inhabitants of Alvechurch and Redditch (their branch line did not open until 1859) and so during the course of 1844, a 2nd class station was erected comprising station house, platforms, signal posts, stables and a 'large entrance gate'! Blackwell, at the summit of the Lickey, was first mooted in May 1841 by Redditch people, and is mentioned as a 3rd class station in July of that year. Between then and the following year it was awarded 2nd class status with buildings, since a clerk is mentioned in the board Minutes. It became a locomotive sub depot in 1842 when McConnell reorganised locomotive working on the Lickey. Watering and refuelling facilities were provided here for engines which shuttled the trains between Birmingham and Blackwell exchanging them there with the Lickey Bankers.

Bromsgrove was the nerve centre of the B&G's traffic throughout its independent existence by virtue of its locomotive works. As such, it survived only until 1847 when the MR centralised upon Derby, after which it became the MR's major wagonworks, a role for which it is probably best remembered.

Bromsgrove station was a railway colony planted a mile or so from Bromsgrove town, but situated in the parish of Stoke Prior. Bromsgrove itself was a thriving country town deserving of a 1st class station which was in fact provided. Whishaw[1] described the station in 1840 as being in a cutting 10ft. deep and approached by a sloped drive off the Bromsgrove road, passing to the rear of the station house and between workmens' cottages and a goods shed, and back by another gateway to the same road.

Accommodation at the station was provided for a booking office, clerk's office, secretary's room, waiting room, ladies room, resident engineer's office and the usual other conveniences. In front of the single storey building was a colonnade extending its whole length, and the whole is of a 'pleasing and most unostentatious appearance'.

The structure demolished in 1973 was long and low with four curious wooden gabled porches, two on brick and two on cast iron columns and reputedly formed part of the colonnade. Returning to Whishaw, the passenger platforms were 10ft. wide and 1ft.6in. high with three tracks of railway separating them. The central line was for holding the bank engine between duties.

For the railway as a whole the locomotive works were of far greater importance than the station. In 1841 and again in 1843 plans were considered to remove the station in the general direction of the village of Stoke Prior to facilitate expansion of the works, but it was the required expenditure which doubtless killed these projects. The removal of the station would have presented no additional problem to would-be passengers as there was already an omnibus link available between the station and the town.

The station area saw an almost continuous series of improvements as new and extended sidings and crossovers were added to facilitate train manoeuvres. When the MR became owners they altered the station to give more room for trains in their descent of the incline, an extra centre road was added to keep through trains off the platform roads. A '. . . very complete set of signals of the most approved description' were put in to control the Lickey, corresponding with the adoption of the telegraph.

A considerable number of men were employed at Bromsgrove – a handful at the station and the majority at the locomotive works. For the key staff who needed to be within easy reach of the railway, two large detached houses and a row of terraced cottages (ten smaller sandwiched between two larger) were built. When J. E. McConnell, the head of the locomotive department, for some reason found his house inadequate, he asked for and gained permission to erect his own house in a more convenient location for the works.

Stoke Prior station, sited near the Salt Works, was designated 3rd class at first, but was soon given 2nd class status. Most of the traffic was generated by the salt and chemical works of the British Alkali Company and Imperial Alkali Company, though the greater part of the output went via the Birmingham and Worcester canal which bisected the two works. A branch line was authorised in 1845 into the works after the B&G had altered the tramway to the docks at Gloucester. Wagons of salt for export could then be ferried right through by rail which had by then become a better proposition than the canal.

Joseph Morris, the clerk, was an 'old hand' and quite a character too. Sworn in as a special constable in August 1840 he was appointed station clerk in October of that year, and had to manage single handed as his requests for an assistant porter or policeman were disregarded. In November 1842 it was reported to the board that he was keeping an ale-house. He was ordered to give it up or be sacked. Morris replied that his only connection with the beer shop was that he had married its proprietress. She had managed it successfully alone for 13 years, and would continue to do so without his help. The board was unimpressed by this reply and sacked him; whereupon they were so heavily bombarded with protests and testimonials from the inhabitants of Stoke that they had to reinstate him. He was still there in 1847 when he was reported for 'inattention to signals'. No details were given of his offence, but his excuse was apparently not good enough and he was fined 10s.

Dodderhill appears on a station list in 1841, but don't look on the OS map for it! Dodderhill parish appears on some of the company's maps, Dodderhill Common is shown on the 1st edition OS map near Pipers Hill on the road between Wytchwood and Hanbury (via Astwood Farm) about 1¼ miles from the railway. No place name exists on the current OS map! Presumably it was an early example of a wayside halt – no platform or buildings – serving whosoever in the vicinity was prepared to walk far enough to catch a train. Not many were though for it failed to gain another mention.

Droitwich Road station was 2 miles from the salt works and spa town of Droitwich. During its short life, expensive coach connections to the town had to be provided and subsidised by the B&G. The station was quite impressive though, and on the 1st class list. Built at a cost of £413 in stone trimmed brick, the four roomed building was mildly Tudor with slender angled chimneys and mullioned windows.[2]

Dunhampstead had at first only a goods siding near the level crossing but it became a 3rd class station in 1841. It was situated near the summit of two minor gradients which occasionally caused operating problems. In 1844 for instance, the up evening goods and passenger train had apparently been loading very well and could not restart on the 1 in 330 upwards grade. McConnell suggested that passengers from the halt be asked to walk 150 yards nearer to Droitwich where the train could stop on the down grade.

The unsuspecting passenger to Worcester might well have wondered why he was being shown from his carriage at Spetchley and helped into a horse-drawn omnibus. We have mentioned above the tribulations the B&G suffered in their dealings with Worcester, which left Spetchley as the main line station for the city until the OWW deviation was opened in 1850. One of the principal objectors to a rail connection to Worcester was Mr Berkeley of Spetchley Park and he was none too pleased with the prospect of having a railway station so near to his home. Such was his influence and authority that plans had to be approved by him before being proceeded with. It was well laid out in keeping with its role as the station for Worcester. Offices, station house, stables and lodge were erected at a cost of £2,716. Prior to opening a further £572 was spent; on the conversion of the stables into two staff cottages and the erection of new stables for ten horses; the improvement of the booking office and ladies' waiting room; the addition of a new water closet and living accommodation for the clerk and an office for the inspector. A refreshment room was provided. This was leased out to a willing party – for instance in 1843 to Mr Dauncey, an ex-member of staff at the station. The station must have been an impressive sight; second only to Cheltenham's station in grandeur, and had the branch to Worcester ever been built it was to have been taken down and rebuilt at the terminus.

The station clerk was Richard Lowe, appointed before the railway opened in 1840 at a salary of £120. After two years he became dissatisfied and asked for a rise in salary, but this was refused. He then started a parcel carrying service as a side-line (in connection with the B&G) which became a success. As business expanded it took him away from his station duties so, as the parcel business was valuable to the B&G, an assistant clerk, Thomas Enoch, was appointed in February 1844.

By September 1845 Lowe having resigned his position at the station. Enoch was appointed station master in his stead. Lowe's parcel business had prospered, and the B&B was paying him a retaining fee of £15 per quarter for the parcels traffic in addition to which he had developed his own cartage business. Further, in March 1846, when Meek & Cobleigh, coach proprietors, objected to the B&B's revised terms for the renewal of their contract, Richard Lowe tendered for the Worcester–Spetchley coach contract at £50 per week, and so continued till the OWW Branch to Worcester from Abbotswood was opened.

Pirton opened as a 3rd class halt in 1841 at the level crossing. Promotion came in 1843 to 2nd class status after protests from the small town of Kempsey (by the Severn and some 2½ miles from the railway). They pleaded for improved travel facilities and were 'rewarded' by the erection of platforms and shelter at Pirton, but traffic was scanty and 'Kempsey' was closed in 1844.

The station at Defford was constructed in a similar style to that at Droitwich Road and was at first given 1st class status. This was not because of the importance of the village, but because the Dowager Queen Adelaide was a frequent visitor to Lord and Lady Coventry at Croome Park, and travelled by special train to Defford in the L&B Royal Coach.

Defford was the scene of the B&G's worst train disaster (see Accidents). As we have seen, the station clerk, J. Dore was really responsible for the accident, but managed to cover himself at the inquest by throwing all the blame on the dead engine driver, Ward. Both Dore and his wife behaved with shocking inhumanity to both Mrs Ward and the injured fireman Baird – it was left to a passenger to attend to them. But, so successful was Dore's cover-up that his salary was raised '. . . in consequence of his good conduct . . .', and his wife was given a gratuity of £5 '. . . for her great attention to sufferers from the accident.' However, most railwaymen knew the real truth and made his life a burden thereafter; so much so, that he was forced away from the main line to Tewkesbury. He couldn't escape there either, and he is last heard of on the BrG at Berkeley Road station.

The fertile Vale of Evesham was a focal point for market garden produce and Defford together with the adjacent stations at Eckington and Bredon sent vast quantities by rail. All three stations had busy goods yards. Eckington and Bredon were 2nd class stations with similar small buildings. Incident and accident occured at both. (see Accidents).

Ashchurch was, and still is, a small village but later in the 19th century it became an important railway centre when the Tewkesbury branch had been extended to Malvern, and the loop from Barnt Green through Reddich and Evesham both joined the main line here. Under the B&G, as the junction for Tewkesbury it was a 1st class station with buildings costing £379. While the branch was horse worked the

junction was relatively safe – though 'Veritas Vincit'[3] thought otherwise when he heard the staff levels were to be cut by the CofE in
1843. '. . . the Day Policeman is to be done away with. This is a place
of utmost importance at which to have men placed to watch the trains
approaching, for the Tewkesbury branch comes in here and collisions
can only be prevented by the vigilance and activity of the engineman.
In foggy weather they must run all the hazards of a 'pitch-in'
occasionally.' A few minor incidents occured here but the first involving a train from the branch came in June 1844 after locomotive
traction had replaced that of Mr Trotman's horses. 'A special train
which was conveying timber and other materials . . . along the line was
met by the engine that works the Tewkesbury branch. The foreparts of
both engines were battered in and considerable injury done to them
. . .'[4] Mr Williams, the coal merchant, set up a depot here in 1842 and
the traffic later warranted the provision of a goods shed and sidings. as
noted above, by the turn of the century the MR had made it a junction
of some importance but details here are beyond our terms of reference.[5]

The villages of Stoke Orchard and Bishops Cleeve were served by a
3rd class halt on the Stoke Road from February 1843. A station building
and siding appeared the next year. A station was first requested in 1839
by Reverend W.L. Townsend to serve Bishops Cleeve. He was told
that a station would be provided only if an agreement to guarantee 500
tons of goods to be sent or received there was made, and if a lesser
amount were handled '. . . the Company would expect to be paid as for
500 tons.' That was enough to silence the Reverend gentleman! The
Stoke Road originally crossed the railway by level crossing which was
replaced by a bridge before the railway opened. A subsequent vestry
meeting at Stoke Orchard requested the removal of the bridge,
substituting a level crossing and a station. All they got was a 3rd class
halt, but local pressure was kept up for a decent station and it paid off.
Aided by a subscription fund initiated by the Reverend Mr Townsend,
a station and siding were constructed and known as Cleeve, policeman
Mayhew being transferred from Cheltenham to take charge.

Badgeworth and Churchdown were small villages between Cheltenham and Gloucester, both some way from the main line but on
direct roads to bridges over it. Local requests initiated by Badgeworth
for a halt were studied by the board who decided that since
Churchdown was the more equidistant from Cheltenham and
Gloucester, it should have a halt. It lasted five weeks. Plans to try
Badgeworth instead were deferred until the following year when two
of the short Cheltenham–Gloucester trains stopped there. Expenditure
of £5.17s.10d. was approved but for what is not recorded, maybe a
pathway from the road above.

REFERENCES

KEY

CE	*Cheltenham Examiner*
GCH	*Gloucestershire Chronicle*
GJ	*Gloucester Journal*
GRO	Gloucester Records Office
H	*Herepaths Railway Journal*
PRO	Public Records Office, Kew; Reference section 'Rail'
PROC ICE	*Proceedings of the Institute of Civil Engineers*
PROC IME	*Proceedings of the Institute of Mechanical Engineers*
RM	*Railway Magazine*
RT	*Railway Times*
TE	*Tewkesbury Examiner*

Chapter 3
1. GJ 17 and 31 October, 7 November 1835
2. GJ 27 February 1836
3. PRO 1075/372

Chapter 4
1. GJ 30 May 1837
2. ibid., 7 October 1837

Chapter 5
1. PRO 37/14 6 December 1837
2. *RT* vol. II p. 341
3. PRO 37/4 9 July 1839

Chapter 6
1. *Autobiography of Herbert Spencer*, Williams and Norgate, 1904
2. *RT* vol.I p. 58
3. *GJ* 10 February 1838
4. *GJ* 29 September 1838
5. ibid., 17 November 1838
6. *RT* 30 November 1839
7. ibid., vol. II p. 76
8. reprinted in *GJ* 30 May 1840
9. ibid.
10. *RT* vol. III p. 15
11. PRO 37/15 21, 28 April 1840
12. *GJ* 30 May 1840
13. Herbert Spencer *op. cit.*.
14. *GJ* 6 June 1840
15. *CE* 1 July 1840
16. Herbert Spencer *op. cit.*.

Chapter 7
1. *GJ* 10 October 1840
2. ibid.
3. *RT* vol. III p. 941
4. Herbert Spencer *op. cit.*

Chapter 8
1. PRO 37/15 M 183
2. PRO 7/4 20 July 1840
3. General Meeting Report August 1842

Chapter 9
1. *RT* vol. 4 pp. 1053, 1102, 1150, 1172
2. Edgell papers, GRO D1406 box 1
3. *RT* vol. 5 p. 544
4. *H* August 1842
5. *GJ* 27 August 1842

Chapter 10
1. *CE* January 25 1843
2. *GJ* 27 August 1842

3. *RT* vol. 6 p. 355
4. *GJ* 8 September 1842
5. *RT* vol. 6 p. 321
6. PRO 37/18
7. 'Veritas Vincit'. letters to the *Railway Times* and *Record* published as 'Railway Locomotive Management', 1847
8. PRO 37/18
9. *GJ* 15 July 1843
10. 'Veritas Vincit' *op. cit.*
11. *RT* vol. 6 p. 809
12. ibid., p. 760
13. ibid., p. 919
14. ibid., p. 1365

Chapter 11
1. *H* 1844 p. 306
2. ibid., p. 794
3. *GJ* 19 October 1844
4. Herbert Spencer *op. cit.*
5. *The Times* 6 October 1850

Chapter 12
1. *History of the Great Western Railway*, MacDermott, republished Ian Allen
2. House of Commons Report, OWW and Oxford and Rugby Railways, 1845
3. *GJ*, 1 February 1845
4. *RT* vol. 8 p. 192
5. PRO 37/6 4 February 1845
6. House of Commons Report, *op. cit.*

Chapter 13
1. PRO 37/15 13 and 20 October 1840
2. *GJ* 17 April 1841
3. Edgell papers *op. cit.*
4. *GJ* 26 February 1842
5. *RT* vol. 5 p. 59
6. ibid., vol. 5 p. 353
7. PRO 37/18
8. ibid.
9. *H* 1844 pp. 306, 764, 794, 904
10. Gauge Commission Report 11 August 1845
11. *GJ* 2 November 1844
12. *GJ* 17 November 1844

13. ibid., 9 September 1843
14. *RT* vol. 7 p. 267

Chapter 14
  1. *GJ* 18 July 1840
  2. ibid., 1 Aug 1840
  3. PRO 37/4 20 July 1840
  4. *H* 1843 p. 562
  5. *History of Cheltenham*, Gwen Hart
  6. *RT* vol. 7 p. 797
  7. *GJ* 13 July 1841
  8. *H* 17 January and February 1843
  9. *RT* vol. 8 p. 1076
10. *GJ* 28 March 1844
11. ibid., 8 May 1841
12. ibid., 20 July 1844
13. ibid., 12 September 1846
14. GCH June 1841
15. *GJ* 7 November 1840
16. ibid., 10 April 1841

Chapter 15
  1. F. Whishaw, *Railways of Gt. Britain and Ireland*, 1842 republished
      David and Charles
  2. ibid.
  3. Herbert Spencer *op. cit.*
  4. 'Veritas Vincit' *op. cit.*
  5. Herbert Spencer *op. cit.*
  6. BoT Report on Level Crossings September 1841
  7. Whishaw *op. cit.*
  8. Herbert Spencer *op. cit.*
  9. Gauge Commission Report *op. cit.*

Chapter 16
  1. 'Veritas Vincit' *op. cit.*
  2. *GJ* 13 September and 8 November 1845

Chapter 17
  1. Diary of David Joy, *Railway Magazine*, July and August 1908
  2. Herbert Spencer *op. cit.*
  3. PRO 37/4 20 July 1840
  4. PRO 37/15 M 635
  5. PRO 37/15 M 119
  6. ibid., M 195

7. ibid., M 244
8. ibid., M 258
9. ibid., M 271
10. ibid., M 414, 420
11. ibid., M 439
12. ibid., M 448
13. Whishaw, *op. cit.* p. 31
14. PRO 37/15 M 635
15. ibid., M 635
16. David Joy, *op. cit.*
17. PRO 37/15 M 640
18. PRO 37/16 M 39, 49
19. ibid., M 72
20. *RT* 1841 p. 439
21. ibid.
22. PRO 37/16 M 2
23. David Joy, *op. cit.*
24. PRO 37/16 M 2
25. ibid., M 523
26. ibid., M 287
27. ibid., M 303
28. *PROC. ICE* vol. II p. 99ff 1843
29. *H* p. 824 1842
30. PRO 37/16 M 750
31. PRO 37/6 M 2003
32. *H* p. 328 1842
33. PRO 37/16 M 750
34. ibid., M 876
35. ibid., M 1013
36. ibid., M 1018
37. *Railway Machinery*, Clark 1855
38. *PROC. ICE op. cit.*
39. 'Veritas Vincit' *op. cit.*
40. ibid.
41. PRO 37/18
42. PRO 37/15 M 1230, 1258
43. ibid., 37/6 M 2799
44. ibid., 74/2 M 916

Chapter 18
1. *The Midland Railway*, F.S. Williams republished David & Charles
2. *The Norris Locomotives in England*, P.C. Dewhurst, Newcomen Society 1947/8
3. *PROC. IME* October 1849, J.E. McConnell

4. PRO 37/15 M 124
5. PRO 37/12 M 986
6. PRO 37/15 M 148, 159
7. ibid., M 284
8. ibid., M 285
9. ibid., November 19 1839
10. *RT* pp. 706, 730, 747, 765 1841
11. Dewhurst *op. cit.*
12. PRO 37/15 M 556
13. Dewhurst *op. cit.*
14. *PROC. ICE* vol. II p. 99ff 1842
15. PRO 37/16 M 985
16. ibid., May 17 1842
17. Clark *op. cit.*
18. David Joy, *op. cit.*
19. PRO 37/15 M 376, 395
20. Described in *Imperial Cyclopaedia of Machinery*, W.Johnson, published William McKenzie
21. PRO 37/15 M 660, 37/16 3 August
22. PRO 37/15 M 284
23. ibid., M 590
24. Dewhurst, *op. cit.*
25. PRO 74/1 M 791
26. PRO 37/5 9, 16 February
27. Dewhurst, *op. cit.*
28. 'Veritas Vincit', *op. cit.*
29. Dewhurst, *op. cit.*
30. *H*, 1842 p. 824
31. PRO 37/17 12 July 1842
32. PRO 37/16 M 1744
33. *RM* vol. xv p. 318
34. Gauge Commission Report, 11 August 1845
35. *Journal of the Historical Model Railway Society*, vol. 8 no. 10
36. House of Lords Enquiry South Wales and Great Western Railway bill 26–30 June 1865
37. *Derby Works and Midland Locomotives*, J.B. Radford, Ian Allan 1971

Chapter 19
1. *H* 1843 p. 562
2. PRO 37/15 10 December 1839
3. Whishaw *op. cit.*
4. *RT* 4 July 1840 p. 528
5. *GJ* 17 October 1840

6. BoT Report 21 October 1840, Capt. Melhuish
7. BoT Report *op. cit.*

Chapter 20
1. *GJ* 13 July 1839
2. ibid., 25 April 1840
3. Herbert Spencer *op. cit.*
4. *PROC. ICE vol. 23 1863/64*
5. *The Engineer* vol. 55, p. 455 1883
6. Biographies exist in Gloucester City Library Local Collection

Chapter 21
1. *GJ* 24 August 1839
2. ibid., 9 May 1840
3. ibid.
4. PRO 37/15 4 August 1840
5. *GJ* 2 September 1843
6. ibid., 8 November 1845
7. PRO 37/15 22 September 1840
8. *GJ* 15 February 1845
9. ibid., 1 May 1841
10. ibid., 4 June 1842
11. *H*, 30 November 1844 vol. 6 p. 1536
12. *GJ* 26 October 1844
13. ibid., 19 July 1845
14. ibid., 27 February 1841
15. *RT* vol. 4 p. 609 1841
16. PRO 37/15 17 and 24 November 1840: *RT* 1840 p. 1013/9: Clark, *op. cit.* and P.C. Dewhurst, *Engineering* December 25 1942
17. *GJ* 14 November 1840
18. PRO 37/15 p.72, *RT* pp. 419, 430, 439 1841
19. *GJ* 23 January 1841, PRO 37/5 26 January 1841
20. 'Veritas Vincit' *op. cit.*
21. *TE* 17 November 1846
22. 'Veritas Vincit' *op. cit.*
23. 'Veritas Vincit' *op. cit.*: *GJ* 6 September 1845
24. PRO 37/15 11 August 1840
25. *GJ* 3 October 1840
26. ibid., 1 May 1841
27. *RT* vol. 5 p. 161 1842

Chapter 22
1. 'Veritas Vincit' *op. cit.*

Chapter 23
1. PRO 37/15 M 617
2. G.P. Neele, *Railway Reminiscences* McQuorquedale 1904
3. PRO 37/16 1 June 1841
4. ibid., M 8
5. Dewhurst *op. cit.*
6. PRO 37/16 M 876
7. ibid., 37/17 M 1261
8. ibid., 37/5 M899
9. ibid 37/5 M992
10. ibid 37/5 8 August
11. 'Veritas Vincit' *op. cit.*.
12. PRO 37/5 March 1844
13. ibid 37/6 M 2247
14. ibid M 2633
15. ibid M 2646
16. *The Times* August 26 1845

Chapter 24
1. *A View of Cheltenham in its Past and Present State*, H. Davies 1843 GRO

Chapter 25
1. D.P. Gowen, Railway Station Postmarks, pub The Railway Philatelic Group, 1978
2. PRO 37/6 M 2434
3. ibid M 2182
4. PRO RT 29/6 pp. 368–375
5. MacDermott *op. cit.* pp. 188, 189
6. Parliamentary Committee Report OWW and O&R Enquiry Q 4948
7. Honeymoon Diary of George and Edna Adeny. Roger Wilson Collection
8. G.P. Neele, *op. cit.*
9. A copy exists in Gloucester City Library Local Collection
10. G.P. Neele *op. cit.*
11. GJ 25 November 1845

Chapter 26
1. PRO 37/11 M 990
2. *TE* August 1839
3. *RT* 5 October 1839
4. *TE* vol. II p. 29
5. ibid p. 45

6.   PRO 37/12 M 1514, 1515
7.   GRO D1406 box 1
8.   PRO 37/18
9.   *TE* vol. III p. 127

Chapter 27
1.   Whishaw *op. cit.*
2.   ibid
3.   'Veritas Vincit' *op. cit.*
4.   *GJ* 22 June 1844
5.   *RM* vol. 26 p. 157 has an in depth article.

BIBLIOGRAPHY AND SOURCE MATERIAL

General References

Railway Times, Herepath's Railway Journal
Gloucester Journal, Gloucester Chronicle
Worcester Journal, Worcester Chronicle
Cheltenham Examiner, Cheltenham Looker-on
Tewkesbury Examiner
Midland Counties Herald, Aris' Birmingham Gazette
Bristol Gazette, Bristol Mercury, Bristol Mirror
Gloucester Records Office (Plans submitted to Parliament, Q/Rum file; Edgell Papers D1406 box 1; CGWU Minutes)
Public Records Office (B&G Minutes PRO RAIL 37–1 to 22; B&B Minutes PRO RAIL 74–1 & 2; BOT RETURNS)
Houses of Parliament Records (Evidence used during the Bills of B&G, CGWU, BRG, MR, etc.)

Further and General Reading

The Rise of the Midland Railway; E.G. Barnes, Allen & Unwin
The Midland Railway, Hamilton Ellis, 1953
Our Iron Roads, F.S. Williams
Locomotive Machinery, Clarke, 1855
The Railways of Great Britain and Ireland, F. Whishaw 1842
Derby Works and Midland Locomotives, J. Radford, Ian Allen 1971
Autobiography of Herbert Spencer, Williams and Norgate 1904
'Diary of David Joy', *Railway Magazine*, 1908 July and August, pp. 48,
  149
The Gloucester and Cheltenham Railway, D.E. Bick, Oakwood Press
The Bristol and Gloucester Railway, C.G. Maggs, Oakwood Press
The Lickey Incline, H.C. Casserley, Oakwood Press
'The Birmingham and Gloucester Railway', *Railway Magazine* vol. 14,
  p. 145
'The Bristol and Gloucester Railway', ibid., vol. 14 p. 221
'West to North by the MR', ibid., vol. 27 p. 1
'MR Train Working', ibid., vol. 44 p. 319

APPENDIX

APPENDIX

GRADIENT PROFILE

	STATION LIST						
NAME	CLASS IN B&G DAYS	DATE OPEN (A)	DATE CLOSED PASSENGERS	DATE CLOSED GOODS	MILEAGE (B) B&G NOV 1841	IMAGINARY B&G MILEPOST	CURRENT MILEPOST (C)
Curzon St (1)	1	–	–	–	–	–	–
Camp Hill	1 (2)	17 12 40	17 8 41(2)	4 10 1965	0	42.7	42.26
Brighton Road	–	?	27 11 1946	–	–	–	42.79
Moseley (MR) (3)	–	11 67	27 11 1946	–	–	–	43.43
Moseley (B&G) (3)	3	19 11 41	27 11 1946	2 5 1966	?	?	44.23
Hazelwell	–	11 67	27 11 1946	1 3 1965	–	–	45.06
Lifford 1st (B&G)	3	19 12 40	11 44	–	4.3.56	46.10	–
Lifford 3rd (MR)	–	?	30 9 1940	6 7 1964	–	–	46.03
Kings Norton	–	?	open	1 9 1964	–	–	46.58
Northfield	–	? 93	open	–	–	–	48.10
Longbridge	3	15 11 41?	open	4 1 1960	7.2.26	49.09	–
Halesowen JC	–	–	–	–	–	–	49.25
Cofton	1	17 9 40	17 12 40	–	8.9.76	50.16	–
Barnt Green	2	6 9 44?	open	6 7 1964	–	–	51.65
Blackwell	2	5 6 41	18 4 1966	3 2 1964	10.46.66	52.57	53.15
Bromsgrove	1	24 6 40	open	5 6 1967	13.24.16	55.31	55.31
Stoke Works JC	–	–	–	–	–	–	57.35
Stoke (Prior)	3 (4)	24 6 40	1 10 55	?	15.54.86	57.62	–
Dodderhill	3	15 11 41	5 3 44?	?	16.25.96	58.33	–
Droitwich Road	1	24 6 40	1 10 55	1 10 1952	18.11.16	60.18	60.19
Dunhampstead	3	15 11 41	1 10 55	1 10 1949	20.2.66	62.10	62.11
Oddingley	3	9 45?	1 10 55	?	–	–	62.58
Bredicot	3	11 45	1 10 55	?	–	–	–
Spetchley	1	24 6 40	1 10 55	2 1 1961	24. 6.91	66.44	66.16
Norton	3	15 11 41	1 10 55	?	25.39.26	67.46	67.51
Abbotswood JC	–	11 50	1 10 55	?	–	–	68.60
Wadborough	3	15 11 41	4 11 1965	–	27.72.86	70.00	69.89
Pirton	3 (5)	15 11 41	11 44	?	28.38.86	70.46	70.52
Besford	3	15 11 41	8 46	?	20.61.56	71.68	–
Defford	3	24 6 40	4 1 1965	1 7 1963	31.27.76	73.35	73.39
Eckington	2	24 6 40	4 1 1965	1 7 1963	32.32.76	74.40	74.47
Bredon	2	24 6 40	4 1 1965	1 7 1963	35.11.26	77.18	77.25
Ashchurch	1	24 6 40	15 11 1971	1 6 1964	37.27.26	79.34	79.39
Tewkesbury (7)	1	21 7 40	14 8 1961	2 11 1964	2. 9.0.(8)	–	–
Cleeve	3	14 2 43	2 2 1950	4 4 1960	–	–	82.34
Swindon	3	15 11 41?	1 10 44	–	–	–	84.23
Cheltenham High St.	–	–	1 7 1910	3 1 1966	–	–	85.60
Cheltenham	1	24 6 40	open	–	44.36.76	86.44	86.56
Badgeworth	3	22 8 43	10 46	–	–	–	–
Churchdown	3	9 8 42 (6)	2 11 1964	–	–	–	89.65
Gloucester B&G	1	17 12 40	12 4 96	–	51.4.91	93.12	–
Gloucester MR	–	12 4 96	(9) 1 12 1975	1 8 1967			99

(A)	day, month, year (18..) or month, year (18..) or as stated
(B)	miles, chains, links (80 chains = 1 mile. 100 links = 1 chain)
(C)	from Derby, miles chains
(1)	L&B station used by B&G (then MR) from 14.8.41 to 1.7.54, then New St. station (opened 1.6.54)
(2)	3rd from Nov 1841, new station on main line opened Dec 1867
(3)	B&G station renamed Kings Heath in 1867 when MR station opened
(4)	2nd from 1843
(5)	2nd from 1843
(6)	Closed 27.9.42. Reopened?
(7)	B&G station closed 16.5.64 & replaced by station on Malvern line.
(8)	Mileage from Ashchurch
(9)	replaced by a rebuilt station on site of Central (GWR) station

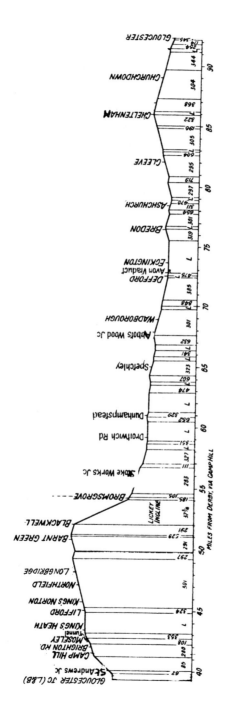

STAFF

Numbers

	Jan–June	July–Dec
1841	803*	347
1842	334	313
1843	294	273

* This, we assume, includes the Engineering Department which was progressively reduced as the railway was completed.

Engineering Department

Engineer in Chief	William Scarth Moorsom 1834–1841
Resident Engineers	F.H.P. Wetherall June 1840–Nov 1843 (Superintendent & Engineer from September 1841)
	James Bayliss Nov 1843–Aug 1845
	W.H. Barlow Aug 1845 (Resident Engineer of the B&B)

Company Secretary

Capt. Bellew	Sept 1836–Feb 1838
William Burgess	Feb 1838–Aug 1841 (Joint Secretary and Superintendent)
George King	Aug 1841–Dec 1843
George Sanders	Feb 1844–Aug 1846

Superintendent – General Manager

William Burgess	Dec 1837–July 1841 (Superintendent & Secretary)
John Kidder	July 1841–Dec 1841 (Temporary post)

F.H.P. Wetherall	Dec 1841–Nov 1843 (Superintendent & Resident Engineer)
Humphrey Brown	Dec 1843–Nov 1844 (Superintendent of Goods & Passenger Traffic)
William Burgess	Dec1844–Feb 1845 (Temporary post)
William Burgess and Wyndham Harding	Feb 1845–April 1845 (B&G worked jointly with BrG)
Wyndham Harding	April 1845–Aug 1846

Locomotive Department

Outdoor Superintendent William Creuze June 1840–April 1841

G.D. Bischopp April 1841–Feb 1842 (post merged)

Works Foreman Joseph Rutherford
June 1840–Nov 1840
Richard Walworth Nov 1840–April 1841
Israel York April 1841–July 1841
James E. McConnell July 1841–March 1842 (post merged)

| Superintendent | James E. McConnell March 1842–Feb 1847 |
| Carriage & Wagon Department Foreman | Edward Lean June 1840–June 1845 (merged with Loco. Dept.) |

Goods department

H.P. Edgell	to Nov 1841 (temporary post)
J.D. Payne	Nov 1841–May 1843
W.D. Brown	July 1843–Dec 1843
Humphrey Brown	Dec 1843–Dec 1844
J.D. Payne	April 1845 (reappointed)

PAY

Examples of the lower grades are given (per week unless stated) in 1840 (if applicable), future rates and the date applicable follow.

Road Police	30s.
Station Inspectors	30s., 35s. (1844), 30s. (1845)
Guards: 1st class, passenger	35s., 20s. (1842)
2nd class, passenger	28s., 15s. (1842) 25s. (1845, post merged)
3rd class, goods	21s.
Train Porters	21s.
Station Porters	18s., 16s. (1843), 10s. (1844)
Station Police	18s.
Gatekeepers	7s.–18s. (1841)
Switchmen	11s.–16s. (1843), 18s. (1844)
Ticket Collectors	30s. (1842), 8s.–15s. (1844)
Permanent Way Overlooker	£80 p.a., £100 p.a. (1845)
Station Clerk	21s., 25s. (1845)
Assistant Clerk	21s. (1843)
Chief Clerk	£100 p.a., £120 p.a. (1841), £140 p.a. (1845)
Clerks, various	£60 p.a., £90 p.a. (1842)
Engine Drivers	40s. (1842), 36s. (1843)
Firemen/Stokers	27s. (1842), 23s. (1843)

ROLLING STOCK

PASSENGER

Details from Whishaw (see ref 15.1)

Carriages 1st class

accommodation 3 abreast × 6 = 18
length of body 17ft.6in.
width of body 7ft.
height of body 5ft.1in.
height
from rails   7ft.8in.
windows   sash window in each door and
                  a fixed light at each side of
                  door.
weight   approx. 3¾ tons (estimate
                  from Gauge Commission)
livery   dark buff, lined black, Com-
                  pany arms on door.
average cost £370

2nd class accommodation 4 a side × 6 = 24
3 Compartments open to each other above
dwarf partitions
length of body 15ft.6in.
width of body 7ft.
height of body 4ft.1in.
windows open until glazing in October 1844
average cost £190

GOODS

Ballast wagons   10ft.3in. × 7ft.9in. × 1ft.5in.. Tare weight 2t,
                  sides and ends hinged, wheels 3in. diam.,
                  wheelbase 4ft.8in. Buffers dumb, wrought iron
                  draw gear, hook-on-chain coupling.
Goods wagons   10ft.3in. × 7ft.9in. × 3ft.5in. Five plank sides and
                  ends. Single lever brake, other details as above.
                  Average cost £60 each.

PERMANENT WAY – 1

Rails	see drawing
Baulks	originally cut from American yellow pine in various lengths at 15ft. minimum, 12in.–14in. square and cut diagonally. Kyanised.
Sleepers	Beech and larch in 8ft. lengths cut from timber as shown. They were incorrectly Kyanised and soon rotted. Sixteen miles of track on embankments were laid on sleepers and had to be completely relaid from 1844. Since the embankments were consolidated by then, longitudinal track replaced the sleepers, the baulks were of Memel pine, Kyanised or creosoted and transoms of creosoted Baltic pine.

Chairs & Saddles see drawing

Ballast	Many varieties were used depending upon local supply. Broken sandstone, broken limestone, gravel or sand were preferred but if unavailable locally, marl or clay were burnt into a sort of rubble. Not the cheapest nor best ballast; it drained badly. Thousands of tons were burnt costing between 1s.8d. to 2s. per cubic yard. Cheaper than bringing in alternatives by horse and cart, but it must have accounted for an awful lot of timber or coal to burn the fires.
Cost of laying	This varied. £5,400 per double track mile is recorded in an 'Account of the Permanent Way of the B&G' G.W.B. Jackson, *Proc. Inst. Civil Engineers* 1842. Capt. W.S. Moorsom reported £5,160 per double track mile in Dec 1839.

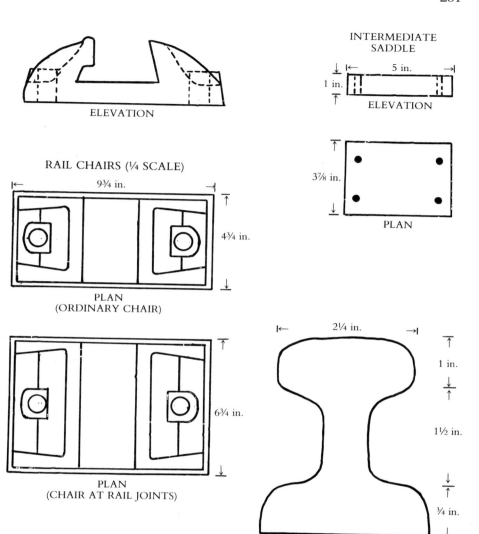

ELEVATION

RAIL CHAIRS (¼ SCALE)

9¾ in.

4¾ in.

PLAN
(ORDINARY CHAIR)

6¾ in.

PLAN
(CHAIR AT RAIL JOINTS)

INTERMEDIATE
SADDLE

5 in.

1 in.

ELEVATION

3⅞ in.

PLAN

2¼ in.

1 in.

1½ in.

¾ in.

¾ in.

2¾ in.

RAIL SECTION (FROM SCIENCE MUSEUM)
56lb. per yard, wrought iron, from Foster
of Stourbridge. In 15ft. lengths

HEADS OF AGREEMENT WITH BrG 14 JAN 1845

1. To unite and become the Bristol & Birmingham Rly Co, and seek an Act to allow the union.
2. Until then the affairs of the United Company to be administered by a Board of Management, seven each from each company, the chairman from the B&G.
3. On passing of Act, Board to be selected by proprietors.
4. Stock of United Company to be £1,800,000; £1,142,125 B&G and £657,875 BrG.
5. Each shareholder of BrG to have option of taking his portion of such allotment and in case he declines, have £50 stock in the combined Company given instead of each share, receiving dividend on the whole and paying 4½ per cent interest to the Co. on unpaid amount. (The BrG originally had 8000 shares of £50 i.e. £400,000 capital, a further £200,000 was authorised in 1842. Only £30 per share was ever paid up.)
6. BrG shareholders who accept, to pay from 1 Jan 1847.
7. Any declined stock to be offered to other proprietors.
8. In case of any BrG shareholders not accepting full stock of 657,875 the proportion unappropriated shall not be created unless approved by the Board.
9. Dividends to be paid on entire £1,800,000.
10. Existing liabilities of each Co. to become those of the United Co.
11. From the 1st Jan 1845 revenue will belong to the joint Co.
12. This is to be binding whether an Act obtained or not.
13. Present agreement to form basis of the Act.

MR HEADS OF AGREEMENT & ACT OF PARLIAMENT

Heads of Agreement 8th Feb 1845

Under the conviction of the absolute necessity of a uniformity of gauge between the Northern manufacturing districts and the Port of Bristol – the amalgamation of the two Companies as per 14 Jan agreement is considered carried into effect.
– the MR to pay the United Co. 6 per cent per annum on the capital of £1,800,000 and undertake liabilities and engagements of £457,000.
– all rolling stock and property etc. becomes property of the MR.
– lease to begin from 1 July 1845.
– MR to have power of purchase after three years of start of lease paying £150 per £100 share.

Absorption Act, 3rd August 1846 9,10 Vict. Cap, 326

Incorporation to come into effect on the Execution of Deeds of Conveyance.
MR to maintain broad gauge between Bristol and Standish.

New shares at present,	B&G has 9374 shares of £100
	8189 shares of £25
	BrG has 7539 shares at £50
	MR has £7,584,906 15s.8d. consolidated stock and shares.

The MR is authorised to create additional shares in Capital to absorb B&B.

9374 @ £100
7539 @ £50
7539 @ £37.5s.0d. (additional)
8189 @ £25

The shares created will be called MR 6 per cent shares; holders not entitled to vote, just to receive 6 per cent per annum. Holders of £50 BrG shares can subscribe to a like number of 6 per cent shares of a nominal value £37.5s.0d. The MR can repurchase all 6 per cent shares after 1849 at 50 per cent more than face value.

B&G TRAFFIC ESTIMATES 1836 (FEBRUARY)

Per Annum

Passengers by coaches, 12 months of 28 days	£ 33,135 4s.0d.
Estimate per railway at double the number of passengers	£ 66,270 8s.0d.
Passengers by Posting, Gigs, Spring Carts, Vans, horsemen, £3000 for 28 days	£ 36,000 0s.0d.
Passengers in total per year	£102,270 8s.0d. *
Merchandise and cattle £2031 10s.2d. per 28 days	£ 24,378 2s.0d.
Coach parcels, 24 long distance coaches @ 20s. daily, 20 short distance coaches @ 10s. daily gives £34 daily	£ 11,424 0s.0d.
Canal and river traffic at present 180,096 Assume only 1/5th by rail	£ 36,019 4s.0d. *
Goods in total	£ 71,821 6s.0d.
Total revenue per annum	£174,091 14s.0d.

'The increase of passengers by railway are estimated only as double the number by present conveyance. If add only half more would be £16,567.12s.0d.'

Total revenue thus	£190,659 6s.0d. *

* The House of Commons report on the B&G proved a traffic of:	
400,000 passengers per annum giving revenue of	£ 90,699
70,000 tons of goods giving revenue of	£ 65,155
expenses of working	£ 52,000
net profit	£103,854

B&G TRAFFIC ESTIMATES AUGUST 1838

Passengers

Route	Weekly journeys	Passenger numbers	Railway miles	Aggregate coach passenger miles
Birmingham–Gloucester	64	520	53	27560
Birmingham–Cheltenham	84	694	46	31464
Birmingham–Worcester	88	656	31	20336
Worcester–Gloucester	12	84	27	2268
Tewkesbury–Cheltenham	26	178	9	1692
Cheltenham–Gloucester	224	1828	7	12796
				96026

Aggregate at 2½d. per mile   £104,028
add 25% for post & parcels   £ 26,007
                                       ─────────
                                       £130,035

No mention of goods traffic but assume 1836 estimates

River and canal goods   £ 36,019
Merchandise and livestock   £ 24,378
                                  ─────────
Total   £190,432

FINANCE: TOTAL COST OF THE LINE

Date	Estimate for (in £1000's)	Total	Excess *	Works	Land	Motive Power	Rolling Stock	Stations Depots	10% Conting.	Notes * over the £950,000 capital
Feb 1836(I)	Birmingham to Gloucester; Cheltenham, Worcs & Docks branch	834	–	584	118	30(1)	9(2)	18	76	(1) Half for locomotive, half for stationary (2) Very low estimate
Feb 1836(II)	as above	930	–	631	174	18(1)	7(2)	7	84	(1) Stationary only quoted! (2) Very low estimate
Sept 1837	Birmingham to Cheltenham; Worcester and Tewkesbury branches	877	–	684	138	18(1)	7(1)	29	–	(1) as Feb 1836 II
Feb 1839	Birmingham to Cheltenham, Worcester branch, Tramroad & Cheltenham–Gloucester line	1069(1) 1109(2)	119(1) 159(2)	664	147	100(3)	(3)	25	–	(1) Burgess' estimate Feb 1839 (see 4).: (2) Actual at March 1841 Audit (see 5): (3) Motive power & rolling stock combined. (4) extra expense for: rolling stock–50: Glos Docks branch–30: misc.–24: works–90: law etc–55. (5) Extra expense for: Chelt/Glos line–60: tramway–15 Law etc–25: Misc.–15: works–14

March 1841									Actual expense at March 1841 Audit. (1) combined: (2) Excess over Feb 1839 estimate. Unavoidable–199: (Chelt/Glos–83: tramway–17.5: interest–14: completing line ahead of schedule etc–5) mismanagement–191: (land–19: works–175)
	Birmingham to Gloucester and Worcester branch	1460	501	893	166	90(1)	(1)	28	—
	As built, Birmingham to Gloucester	1500 (3)	550	1081 (3)	176	98(1)	(1)	(2)	— (1) combined (2) included in (1) (3) Includes Cheltenham to Gloucester line, £100,000 of which was later repaid by GWR

FINANCE HALF YEARLY REPORTS

Period (1)	Total Capital (2) £	Shares Paid up s.	Shares Value s.	Revenue/Receipts £ Total (8)	Passengers (9)	Goods (10)	Expenses £ Total	General	Interest	Loco	Perm. Way	% of Receipt To Expense	Profit £	Dividend £ s.
1836a	52875	5	?											
1836b	73578	10	?											
1837a	90915	12½	5½											(3)
1837b	112529	20	9½											
1838a	169057	40	24½											
1838b	317636	50	29											
1839a	468487	70	46½											—
1839b	641235	80	75											
1840a	1005004	100	77½	249	?	?	?	?	(6)	?	(6)	?	?	0
1840b	1217147	100	60	21769	20175	1594	22381	13192	(6)	9189	(6)	111	−162	0
1841a	1320717	100	64	38214	28964	8152	28860	10207	7988	10138	524+6	76	9354	0
1841b	1392649	100	43	50114	36766	11902	39381	12887	10292	10235	5967	79	10783	1.11. (4)
1842a	1438371	100	48	41967	28436	12197	40352	13028	12054	9648	5622	96	1615	0
1842b	1460650	100	53½	50319	33912	15147	41694	13971	12963	8959	5801	83	8625	1. 5.
1843a	1470730	100	65½	42619	29100	13518	38352	11281	12792	7835	6444	90	4266	0.12.
1843b	1481395	100	114	51350	36256	15093	37639	10197	13764	7639	6039	73	13763	1.10.
1844a	1500807	100	103	53203	30975	21998	39262	14481	10621	8261	5899	74	13941	1. 5.
1844b	1527267	100	133½	70096	44274	25008	44739	21115	9037	10390	4317	64	25357	2. 0.
1845a	1527267	100	130	90433	58847	30842	53458 (7)	?	?	?	3190	59?	?	1.16.
1845b		100	130	114208	75696	37886	57582 (7)	?	?	?	4951	50?	?	3. 0.
1846a		100	129	100098	64119	35979	?	?	?	?	?	?	?	3. 0. (5)
1846b		100		107968	75268	32700	?	?	?	?	?	?	?	?

(1) a=Jan to June
     b=July to Dec
(2) Share and loan capital
(3) Constuction
(4) Worked by B&G
(5) Worked jointly with BrG

(6) Charged to capital
(7) Interest excluded
(8) Goods and passenger and miscellaneous
(9) Includes luggage, horses, carriages and dogs
(10) Goods, coal, Mail, parcels, livestock

FINANCE – MONEY ACT 27 June 1843, 6 – 7 Vic Cap 53

'An Act to enable the B&G Rly. Co. to raise a further sum of money'.

The Bill launched by the B&G was to legalise the Scrip and Loans authorised by the Special General Meeting of May 1841. These were to raise:
– £175,000 in Scrip of £17 10s.0d. each, and to be exchanged for a Quarter-Share of £25 at a later date (thus raising the Share Capital by £250,000 whilst only raising £175,000 in cash).
– £60,000 in Loan Notes. By the time the Bill was launched 8189 Scrip were issued raising £143,307 10s.0d. and £42,020 was raised in Loan Notes.
The Act authorised the B&G to:
– Create 8189 Quarter-Shares
– Raise by subscription (in shares of equal amount) £106,692 10s.0d. (the difference between the £250,000 extra share capital sought and the money raised by the 8189 Scrip.)
– Exchange the Loan Notes for Bond or Mortgage.
– Convert all or part of the Loan powers to Capital
– Consolidate Shares into Stock

APPENDIX

GOODS STATISTICS

Year	Parcels Receipts £	Mail Receipts £	Goods		Coal	
			Receipts £	Tonnage	Receipts £	Tonnage
1841	2799	9345	9860	17145	(2)	–
1842	2998	10156	12791	24288	1167 (2)	5003
1843	3060	10156	12240	28281	2789	11643
1844	3677	4144	34614	95481	2740	10421
1845(1)	5951	2759	52056	117990	7932	83997 (3)
1845(2)	–	2759	56374	124290	7928	100405 (3)

(1) Worked jointly with the BrG
(2) May have been included in 'Goods' up to July 1842
(3) Mostly worked between Coalpit Heath and Bristol (7 miles)

TOLLS AND RATES OF TONNAGE BY ACT OF PARLIAMENT
23 APRIL 1836

For all dung, compost and all sorts of manure, lime, limestone and salt for the purpose of manure and all undressed materials for the repair of roads and highways   . . . 1*d.* per ton per mile.

Coals, coke, culm, charcoal, cinders, building, pitching and paving stone dressed, bricks, tiles, slates, clay sand, limestone, iron ore, pig, bar, rod, hoop, sheet and all other similar description of wrought iron, and castings not manufactured into utensils or . . . merchandise
. . .3*s.*4*d.* per ton per mile.

Sugar salt, grain, corn, flour, dyewoods, earthenware, timber, staves and deals, metals (except iron), rails, anvils, vices and chains
. . . 2*d.* per ton per mile.

Cotton and other wools, hides, drugs, manufactured goods and all other wares, merchandise, articles, matters and things
. . . 3*d.* per ton per mile.

For every horse, mule, ass or other beast of draught and burthen and for every ox, cow, bull, or meat cattle   . . . 3*s.*4*d.* per mile.
    calf or pig   . . . 1*s.*2*d.* per mile.
    sheep or lamb or other small animal   . . . 1*s.*4*d.* per mile.

Tolls and rates are exclusive of any charges for locomotive power loading, unloading, sheeting, storage, etc.

BIRMINGHAM AND GLOUCESTER
RAILWAY.

CLASSIFICATION AND RATES FOR GOODS
BETWEEN

CAMP-HILL STATION, BIRMINGHAM, & GLOUCESTER & BRISTOL,
AND BETWEEN

LIVERPOOL & MANCHESTER, GLOUCESTER & BRISTOL,
EXCLUSIVE OF COLLECTION OR DELIVERY.

6d FOR RATES TO NEWPORT, CARDIFF, AND SWANSEA.—SEE OTHER SIDE.

FIRST RATE. *Per Ton.*

	s. d.				
Birmingham to Gloucester	8 0	Boiler Plates	Flour	Potatoes	Stone
Birmingham to Bristol (*Water Conveyance between Gloucester and Bristol*)	12 0	Bricks, common	Grain	Salt	Tiles
		Coal	Iron, Bar and Rod	Slates	Timber

SECOND RATE. *Per Ton.*

	s. d.				
Birmingham to Gloucester	9 0	Alabaster	Bottles in cases	Iron Hoops	Seeds, Hemp, Flax, &c.
Birmingham to Bristol (*Water Conveyance between Gloucester and Bristol*)	13 6	Anvils	Brimstone	Iron Pipes	Spelter or Zinc
		Argols	Cement	Lead	Staves
		Ashes	Clover Seed	Linseed	Tallow
		Bath Bricks	Copper and Metals	Mahogany Logs	Tin Plates
		Blocks	Grind-stones	Nails	Wire, Iron

THIRD RATE. *Per Ton.*

	s. d.				
Birmingham to Gloucester	12 0	Ale and Porter	China in Casks	Molasses	Soda
Birmingham to Bristol (*Water Conveyance between Gloucester and Bristol*)	17 0	Alum	Cider and Perry	Rice	Sugar
Liverpool or Manchester to Gloucester	25 0	Bones	Earthenware in	Sad Irons	White Lead
Liverpool or Manchester to Bristol (*Water Conveyance between Gloucester & Bristol*)	32 6	Casks	Crates	Shumac	Wire, Brass
		Cheese	Hardware Goods	Soap	Wire, Bright

FOURTH RATE. *Per Ton.*

	s. d.				
Birmingham to Gloucester	15 0	Aloes	Coffee	Hides, Wet	Pins
		Anchovies	Cordage	Hoofs, Hogsheads	Pumice-stone
Birmingham to Bristol (*Water Conveyance between Gloucester and Bristol*)	22 6	Arrow Root	Cotton	or Bags	Quicksilver
		Bacon	Cream of Tartar	Indigo	Rotten-stone
Ditto Ditto (*Land Conveyance*)	35 0	Baggage, Military	Currants	Iron Liquor	Saltpetre
		Bales	Drysaltery	Iron Tubing	Shot
Liverpool or Manchester to Bristol (*Water Conveyance between Gloucester & Bristol*)	40 0	Barilla	Dye Woods	Juniper Berries	Tarpaulins
		Bark	Eggs	Kelp	Tea
Ditto ditto (*Land Conveyance*)	52 6	Bees Wax	Emery	Leather	Tobacco Leaf
		Blacking	Fish, Salt	Lignumvitæ	Twist
		Black Lead	Flax	Liquorice	Veneers
		Boilers	Fruit, Dry	Needles	Weighing Machines
		Boxwood	Ginger	Nuts	Wine and Spirits, in
		Bristles	Glass in Boxes	Ocre	Casks
		Broom Handles	Grapes	Oil	Wool
		Butter	Groceries	Oranges and Lemons	Woollen Goods
		Candles	Gum	Packs	
		Canvas	Hair in Mats	Paper, Coarse	
		Cases	Hams	Pepper	

FIFTH RATE. *Per Ton.*

	s. d.				
Birmingham to Gloucester	22 6	Apples in Casks	Haberdashery	Oil, in Boxes or Jars	Silks
Birmingham to Bristol (*Water Conveyance between Gloucester and Bristol*)	32 6	Berries, Dyers'	Hops	Onions	Snuff
Ditto Ditto (*Land Conveyance*)	42 6	Cochineal	Lamp Black	Paper, Fine	Teazles
Liverpool or Manchester to Gloucester	50 0	Crocks, Butter	Lance Wood	Pigs, Dead	Tobacco, Manufactured
Liverpool or Manchester to Bristol (*Water Conveyance between Gloucester & Bristol*)	60 0	Drugs	Luggage, Passengers	Poultry, Dead	Toys
Ditto Ditto (*Land Conveyance*)	70 0	Flocks	Marble Slabs	Rhubarb	
		Fruit, Ripe	Mats in Bundles	Sasafras	

Furniture, Hats, Millinery, &c. by Special Agreement.

Collection or Delivery in BIRMINGHAM .... 2s. 0d. per Ton.
——　　——　　GLOUCESTER .... 1s. 0d. ——

AGENTS.

Grand Junction Railway Company,		{ Liverpool. / Manchester. / Birmingham.
Mr. J. Kidder,	Birmingham and Gloucester Railway,	Birmingham.
— H. P. Edgell,	ditto　　　　ditto	Gloucester.
Messrs. H. Southan & Son,		Gloucester.
— Southan, Evans & Co.,		Bristol.

November 10, 1841.

(Gloucester Records Office)

REVISED CLASSIFICATION MAY 1842

Rate per ton is Birmingham to Gloucester

Class 1 (7s.)	Iron, wrought and cast, timber, grain, slates, empty packages and other heavy packages in bulk.
Class 2 (7s.6d.)	Metals, wire, brass and copper, nails, tin-plates, oil, wet hides, fancy goods, mahogany, bones and hoofs, brown paper, machinery, cement, porter, cider, perry, ale.
Class 3 (9s.)	Drysaltery, provisions, earthenware, hardware, groceries, leather, doghides, pins, bright wire.
Class 4 (12s.6d.)	Glass in crates and boxes, bale goods, wool, hops, wine and spirits in cases, fish, salt and dried, dead meats and orange.
Special (20s.)	Fresh fish, furniture, hats, luggage, teasles. (20s.)

REVISED CLASSIFICATION AUGUST 1843 (CofE)
(per ton Birmingham to Gloucester – no more details)

Class 1 6s.
Class 2 8s.
Class 3 11s.

REVISED CLASSIFICATION, 1ST FEB 1844
(Rate is Birmingham–Gloucester)

Class 1 (5s.6d.)	Iron, pig, bar and sheet, nail rods, nail in quantity, iron pipes, bricks, grain
Class 2 (7s.6d.)	Alabaster, anvils, crates, empty bottles, bones, cement, seeds, grindstoneas, lead, linseed oil, mahogany, staves, tallow, flour, bran, earthenware, paint, pitch, tar, currants, hides, palm oil, brimstone, castings
Class 3 (8s7d.)	Ale and porter, alum, cheese, cider, perry, butter, salt, groceries, thumac, soap, soda, candles, leather, hardware, paper, machinery, Manchester bales and packs, oysters in hogsheads or bags, plaster of Paris
Class 4 (11s.)	Haberdashery and cotton goods, hosiery and canvas, lemons, oranges, ripe fruit, vegetables, hams, wool, apples, hops, tobacco, loose oysters
Class 5 (15s.)	Wines and spirits, drugs, glass, flock, furniture, hats and anything else not mentioned

PASSENGER TIMETABLE

Date	Number each way	Average time (hrs)	Type (see key)	Notes
24.6.40	2	3.5	–	Train from Cheltenham to Bromsgrove, thence by coach
8.7.40	5	3.4	3a,2b	as 24.6.40
17.9.40	5	3.0	2a,b,2c	Open to Cofton, thence by coach to Birmingham
4.11.40	4	3.4	a,b,2c	Open to Gloucester, 4 'short trains' each way between Cheltenham and Gloucester
17.12.40	4	2.6	a,b,2c	Open to Camp Hill, Birmingham; short trains as 4.11.40
6.2.41	6	2.6	2a,b,c,2d	as 17.12.40
14.8.41	8	2.7	3a,b,c,2d	Open to Curzon St. Birmingham 'short trains' withdrawn
14.9.41	8	2.7	3a,b,2c,2d	Through booking to London via Birmingham
15.11.41	8	–	2a,2b,2d,2e	7 'short trains' each way till Jan. 1842; London as 14.9.41
9.5.42	7	–	3a,c,2d,e	London as 14.9.41
1.6.42	8	–	3a,c,2d,e,f	2 'short trains' each way; London as 14.9.41
14.11.42	8	–	4a,2d,2f	Short trains as 1.6.42; thro. 1st class coach to London each way
1.8.43	8	–	4a,2d,2f	4 'short trains' each way; 1st & 2nd class coach to London each way
4.11.44	8	2.7	a,b,2c,d,2f,g	as 1.8.43. Thro. connection to Bristol on most trains
1.1.46	8	2.6	a,c,d,e,3f,g,h	B&B Timetable. Bristol connection to each train. 3 'short trains'

Key	Stations Served*	Passengers Carried
a	1st class	1st and 2nd class
b	all	1st and 2nd class
c	all	1st, 2nd, 3rd
d	1st	Mail train, 1st and 2nd
e	all	Goods train+, 1st, 2nd, 3rd
f	all	Goods train+, 3rd
g	1st and 2nd class	1st and 2nd
h	1st class	Express train 1st

* see station list appendix 1
+ to Camp Hill, Birmingham only

PASSENGER FARES

Journey	1840 Class			1842 Class			1845 Class		
	1	2	3	1	2	3	1	2	3
Gloucester–Birmingham	13s. 6d.	9s.	5s. 6d.	14s.	10s.	5s. 6d.	14s.	10s. 6d.	–
Cheltenham–Birmingham	11s. 6d.	8s.	5s.	12s.	9s.	5s.	–	–	–
Cheltenham–Gloucester	2s.	1s.	0s. 8d.	2s.	1s. 6d.	0s. 8d.	–	–	–
Gloucester–London	–	–	–	36s.	24s.	–	30s.	20s.	9s. 5d.

APPENDIX

LOCOMOTIVE STATISTICS

Period *	Expenses £	Total Locomotives	Main line costs/mile s. d.	Lickey cost/ mile s. d.	Total/mile s. d.	Coke consumption lb/mile
1840 b	9189	23	?	?	2s.9d.	49
1841 a	10138	28	?	?	1s.11¾d.	48
1841 b	10235	30	1s.5½d.	17s.6¼d.	1s.6d.	40
1842 a	9648	34	1s.3d.	10s.5¾d.	1s.3¾d.	38
1842 b	8959	34	1s.½d.	7s.11½d.	1s.¾d.	33
1843 a	7835	34 (1)	11½d.	6s.3d.	0s.11½d.	31
1843 b	7639	33 (1)	11½d.	5s11d.	?	?
1844 a	8261	35	?	?	?	?
1844 b	10390	36	?	?	?	?
1845 a	?	36	?	?	?	?
1845 b	?	37	?	?	?	?

* a = January–June
  b = July–December
(1) 15 spare in working order

LOCOMOTIVE LISTS

Name	B&G No.	MR. No. Feb 1847	Maker	Cost £	Wheel arr.	Leading	Driving	Trailing	Cylinders inches o=out i=insd	Working weight empty in ()	Built	Delivered	Disposed	Notes ?=not known/assumed -=not applicable
Bromsgrove	1	244?	G. Forrester	1660	2–2–2	4ft.	5ft.6in.	3ft.	o,13	12t5c	as delvd	Nov 1838	Mar 1851	*Whishaw said 4ft. Ahrons 3ft.6in. copper fireboxes, brass tubes, 130 @ 1⅝ dia.
Tewkesbury	2	–	"	"	"	"	"	"	"	"	"	Sept 1839	7/45 to 2/47	
Worcester	3	243?	"	"	"	"	"	"	"	"	"	May 1839	Feb 1851	
Cheltenham	4	–	Norris type B	"	4–2–0	2ft.6in.	4ft.	–	o,10½ × 18		"	Nov 1838	2/45 to 2/47	
England	5	–	"	1525	"	"	"	–	18	9t4c (8t)	"	Mar 1839	8/42 to 7/45	Dec 1845 sold to Disc Engine Co, allegedly seen at a Notts colliery in Jan 1851
Victoria	6	277?	" type A	1200	"	"	"	–	o,11½ × 18	10t15c (10t)	"	July 1839	1848?	In MR stationary stock 1848
Atlantic	7	–	" type B	1525	"	"	"	–	o,10½ × 18	9t4c (8t)	"	Nov 1839	July 1846	Sold to Mr Cardew for £600, Leased to TVR Jan 1847 sold Sept 1852 for £250
Columbia	8	–	"	"	"	"	"	–			"	Nov 1839	Jan 1846	Sold to Aberdare Rly £530
Birmingham	9	–	"	"	"	"	"	–			"	by Aug 1840	April 1846	Sold to Mr Worswick £650
Gloucester	10	–	"	"	"	"	"	–			"	June 1840	Oct 1845	Sold to TVR £650, scrapped 1859. New firebox of copper fitted Sept 1840 after 600 miles
W. S. Moorsom	11	–	"	"	"	"	"	–			"	June 1840	Sept 1845	Sold to TVR £400. Out of use Aug 1849, scrapped 1854
Washington	12	–	"	"	"	"	"	"			"	by Aug 1840	Nov 1846	Sold to English Copper Co. £720
Philadelphia	13	271	" type A Extra	1762	"	"	"	–	o,12½ × 20	13t4½c (12t)	"	May 1840	June 1856	Saddletanked March 1842

Name	B&G No.	MR No. Feb 1847	Maker	Cost £	Wheel arr.	Wheel dimensions			Cylinders inches o=out l=insd	Working weight empty in ()	Built	Delivered	Disposed	Notes ?=not known/assumed –=applicable
						leading	driving	trailing						
Boston	14	272	"	1500	"	"	"	–	"	"	"	Aug 1840	June 1856	Saddletanked by March 1842
Baltimore	15	281	type A		4-2-0	2ft.6in.	4ft.	–	o,11½ × 20	10t15c (10t)	"	Sept 1840	1847/48?	Into MR stationary stock 1847–8. Then sold to Mr Pickering £100
Moseley	16	–	type B	1350	"	"	"	–	o,10½ × 18	9t4c (8t)		Feb 1840	Dec 1843	Original owner Banks of Manchester. Fitted with Disc engine May 1841. Out of use Aug 1842. Sold to Disc Co. Dec. 1843 (with *England?*)
Pivot	17	278	"	"	"	"	"	–	"			July 1840	1847/48?	Owner as above. Into MR stationary stock 1847–8
Bredon	18	279?	Hick type A	1032	4-2-0	2ft.6in.	4ft.	–	o,11½ × 20	10t15c (10t)	"	Oct 1840	1847/48?	as above
Defford	19	280?	Nasmyth type A Mk 1	1050	"	"	"	–	"	"		"	"	"
President	20	282	Norris type A	1465	"	"	"	–?	"			Dec 1840	Mar 1852	5ft. wheels fitted Feb 1842. Into stationary stock 1847/48. Sold Mr Pickering £100
William Gwynn	21	273	Norris type A Extra	1785	"	"	"	–	o,12½ × 20	13t4½c (12t)		Dec 1840	May 1852	Saddletanked by Aug 42. Sold Mr Knox £250
Leicester	22?	–	R. Stephenson	500	0-4-0	–	5ft.	–	l,12 × 16	?	5/32	Oct 1838	7/45 to 1/46	From Leicester and Swannington Rly. Out of use by Aug 1842. Replaced 1846 by *Stratford*
Southampton	23	–	John Jones	900	0-4-2	–	5ft.?	?	l,12 × 18	?	5/37	Jan 1839	Mar 1847	From London and Southampton Rly. Sold Tos. Hale £1000. Replaced March 1846 by *Atlas*
Spetchley	24	283?	Hick type A	1032	4-2-0	2ft.6in.	4ft.	–	o,11½ × 20	10t15c (10t)		Feb 1841	Mar 1847	Sold to Wykes I Porter £1000

Name	No.	No.	Maker / Type	Works No.	Wheels		Driving wheels		Cylinders			Into service		Withdrawn	Notes
Eckington	25	—	"	"	"	"	"	—	"	"		Mar 1841		Oct 1846	Drivers changed to 5ft. Sold to B&H Sherwood £1300
Ashchurch	26	—	Nasmyth type A Mk 1	1050	"	"	"+	—	"	"		Jan 1841		Aug 1846	Drivers changed to 5ft. Feb 1842. Sold to G. Wythes (Brighton Rly contractor) £1300
Droitwich	27	284?	"	"	"	"	"+	—	"	"		Jan 1841		1847/48	Into MR stationary stock 1847/48
Pershore	28	—	Nasmyth type A MKII	"	"	"	"	—	"	"		June 1841		April 1846	Sold to Lord Ward, colliery owner £1200
Upton	29	285?	"	"	"	"	"	—	"	"		July 1841		Mar 1847	Sold to T. Leather £1000
Lifford	30	286?	"	"	"	"	"	—	"	"		Aug 1841		Oct 1847	Sold to Wykes & Co £600
Niagara	31	274?	Norris type A Extra	1000	"	"	"	—	o,12½ × 20	13c4½ × (12c)		May 1842		May 1851	Saddle tanked. Believed sold to C.H. Smith, Swansea £200
New York	32	275?	"	"	"	"	"	—	"	"		May 1842		April 1855	Saddle tanked. Sold John Wood, Derby £200
Evesham	33	118	Bury	1355,200 tender	2-2-0	?	5ft.	—	I,13 × 18	?		June 1842		June 1855	Withdrawn Jan 1954 scrapped June 1855
Kempsey	34	119	"	"	"	?	"	—	"	?		June 1842		June 1855	Scrapped June 1855
Wadborough	35	296	Sharp Bros	1050	0-4-2	—	4ft.6in.	?	I,14 × 20	?	2/43	Jan 1844		Nov 1852	
Bristol	36	167	Jones & Potts 'long boiler'	1357	0-6-0	—	4ft.6in.	—	I,15 × 24	?		June 1844		June 1860	Rebuilt Oct 1848 & 1856 with 5ft. wheels & 16×24 cyls. Alleged rebuilt as 222A in 1889, scrapped 1894
Hercules	37	168	"	"	"	—	"	—	"	?		June 1844		Sept 1862	Rebuilt 1855 5ft. wheels 16×24 cyls. alleged rebuilt 1889
Great Britain	38	276	Birmingham I Gloucester Rly	?	0-6-0 saddle-tank	—	3ft.10in.	—	o,18 × 26	30t		June 1845		July 1862	Rebuilt as well-tank 1853 cyls. 16×24 Withdrawn Oct 1862

ADDITIONS BY BIRMINGHAM AND BRISTOL RAILWAY (excluding those paid for by MR and taken direct into MR stock)

Name	No.	No.	Maker / Type	Works No.	Wheels		Driving wheels		Cylinders			Into service		Withdrawn	Notes
Camilla	5	104	Nasmyth Gaskell	?	2-2-2	?	5ft.	?	?14 × 18	?	40?	12/45		6/55	From Hargreave of Bolton Withdrawn 2/54
Gloucester	10	?	Bury	?	6 wheel	?	5ft.	?	?12 × 18	?	?	?		?	
?	11	?	"	?	"	?	"	?	?	?	?	?		?	
Strafford	22	53	Sharp Bros.	2250	2-2-2	3ft.3in.	"	3ft. 3in.	I,15 × 20	25t inc tender		Jan 1846		Feb 1861	No details

Name	B&G No.	MR. No. Feb 1847	Maker	Cost £	Wheel arr.	Wheel dimensions leading	driving	trailing	Cylinders inches o=out l=insd	Working weight empty in ()	Built	Delivered	Disposed	Notes
														?=not known/assumed -=applicable
Atlas	23	54	"	"	"	"	"	"	"	"		Mar 1846	June 1860	Possibly renamed *Stephenson*
Wellington	39	245	Tayleur, Vulcan Foundry	?	0-4-2	-	5ft.6in.	?	?,13 × 18	?	1836	Dec 1845	July 1849	Rebuilt 4ft.8in. drivers by 1841 & 14×18 cyls in 1845. Bought from Hargreaves of Bolton. Rebuilt by 1849 as 2-2-2, 5ft. drivers (ex Bolton & Leigh) Sold 1849 to Hoof & Hill £500
Pandora	40	247	"	?		-	"	?	"	?	1838	Dec 1845	July 1854	Rebuilt 4ft.8in. drivers by 1841; with 4ft.4in. drivers 1 14×20 cyls in 1845. Bought from Hargreaves (ex Bolton & Leigh). Rebuilt by 1849 as 2-2-2 5ft. drivers, 14×18 cyls. Sold £500 Fairbanks & Co
?	50	301	Bury	?	0-6-0	-	5ft.	-	?16×24	?		Feb 1846	May 1852	Sold Brown, Marshal & Co
?	?	88	Tayleur, Vulcan Foundry	2000 + 400(t)	4-2-0	3ft.6in.	6ft.	-	o.15×24	?		April 1846	Aug 1859	altered by E.B. Wilson c 1849 to *Jenny Lind* type 15 × 20 cyls 2-2-2
?	?	89	"	"	"	"	"	-	"	?		"	Jan 1861	withdrawn – see 88
?	?	90	"	"	"	"	"	-	"	?		"	July 1858	June 1846 see 88
Vulcan?	?	169	"	?	0-6-0	-	4ft.7in.	?16×24	?	?	May	Aug 1846	Jan 1863	
Proserpine?	?	170	Tayleur, Vulcan Foundry	?	0-6-0	-	4ft.7in.	-	?16×24	?		May 1846	July 1858	
?	?	165	"	2167	2-4-0	?	5ft.6¾in.	-	?16×22	?		June 1846	July 1858	
?	?	166	"	2098	"	?	"	-	"	?		"	July 1858	

RULES FOR WORKING THE LICKEY

Ref. PRO RAIL 37/15 M617

'The Secretary reported that the necessary alterations (to the brakes of all vehicles) had been made, and that the Engineer and he had drawn up a set of rules for working the Inclined Plane.'

DESCENDING

(1) At a point half a mile from the summit, there is a timber arched bridge, painted white. All engines must have their steam shut off here.

(2) Near the top of the Plane there is a post on which a white light is kept burning. Trains must stop here.

(3) Before stopping the driver will whistle for the Brakesmen, as well as giving three sharp whistles for the application of brakes by the Train Guards.

(4) The Switchman is also to ring a bell as a signal to the Brakesmen as soon as the train is in sight.

(5) The train having stopped the Brakesmen will mount and take complete charge of the train.

(6) The First Brakesman will mount the middle carriage. The Second Brakesman and others (Travelling Porters who may be on the train) will all take their orders from the First Brakesman, to distribute themselves – at least one to every three wagons of a wagon train. The Fireman will station himself at the tender brake.

(7) It is hereby positively ordered that the Enginemen, Guards, Porters etc. shall submit to, and implicitly obey the First Brakesman. They are to keep the brakes positively and firmly in hand ready to act.

(8) No train shall descend without a Brakesman.

(9) If the First Brakesman cannot accompany the train, the Second Brakesman will take charge.

(10) The speed for a descending coach train shall never exceed 20 miles per hour in dry weather, or 16 miles per hour in slippery weather. The descending speed of wagon trains shall in no case exceed 10 miles per hour.

(11) The First Brakesman shall make use of the following signals:-

One blast of the whistle:	Start the train
Two " " "	Driver to shut off steam when the train has started.

Three   "   "   "   Apply brakes.

Note. This signal applies anywhere on the plane and if repeated elsewhere than on the summit it means:- Apply brakes more forcibly, but gradually. One blast of the whistle (when on the Plane): Ease brakes gradually. Five blasts on the whistle means: Obstruction, Danger.

Note. In daylight, warning of danger will be given by the showing of a red flag. At night, a red lamp will be shown.

ASCENDING

(1)   All trains stop at Bromsgrove.

(2)   When an Up train is in sight, the policeman shall ring a bell.

(3)   The bell shall be a signal for the bank engineman to place his engine under the bridge at the foot of the Plane on the west line.

(4)   When the train stops, the fireman of the bank engine will connect his engine to the train, which will then start when signalled by the Guard.

(5)   It is the special duty of the policeman at Bromsgrove to see that the carriages and wagons are properly connected both by centre and side chains, also that the last carriage or wagon has a brake attached.

(6)   The Guards are to stand to the brakes in ascending the Plane, keeping them constantly ready for use. A Guard or Porter must invariably ride on the last carriage or wagon.

(7)   As soon as the tail of the train reaches the summit of the Plane, the fireman of the bank-engine will throw off his engine from the train, and at the same moment the train engine is to slacken speed by shutting off steam, and thus allow the bank-engine to go at least 30 yards ahead, and turn into the siding prepared for the purpose.

(8)   When the train has passed on, the bank-engine will descend the Plane on the east line at a speed not exceeding 12 miles per hour.

(9)   Any obstruction at the top of the Plane will be notified, in clear weather, by the showing of a red flag. At night or in fog, a bright red light will be shown.

(10)   It is the duty of the switchmen both at the summit and at the foot of the Plane to keep the lines of way constantly clear.

ANY SERVANT OF THE COMPANY DISOBEYING THESE
RULES WILL NOT ONLY MEET WITH INSTANT DISMISSAL
AND LOSS OF ANY PAY DUE TO HIM, BUT WILL ALSO BE
PROSECUTED AT LAW FOR NEGLECT OF DUTY.

By order of the Directors

Willm. Burgess
Gnl. Superintendent

EDWARD BURY ON THE LICKEY. Aug 3 1841

Note. These particulars come from the Company Minutes (PRO RAIL 37/16 M 367) and also from a letter written by Capt. W.S. Moorsom to William Norris after the trial of engines. This letter is quoted by Mr P.C. Dewhurst in his paper read before the Newcomen Society. ('Norris Locomotives in England' p.26)

The trials began with an attempt by Bury's engine to haul his six wagons and the coach, a total weight of 45 tons. Bury's engine, L&B 0-4-0 No. 65, stalled at the foot of the Incline.

Next she attempted the climb with four wagons and a coach, a total weight of 31 tons 10 cwt. No. 65 stalled this time after travelling 270 yards. She climbed successfully with the following:

Load			Weight			Time	Speed
Wagons	Carrs	Passrs	Tons	Cwt	Qrs	(seconds)	m.p.h.
3	1	15	24	12	1	840	8.7
2	1	15	17	18	2	524	14.0
1	1	15	11	4	3	349	21.0
0	1	15	4	10	0	297	24.7

With the same loads *Philadelphia*'s times and speeds were:-

483	15.2
446	16.4
421	17.4
347	21.1

It was ordered in the Minutes 'that a copy of the Chairman's Report be sent to Mr Bury'.

Mr P.C. Dewhurst (*op. cit.*) quotes from a letter written to Norris by Capt. Moorsom, and after stating the weights of the two engines empty, he also mentions the attempts with six and four wagons respectively. His letter gives neither the weight in working order nor the boiler pressure of *Philadelphia*. (which Mr Dewhurst calculated was 55lb. p.s.i. as compared with No. 65's rating of 56lb. p.s.i..)

Capt. Moorsom then goes on to state that he had asked Bury if the latter had any objection to the publication of the report of the trials, and the latter had replied that he 'positively objected . . . to publish trials of engines of different dimensions, and especially where there is no means of treating accurately the pressure of steam used by one of the engines'. Moorsom added in his letter to Norris, '. . . I think, in this instance, Mr Bury's insinuation is a most unfair one as to pressure . . . .after his reply to the question 'which pressure shall we use?' – 'Use any pressure you please, up to the utmost you think your boiler will bear'.'

John Donahue was the driver of the *Philadelphia*.